MW01041768

Verbal Encounters:
Anglo-Saxon and Old Norse Studies
for Roberta Frank

Roberta Frank. Photograph by Alexander C. Murray.

Verbal Encounters

Anglo-Saxon and Old Norse Studies for Roberta Frank

Edited by

Antonina Harbus and Russell Poole

UNIVERSITY OF TORONTO PRESS
Toronto Buffalo London

ISBN 0-8020-8011-1

Printed on acid-free paper

Library and Archives Canada Cataloguing in Publication

Verbal encounters: Anglo-Saxon and Old Norse studies for Roberta
Frank / edited by Antonina Harbus and Russell Poole.

(Toronto Old English series)
Includes bibliographical references and index.
ISBN 0-8020-8011-1

1. English philosophy – Old English, ca. 450–1100 – History and criticism.
2. Old Norse poetry – History and criticism.   I. Frank, Roberta   II. Harbus, A.
(Antonina)   III. Poole, Russell Gilbert

PR176.V47 2005   429   C2004-904042-1

University of Toronto Press acknowledges the financial assistance to its publishing
program of the Canada Council for the Arts and the Ontario Arts Council.

University of Toronto Press acknowledges the financial support for its publishing
activities of the Government of Canada through the Book Publishing Industry
Development Program (BPIDP).

CONTENTS

Preface

We are grateful to all those who have helped bring this volume to fruition. In particular our thanks go to our good-natured and productive contributors; to Grace Desa, Ruth Harvey, and Walter Goffart for advice and information; to Alexander C. Murray for photographing our honorand and providing technical advice; to Debbie Rayner and Andrew Gillett for their support and practical assistance throughout the genesis and development of this book; and to Roberta herself for kind help in so many ways.

LIST OF ABBREVIATIONS

ANQ	*American Notes and Queries*
ASE	*Anglo-Saxon England*
ASPR	Anglo-Saxon Poetic Records, ed. G.P. Krapp and E.V.K. Dobbie (New York 1931-53)
AASS	Acta sanctorum (Antwerp etc. 1643-1940; Paris 1863-7)
BHL	Bibliotheca hagiographica latina antiquae et mediae aetatis, ed. Bollandists, Subsidia hagiographica 6 (Brussels 1898-1901); Novum Supplementum, ed. H. Fros, Subsidia hagiographica 70 (Brussels 1986)
BT, BTS	J. Bosworth and T.N. Toller, *An Anglo-Saxon Dictionary* (Oxford 1898); T.N. Toller *Supplement*, (Oxford 1921); A. Campbell, *Enlarged Addenda and Corrigenda* (Oxford 1972)
CCCC	Corpus Christi College, Cambridge
CCCM	Corpus christianorum continuatio mediaevalis
CCSL	Corpus christianorum series latina
Cleasby-Vigfusson	Richard Cleasby and Gudbrand Vigfusson, *An Icelandic-English Dictionary*, 2nd edn, rev. William A. Craigie (Oxford 1957; repr. 1993)
CSASE	Cambridge Studies in Anglo-Saxon England
CSEL	Corpus scriptorum ecclesiasticorum latinorum
DOE	*The Dictionary of Old English*
EETS	Early English Text Society (os - original series; ss – supplementary series)
ES	*English Studies*
Fritzner	Johan Fritzner, *Ordbog over Det gamle norske Sprog*, 2nd edn, 3 vols (Oslo, 1883-96; repr. 1954; vol. 4, ed. Finn Hødnebø, 1972)
FSN	*Fornaldar sögur norðurlanda*, ed. Guðni Jónsson, 4 vols (Akureyri 1954)
GL	*Grammatici Latini*, ed. H. Keil, 8 vols (Leipzig 1857-80)
Go	Gothic
Gr	Greek

Grágás Ia	*Grágás: Islændernes Lovbog i Fristatens Tid, udgivet efter det kongelige Bibliotheks Haandskrift*, 1st part (Copenhagen 1852; repr. Odense 1974)
ÍF	Íslenzk fornrit
JEGP	*Journal of English and Germanic Philology*
Lat	Latin
LGer	Low German
LP (1860)	*Lexicon poëticum antiquæ linguæ septentrionalis*, ed. Sveinbjörn Egilsson (Copenhagen 1860)
LP (1913-16)	*Lexicon poeticum antiquæ linguæ septentrionalis: Ordbog over det norsk-islandske Skjaldesprog*, ed. Sveinbjörn Egilsson, rev. Finnur Jónsson (Copenhagen 1913-16)
MÆ	*Medium Ævum*
MED	*Middle English Dictionary*
MGH	Monumenta Germaniae historica (SS - Scriptores)
MHG	Middle High German
MM	Maal og Minne
Neo	*Neophilologus*
NGL	*Norges gamle Love indtil 1387*, ed. R. Keyser and P.A. Munch et al., 5 vols (Christiania 1846-95)
NM	*Neuphilologische Mitteilungen*
NQ	*Notes and Queries*
OE	Old English
OED	*Oxford English Dictionary*
OFris	Old Frisian
OHG	Old High German
OI	Old Icelandic
OIr	Old Irish
ON	Old Norse
OS	Old Saxon
PL	Patrologiae cursus completus, Series latina, ed. J.-P. Migne et al., 221 vols (Paris 1841-64)
RES	*Review of English Studies*
STUAGNL	Samfund til Udgivelse af gammel nordisk Literatur

NOTES ON EDITIONS

1. With the exception of *Beowulf*, ed. F. Klaeber, 3rd edn (Boston/Lexington 1950), the OE editions and short titles cited are those used by the *DOE*, listed in A.diP. Healey and R.L. Venezky, *A Microfiche Concordance to Old English: The List of Texts and Index of Editions* (Toronto 1980), incl. revisions published with fascicles (ongoing).

2. The Latin editions and short titles are those used in Pauline A. Thompson, *Dictionary of Old English: Abbreviations for Latin Sources and Bibliography of Editions* (Toronto 1992; rev. 1998).

3. The OI/ON editions and short titles cited are those listed in the *Editors' Manual* prepared for the new international edition of skaldic poetry at the website: http://www.arts.usyd.edu.au/Arts/departs/medieval/skaldic/manual (contained under 'Sigla for Sources' and 'General Conventions and Abbreviations').

4. Unless stated otherwise, all translations are those of the individual authors of the articles below.

Introduction

ANTONINA HARBUS AND RUSSELL POOLE

> Non semper breuitas sermonem deturpat
> sed multotiens honestiorem reddit.[1]
>
> Brevity does not always disfigure speech
> but often renders it more distinguished.

As of speech, so of scholars. Although a wealth of things could be said of Roberta Frank, here we shall abide by Ælfric's dictum and maintain a fitting brevity.

Roberta herself has contributed so much, in the classroom, in publications, and in fora of other kinds, and she has made these contributions with a graceful unassuming lightness of touch. At their centre lie a love of both words and people, perhaps necessarily accompanied by a fascination with the words of love, engagement, understanding, and reconciliation that people have used down the centuries and a gentle deprecation of bellicose attitudes towards life and literature.

The current volume aims to recognize and celebrate these qualities through a series of papers written by Roberta's former doctoral students at the Centre for Medieval Studies and Department of English at the University of Toronto. These papers represent new work by a variety of scholars at various stages in their careers, but in common is the theme of 'verbal exchanges,' reflecting the honorand's own abiding interest in cultural and linguistic exchange in Old Norse, Old English and medieval Latin literature.

Roberta Frank was born in New York on 9 November 1941. After taking her BA degree at New York University in 1962, she went on to do her MA (1964) and PhD (1968) at Harvard. Her doctoral thesis, 'Wordplay in Old English Poetry,' formed the basis of her seminal article, 'Some Uses of Paronomasia in

---

[1] Ælfric, 'Preface,' ed. W.W. Skeat, *Lives of the Saints*, 2 vols, EETS, os 76 and 82 (London 1881; repr. 1966), 1.4, ll. 28-9.

Old English Scriptural Verse,' now a classic in the field. From Harvard, Roberta took up an assistant professorship at the University of Toronto in 1968, where she remained until 2000 with promotion to Associate Professor in 1973, Professor in 1978, and University Professor in 1995. In 2000 she left Toronto to assume her current position as the Douglas Tracy Smith Professor of English at Yale University.

Roberta's 1978 book on Old Norse court poetry has proved a source of inspiration for its rigorous philology, its imaginative and eclectic literary criticism, and its broadly comparative spirit. Structured as it is around a series of sharp insights about individual skaldic stanzas, it shares with those medieval texts qualities of poise, stylistic fluency, and succinctness – artistry within strictly defined limits. Fittingly, as can be seen in the bibliography printed below, Roberta is a self-professed and extremely prolific 'article person.' Such title keywords as 'onomastic play,' 'anatomy of a skaldic double-entendre,' 'hand tools and power tools,' 'skaldic tooth,' and 'an aspirin for *Beowulf*' testify to her scholarly verve, verbal playfulness, and creativity in finding or devising telling aphorisms and epigrams. But lightness of touch in no way means lightness of learning: the large number of items in the Bibliography that have been selected for reprinting and translation or otherwise anthologized attests to the enduring value of her writings as well as to their wide appeal.

What the bibliography does not show is Roberta's leadership in some highly significant editorial projects. Most notably, between 1976 and 2002 she was the General Editor for the Toronto Old English Series (University of Toronto Press) and, between 1985 and 2002, for Publications of the Dictionary of Old English (Pontifical Institute of Mediaeval Studies). In order to keep the Bibliography to a manageable length, we have omitted these, as well as Roberta's numerous public lectures and scores of book reviews for a wide range of scholarly journals – genres in which she excels.

The field of Old English studies has benefited immeasurably from her passionate and energetic support. Among Roberta's longest-lasting achievements is her ongoing role as a member of the international advisory committee of the Dictionary of Old English project. In addition, Roberta was the cofounder of the International Society of Anglo-Saxonists in 1981, first vice-president (1982-5), president (1986-8), and most recently the (anonymous) winner of its logo competition. Her service and initiative on countless advisory boards and steering committees has directed the discipline perhaps as much as anyone else of her generation might be said to have done.

As influential for the field, during thirty-two years in Toronto Roberta Frank supervised more than a score of graduate students and served as Director of the Centre for Medieval Studies from 1995 until 1999. Her inter-disciplinary interests and inspiring teaching in Old Norse and Old English literature attracted students from a range of undergraduate departments and from around the world to the Centre and likewise to the Department of English. The papers printed below give some indication of the range of deployments to which Roberta's teaching and counsel have been put.

In Part I, entitled 'On Words,' Christopher A. Jones takes Chaos as his theme and traces the development of medieval and early modern understandings of this curiously seminal concept. Appropriately, the two papers that follow consider the complementary concepts of articulation and creation. Don Chapman analyses Anglo-Saxon understandings of the formation of compound words, demonstrating that to medieval grammarians process was key, not product. Pauline Head points out how the concepts of birth and knowledge are strangely entangled in Old English in the one polysemous word *cennan*, 'to cause to be born'/'to cause to know.' Another polysemous word, *mōd*, is analysed by Soon-Ai Low, with the proposal that connotations such as pride and anger, suggested by its occurrence in *Genesis A* and other accounts of famous falls, are not necessarily intrinsic to its meaning.

In Part II, 'On Anglo-Latin and Old English Prose,' the authors focus on two expressions of the teacherly spirit in Anglo-Saxon England. Carin Ruff shows how grammarians writing in and about the Latin language sometimes enlivened their austere subject matter and sought to intrigue their *leorningcnihtas*. Dorothy Haines, considering homiletic instruction and preparation for the last days, notes preachers resorting to a form of dramatic monologue for greater immediacy and impact.

In Part III, 'On Old English Poetry,' Karin Olsen continues on this line of enquiry by analysing how vistas of devastation were used by the poet of *Genesis A* to impress upon his audience the perils of rebellion against the Almighty. Antonina Harbus takes up the theme of effective speaking by examining the processes by which thoughts determine speech and speech determines action in *Juliana*. Turning to that altogether less transparent form of discourse, the runes, Robert DiNapoli argues that their very arcaneness kept them in currency in verbal exchange and conferred on them a special appeal and instructive value for poets and readership alike. In the case of *Beowulf*, instruction extends to the hero himself. Haruko Momma traces the process of his education and acculturation so as to conform to the mores of a Danish leisure society.

In Part IV, 'On Old Norse Literature,' Martin Chase shows how the twelfth-century poet Einarr Skúlason benefited from traditional teaching while creatively adapting inherited doctrines and verbal formulas to new use in a Scandinavian context. Similarly for prose, Bernadine McCreesh investigates how motifs in mainstream European hagiography could be adapted to serve the needs of Icelandic ecclesiastical history and advocacy. On the less decorous side, Oren Falk focuses on a brief exchange of verbal insults in *Gísla saga*, revealing the wealth of innuendo and implication that lies within this brevity. Finally, Russell Poole shows how two poets of the Conversion period handled the verbal side of their exchanges with two missionary kings so as to elicit gifts of property and comradeship.

This, then, is our gift and expression of thanks to Roberta and with it we wish her all happiness and prosperity.

Roberta Frank: Bibliography, 1970-2003

1970

Coeditor with Angus Cameron and John Leyerle. *Computers and Old English Concordances*. Toronto Old English Series 1. Toronto 1970.
'Onomastic Play in Kormakr's Verse: The Name Steingerðr.' *Mediaeval Scandinavia* 3 (1970): 7-30.

1972

'Anatomy of a Skaldic Double-Entendre: Rognvaldr Kali's *Lausavísa* 7.' In *Studies Offered to Einar Haugen*, ed. E.S. Firchow et al., 227-35. Janua Linguarum, series maior, 59. The Hague 1972.
'Some Uses of Paronomasia in Old English Scriptural Verse.' *Speculum* 47 (1972): 207-26. Repr. in *The Poems of MS Junius 11: Basic Readings*, ed. R.M. Liuzza, 69-98, London 2002.

1973

Coeditor with Angus Cameron. *A Plan for the Dictionary of Old English*. Toronto Old English Series 2. Toronto 1973.
'Marriage in Twelfth- and Thirteenth-Century Iceland.' *Viator* 4 (1973): 473-84.

1976

'The Dróttkvætt Stanza.' In *Medieval Studies in Honor of Lillian Herlands Hornstein*, ed. Jess B. Bessinger Jr. and Robert R. Raymo, 123-40, New York 1976.

1978

Old Norse Court Poetry: The Dróttkvætt Stanza. Islandica 42. Ithaca 1978.

1979

'Old Norse Memorial Eulogies and the Ending of *Beowulf*.' In *The Early Middle Ages*, ed. W.H. Snyder, 1-19. *ACTA* 6. Binghampton 1982.

1981

'Skaldic Verse and the Date of *Beowulf*.' In *The Dating of Beowulf*, ed. Colin Chase, 123-39, Toronto 1981. Repr. in paperback 1997. Repr. in *Beowulf: Basic Readings*, ed. Peter S. Baker, 155-80, New York and London 1995.
'Snorri Sturluson and the Mead of Poetry.' In *Speculum Norroenum, Norse Studies in Memory of Gabriel Turville-Petre*, ed. Ursula Dronke et al., 155-70, Odense 1981.

1982

'The *Beowulf* Poet's Sense of History.' In *The Wisdom of Poetry: Essays in Early English Literature in Honor of Morton W. Bloomfield*, ed. L. D. Benson and S. Wenzel, 53-65, 271-7, Kalamazoo 1982. Repr. in *Beowulf: Modern Critical Interpretations*, ed. Harold Bloom, 51-62, New York 1987. Repr. in *Beowulf – A Prose Translation*, trans. E. Talbot Donaldson, ed. Nicholas Howe, 98-111, New York 2002. Repr. in *Beowulf – A Verse Translation*, trans. Seamus Heaney, ed. Daniel Donoghue, 167-81, New York 2002.

1983

Dictionary of the Middle Ages. New York. Vol. 2 (1983): 'Bjarni Kolbeinsson' (255-6); 'Bragi Boddason the Old' (359-60).

1984

'Viking Atrocity and Skaldic Verse: The Rite of the Blood-Eagle.' *The English Historical Review* 99, no. 391 (April 1984): 332-43.
Dictionary of the Middle Ages. New York. Vol. 4 (1984): 'Dróttkvætt' (294-5); 'Eddic Meters' (384-5); 'Egill Skallagrímsson' (400-1); 'Eilífr Goðrúnarson' (409-10); 'Einarr Helgason Skálaglamm (410-11); 'Eyvindr Finnsson Skáldaspillir' (570).

1985

'Skaldic Poetry.' In *Old Norse-Icelandic Literature: A Critical Guide*, ed. Carol J. Clover and John Lindow, 157-96. Islandica 45. Ithaca 1985. *Dictionary of the Middle Ages*. New York. Vol. 5 (1985): 'Flokkr' (91); Vol. 6 (1985): 'Háttalykill' (112); 'Haukr Valdísarson' (113-14).

1986

'Hand Tools and Power Tools in Eilífr's *Þórsdrápa*.' In *Proceedings of the Sixth International Saga Conference*, Copenhagen 1985, I:347-72. Repr. in *Structure and Meaning in Old Norse Literature: New Approaches to Textual Analysis and Literary Criticism*, ed. John Lindow, Lars Lönnroth, and Gerd Wolfgang Weber, 94-109, Odense 1986.

'*Mere* and *Sund*: Two Sea-Changes in *Beowulf*.' In *Modes of Interpretation in Old English Literature: Essays in Honour of Stanley B. Greenfield*, ed. P.R. Brown, G.R. Crampton, and F.C. Robinson, 153-72, Toronto 1986.

Dictionary of the Middle Ages. New York. Vol. 7 (1986): 'Kenning' (230-1); 'Kormáks Saga' (299-300); 'Kviðuháttr' (311-12); 'Lausavísa' (387).

1987

'A Note on Old English *Swigdagas* "Silent Days."' In *Studies in Honour of René Derolez*, ed. A.M. Simon-Vandenbergen, 180-9, Ghent 1987.

'Did Anglo-Saxon Audiences Have a Skaldic Tooth?' *Scandinavian Studies* 59, no. 3 (1987): 338-55. Repr. in *Anglo-Scandinavian England: Norse-English Relations in the Period before the Conquest*, ed. John D. Niles and Mark Amodio, 53-68, Old English Colloquium Series 4, Lanham, MD 1989.

'Pre-Christian Beliefs and Rites.' In *The Christianization of Scandinavia: Report of a Symposium held at Kungälv, Sweden, 4-9 August 1985*, ed. Birgit Sawyer, Peter Sawyer, and Ian Wood, 26-7, Alingsås 1987.

'Searching for System in Skaldic Verse.' *Scandinavian Studies* 59 (1987): 370-1.

Dictionary of the Middle Ages. New York. Vol. 8 (1987): 'Málsháttakvæði' (65-7); 'Merlínússpá' (275-6).

1988

'The Blood-Eagle Again.' *Saga-Book of the Viking Society for Northern Research* (*Notes and Reviews*) 22, no. 5 (1988): 287-9.

'Interdisciplinary: The First Half-Century.' In *Words for Robert Burchfield's Sixty-Fifth Birthday*, ed. E.G. Stanley and T.F. Hoad, 73-8, Cambridge 1988. Repr. in *Items* 42, no. 3 (1988): 73-8. Repr. in *Issues in Integrative Studies* 6 (1988): 139-51.

'Medieval English Studies at the University of Toronto.' *Mediaeval English Studies Newsletter* (University of Tokyo) no. 19 (December 1988): 3-6. Repr. in *Mediaeval English Studies Past and Present*, ed. A. Oizumi and T. Takamiya, 154-7, Tokyo, 1990.

'What Kind of Poetry is *Exodus*?' In *Germania: Comparative Studies in the Old Germanic Languages and Literatures*, ed. Daniel G. Calder and Craig Christie, 191-205, Cambridge 1988.

Dictionary of the Middle Ages. New York. Vol. 11 (1988): 'Skáldatal' (316); 'Skaldic Poetry' (316-23).

1989

'Denton Fox, 1930-1988.' In *Mediaeval English Studies Newsletter* (University of Tokyo), no. 20 (July 1989): 9-11. Repr. in *Mediaeval English Studies Past and Present*, ed. A. Oizumi and T. Takamiya, 230-3, Tokyo 1990.

Dictionary of the Middle Ages. New York. Vol. 12 (1989): 'Þjóðólfr ór Hvíni' (32); 'Ulfr Uggason' (245-6).

1990

'Anglo-Scandinavian Poetic Relations.' In 'Old English Studies: Current State and Future Prospects.' *NQ: A Quarterly Journal of Short Articles, Notes and Reviews*, n.s. 3, no. 2 (April 1990): 74-9.

'Ornithology and the Interpretation of Skaldic Verse.' *Saga-Book of the Viking Society for Northern Research* 23, no. 2 (1990): 81-3.

'Why Skalds Address Women.' In *The Seventh International Saga Conference, 4-10 sett. 88*, 67-83, Spoleto 1990.

1991

'*The Battle of Maldon* and Heroic Literature.' In *The Battle of Maldon A.D. 991*, ed. D.G. Scragg, 196-207, Oxford 1991.

'Germanic Legend in Old English Literature.' in *The Cambridge Companion to Old English Literature*, ed. Malcolm Godden and Michael Lapidge, 88-106, Cambridge 1991. Spanish trans.: 'Las leyendas germanicas en la literatura inglesa Antigua.' *Acta Poetica: Revista del Seminario de Poética* (Universidad Nacional Autonoma de México) 16 (1995): 159-82.

'The Ideal of Men Dying with their Lord in *The Battle of Maldon*: Anachronism or *Nouvelle Vague*.' In *People and Places in Northern Europe 500 - 1600: Essays in Honour of Peter Hayes Sawyer*, ed. Ian Wood and Niels Lund, 95-106, Woodbridge 1991.

1992

'*Beowulf* and Sutton Hoo: The Odd Couple.' In *Voyage to the Other World: The Legacy of Sutton Hoo*, ed. Calvin B. Kendall and Peter S. Wells, 47-64. Medieval Studies at Minnesota 5. Minneapolis 1992. Repr. in *The Archaeology of Anglo-Saxon England*, ed. Catherine E. Karkov, 317-38. Basic Readings in Anglo-Saxon England 7. New York 1999.

'Late Old English *þrymnys* "Trinity": Scribal Nod or Word Waiting to be Born?' In *Old English and New: Studies in Language and Linguistics in Honor of Frederic G. Cassidy*, ed. Joan H. Hall, Nick Doane, and Dick Ringler, 97-110, New York 1992.

'Old English *Æræt*: "Too Much" or "Too Soon"?' In *Words, Texts and Manuscripts: Studies in Anglo-Saxon Culture Presented to Helmut Gneuss on the Occasion of His Sixty-Fifth Birthday*, ed. Michael Korhammer, 293-304, Woodbridge 1992.

1993

Editor. *The Politics of Editing Medieval Texts*. Twenty-Seventh Conference on Editorial Problems: University of Toronto, 1-2 November 1991. New York 1993.

'*The Battle of Maldon*: Its Reception 1726-1906.' In *Heroic Poetry in the Anglo-Saxon Period: Studies in Honor of Jess B. Bessinger, Jr.*, ed. Helen

Damico and John Leyerle, 29-46. Studies in Medieval Culture 32. Kalamazoo 1993. Repr. in *The Battle of Maldon: Fiction and Fact*, ed. Janet Cooper, 137-47, London and Rio Grande 1993.

'The Search for the Anglo-Saxon Oral Poet.' *Bulletin of the John Rylands University Library of Manchester* 75, no. 1 (1993): 11-36; and printed separately by the Manchester Centre for Anglo-Saxon Studies. Repr. (with postscript) in *Textual and Material Culture in Anglo-Saxon England: Thomas Northcote Toller and the Toller Memorial Lectures*, ed. Donald Scragg, 137-60, Woodbridge 2003.

1994

'King Cnut in the Verse of His Skalds.' In *The Reign of Cnut, King of England, Denmark and Norway*, ed. Alexander R. Rumble, 106-24, Leicester 1994. Repr. in paperback 1999.

'Old English Poetry.' In *The Columbia History of British Poetry*, ed. Carl Woodring, 1-22, New York 1994.

'On a Changing Field: Medieval Studies in the New World.' *The Southern African Journal of Medieval and Renaissance Studies* 4, no. 1 (1994): 1-20. Also in '*Tis all in Peaces, all cohaerence gone*': *Change and Medieval and Renaissance Studies*, ed. Rosemary Gray and Estelle Maré, 1-13. Miscellanea Congregalia 47. Pretoria 1995.

'On the Field.' In *The Past and Future of Medieval Studies*, ed. John Van Engen, 204-16. Notre Dame Conferences in Medieval Studies 4. Notre Dame 1994.

'Poetic Words in Late Old English Prose.' In *From Anglo-Saxon to Early Middle English: Studies Presented to E.G. Stanley*, ed. M. Godden, D. Gray, and T. Hoad, 87-107, Oxford 1994.

'When Poets Address Princes.' In *Sagnaþing helgað Jónasi Kristjánssyni sjötugum, 10. apríl 1994*, ed. Gísli Sigurðsson, Guðrún Kvaran, and Sigurgeir Steingrímsson, 189-95, Reykjavík 1994.

1995

'The Centre for Medieval Studies at the University of Toronto.' *Mediaeval English Studies Newsletter* (University of Tokyo) no. 33 (1995): 12-14.

'*Quid Hinieldus cum feminis?* The Hero and Women at the End of the First Millennium.' In *La Funzione dell'Eroe germanico: Storicità, Metafora, Paradigma*, ed. Teresa Pàroli, 7-25. Atti del Convegno Internazionale di studio, Roma, Università La Sapienza. Rome 1995.

1997

'Old English *Orc* "cup, goblet": A Latin Loanword with Attitude.' In *Alfred the Wise: Studies in Honour of Janet Bately on the Occasion of her Sixty-Fifth Birthday*, ed. Jane Roberts, Janet L. Nelson, and Malcolm Godden, 15-24, Woodbridge 1997.

'The Unbearable Lightness of Being a Philologist.' *JEGP* 96 (1997): 486-513.

1998

'When Lexicography Met the Exeter Book.' In *Words and Works: Studies in Medieval English Language and Literature in Honour of Fred C. Robinson*, ed. Nicholas Howe and Peter S. Baker, 207-22, Toronto 1998.

2000

'The Invention of the Viking Horned Helmet.' In *International Scandinavian and Medieval Studies in Memory of Gerd Wolfgang Weber: Ein runder Knäuel, so rollt' es uns leicht aus den Händen*, ed. Michael Dallapiazza, Olaf Hansen, Preben Meulengracht-Sørensen, and Yvonne S. Bonnetain, 199-208, Trieste 2000.

2001

'Masters on Masters.' *The Yale Literary Magazine* 13 (2001): 5-7.

'Old English *ancor* "anchor": Transformation of a Latin Loanword.' In *Medieval Reconstructions: Germanic Texts and Latin Models*, ed. K.E. Olsen, A. Harbus, and T. Hofstra, 7-27. Germania Latina 4. Leuven 2001.

2002

'An Aspirin for *Beowulf*: Against Aches and Pains (*ece* and *wærc*).' *ANQ* 15, no. 2 (2002): 58-63.

'North-Sea Soundings in *Andreas*.' In *Early Medieval Texts and Interpretations: Studies Presented to Donald G. Scragg*, ed. Susan Rosser and Elaine Treharne, 1-11. Medieval and Renaissance Texts and Studies. Tempe 2002.

'Ongendus.' In *Reallexikon der germanischen Altertumskunde*. Berlin 2002.

2003

'The Discreet Charm of the Old English Weak Adjective.' In *Anglo-Saxon Styles*, ed. Catherine Karkov and George H. Brown, 239-52, Albany 2003.

'Sex in the *Dictionary of Old English*.' In *Unlocking the Wordhord: Anglo-Saxon Studies in Memory of Edward B. Irving, Jr.*, ed. Mark C. Amodio and Katherine O'Brien O'Keeffe, 302-12, Toronto 2003.

Forthcoming

'The Boar on the Helmet.' In *Essays in Honor of Rosemary Cramp*, ed. C. Karkov, Kalamazoo.

'The Lay of the Land in Skaldic Praise Poetry.' In *Myth in Early Northwest Europe*.

'Old Norse-Icelandic Women Poets (*Skaldkonur*).' In *Women in the Middle Ages: An Encyclopedia*, ed. Katherine Wilson and Nadia Margolis, Westport, CT and London 2004.

'Three "Cups" and a Funeral in Beowulf.' In *Anglo-Saxon Literature*, ed. Katherine O'Brien O'Keeffe and Andy Orchard.

'The Incomparable Wryness of Old English Poetry.' In *Blackwell's Concise Companion to Old English Poetry*.

'*Málsháttakvæði*: A Translation.' In *A Festschrift for Helen Damico*.

Part I — On Words

Early Medieval *Chaos*

CHRISTOPHER A. JONES

> Mirum et humanae rationi imperscrutabile
> quale illud chaos fuerit ...'
>
> What sort of chaos that was remains a wonder,
> impenetrable to human understanding ...

'For a philologist, even a small word can mask a shaft so bottomless that probes dropped into it produce no more than an echo.'² In essays on the Old English loanwords *orc* 'drinking vessel' and *ancor* 'anchor,' Roberta Frank has led the way through histories not only deep but mazy with the turns of medieval etymology and wordplay.³ Similar forces operated no less often, but have drawn less attention, in medieval Latin vocabulary.⁴ The following essay explores a few of the stranger legacies of early medieval erudition about another deceptively small word, *chaos*. Unlike orcs and anchors, *chaos* did not become a full English citizen until the Renaissance,⁵ but earlier etymologies, glosses, puns, and vernacular translations of the word betray a deep pit indeed beneath its familiar Greco-Roman surface. The echoes from its depths record

---

¹ Heiric of Auxerre, Homily 2.17; Riccardo Quadri, ed., *Heirici Autissiodorensis Homiliae per circulum anni*, 3 vols, CCCM 116, 116A, and 116B (Turnhout 1992-4), 3:149-60, at 154.
² R. Frank, 'The Unbearable Lightness of Being a Philologist,' *JEGP* 96 (1997): 486-513, at 496.
³ 'Old English *Orc* "cup, goblet": A Latin Loanword with Attitude,' in Jane Roberts et al., eds, *Alfred the Wise: Studies in Honour of Janet Bately on the Occasion of her Sixty-Fifth Birthday* (Rochester 1997), 15-24; and 'Old English *ancor* "anchor": Transformation of a Latin Loanword,' in K.E. Olsen, A. Harbus, and T. Hofstra, eds, *Germanic Texts and Latin Models: Medieval Reconstructions*, Germania Latina 4 (Leuven 2001), 7-27.
⁴ See the survey by Peter Stotz, *Handbuch zur lateinischen Sprache des Mittelalters, II: Bedeutungswandel und Wortbildung* (Munich 2000), 95-106 (§§ 43-7) and 171-84 (§§ 84-7).
⁵ The earliest quotation in the *OED*, s. *chaos*, is dated 'c. 1440' but comes from Walter Hilton (d. 1394), *Scala perfectionis*, translating Luke 16:26, on which see below, n. 68. All other citations in the *OED* are from the sixteenth century and later. The picture is similar for French and German; see Walther von Wartburg, ed., *Französisches etymologisches Wörterbuch* (Bonn 1928-), 2:622-3, and H. Schulz et al., eds, *Deutsches Fremdwörterbuch* (Berlin 1995-), 3:609-14.

how *chaos*, tantalizingly old and obscure, beckoned clever medieval philologists down some bizarre paths.

Appropriately, clashes over the meaning of *chaos* go back to the beginnings. The sense usual in modern English — tumultuous disorder, utter confusion — attached to the word almost as soon as it was borrowed, in the sixteenth century.[6] Among its humanist sponsors the term inevitably recalled the contexts of Greek and Roman cosmogony, whether in themselves or superimposed on the biblical creation story.[7] Some of the earliest instances of *chaos* in English specify a confusion of formless, primal matter, and do so in terms plainly indebted to what was, for the later Middle Ages and the Renaissance, the locus classicus in Ovid. Near the beginning of the *Metamorphoses*, Chaos roils as the

> rudis indigestaque moles
> Nec quicquam nisi pondus iners congestaque eodem
> Nec bene iunctarum discordia semina rerum.[8]

Translators have taken to the lines with metamimetic relish, from Arthur Golding (1567):

> a huge rude heape, and nothing else but even
> A heavie lump and clottred clod of seedes together driven,
> Of things at strife among themselves, for want of order due,[9]

all the way down to Ted Hughes (1997):

> A huge agglomeration of upset.
> A bolus of everything — but
> As if aborted.
> And the total arsenal of entropy
> Already at war within it.[10]

---

[6] *OED*, s. *chaos*, senses 3a-b.

[7] Ibid., senses 2a-b.

[8] OVID. Met. 1.7-9; cf. also Met. 2.299, 10.30, 14.404; Fasti 1.103, 4.600, 5.11; Ars 2.470; Pont. 4.8.57 and 84.

[9] John Frederick Nims, ed., *Ovid's Metamorphoses: The Arthur Golding Translation, 1567* (Philadelphia 2000), 3. Uglier still is George Sandys's version (1626): 'An undigested lump; a barren load; / Where jarring seeds of things ill-joyn'd aboad' (*Ovid's Metamorphosis Englished, Mythologiz'd, and Represented in Figures* [London 1640], 1).

[10] *Tales from Ovid* (New York 1997), 3.

Jarring by intention, these images of chaos, like Ovid's before them, reflect a kind of popular or literary *doctrina communis* rather than an internally consistent cosmogony." Milton reassembled many images of this tradition into what has become the most memorable literary depiction of Chaos, his

> wilde Abyss,
> The Womb of nature and perhaps her Grave,
> Of neither Sea, nor Shore, nor Air, nor Fire,
> But all these in thir pregnant causes mixt
> Confus'dly, and which thus must ever fight."

That Milton's Chaos transformed the commonplaces is generally agreed, though his ultimate designs for the construct remain disputed." If Ovid's description, down to its very wording, exerted so strong a pull on Milton, its dominance over the less original or less ambitious can hardly be overstated. This is the familiar *chaos* that echoes among the poets and antiquaries, not to mention among the classically trained founders of comparative mythology, who assimilated to the Greek categories of *chaos* and *cosmos* stories from traditions as diverse as the Egyptian, Babylonian, Vedic, and Zoroastrian."

" The distinction of popular from technical senses is common; see U. Dierse and R. Kuhlen, 'Chaos,' in Joachim Ritter, ed., *Historisches Wörterbuch der Philosophie*, 11 vols (Stuttgart 1951), 1:980-4, at col. 980; J. Ternus, 'Chaos,' in T. Klauser, ed., *Reallexikon für Antike und Christentum* (Stuttgart 1950-), 2:1031-40, at cols 1034-5.
" *Paradise Lost* (1674) bk. 2, ll. 910-14, quoted from *Complete Poems and Major Prose*, ed. Merritt Y. Hughes (New York 1957), 253.
" See Walter Clyde Curry, *Milton's Ontology, Cosmogony, and Physics* (Lexington, KY 1957), 74-91; A.B. Chambers, 'Chaos in *Paradise Lost*,' *Journal of the History of Ideas* 24 (1963): 55-84; Robert M. Adams, 'A Little Look into Chaos,' in Earl Miner, ed., *Illustrious Evidence: Approaches to English Literature of the Early Seventeenth Century* (Berkeley 1975), 71-89. More recently, see John Rumrich, 'Milton's God and the Matter of Chaos,' *PMLA* 110 (1995): 1035-46; Catherine Gimelli Martin, 'Fire, Ice, and Epic Entropy: The Physics and Metaphysics of Milton's Reformed Chaos,' *Milton Studies* 35 (1997): 73-113; see also below, n. 92.
" See Norman Cohn, *Cosmos, Chaos and the World to Come: The Ancient Roots of Apocalyptic Faith* (New Haven 1993).

1. Greek *khaos*

Those who wish to pin down *chaos* in any of its modern popular, literary, or scholarly senses will get little help from the ancient Greeks.[15] Every classicist knows the debut in Hesiod's *Theogony* 116: 'first of all *Chaos* came into being' (êtoi men prôtista Khaos genet[o]).[16] After Chaos, Hesiod continues, appeared Earth, the gloomy nether regions (Tartara t' êeroenta) and the god Eros; Chaos itself then spawned Erebos and Night. What exactly Hesiod meant by *khaos* is still disputed.[17] Many modern commentators follow those ancients who tried to graft its root onto that of Greek *khaskein*, 'to gape, stand open.'[18] The verb descends from IE *ghē-*, a prolific source of 'gaping'-words, whether on the landscape (OE and ON *gin* or *gill*, ON *gap*, *gjá*, *geisa*), or on the face of creatures when yawning (Lat. *hiare*, OE *ginian*, ON *gina* etc.), gasping for air (OE *gipian*; cf. ON *geipa*), devouring voraciously as the glutton (OE *gīfer*) and the vulture (OE *gīw*, OHG *gīr*), or making unintelligible noises (LGer. *Geck*, ?ModE *geek*).[19] Most important, the root also appears in the Greek noun *khasma* 'chasm,' identified by some critics as a synonym for *khaos* at *Theogony* 740 and ever after.[20] Etymologically correct or not, chaos as 'yawning chasm, abyss' spawned its share of puns and metaphors in Greek antiquity: pseudo-Oppian made the crocodile's open jaws a 'vast chaos'; a Byzantine encyclopedist traced monstrous 'Charybdis' to *eis khaos bainon* 'going into an abyss'; and for centuries the Chaones, a Thracian tribe, had to endure a predictable joke about gaping holes. Even the translators of the Septuagint, it

---

[15] See O. Waser, s. 'Chaos,' in Georg Wissowa, ed., *Paulys Real-Encyclopädie der classischen Altertumswissenschaft*, 49 vols plus supplements (Stuttgart 1894-1963), 3:2112-13.

[16] M.L. West, ed., *Hesiod: Theogony* (Oxford 1966), 116.

[17] For overviews, see Robert Mondi, 'ΧΑΟΣ and the Hesiodic Cosmogony,' *Harvard Studies in Classical Philology* 92 (1989): 1-41, at 1-4; Luciano Cordo, *ΧΑΟΣ: Zur Ursprungsvorstellung bei den Griechen*, Beiträge zur Philosophie 101 (Idstein 1989), 13-66; Thomas Kratzert, *Die Entdeckung des Raums: Vom hesiodischen 'χάος' zur platonischen 'χώρα,'* Bochumer Studien zur Philosophie 26 (Amsterdam 1998), esp. 18-21.

[18] Or from synonymous *khainein* (aorist root *khan-*); see West, *Theogony*, 192-3, and the cautious treatments s. *khaos* in Hjalmar Frisk, ed., *Griechisches etymologisches Wörterbuch* (Heidelberg 1960-70; repr. in 3 vols, 1973), 3:1072-3; Pierre Chantraine, ed., *Dictionnaire étymologique de la langue grècque: Histoire des mots*, 2 vols (Paris 1983-4), 2:1246.

[19] Julius Pokorny, ed., *Indogermanisches etymologisches Wörterbuch*, 3rd edn, 2 vols (Tübingen 1994), 1:419-22 (*ghē-* 2); cf. 411 (*ghan-*); for *khaos*, see 449 (*ghēu-*).

[20] West, *Theogony*, 192; cf. his own trans. 'the Chasm' for *Theogony* 116, 123, 700, and 814, in M.L. West, trans., *Hesiod: Theogony, Works and Days* (Oxford 1988), 6, 24, and 27.

has been argued, may have employed the relatively rare Greek word because they perceived in it some link to Hebrew *gay'*, 'valley.'[21]

Parting ways with the poets, Aristotle, Sextus Empiricus, and — at least by one scholiast's account — Plato took *khaos* for a primal empty space, etymologically justified by *khadein* (aorist of *khandanein* 'to contain, hold') or *khôra* 'space, area.'[22] Other early Greek authorities, no less learned, wanted to make the essential referent of *khaos* a substance rather than space. The text of the *Theogony* cooperated, hinting that chaos was 'dark' (zopheroio 814) and could catch fire (at line 700). The implication — that Hesiod's *khaos* had something in it — still left unanswered what that substance might be. In *The Birds*, Aristophanes plainly equates *khaos* with the *aêr* 'lower air, denser atmosphere,' and traces of a similar view survive in a Euripidean fragment and in lyrics by Bacchylides and Ibycus. These hints, teased out by scholia and canonized in the Byzantine *Suda*, have raised a suspicion that Hesiod too understood *khaos* as the dusky *aêr*.[23] To support a cosmogonic primacy of *aêr*, the etymologists (this time the Stoics) joined *khaos* to *kheisthai* 'to be poured out,' and to its derived noun *khysis* (cf. Lat. *fusio*). Creation, by this view, first involved the 'pouring out' of a primal substance identified by some as a dark *aêr* or mist, by others as water, and by others as fire or a dark cloud of heat and

---

[21] For pseudo-Oppian's *Cynegetica*, see Henry George Liddell et al., eds, *A Greek-English Lexicon*, 9th edn with rev. supp. (Oxford 1996), s. *khaos*, sense 4. For 'Charybdis,' see Thomas Gaisford, ed., *Etymologicon magnum* (Oxford 1848), 807. For 'Chaones,' see Ada Adler, ed., *Suidae lexicon*, 5 vols (Leipzig 1928-38), 4:786, citing Aristophanes, *Knights* 74-8; cf. the more edifying pun claimed by Michael Paschalis, *Virgil's Aeneid: Semantic Relations and Proper Names* (Oxford 1997), 132 (to *Aen.* 3.290-3). The Septuagint loci are Mic. 1:6 and Zech. 14:4; on the alleged echo of Hebr. *gay'*, see G.B. Caird, 'Homoeophony in the Septuagint,' in Robert Hamerton-Kelly and Robin Scroggs, eds, *Jews, Greeks and Christians: Religious Cultures in Late Antiquity: Essays in Honor of William David Davies* (Leiden 1976), 74-88, at 86.

[22] See Cordo, *XAOΣ*, 106-14; Kratzert, *Entdeckung des Raums*, 88-115; and Hans Joachim Waschkies, 'Χάος κενόν χώρα ὕλη: Das Unbestimmbare in der Kosmologie der Griechen und seine Rezeption bei Descartes,' *Antike Naturwissenschaft und ihre Rezeption* 7 (1997): 145-74, at 151 and 156-7; these scholars all accept that *khôra* was in some degree material ('stofflich') as well as spatial ('räumlich'). For etymologies of *khaos* through *khôra* etc., see Cordo, *XAOΣ*, 113, and citations s. *khaos* in Wilhelm Dindorf and Ludwig Dindorf, eds, *Thesaurus Graecae linguae ab Henrico Stephano constructus*, 8 vols (Paris 1831-65), 8:1302-4, at cols 1303C-1304A.

[23] Werner Karl, 'Chaos und Tartaros in Hesiods Theogonie' (diss. Erlangen-Nuremberg 1967), 9-20 (cf. Cordo, *XAOΣ*, 50-2, 78-104). On *aêr* as distinct from the purer upper *aithêr*, see Bruno Snell, ed., *Lexikon des frühgriechischen Epos* (Göttingen 1955-), s. *aêr* and literature there cited.

moisture.²⁴ Eventually the *khaos-khysis* etymology merged with Empedoclean schemes of elemental strife, and only a simple prefix was required to change 'outpouring' (*khysis*) into a disordered 'pouring together' or 'mixture' (*sygkhysis*, Lat. *confusio*).²⁵

2. *Chaos* in Classical and Patristic Latin

A number of Greek etymologies journeyed with *khaos* into Latin. Drawing on the work of Verrius Flaccus (first century B.C.), the second-century grammarian Festus repeated the commonplace derivation from *khaskein* and based on it a parallel origin of *Ianus*, god of openings, from *hiare*. Varro's *De lingua latina* likewise claimed that *chaos*, as a concavity or void, lay at the root not only of *cavus* 'hollow' but *caelum* 'heaven' through its poetic synonym *cohum*.²⁶ *Cavus* and *cohum* begin a long list of Latin words, or Greek loans into Latin, invoked to demystify *chaos*. Associated since Hesiod with cosmic beginnings, the noun was inevitably foisted upon the root of Lat. *incohare* 'to begin,' an etymology repeated in the Middle Ages and no doubt encouraged by frequent variant spellings such as *cahos* and *chahos*.²⁷ Also common was the assimilation of *chaos* (third-declension neuter in Greek) to the Latin second declension. The resulting forms, *chaus* or *caus*, occasionally suggested to the eyes of medieval glossators some etymological link to *cauma* (Gr *kauma*) 'heat' and likewise to *cauter* (Gr *kautêr*) 'brand, branding iron.'²⁸ More popular and

---

²⁴ Ternus, 'Chaos,' cols 1032-3, and esp. Friedrich Börtzler, 'Zu den antiken Chaoskosmogonien,' *Archiv für Religionswissenschaft* 28 (1930): 253-68, at 254-9. The etymology by 'pouring out' was occasionally used to interpret *khaos* by *to kenon* 'emptied [space]'; see s. *chaos* in Johann Albert and Moitz Schmidt, eds, *Hesychii Alexandrini lexicon*, 5 vols (Jena 1858-68), 4:274.
²⁵ Börtzler, 'Chaoskosmogonien,' 263-6.
²⁶ FEST. Verb.sign. 45; for Varro, see Georg Goetz and Friedrich Schoell, eds, *M. Terenti Varronis De lingua latina quae supersunt* (Leipzig 1910; repr. Amsterdam 1964), 8 (V.19-20). On chaos and Ianus, see Friedrich Börtzler, 'Janus und seine Deuter,' *Schriften der Bremer Wissenschaftlichen Gesellschaft, Abhandlungen und Vorträge* 4 (1930): 101-96, at 133-7.
²⁷ See citations s. *incoho* in Robert Maltby, ed., *A Lexicon of Ancient Latin Etymologies*, ARCA Papers and Monographs 25 (Leeds 1991), 299; also Sedulius Scottus, *In Donati Artem maiorem*, ed. Bengt Löfstedt, CCCM 40B (Turnhout 1977), 208; Remigius of Auxerre, *In Artem Donati minorem commentum*, ed. W. Fox (Leipzig 1902), 47. On the form *c(h)ahos*, see Peter Stotz, *Handbuch der lateinischen Sprache des Mittelalters, III: Lautlehre* (Munich 1996), 162 (§121.1).
²⁸ For *cauma*, see Scott Gwara, ed., *Aldhelmi Malmisbiriensis Prosa de virginitate*, 2 vols, CCSL 124 and 124A (Turnhout 2001), 2:366, ll. 184-5; note that this etymology (or mistake) affected *chasma*

appealing, however, was a perceived tie between *c(h)aus* and Lat. *causa*, whose range of meanings included 'origin' and eventually 'dispute, conflict,' both attributes of literary *chaos*.[29] The etymology by *causa* may not go all the way back to antiquity, but Sedulius Scottus and Remigius of Auxerre repeat it in the ninth century,[30] and it would explain the rendering, usually considered erroneous, of *c(h)aus* by OHG *sahha* 'dispute' in the eighth-century *Abrogans* glossary.[31] With this entry in the *Abrogans*, the interlingual engagements of *chaos* start to broaden, increasingly exploiting nonclassical languages. Among synonyms and glosses grouped beneath the *Abrogans*-lemma *caus* appears *duncali kacoz*, translating *caligo confusa* within a longer phrase. Transposing the functions of noun and adjective in the lemma, the glossator's chosen substantive *kacoz* (normalized *gigôz*), 'flow, (out)pouring,'[32] offered a semantically exact analysis of half the lemma (-*fusa*) and the bonus, perhaps, of homeophony with *cha(h)os*. A medieval Irishman, too, could hear in *chaos* something like a native word: the etymological glossary of Bishop Cormac Úa Cuilennáin (d. 908) seems to relate the Greek noun to OIr. *ceó* 'mist, fog.'[33] Similarity of sound probably

---

too; see D. Howlett et al., eds, *Dictionary of Medieval Latin from British Sources* (London 1975-), s. *chasma* (b). For the perceived link to *kautêr*, see Herbert Dean Meritt, ed., *The Old English Prudentius Glosses at Boulogne-Sur-Mer* (New York 1967), 80 (no. 760).

[29] Bayerische Akademie der Wissenschaften, eds, *Mittellateinisches Wörterbuch* (Munich 1959), s. *causa*, senses I.A and II.A.2.d. Grammarians sometimes took *c(h)aos* and *c(h)aus* as two different words (see Cyrille Lambot, ed., *Oeuvres théologiques et grammaticales de Godescalc d'Orbais*, Spicilegium Sacrum Lovaniense 20 (Leuven 1945), 383) or distinguished senses by grammatical gender (e.g., 'Chaos quando mortem sign[ificat] masculi[nu]s est. quando uero uallem neutru[m] est'; marg. gloss in Edinburgh, National Library of Scotland, Advocates' MS 18.7.7 (English s. X), fol. 8r, at CAEL.SED. Carm.pasch. 1.103).

[30] Sedulius, *In Donati Artem maiorem*, 282; Remigius, *In Artem Donati minorem*, 76.

[31] In one manuscript the scribe actually wrote *causa* but the last two letters have been erased; see Elias Steinmeyer and Eduard Sievers, eds, *Die althochdeutschen Glossen*, 5 vols (Berlin 1879-1922), 1:72-3. Modern studies usually regard the gloss *sahha* as erroneous; see Jochen Splett, *Abrogans-Studien: Kommentar zum ältesten deutschen Wörterbuch* (Wiesbaden 1976), 134-5.

[32] Steinmeyer-Sievers, *Die althochdeutschen Glossen* 1:72, ll. 36-7: 'Profundum uel confusio uel caligo confusa omnium rerum / tiuffi higoz edo duncali kacoz allero sahhono' (from Paris, Bibliothèque nationale, MS. lat. 7640); cf. discussion s. *gi-gôz*, sense 2 (s. *gôz*), in Elisabeth Karg-Gasterstädt et al., eds, *Althochdeutsches Wörterbuch* (Berlin 1968-).

[33] Kuno Meyer, ed., *Sanas Cormaic: An Old-Irish Glossary*, Anecdota from Irish Manuscripts 4 (Halle 1912), 20 (no. 226): 'Ceu *graece* ceus .i. nubs.' The text is obscure; I take 'ceus' as an etymological respelling of *caus*, and 'nubs' as *nubes* 'cloud' (similar in sense to *aêr*). On the range of *ceó*, see E.G. Quin, ed., *A Dictionary of the Irish Language, Based Mainly on Old and Middle Irish*

also explains a Latin etymology 'chaos' for Hebrew *ha'Ai* (*Ahi* in the Vulgate), the name of a city overthrown by the Israelites in Josh. 7-8.[34] Most exotic of all, in the thirteenth century Ramón Lull would regard *chaos* as a cosmogonic term indebted in sense and sound to Arabic *qaws*, 'bow, arc,' the word used by Ibn al-'Arabî to describe the circular bounds of creation.[35] The assimilation of *chaos* to the vernaculars, one should also note, did not end with the Middle Ages: in modern times, French speakers have been known to collapse *chaos* with homonymous *cahot*, a word in use since perhaps the thirteenth century to mean the 'shaking' or 'jostling' felt by passengers conveyed over rough terrain.[36]

Uncertainties about derivation and spelling registered and ultimately deepened the semantic obscurity of Latin *chaos*. Its identification as disordered primal matter, though neither the earliest nor the commonest in Greek, prevailed in literary usage among Roman authors through the late empire. But the most popular source, Ovid's lines from the *Metamorphoses*, had less impact on the earlier than the later Middle Ages, and the period from (roughly) Isidore to the twelfth century tolerated more varied and complex meanings for *chaos* than the dictionaries imply. The *Thesaurus linguae latinae* (*TLL*) takes as the leading sense of *chaos* 'confusio rerum atque elementorum, quae erat ante mundum conditum,' and draws supporting examples from Ovid, Vergil, Seneca, Lucan, Statius, Valerius Flaccus, and Martianus Capella, as well as Christian authors Augustine, Prudentius, Dracontius, Ennodius, Avitus, Sedulius, and Isidore.[37] The remaining divisions in the *TLL* naturally mirror developments in the Greek, namely the senses: (2) *inferi* 'the nether-regions or underworld,' Tartarus or Hades, eventually merging with the hell of Christian

---

Materials, compact edn (Dublin 1983), 133-4, and J. Vendryes et al., eds, *Lexique étymologique de l'irlandais ancien* (Dublin 1959-), Part C, 68-9.

[34] Hrabanus Maurus, *Commentaria in Iesu Nave* 1.10 (PL 108, 1029B-1036B, at col. 1030C). The 'chaos'-etymology for 'Ai' arose from a confusion of the name with Iye (Num. 33:44-5), transliterated as Lat. *Gai* and interpreted as 'chaos' in Rufinus's trans. of Origen's Homily 27 on Numbers; see Louis Doutreleau, ed., *Origène: Homélies sur les Nombres*, 3 vols, Sources Chrétiennes 415, 442, and 461 (Paris 1996-2001), 3:338. Cf. HIER. Interpr.hebr.nom. 126.16: 'Ahi quaestio uel uallis siue uiuit' (cf. again 88.18: 'Ain quaestio'; 87.23: 'Gai uorago').

[35] Charles Lohr, 'The Arabic Background to Ramon Lull's *Liber chaos* (ca. 1285),' *Traditio* 55 (2000): 159-70, at 169.

[36] On the confusion see Paul Imbs, ed., *Trésor de la langue française*, 16 vols (1971-94), 5:7 (s. *cahot*) and 518 (s. *chaos*).

[37] *Thesaurus linguae latinae* (Leipzig 1900-). The sense 'primal confusion [of matter, elements, etc.]' was also current in glosses; see the conspectus in Georg Goetz, ed., *Corpus glossariorum latinorum*, 7 vols (Leipzig 1888-1923), 6:206-7.

scripture or the Jewish pseudepigrapha;[38] (3) *tenebrae* 'darkness'; and (4) *profundum* 'the deep.' For their treatment of the word, the editors of the Munich *Mittellateinisches Wörterbuch* accepted much the same divisions but reduced the number of main headings to three: (1) the disordered state of primal creation; (2) an abyss or chasm, including the pagan netherworld or Christian hell; and (3) darkness.

However expedient, these classifications rest precariously atop their supporting data. If the asserted contrasts tend to vanish under scrutiny,[39] often they do so simply because Latin authors enjoyed the polysemy of *chaos*. Some Hellenistic Greek poets had begun the trend, as when Apollonius of Rhodes described a supernatural darkness besetting the Argonauts:

> The stars pierced not that fatal night nor the beams of the moon, but black chaos (*melan khaos*) descended from heaven, or haply some other darkness came, rising from the nethermost depths. And the heroes, whether they drifted in Hades or on the waters, knew not one whit.[40]

The lexicon of Liddell and Scott takes *khaos* here simply as 'darkness,' but the word's function in situ is more complex, linked to images of vast water and thick Stygian murk. This type of suggestiveness can be seen even more frequently among Roman poets. Thus in book 6 of Lucan's *De bello civili*, the Thessalian witch Erichtho prays to 'Chaos, who longs greedily to plunge countless worlds into confusion' (Chaos innumeros avidum confundere mundos).[41] This invocation of Chaos, though immediately dependent on Vergil (*Aeneid* 6.265), was evidently a real feature of some magical incantations from antiquity.[42] Lucan's context enriches the word, however,

---

[38] See esp. the 'chaos of fire' at Enoch 10:13, in M. Black, ed., *Apocalypsis Henochi graece*, Pseudepigrapha veteris testamenti graece 3 (Leiden 1970), 25; cf. R.H. Charles et al., eds and trans., *The Apocrypha and Pseudepigrapha of the Old Testament in English*, 2 vols (Oxford 1913), 2:194.

[39] The fragility of some sense-divisions for *chaos* in the *TLL* was noted by D. de Bruyne, 'Notes de philologie biblique 1: Chasma (Luc 16, 26),' *Revue biblique* 30 (1921): 400-5, at 400.

[40] *Apollonius Rhodius: The Argonautica*, ed. and trans. R.C. Seaton (Cambridge, MA 1912), 409 and 411 (4.1696-1700).

[41] LVCAN. Phars. 6.696.

[42] See *P. Vergilius Maro: Aeneis Buch VI*, ed. Eduard Norden, 9th edn (Stuttgart 1995), 209. Despite the context, Servius treated *chaos* at Aen. 2.265 as a cosmogonic term and glossed it

since it follows a description of the precipice over which Erichtho chants, a chasm so deep that it reaches almost to Dis itself and smothers all natural light.[43] *Chaos* here and elsewhere in Lucan's poem, moreover, retains its mythic scale, so darkly do Stoic images of cosmic dissolution loom over the account of the civil wars.[44]

Despite its exotic pagan history, *chaos* received the warmest of welcomes among Christian scholars of late antiquity. The very imprecision of the term eased its transfer to the primal 'deep' and 'darkness' of Genesis,[45] as well as to the gloomy pits of biblical Gehenna or hell (*chaos inferni* or *infernale*). Much like Apollonius or Lucan, a Christian author such as Sedulius could construct a passage to draw out multiple senses of the word. When Lot flees 'the chaos of Sodom,'[46] the term captures both the figurative confusion of morals in the city and the scene of its literal dissolution; the burning sulphur and black smoke (cf. Gen. 19:23 and 28) make Sodom a vision of hell. If Sedulius knew the etymological link to *khysis* and *(con)fusio*, a prophetic pun may lurk here too, based on the exegetical tradition that the ruins of Sodom were inundated by the Dead Sea, also famous in medieval lore as a place where elements war against their natural bonds.[47] Such density of association would not be exceptional.

Consider another example of *chaos* wittily exploited in Christian Latin poetry, this time in Arator's retelling of Acts 20:7-12, the episode of the young disciple Eutychus at Troas. Perched in the sill of a third-storey window while Paul preaches late into the night, Eutychus dozes off and tumbles out to his death, at which the poet erupts, 'Why, O young man, do you seek out the vacant chaos of a window? Why rest in this spot from which you're bound to

---

'elementorum confusio'; see Georg Thilo and Hermann Hagen, eds, *Servii grammatici qui feruntur in Vergilii carmina commentarii*, 3 vols (Leipzig 1881-7), 2:46.

[43] LVCAN. Phars. 6.642-51.

[44] E.g., LVCAN. Phars. 1.72-82 (at 74) and 5.625-36 (at 634); see Michael Lapidge, 'Lucan's Imagery of Cosmic Dissolution,' *Hermes* 107 (1979): 244-70, at 359-63.

[45] See below, p. 35, as well as N. Joseph Torchia, *'Creatio ex nihilo' and the Theology of St. Augustine: The Anti-Manichaean Polemic and Beyond*, American University Studies 7, no. 205 (New York 1999), 30-7.

[46] CAEL.SED. Carm.pasch. 1.121-2: 'Loth Sodomae fugiente chaos, dum respicit uxor, / In statuam mutata salis, stupefacta remansit' (cf. Gen. 19:15-29).

[47] E.g., Gregory of Tours, *Libri miraculorum* I.17 (PL 71, 721C); Remigius of Auxerre, *Commentarius in Genesim*, cap. XIV (PL 131, 84C); in the vernaculars as early as the Old Saxon *Genesis* (at 320-5), but most famously in the Middle English poem *Cleanness* (at 1015-24).

plummet?' (quid inane fenestrae / Quaeris, adulte, chaos? quidve hac in parte quiescis, / Qua ruiturus eris?).[48] The description of the open window as *inane chaos* first evokes the familiar and etymologically justified meaning 'chasm,' but further associations also crowd the passage. For Eutychus the window opens onto death and the threat of hell; he is compared to a sheep falling into the (naturally) gaping jaws of the wolf (line 776). The scene also pointedly contrasts the external darkness that receives him with the brightly lit upper room (a detail from Acts 20:8). More remarkably, Eutychus's resurrection also reenacts a genesis out of that dark void: in a highly suggestive phrase, Arator's Paul 'pours out' the life-giving word (at line 819) and the boy rises re-created out of the 'chaos' into which he had plunged.

Christian verse could provide more examples. Prose offers rather fewer. A pseudo-Augustinian sermon comments on Rom. 5:12 ('Wherefore, as by one man sin entered into the world, and death by sin; and so death passed upon all men, for that all have sinned'): 'Therefore [Adam], being mindless of sin, had henceforth poured out (*infuderat*) some sort of chaos between the divine nature and that of man.'[49] The odd choice of verb recalls the etymology of *khaos* from *khysis*; by this subtle play, Adam's disobedience results in a parody of Creation, wherein that which is poured out alienates rather than unites creature and creator. The strange indeterminacy of this product 'chaos quoddam,' as well as its strongly separative effect, finally calls attention to yet another complicating factor among late antique and medieval ideas of chaos.

3. *Chaos* in Luke 16:26: Dives and Lazarus

Already associated with the dark underworld of Hades, the term required little adaptation to suit the Christian hell. But an important authority also named as *chaos* the space or substance, or both, standing between the righteous and the damned in the next world. This belief depended on a reading nearly universal in manuscripts of the Vulgate at Luke 16:26, in the story of the Rich Man (Dives) and the beggar Lazarus (Luke 16:19-31).[50] The rich man dies and is

---

[48] ARATOR. Act.apost. 2.767-9.

[49] Sermon 84 in Angelo Mai, ed., *Nova patrum bibliotheca*, 10 vols (Rome 1852-1905), 1:163-5, at 163: 'Ex illo igitur chaos quoddam inter divinam humanamque naturam, scelerum securus infuderat.'

[50] For recent analyses, see F. Schnider and W. Stenger, 'Die offene Tür und die unüberschreitbare Kluft,' *New Testament Studies* 25 (1978-9): 447-63; Ronald F. Hock, 'Lazarus and Micyllus:

carried down to hell; there he looks up (elevans oculos) from his torment to behold Lazarus, whose poverty he scorned in life, now comforted in the bosom of Abraham. Dives begs mercy of the patriarch, who in turn rebukes him: not only does justice now forbid leniency, Abraham explains, but 'a great *chaos*' has been fixed between them, which the spirits of the dead may not traverse ('et in his omnibus inter nos et vos chasma [*vars.* chas; chaos] magnum firmatum est ut hii qui volunt hinc transire ad vos non possint neque inde huc transmeare').[51]

Accepting 'khasma mega' (a great chasm) as the reading of the Greek *textus receptus*, scholars since Bentley have argued that 'chasma magnum' must also have stood in the earliest Latin translations. Early and often, haplography corrupted this to *chas magnum* (actually attested in some copies), which later scribes wrongly restored to *chaos magnum*, the reading found in the vast majority of Vulgate manuscripts and patristic quotations.[52] Plausible thus far on its own terms, the argument becomes problematic when it asserts that the error *chaos* was limited to Latin translations or that *chaos* could not be an original reading because the word in Latin meant 'confusion' (as in Ovid) but not 'gulf, abyss.' In fact the Greek fathers, especially Chrysostom, often quoted the relevant verse as 'khaos mega'[53] and, as we have seen, literary Latin exploited the full range of senses for *chaos*, including 'gulf.' If chaos and chasm were already near-synonyms in Greek and Latin, there is probably little point in trying to locate the origin of the Vulgate's *chaos* at Luke 16:26. If their synonymy was not common, the context of the Lukan passage must certainly have promoted it, since *chaos* there strongly suggests some spatial barrier between the speakers.[54]

Greco-Roman Backgrounds to Luke 16:19-31,' *Journal of Biblical Literature* 106 (1987): 447-63; Richard Bauckham, 'The Rich Man and Lazarus: The Parable and the Parallels,' *New Testament Studies* 37 (1991): 225-46.

[51] Robert Weber et al., eds, *Biblia sacra iuxta vulgatam versionem*, 3rd ed. (Stuttgart 1983).

[52] For this account, see De Bruyne, 'Notes de philologie,' and John Wordsworth and Henry Julian White, eds, *Nouum testamentum Domini nostri Iesu Christi latine secundum editionem sancti Hieronymi, pars prior: Quattuor euangelia* (Oxford 1889-98), 425 and apparatus to Luke 16:26.

[53] See The American and British Committees of the International Greek New Testament Project, eds, *The New Testament in Greek: The Gospel According to St. Luke*, 2 vols (Oxford 1984-7), 2:66 and apparatus to Luke 16:26.

[54] The 'chasm' in the story might have suggested a common feature of the Palestinian landscape, the wadi; see Eric F.F. Bishop, 'A Yawning Chasm,' *Evangelical Quarterly* 3 (1975): 3-5.

Interpreting *chaos* precisely in this passage mattered for an obvious reason. The story of Dives and Lazarus included one of the few descriptions of the afterlife spoken by Christ himself. Exegetes therefore sifted the narrative for its implications regarding some urgent problems in Christian eschatology: What happened to the righteous who died before Christ's resurrection? Did an interim paradise or limbo exist, and if so how did it differ from hell? Did further rewards or punishments remain suspended until the Last Judgment?[55] In light of Jewish tradition, the story of Dives and Lazarus likely intended the 'bosom of Abraham' as a place of final reward for the righteous, entirely separate from that of perpetual torment for the wicked. Some Christian exegetes drew the same conclusion and did not press the point further. Gregory the Great's homily on the pericope seems to equate Lazarus's reward with heaven itself, the 'seat of the blessed' and 'the share of beatitude.'[56] But elsewhere Gregory and, indeed, most of the fathers would state that, because the story takes place before Christ's harrowing of hell, neither Lazarus nor Abraham nor any Old Testament figure could have enjoyed the full reward of heaven. According to this view, the 'bosom of Abraham,' while clearly separate from hell and its torments, represents at best some kind of lesser heaven or interim paradise.[57] Still others argued that the relation of 'paradise' to hell described in Luke 16 must be taken figuratively, for it makes no literal sense to speak of a '*chaos* that is so slight that words can pass back and forth between those to either side, and [at the same time] so vast that it cannot be crossed.'[58]

Beyond posing a challenge to commentators, the polysemy that so endeared *chaos* to early medieval poets raised acute difficulties for glossators and translators, most of whom were concerned with the instance in Luke's gospel. The work of these scholars required choosing among several available senses for a lemma based on its context or etymology or some other linguistic criterion. *Chaos* in Luke 16:26, however, was neither etymologically nor contextually transparent. This is easily forgotten because most vernacular

---

[55] See Ananya Jahanara Kabir, *Paradise, Death and Doomsday in Anglo-Saxon Literature*, CSASE 32 (Cambridge 2001).
[56] GREG.MAG. Hom.evang. 40.404.263-74.
[57] For representative formulations, see AUG. Gen.litt. 12.33; also PETR.CHRYS. Serm. 66.5; GREG.MAG. Moral.Iob 4.29.47-57; IUL.TOL. Progn.fut.saec. 2.1-4.
[58] *De statu animae* 3.9: August Engelbrecht, ed., *Claudiani Mamerti opera*, CSEL 11 (Vienna 1885), 170; and similarly Heiric of Auxerre, Homily 2.17 (cited above, n. 1).

Bibles since the Reformation void the issue, returning to the Greek and its unambiguous *khasma*: hence the now-proverbial 'great gulf fixed' of the Authorized Version (1611), echoing the 'great gulfe set' of the Geneva Bible (1557) and the sense, if not the wording, of Tyndale's 'greate space set' (1526).[59] The Rheims New Testament (1582) clung to the Vulgate reading but, in its own way, also sidestepped the problem by leaving the hard word untranslated: 'there is fixed a great chaos.'

4. *Chaos* in Early Germanic Translations and Glosses

Unlike the later translations, those of the earlier Middle Ages did not often have the luxury of appeal to the Greek. Some chose simply to substitute a noncommittal vernacular word for the troublesome Latin one, as in the Old High German Tatian, where *chaos* receives a vaguely contextual translation *untarmerchi*, probably 'boundary-line, border.'[60] But elsewhere glosses and translations took a more definite stand on *chaos*, with Old English providing the most abundant evidence, followed distantly by Old High German and Old Norse. The solutions show remarkable range and often return, in surprising ways, to the philological traditions about the word in secular literature.

A typical response appears in the eleventh-century Old English translation within the so-called West-Saxon Gospels:

> And on eallum þissum betwux us and eow is mycel dwolma getrymed. Þa ðe willað heonon to eow faran ne magon, ne þanun faran hidere. (Luke [WSCp] 16.26)

> And in all these respects a great 'dwolma' is set between us and you. Those who wish to go from here to you cannot do so, nor come here from there.

---

[59] Tyndale's wording may echo still earlier traditions; cf. the 'expanded version' of the Northern Homily Cycle (c. 1400), lines 14,898-9: 'A mekil space es ordaind now / To be ay bitwix vs and þow'; Saara Nevanlinna, ed., *The Northern Homily Cycle: The Expanded Version in MSS Harley 4196 and Cotton Tiberius E vii*, 3 vols, Mémoires de la Société Néophilologique de Helsinki 38, 41, and 43 (Helsinki 1972-84), 2:273.
[60] Eduard Sievers, ed., *Tatian: Lateinisch und altdeutsch mit ausführlichem Glossar*, Bibliothek der ältesten deutschen Literatur-Denkmäler 5 (Paderborn 1892), 154 (107.3); see s. *untarmerchi* in Rudolf Schützeichel, ed., *Althochdeutsches Wörterbuch*, 5th edn (Tübingen 1995).

The context tempts us to make *dwolma* a simpler word than it actually is. Old English *dwolma* glosses *chaos* ten times and in three of these the lemma in context pertains to the 'state of primal confusion' as common in post-Ovidian literary use.[61] As an equivalent for *chaos* in the sense '[elemental] confusion,' OE *dwolma* perhaps joins Old High German glosses *gimischida* 'mixture, confusion' and the already mentioned *gigôz*.[62] For all other occurrences of *dwolma*, however, either the context is unknown or the Old English collocations are too vague to permit distinction between 'confused-ness' in the abstract or the matter subsisting in that state. At base *dwolma* is related to a family of Old English terms for 'wandering' and 'error' (verbs *dwellan, dwelian, dwolian*; nouns *dwala, dwola, gedwyld*) and has a large number of Germanic cognates spanning ideas from 'foolishness' (Go. *dvals*) to 'delaying, lingering' (ON *dvala* and *dvelja*, OHG *twalên, twalôn, twellen*), or the state of 'being numbed, stunned' (OHG *twalm*, OS *dwalm*). The same root, IE **dheu-*, shows many derivatives fundamentally related to the idea of '"rising in a cloud," as dust, vapor, or smoke,' and hence 'notions of breath, various [dark] color adjectives, and forms denoting defective perception or wits.'[63] Traces of this historical range survive about OHG-MHG *twalm*, used not only for the abstract condition of being disoriented but also for the obfuscating substance responsible, such as 'thick smoke' or 'vapour,' even 'drink.'[64] A few citations of OE *dwolma* suggest that it too requires a definition 'darkness' not as the mere absence of light but as a turbid, obscuring substance.[65]

---

[61] *DOE*, s. *dwolma*, sense 1, citations from CorpGl 2 3.361, AldV 13.1 2483, and AldMV 5.1 9; see also *gedwolma* at ClGl 1 1459.

[62] Steinmeyer-Sievers, *Die althochdeutschen Glossen*, 2:654.17; for *gigôz*, see above, p. 21.

[63] See Calvert Watkins, ed., *The American Heritage Dictionary of Indo-European Roots* (Boston 2000), s. *dheu-* 1; cf. Jan de Vries, ed., *Altnordisches etymologisches Wörterbuch*, 2nd edn (Leiden 1962), s. *dvala* and *dvelja*; Ferdinand Holthausen, ed., *Altenglisches etymologisches Wörterbuch*, 2nd edn (Heidelberg 1963), s. *dwala* etc.; and Pokorny, *Indogermanisches etymologisches Wörterbuch*, 1:261-7 (*dheu-* 4).

[64] See s. *twalm* in Oskar Schade, ed., *Altdeutsches Wörterbuch*, 2nd edn, 2 vols (Halle 1872-82), 2:973; s. *TWILL* in Georg Benecke et al., eds, *Mittelhochdeutsches Wörterbuch*, 3 vols (Leipzig 1864-81), 3:160 (cf. Scots *dwalm*, at *OED*, s.). But note that OHG *twalm* and OE *dwolma* are morphologically distinct, derived by Germanic abstractive suffixes **-ma* (strong) and **-man* (weak) respectively; see Friedrich Kluge, *Nominale Stammbildungslehre der altgermanischen Dialekte*, 3rd edn (Halle 1926), 80 (§152) and 81 (§154).

[65] See *DOE*, s. *dwolma*, sense 1, citations from JDay II 104 (with HomU 26 82) and Met 5.42; cf. AldMV 5.1 9 'chaos i[d est] tenebre, sax[onice] dwolma.'

The identification of *chaos* with 'darkness,' familiar from classical and Christian poetry, explains not only some overlooked dimensions of OE *dwolma* but many other glosses and translations. Two early Old English glossaries attach to the ablative form *chao* the strangely specific *dimnesse gastas* 'spirits of darkness,' carrying further associations with the underworld and shades.[66] In other instances the equation with darkness is plainer, from the *Abrogans* glosses *immensae tenebrae / mihil finstar*, to the Wycliffite translation (1380) of Luke 16:26 as 'a greet derk place.'[67] Walter Hilton cites the verse in his fourteenth-century *Scala perfectionis*: 'There is a gret chaos (that is a grete myrkenesse to sai).' Early printed versions substitute 'a thycke derkenes'; one also misprints (or re-etymologizes?) 'gret chaos' as 'great cause.'[68]

Others went further to stress that the darkness of *chaos* had palpable form. The most jarring example falls in an Old English homily by Ælfric of Eynsham (d. ca. 1010) for the second Sunday after Pentecost. Translating the story of Dives and Lazarus, Ælfric has Abraham say of the notorious *chaos magnum*, 'And betwux us is micel þrosm gefæstnod,' and later in the same piece, 'betwux us and eow is gefæstnod micel þrosm.'[69] Nothing in Ælfric's principal source for this homily, Gregory the Great's Latin exposition of the same pericope, explains what is, in context, this rather surprising translation of *chaos*. Just like *dwolma*, the noun *þrosm* defies easy reduction to a one-word gloss. The *Anglo-Saxon Dictionary* of Bosworth and Toller attempts to split the sense 'smoke, vapour' from that of 'darkness,'[70] but as the word typically appears in context those qualities are inseparable. Apart from the two instances in Ælfric's homily, *þrosm* occurs as a simplex fifteen times.[71] Twelve of those

---

[66] ClGl 1 (Stryker) 1327 and ClGl 3 (Quinn) 1991. The lemma may be either VERG. Georg. 4.347 or CAEL.SED. Carm.pasch. 1.103.

[67] Steinmeyer-Sievers, *Die althochdeutschen Glossen*, 1:73.33; Josiah Forshall and Frederic Madden, eds, *The Holy Bible ... in the Earliest English Versions Made from the Latin Vulgate by John Wycliffe and His Followers*, 4 vols (Oxford 1850), 4:203; some versions add 'ether depthe.'

[68] Walter Hilton, *The Scale of Perfection*, 1.77, ed. Thomas Bestul, TEAMS Middle English Texts (Kalamazoo 2000), 119 (for the early printings, see quotation at *OED*, s. *chaos*, sense 1); on this 'myrknesse' as Hilton's metaphor for separation from God, see Bestul's introduction, 2 and 6.

[69] ÆCHom I, 23   365.18 and 368.85.

[70] BT, s. *þrosm*, senses I-II. Campbell (BTS-Addenda, s. *þrosm*) questioned BT sense III, 'gl[ossing] chauterem' [at PrGl 1 (Meritt) 760]; but there the glossator probably understood the first element of the lemma (*cau*-) as related to *chaos*, as Meritt has noted (see n. 28 above).

[71] Its derivatives are few, including an adjective *þrosmig* and a compound *sweflþrosm* (glossing *sulphur*). The verbs *ā-, for-, of-þrysm(i)an* all incorporate the idea 'suffocating, smothering' and perhaps 'darkening, blackening' with cloud or smoke (as Lat. *obnubilare*); cf. verbs OFris. *thresma*,

refer unambiguously to the conditions of hell, wherein *þrosm* is difficult to distinguish from smoke, fire or heat, and covering darkness.[72] It is rather all of these, a synaesthetic concept of darkness as a roiling, asphyxiating, black cloud.[73] This definition also suits on the rare occasions when the word does not apply to hell. The second stanza of the Sunday Vespers hymn, *Lucis creator optime*, poetically describes the onset of night as a 'descent of chaos' (tetrum chaos inlabitur), which a glossator, probably working at Winchester in the later tenth century, has translated 'sweart þrosm on aslit.'[74] The image bears close comparison with the 'Sun and Moon' Riddle in *The Exeter Book,* where the words 'Dust stonc to heofonum' (Rid 29, 12) (Dust [or smoke] wafted to the heavens) describe the lifting of darkness with the sunrise.

A suspicion inevitably arises that *þrosm* used as an equivalent for *chaos* in both the hymn glosses and in Ælfric's homily points back to a Winchester school tradition. If so, the proposed synonymy was all the more remarkable for the way it complicated exegesis of the gospel story. As a stifling, opaque turbidity, OE *þrosm* is an odd choice at Luke 16:26 where Dives, it is said, can 'raise his eyes' and see Lazarus across or through the *chaos*, whatever that is. The widespread association of *þrosm* with hell, where the rich man finds himself, may have determined Ælfric's choice, but an equally likely explanation lies in a Winchester glossing tradition, as attested in the hymnals. In either case, Ælfric evidently saw no contradiction in making the barrier between Dives and Lazarus an opaque substance rather than a yawning gap.

MLG *drüs(se)men*; see Holthausen, *Altenglisches etymologisches Wörterbuch*, s. *for-þrysman*, and BTS, s. *for-þrysmian*.

[72] In poetry the word alliterates with *þystro* 'darkness,' *beþeccan* 'cover, enshroud,' and *þracu* 'pressure, force'; see GenA,B 323-6; El 1297-8; ChristA,B,C 109; JDay II 191. Other uses, all in descriptions of hell, are: JDay II 197; HomS 27 65; HomU 3 (Irv 7) 46-7; HomU 9 (ScraggVerc 4) 41-2; HomU 15.1 (Scragg) 16-17; HomU 26 (Nap 29) 139; HomU 32 (Nap 40) 74; Bede 5, 13.426.25.

[73] A further quality, heat, may only be incidental to the use of *þrosm* in descriptions of hell: see esp. HomU 9 (ScraggVerc 4) 41-2, 'næfre ... þurst aceled biþ þære helle þrosmes,' 'never ... will the thirst of [= caused by?] the *þrosm* of hell be quenched.' In addition to context, a perceived link to Gr *kauma* (see n. 28) would reinforce the idea that heat is intrinsic to *chaos* and thus perhaps to *þrosm*.

[74] HyGl 2 (Milfull) 13.2; cf. the same gloss in the prosified version HyGl 3 (Gneuss) 13.2. On the date and Winchester backgrounds of these glosses, see Inge B. Milfull, *The Hymns of the Anglo-Saxon Church: A Study of the 'Durham Hymnal,'* CSASE 17 (Cambridge 1996), 37 and 78. On *taetrum chaos* in the Latin original, see Clemens Blume, *Unsere liturgischen Lieder: Das Hymnar der altchristlichen Kirche* (Regensburg 1932), 161, and Leo Eizenhöfer, 'Taetrum chaos illabitur,' *Archiv für Liturgiewissenschaft* 2 (1952): 94-5.

Perhaps Ælfric is simply keeping company with commentators such as Claudianus Mamertus, who had cautioned that any overly literal reading of details in the passage would lead to hopeless contradictions.[75] As a kind of one-word riddle, *chaos* already held in tension the opposed ideas of destruction and creation, void and matter, confusion and order, death and salvation, so why not opacity and transparency? However they reconciled it, some interpreters clearly did regard Luke's *chaos* as an impenetrable dark cloud. In the eighth century, Ambrosius Autpertus went so far as to associate the '*chaos* fixed' between Dives and Lazarus with the pillar of cloud that separated Egyptians from Israelites through the night before the crossing of the Red Sea. That cloud not only kept Pharaoh's army at a safe distance but also plunged it into immobilizing darkness, while its opposite face bathed Israel in light (Exod. 14:19-20). The Egyptians' plight, Ambrosius explains, anticipates both the 'outer darkness' (tenebrae exteriores) that awaits the ill-attired wedding guest at Matt. 22:13 and also the impenetrable *chaos magnum* of Luke 16:26.[76]

Sometimes the thing separating the damned from the saved took more solid form. A few readers, faced with the indeterminacy of *chaos* at Luke 16:26, evidently made much of the lone clue to its nature in the accompanying passive participle *firmatum* (Gr *estêriktai*; 'fixed' in the Authorized and Rheims versions). Among several possible glosses for *chaos*, Haymo of Auxerre included the participial substantives 'pactum vel firmatum,' ([something] fixed or established).[77] In the vernaculars, an Old High German gloss makes of *chaos* a *festi(n)* 'that which provides protection,' or 'defensive wall,'[78] while a late medieval Latin-German dictionary renders the term (outside the Lukan context) as *ein vnderwall*, evidently an '(outer) defensive embankment.'[79] The

---

[75] See above, p. 27, esp. n. 58.
[76] Robert Weber, ed., *Ambrosii Autperti Expositio in apocalypsin*, 3 vols, CCSL 27, 27A, and 27B (Turnhout 1975-9), 1:51-2 (to Apoc. 1:7 'Ecce venit cum nubibus').
[77] *Homiliae de tempore*, Homily 110, at PL 118, 596B.
[78] Steinmeyer-Sievers, *Die althochdeutschen Glossen*, 1:813.4; see Karg and Gasterstädt, *Althochdeutsches Wörterbuch*, s. *festi(n)*, sense 8.b 'Schutzwall.' Cf. the MHG (13th-century?) sermon on Dives and Lazarus in Anton E. Schönbach, ed., *Altdeutsche Predigten*, 3 vols (Graz 1886-91), 2:117-20, at 119: 'ez wær ein so getan vest enzwischen in von got gemacht.' On the other hand, the OE cognate *fæsten* is used of [the enclosure of] hell at Whale 71 and perhaps Ex 49; might a similar association explain OHG *festin* for *chaos*?
[79] Cited s. *Chaos* in Lorenz Diefenbach, ed., *Glossarium latino-germanicum mediae et infimae aetatis* (Frankfurt am Main 1857), 96. *Vnderwall* occurs in lexica of military terms; see Jacob and Wilhelm Grimm et al., eds, *Deutsches Wörterbuch*, 33 vols (Leipzig 1854-1971; repr. Munich 1971), 24, col. 1884.

same impulse would appear in occasional Middle English paraphrases of 'chaos magnum ... firmatum' as 'sykernes' and 'mechil firmament,' the latter perhaps intending to sound a cosmogonic note as well.[80] The most oddly explicit witness to this pattern nevertheless appears back in Old English: the Northumbrian glossator of the Rushworth Gospels explained the cause of 'fixity': 'Bitwih iow & usih ðonne pæð miclum cele gifæstnad is.'[81] However misguided, 'miclum cele gifæstnad' (hardened or made firm by great cold) indicates explicitly how the glossator pictured the scene, with the dividing substance frozen solid. (Many visions of hell described among its torments simultaneous extremes of heat and cold, so there would be no contradiction in the rich man's complaints of parching thirst.)

The other striking feature of the Rushworth gloss, its translation of *chaos* as 'pæð,' has long caught the attention of lexicographers. Aldred interprets the same lemma (*chaos magnum*) in the Lindisfarne Gospels as 'dene [ue]l pæð micel.'[82] These two instances, along with evidence from later northern English and place names, allow that *pæð* in Anglian could mean 'ravine, valley,' particularly where these served as narrow passages up or down a slope.[83] Since Dives sits not only far from but apparently lower than Abraham — or so many exegetes understood 'elevans oculos' at 16:23 — 'path' in the sense 'ravine-like passage [up the acclivity]' would be topographically apt. Implied reference to some northern landscape would also explain 'miclum cele gifæstnad' as where the muddy floor of a gully can freeze hard. The tendency to make of *chaos* a passageway, however cold and arduous, probably arose by anticipation of Abraham's words in the remainder of the verse: 'so that they who would pass from hence to you, cannot, nor from thence come hither' (Rheims 1582). Latin sermons provide occasional analogies for *chaos* as a space for journeying through. 'Eusebius Gallicanus' describes the doomed soul's passage 'along paths of darkness' (per semitas tenebrarum), which

---

[80] See O.S. Pickering, ed., *The South English Ministry and Passion* [c. 1270-85], Middle English Texts 16 (Heidelberg 1984), 130 (line 1317); Frederick Furnivall, ed., *Robert of Brunne's 'Handlyng Synne'* [c. 1300], 2 vols, EETS, o.s. 119 and 123 (London 1901-3), 1:216 (line 6689). See also *MED*, s. sikernes(se, sense 2.c.

[81] LkGl (Ru) 16.26. I follow the parsing of Uno Lindelöf, *Glossar zur altnorthumbrischen Evangelienübersetzung in der Rushworth-Handschrift (die sogenannte Glosse Rushworth 2)*, Acta Societatis Scientiarum Fennicae 22, no. 5 (Helsinki 1897), 13 (s. *cele*).

[82] LkGl (Li) 16.26.

[83] See *OED*, s. *path*, sense 2, and H.W. Bailey and Alan S.C. Ross, 'Path,' *Transactions of the Philological Society* (1961): 107-42, at 108-10.

simultaneously constitute the vast, void *chaos* that separates the domains of life and death.[84] Some apocryphal accounts of the next world feature a treacherous passage in the form of a 'bridge of hell,' and according to the motif known as the 'three utterances,' a condemned soul cries out, 'Harsh is the journey' (Asperum est iter) or, in one Old Irish version, 'Steep is the road.'[85]

The plainest example of *chaos*-as-passage survives in the Old Norse translation of Gregory the Great's homily on Dives and Lazarus, where Abraham declares: 'En torleiþi er sett micit a meþal var oc yþvar.'[86] With its synonym *torfæra* (or *torfæri*), ON *torleiði* means 'a difficult, dangerous passage or road.'[87] Another Old Norse translation of *chaos* may also belong to the 'passage'-group: the Saga of the Apostles John and James repeats the story of Dives and Lazarus entire, including the relevant verse, translated 'Sva er ok mikit forat [*var.* forad] sett ok skipat milli vár.'[88] All occurrences of ON *forað* convey the essential idea of 'peril,' whether belonging to a place (a precipice, abyss, or bog), to a creature (the hell-hound Garmr in Snorri's *Edda*), or more generally to any dangerous person or situation.[89] But a plausible case has been made that the original sense of *forað* was something like 'difficult or dangerous [place of] passage.'[90] Etymological definitions aside, the medieval traditions of *chaos* as 'danger' or a 'hazardous passage' are sufficiently well established to allow that *forað* may not simply mean 'chasm' in the *Jóns ok Jacobs saga*.[91]

---

[84] EUSEB.GALL. Collect.hom. 36.27-24, continuing: 'in illud inane ac uacuum [cf. Gen. 1:2] ... atque illud magnum chaos, quod uitae mortisque regionem discernit.'

[85] On the 'bridge of hell,' see Charles D. Wright, *The Irish Tradition in Old English Literature*, CSASE 6 (Cambridge 1993), 122-4; on the 'three utterances,' see Rudolf Willard, *Two Apocrypha in Old English Homilies*, Beiträge zur englischen Philologie 30 (Leipzig 1935), 44-5, with discussion at 113-21; for updated bibliography, see Wright, *Irish Tradition*, 215-18.

[86] Þorvaldur Bjarnarson, ed., *Leifar fornra kristinna fræða íslenzkra: Codex Arna-Magnæanus 677 4to* (Copenhagen 1878), 37; cf. 43. The manuscript was copied in the earlier thirteenth century. Later medieval and early modern Icelandic translations, like their English counterparts, tend to reflect the 'restored' reading *chasma* for *chaos*: thus *hvelfi* in Oddur Gottskálksson's New Testament (1540); or *djup* in the Icelandic New Testament of 1644.

[87] The definition in Cleasby-Vigfusson, s. *tor-færa*; see also Fritzner, s. *torfæra*: 'besværlig Passage, Sted hvor det er vanskeligt at komme frem.'

[88] C.R. Unger, ed., *Tveggja postola saga Jons ok Jacobs*, in *Postola sögur* (Christiania 1874), 539-711, at 650.

[89] See citations in Fritzner and Cleasby-Vigfusson.

[90] See s. *forað* in de Vries, *Altnordisches etymologisches Wörterbuch*, and Axel Kock, 'Studier i de nordiska språkens historia,' *Arkiv för nordisk filologi* 14 (1898): 213-70, at 262-4.

[91] The Latin (contextual) gloss *periculum* also attaches to *chaos*; see A.P. Orbán, 'Ein anonymer Aratorkommentar in Hs. London, Royal MS. 15 A. V,' *Sacris Erudiri* 38 (1998-9): 317-51, and 40

5. Postscript: *Chaos* in Later Centuries

As soon as 'hazardous passage-way' joins the possible senses for literary *chaos*, it is hard for the mind not to leap forward to Milton's Satan 'treading the crude consistence' between heaven and hell:

> So eagerly the fiend
> O'er bog or steep, through strait, rough, dense, or rare,
> With head, hands, wings, or feet pursues his way,
> And swims or sinks, or wades, or creeps, or flies.[92]

The conceptual parallel is surely coincidental; much further, tortuous history would separate the early medieval philologists from Milton. Vaguely poetic *chaos* lost little of its popularity in the later Middle Ages, but in the twelfth and thirteenth centuries proponents of the new learning tried to reclaim the word for serious cosmogonic discussion. Even this was not altogether new; understood as *prima confusio* or *inanitas*, the word *chaos* had seen occasional if superficial duty in early medieval commentary on Gen. 1:2 ('et terra erat inanis et vacua') and Wis. 11:18 ('qui fecisti mundum de materia informi'). Expounding these crucial verses, Augustine, Isidore, and others had already nodded to the Greco-Roman concept of *chaos* and associated terms for primal matter (Gr *hylê*; Lat. *materia*, *silva*).[93] But the full potential of *chaos* for Christian cosmology would remain relatively unexploited until adopted by the likes of Alanus de Insulis, Bernardus Silvestris, Hugh of St Victor, William of Conches, Thierry of Chartres, Albertus Magnus, Thomas Aquinas, and Ramón Lull.[94] No less momentous for the history of *chaos*, Ovid returned

---

(2001): 131-229, at 200. For this lemma (the Eutychus episode, at ARATOR. Act.apost. 2.767-9), see also above, pp. 24-5.

[92] *Paradise Lost*, bk. 2, ll. 947-50, on which passage see Regina M. Schwartz, *Remembering and Repeating Biblical Creation in* Paradise Lost (Cambridge 1988), 17.

[93] Augustine, *De Genesi contra Manichaeos* 5 (PL 34, 173-220, at col. 178); idem, *Contra epistulam Manichaei quam uocant fundamenti* 29 (PL 42, 173-206, at col. 195); ISID. Diff.rer. 11.29-30. These discussions all further associate Gen. 1:2 with Wis. 11:18.

[94] This phase of the history lies beyond the study at hand, but see refs at Dierse and Kuhlen, 'Chaos' (at n. 11), 981, as well as Simone Viarre, 'Cosmologie antique et commentaire de la creation du monde: Le chaos et les quatre elements chez quelques auteurs du haut moyen âge,' in *La cultura antica nell'occidente latino dal VII all'XI secolo*, 2 vols, Settimane di studio del Centro italiano di studi sull' alto Medioevo 22 (1975) II, 541-73; and Lenka Karfíková, 'Die Gestaltung des Chaos:

triumphantly to school curricula.[95] From the eleventh and twelfth centuries, the associations of *chaos* would therefore divide and overlap even more subtly, and few safeguards were left to discourage confusion between technical and 'popular' senses of the word.

Nor did the wealth of medieval traditions simply fade when the humanists' revival of *chaos* fixed the word permanently in the vernaculars. To many who knew it as more than a simple allusion to Ovid, the mysteries and possibilities of the term carried on productively as ever. It is well known, for example, that Paracelsus (1493-1541) used *chaos* not just for the primal stuff of creation but for the atmospheres proper to creatures of the divers elements; earth constitutes the 'Chaos' of Gnomes, fire that of Salamanders, and so on.[96] From *chaos* probably in this Paracelsan sense 'element,' the Dutch chemist Van Helmont (1577-1644) derived the term *gas*, which quickly entered the vernaculars of Europe.[97] *Gas* not only continued the generative pattern of *chaos* across languages but, coincidentally, began life as something oddly reminiscent of Old English *þrosm*: the earliest known use of Van Helmont's coinage in English, by Richard Francke (1658), describes the atmosphere about Dundee as 'Gass,' or 'embodied Mists' with 'such pernicious Vapours as nauseate the Air.'[98]

In broader perspective, even as Milton worked to remythologize literary *chaos*, the word was entering a new period of contest among poets, scientists, and philosophers. Their competing claims, like the polysemy of the very term, have shown no signs of diminishment as, in the nineteenth and twentieth centuries, specialists in many fields have claimed the word as their own. Philosophers since Nietzsche and Heidegger have held up chaos as an abstraction of pure, amoral potentiality, with resonances of Greek *dynamis*.[99]

Das kosmogonische Paradigma bei Hugo von St. Viktor und Wilhelm von Conches,' *Graecolatina Pragensia* 15 (1997): 47-71.
[95] OVID. Met. I.7-9 has been quoted above (p. 16); for typical high-medieval commentary, see Frank Coulson, ed., *The 'Vulgate' Commentary on Ovid's* Metamorphoses: *The Creation Myth and the Story of Orpheus*, Toronto Medieval Latin Texts 20 (Toronto 1991), 35-41.
[96] Theophrastus von Hohenheim, genannt Paracelsus, *Liber de nymphis, sylphis, pygmaeis et salamandris et de caeteris spiritibus*, ed. Robert Blaser, Altdeutsche Übungstexte 16 (Bern 1960), 16-21 (Tractate II).
[97] 'halitum illum *Gas* vocavi, non longe a Chao veterum secretum'; quoted from his *Ortus medicinae* (1652 edn) at *OED*, s. gas n.I.
[98] *Northern Memoirs, Calculated for the Meridian of Scotland* ... (London 1694), 202.
[99] See refs at Dierse and Kuhlen, 'Chaos' (at n. 11), 983-4.

For their part, artists and poets redefined a formalism based on order-in-disorder. One of the modernists' more familiar devices, labelled 'chaotic enumeration' by Spitzer, embodies a critique not only of traditional aesthetics but of traditional ways of knowing and reasoning; hence the deep significance of 'chaos' to a poet such as Wallace Stevens, who distils the idea in memorable and prescient terms as 'A small relation expanding like the shade / Of a cloud on sand.'[100] The image of cloud shapes mutating in seemingly unpredictable patterns foreshadows the latest, noisiest arguments over *chaos*, namely those swirling about 'Chaos Theory.'[101] Even this 'new' controversy, however, turns out to involve a misunderstanding between technical and popular senses of *chaos*. To the scientist, 'chaotic' describes not utter disorder or indeterminacy, but the effective unpredictability of a system in which infinitesimal changes to one part will produce drastically different outcomes. Far from *chaos* in the popular sense, this type of system is entirely determined; its outcomes would be predictable, could the variables be measured with perfect accuracy.[102]

Simply put, the most recent technical definition effectively inverts the popular one. The result has been no little confusion about what Chaos Theory actually claims or how (if at all) its applications reach beyond the sciences.[103] Yet within the longer history of the word, this kind of semantic turnabout should come as no surprise. Between antiquity and the early Middle Ages, *chaos* often changed shape before the curious eyes of poets and grammarians. Their learned preoccupations alone can account for some of the more arresting treatments of Luke 16:26, as well as for the proliferation of etymologies and puns within or across languages. Like the shadow cast by

---

[100] Leo Spitzer, 'La enumeración caótica en la poesía moderna,' in his *Lingüística e historia litteraria* (Madrid 1961), 295-346. Wallace Stevens, 'Connoisseur of Chaos,' first publ. in *Parts of a World* (1942), reprinted in *The Collected Poems of Wallace Stevens* (New York 1954), 215-16.
[101] 'Chaos' the mathematical term and 'chaos theory' were included among additions to the *OED* in 1997, with supporting quotations dating back to 1960. 'Chaos theory' was popularized in North America mainly through James Gleick's best-selling *Chaos: Making a New Science* (New York 1987).
[102] I have found helpful Nina Hall, ed., *The New Scientist Guide to Chaos* (London 1992) and Stephen H. Kellert, *In the Wake of Chaos: Unpredictable Order in Dynamic Systems* (Chicago 1993).
[103] For the advent of 'chaos' in literary theory, see N. Katherine Hayles, *Chaos Bound: Orderly Disorder in Contemporary Literature and Science* (Ithaca, NY 1990), and Harriett Hawkins, *Strange Attractors: Literature, Culture, and Chaos Theory* (New York 1995); cf. the strong objections of Carl Matheson and Evan Kirchhoff, 'Chaos and Literature,' *Philosophy and Literature* 21 (1997): 28-45; Willie van Peer, 'Sense and Nonsense of Chaos Theory in Literary Studies,' in Elinor S. Shaffer, ed., *The Third Culture: Literature and Science* (Berlin 1997), 40-8.

Stevens's shape-shifting clouds, 'relation appears' among the referents with seemingly limitless complexity: from the primal 'something,' whether a void or confusion of matter; to the underworld (pagan, Jewish, or Christian); to darkness palpable in the forms of cloud, mist, fog, vapour, or dust; to a liminal space between life and death, heaven and hell, or upper and nether hells; to a hazardous trail connecting worlds; or to some barrier, material or moral, separating them.[104]

[104] It is fitting that all who have generously provided help during the writing of this essay — Ian and David MacDougall, Anna Grotans, and Nicholas Howe — share the author's deep appreciation of Roberta. Though mindful that she would have made from *chaos* a much wittier, more learned essay, I offer this with thanks for years of selfless, patient, and good-humoured mentoring, *matre dea monstrante viam.*

2

Composing and Joining: How the Anglo-Saxons Talked about Compounding

DON CHAPMAN

In the course of her career, Roberta Frank has repeatedly illuminated the Anglo-Saxons' ways with words, whether poetic words like *wiga* and *hyge* in prose, blends like *þrymnes*, or play on words like *weard*, *werod*, and *word*.[1] Indeed, the writings of Anglo-Saxons show much creativity with words. The creative compounds in Old English poetry and the neologisms in hermeneutic Latin prose are both well known.[2] As outsiders, we certainly are aware of such neologisms and creative coinages when we encounter them. But how aware were the Anglo-Saxons? What self-conscious attitudes would learned Anglo-Saxons have had towards the words they created and encountered? Not that they would have needed an awareness of creativity to be creative, but a better understanding of how Anglo-Saxons would have regarded new word creations will let us gauge more accurately the differences between their perceptions and ours. Trying to grasp their perceptions is part of the philological task of understanding what words would have meant and what effect they would have had at the time they were used.[3]

Ideally such an understanding would come from some kind of poetics or rhetoric of word formation. Unfortunately, no early medieval poetics for

[1] Roberta Frank, 'Poetic Words in Late Old English Prose,' in Malcolm Godden et al., eds, *From Anglo-Saxon to Early Middle English: Studies Presented to E.G. Stanley* (Oxford 1994), 87-107; 'Late Old English *þrymnys* 'Trinity': Scribal Nod or Word Waiting to Be Born?' in Joan H. Hall et al., eds, *Old English and New: Studies in Language and Linguistics in Honor of Frederic G. Cassidy* (New York 1992), 97-110; and 'Some Uses of Paronomasia in Old English Scriptural Verse,' *Speculum* 47 (1972): 207-26.
[2] For compounds, see Otto Krackow, *Die Nominalkomposita als Kunstmittel im altenglischen Epos* (Weimar 1903); and Arthur Gilchrist Brodeur, *The Art of Beowulf* (Berkeley 1959). For Latin neologisms, see Michael Lapidge, 'The Hermeneutic Style in Tenth-Century Anglo-Latin Literature,' *ASE* 4 (1975): 67-111.
[3] Roberta Frank, 'The Unbearable Lightness of Being a Philologist,' *JEGP* 96 (1997): 486-513.

word formation is extant for either Old English or Latin. For Old English poetry, we derive some benefit from Snorri's poetics, which expounds categories for appellations (e.g., *kend heiti, ōkend heiti,* and *kenning*) and reveals his attitudes towards neologisms in Old Icelandic poetry.[4] But notwithstanding the many connections between Anglo-Saxon England and Scandinavia and the suitability of Snorri's categories to Old English poetry, it is not clear how much Anglo-Saxons would have shared Snorri's self-conscious understanding of poetic diction.

Similarly, we can make some headway in the Latin hermeneutic tradition with remarks from classical rhetoric about the creation of new words. Cicero and Quintilian both speak of the potential effects of new words and their appropriateness for particular styles.[5] But again there is very little evidence that Cicero's and Quintilian's treatises were known among the Anglo-Saxons.[6]

The doctrines on language that we know the Anglo-Saxons knew come instead from the grammatical tradition. This tradition, which became the principal approach to language study in the early Middle Ages,[7] does not provide an explicit poetics of word formation, but it does present several statements about the creation of new words. Even though grammatical doctrines may not be the best indicator of self-conscious attitudes towards the use of new words, they still tell us what educated Anglo-Saxons would have learned about word formation. From the statements in the medieval *artes grammaticae,* perhaps we can tease out, albeit tentatively, what a poetics might have looked like, or at least what self-conscious attitudes about new words might have existed in Anglo-Saxon England.

Anglo-Saxons schooled in Latin grammar would have known explicitly about two major methods of word formation, namely compounding and derivation. Of the two, compounding is consistently presented more directly. In medieval grammars, the form of a word — whether it was a compound or simplex — was considered one of its features of accidence. So, just as students

---

[4] Brodeur, *The Art of Beowulf;* cf. Frank, 'Unbearable Lightness,' 506.

[5] Jaana Vaahtera, *Derivation: Greek and Roman Views on Word Formation* (Turku 1998), 37-51.

[6] Gabriele Knappe, *Traditionen der klassischen Rhetorik im angelsächsischen England* (Heidelberg 1996), 112-18. The relevant classical texts — *De oratore* and *Orator* by Cicero and *Institutio oratoria* by Quintilian — are not listed in Helmut Gneuss, *Handlist of Anglo-Saxon Manuscripts: A List of Manuscripts and Manuscript Fragments Written or Owned in England up to 1100* (Tempe 2001).

[7] Martin Irvine, *The Making of Textual Culture* (Cambridge 1994).

learning Latin today are expected to know the gender, number, or case of a noun, medieval students were also expected to know the *figura*, or compound status.[8] The treatment of derivation, on the other hand, is much more diffuse and incidental, as the categories comprising derivations (diminutives, patronymics, deverbal nouns, etc.) are scattered among several semantic categories (concrete and abstract words, relational opposites, etc.). This paper will focus on the more prominent category of *figura*, or compounding.

The medieval notions of *figura*, however, are not identical to our notions of compounds,[9] and equating *figura* with our term *compounding* would efface subtle differences in medieval terminology — differences that may well reflect a different perception of words formed by compounding. There is a sense in the Latin terminology of creating, fashioning, or forming that is missing from our terms. The difference can be seen in the grammatical forms used to refer to compounding: today we speak of a word as being a **compound**, whereas medieval descriptions usually speak of a word as being **composed** (*compositum*). Likewise, we refer to compounds as substantives, and our definitions generally emphasize the result of the compounding process, not the process itself. A typical general definition, for example, is, 'A "compound" is a word that consists of more than one word.'[10] Current linguistic research certainly is concerned with the processes that generate compounds, but the

---

[8] *Figura* is also used in medieval grammatical and paragrammatical texts to refer to rhetorical figures, such as assonance and rhyme. This essay, including the quotations below from medieval grammatical commentaries, treats only the use of *figura* as a feature of grammatical accidence.

[9] Today most linguists are careful to define compounds against derivations on the one hand and syntactic phrases on the other. The classical notions of compounds that the medievals inherited, however, included structures that we would call prefixed words, like *indoctus* and *impius*, and collocations, like *res publica* and *tribunus plebis*. For a comparison of medieval and modern concepts of compounds, see Don Chapman, 'Notions of Compounding in Priscian's *Institutiones*,' in *History of Linguistics 1996*, vol. 1, ed. D. Cram, A. Linn, and E. Nowak (Amsterdam 1999), 23-30.

[10] G.P.J. Wamelink-van Lint, 'Compounds: Semantics and Pragmatics,' in *The Encyclopedia of Language and Linguistics*, vol. 1, ed. R.E. Asher (Oxford 1994), 657-9. Even in more specialized discussions of compounds, the emphasis is usually on a structure consisting of two or more components, as in the following definition:

An H-compound is a structure [X Y]z or [Y X]z, such that:
  * The denotation of Z is a subset of the denotation of Y;
  * If S is a possible way of specifying Y, the denotation of Z is determined by the range of S's that are compatible with the semantics of X;
  * X does not have independent access to the discourse.

See also Pius ten Hacken, *Defining Morphology* (Hildesheim 1994), 74; and Laurie Bauer, *The Grammar of Nominal Compounding* (Odense 1978), 48-54.

result of those processes (a compound) is still referred to as a substantive, and its structure is still emphasized as its salient characteristic, not the fact that it has been produced. Perhaps current linguistic theory comes closest to emphasizing the formation process in the debate over whether compounds reside in an individual's lexicon or are created anew each time an individual uses them."

There are good indications that the verbal, participial force of *compositum* was primary, or at least salient for medieval writers. Instead of occurring by itself as a substantive, *compositum* nearly always agrees with nouns or pronouns, as in the following passage from Donatus: 'In declinatione conpositorum nominum animaduertere debemus, ea, quae ex duobus nominatiuis conposita fuerint' (*Ars maior*, ii. 8)¹² (In the declension of composed nouns, we should note those which have been composed from two nouns in the nominative case). Only rarely does *compositum* occur on its own as an absolute term.¹³ More telling, *compositum* often occurs with the preposition *ex* or *ab* denoting the components of the compounds, as in 'Notandum sane quod osanna uerbum hebraicum compositum est ex duobus corrupto et integro'¹⁴ ('It must be noted that *hosanna*, a Hebrew word, is composed from two parts: a deficient part and an intact part). The ablative of material, more typical of verbs than nouns, confirms the verbal force of *compositum*.¹⁵ It would be hard to translate this construction into English without using a participle. We might say 'words *composed* of,' or 'words that are compounds *formed* from' or even 'words *compounded* from,' but we use a participle to admit the components from which the compound was formed.

---

¹¹ See Pavol Stekauer, *English Word Formation: A History of Research (1960-1995)* (Tübingen 2000).

¹² Louis Holtz, ed., *Donat et la tradition de l'enseignement grammatical: Étude sur l'Ars Donati et sa diffusion (IVe - IXe siècle)* (Paris 1981), 624.

¹³ There are several cases in which *compositum* could have been regarded either as a substantive or a participle, but there are few unambiguous cases in which the form of *compositum* does not agree with some noun. The following from Priscian's *Institutiones grammaticae* is probably such a case: 'In compositis quoque idem solet fieri' (GL 3 110.24) (In composed words the same thing also often happens) (see n. 37 below), but even here *compositis* could be in agreement with an unstated term like *verbis* or *dictionibus*.

¹⁴ Bede, *In Marci Euangelium Expositio*, ed. D. Hurst, CCSL 120 (Turnhout 1960), bk 3, ll. 1278-9.

¹⁵ J.B. Greenough et al., *Allen and Greenough's New Latin Grammar* (New Rochelle, NY 1983), §403. Cf. Randoph Quirk et al., *A Comprehensive Grammar of the English Language* (London 1985), §7.16.

Ælfric also uses a participle for *compositum* in his grammar, namely *gefēged*, the past participle of *gefēgan*, 'to join.' His choice is interesting, since it gives us some idea of how an educated Anglo-Saxon would have regarded Latin grammatical terminology. Not only does Ælfric's term closely resemble *compositum*, but Ælfric also imitates the *compositum ex/ab* formula from Latin grammars by using *of* with *gefēged*. This would be an unusual use of 'to join' in today's English. We can speak of two things being joined together, as in '*in* and *doctus* are joined,' or 'someone joined *in* and *doctus* together' or '*in* joins *doctus*,' or we can even speak of joining something **to** something else, as in '*in* is joined to *doctus*,' but we do not speak of having something joined **from** something else, as in 'a word is joined from *in* and *doctus*.'[16] We would probably employ a verb like *combine* or *compose* instead. It must have been a strange construction in Ælfric's day as well, for outside Ælfric's grammar *of* is never collocated with *gefēgan* but within the grammar *of* is used about sixty of the seventy-odd times that *gefēged* is used.[17] Ælfric's unusual collocation, then, also highlights the verbal force of *gefēged*. Since both Latin and Old English terminology uses participles, perhaps it is slightly misleading to translate the terms with our present-day term 'compound.' Perhaps we too should use a participle, like 'composed' (words), to echo the process evoked by the medieval terminology.

The senses of the terms used for compounding may also highlight a difference in perspective. The more general senses of the medieval terms *compono* and *compositum* include 'building, fashioning, forming, fitting together, making something fitting or suitable.'[18] To be sure, *compositum* is a technical term used in opposition to *simplex* in medieval grammars, but the technical sense derives from a broader range of senses for building and forming things.[19] These broader senses can be seen in the Anglo-Saxon glosses of

[16] Morton Benson, Evelyn Benson and Robert Ilson, *The BBI Dictionary of English Word Combinations* (Amsterdam 1997), s. *join*. The *OED* lists no definition or quotation for *join* that includes a term denoting source, like 'from.'

[17] All Old English word searches were performed using A. diP. Healey et al., *The Dictionary of Old English Corpus in Electronic Form* with the first TEI-P3 conformant conversion by Takamichi Ariga and John Price-Wilkin (Toronto 1995).

[18] Charlton T. Lewis, *A Latin Dictionary* (Oxford 1879), s. *compono, compositum*. Cf. R.E. Latham and D.R. Howlett, eds, *Dictionary of Medieval Latin from British Sources* (London 1975-7), s. *componere*.

[19] Ideally a technical term will be limited to a single concept, but when the term has been borrowed from general language, as the medieval grammatical terms were, associations easily crop up between

compono and *compositum* when they occur outside grammar. In one gloss we see several words for forming and fashioning clustered with *componat*, including the Old English word for building: 'texat, componat, struat timbreð' (PrudGl 6 [Nap-Ker] 58). In another gloss we see the sense of finishing or making something ready: 'Conficior i compono' (AntGl 4 [Kindschi] 186). We even see *compositum* opposing *simplex* in a nongrammatical context: 'Conditum scilicet uinum uocatum quod non sit simplex sed commixtione pigmentorum compositum' (HlGl [Oliphant] C1777) (*Conditum*, namely wine that is not simple but composed of a mixture of juices).

These glosses reveal a range of senses for combining and fashioning that the Anglo-Saxon glossators certainly recognized. Other uses of *compositum* in prose likewise reveal the general sense of building or fashioning. Bede, for example, uses *compono* when discussing the building and restoration of Solomon's temple:

Post fundamentum uero talibus ac tantis lapidibus compositum aedificanda est domus praeparatis diligentius lignis ac lapidibus ac decenti ordine collocatis.

But after the foundation, which is made up of stones of such quality and size, the house must be built with wood and stones very carefully dressed in proper arrangement.[20]

Laquearia sunt tabulata quae magno decore composita et ornata ab inferiori parte trabibus adfiguntur ...

Ceilings are boardwork constructed and adorned with great beauty and fixed to the beams on the lower side ...[21]

---

the term in its technical sense and its general use. Cf. Fred Riggs, 'Social Science Terminology: Basic Problems and Proposed Solutions,' in Helmi B. Sonneveld and Kurt L. Loening, eds, *Terminology: Applications in Interdisciplinary Communication* (Amsterdam 1993), 195-222; Rita Temmerman, *Towards New Ways of Terminology Description* (Amsterdam 2000), 125-39; and Elizabeth Closs Traugott and Richard B. Dasher, *Regularity in Semantic Change* (Cambridge 2002), 11-16.

[20] Bede, *De templo libri ii*, ed. D. Hurst, CCSL 119A (Turnhout 1969), bk 1, ll. 356-9; trans. Seán Connolly, *Bede: On the Temple* (Liverpool 1995), 16.

[21] Bede, *De templo*, bk 1, ll. 832-4; trans. from Connolly, *Bede*, 32.

Vnde colligitur hoc altare multum citato opere de lapidibus impolitis compositum.[22]

And so this altar was assembled in very hasty work, composed of rough stones.

The grammatical term *figura* also derives from notions of creating or making. *Figura* derives from *fingo*, meaning 'to fashion, to create.' Our modern term *figure* captures that sense only distantly, if at all, when it is used to mean a representation in a painting or statue,[23] whereas the Latin term *fingo* is directly associated with *compono*. In a couple of Anglo-Saxon glosses that apparently have nothing to do with grammar, *fingo* and *compono* appear together:

Pango pepegi i fingo compono inde pangere uersus et arbores dicuntur. (AntGl 7 [Kindschi] 289)

Pango pepegi, i.e., 'make up, compose,' whence we speak of disseminating verses and propagating trees.

Componendus fingendus. Compositores luti figulos uocamus. (HlGl [Oliphant] C1326 [- C1328])

Composing, making. We call those who fashion clay '*figuli*' [potters].

The implication of these glosses is that the notion of forming and fashioning found in *compono* is echoed in *fingo*, so that the category name *figura* does not simply refer to the form of the words but to their having been fashioned or created.

The OE term *gefēgan*, used to render Latin *compositum*, also has a core sense of joining or putting together, which shades into senses of building, forming, creating. Some uses of *gefēgan* follow:

---

[22] Bede, *In Ezram et Neemiam libri iii*, ed. D. Hurst, CCSL 119A, bk 1, ll. 1191-3.
[23] *OED*, s. *figure*, sense II.

Hit is gecueden ðætte ða stanas on ðæm mæran temple Salomonnes wæron sua wel **gefegede** & sua emne gesnidene & gesmeðde, ær hie mon to ðæm stede brohte ðe hie on standan scoldon, ðætte hie mon eft siððan on ðære halgan stowe sua tosomne gesette ðæt ðær nan monn ne gehierde ne æxe hlem ne bietles sueg. (CP 36.253.12-17)

It is said that the stones in the famous temple of Solomon were so well fitted, and so evenly cut and polished before being brought to the place where they were to stand, that they were afterwards so joined together in the holy place, that no man heard there the sound either of axe or hammer.[24]

> Con he sidne ræced
> fæste **gefegan** wiþ færdryrum. (Gifts 47b-8)

He knows how to truss the spacious edifice securely against sudden collapses.[25]

Ærest man asmeað þæs huses stede, and eac man þæt timber beheawð, and þa syllan fægere **gefegð** and þa beamas gelegð and þa ræftras to þære fyrste gefæstnað and mid cantlum underwriðað and syððan þæt hus wynsumlice gefrætwað. (ByrM 1 3.1.114-18)

We first of all survey the site of the house, and also hew the timber into shape, and neatly fit together the sills and lay down the beams, and fasten the rafters to the roof, and support it with buttresses, and afterwards delightfully adorn the house.[26]

Soðlice se sealmsceop awrat be criste þæt he is se hyrnstan þe **gefegð** þa twegen weallas togædere. for þan ðe he geþeodde his gecorenan of iudeiscum folce. & þa geleaffullan of hæþenum: swilce twegen wagas to anre gelaðunge. (ÆCHom I, 7 106.11-15)

---

[24] Translation from OE edition of CP, 253. Bold face emphasis in this and the following passages is added.

[25] Trans. S.A.J. Bradley, *Anglo-Saxon Poetry: An Anthology of Old English Poems in Prose Translation* (London 1982), 327.

[26] Translation from OE edition, 143.

For the psalmist wrote concerning Christ, that he is the corner-stone which joins the two walls together, because he united his chosen of the Jewish people and the faithful of the heathen, as two walls, to one church.[27]

While most uses of *gefēgan* can still be interpreted in terms of the primary sense 'to join,' one notes the frequent association of *gefēgan* with building.

Ælfric's term for *figura* similarly captures the notion of forming or making. He first uses the term *hīw*, which like the modern English term *figure* or *shape*, characterizes the appearance or state of an object, not necessarily the process that produced it. But Ælfric soon switches to his own neologism *gefēgedness* (joinedness) because he needed *hīw* for the closely related category of *species*.[28] Though perhaps clumsy, Ælfric's term for *figura* preserves the notion of forming.

Our modern term *compound*, on the other hand, has a more limited range of senses outside grammar. The *OED* lists just one general definition each for the nominal and adjectival uses of *compound*: 'A union, combination, or mixture of elements' and 'made up by the combination of several elements or ingredients.' The rest of the senses in the *OED* are specialized to medicine, chemistry, mathematics, architecture, and so on. The use of the term *compound* in various electronic corpora of modern English confirms the specialization of *compound*, as the distribution shows an overwhelming preference for technical senses.[29] We find 'hydroxil-rich compound,' 'fluorescent compound,' 'compound-engine planes,' 'compound cuts' (in woodworking) and 'compound interest,' among other uses of *compound*. Only six of the ninety-one instances of *compound* are used in a general sense of 'mixture' or 'combination,' as in 'the household is a compound of "unlike persons" — man, woman, servants, and children.'[30] And the sense common to nearly all uses of *compound*, general and technical, is that something is a

---

[27] Translation from Benjamin Thorpe, trans., *The Homilies of the Anglo-Saxon Church* (London 1844-6), 1:107.
[28] Lawrence Kennedy Shook, 'Ælfric's *Latin Grammar*: A Study in Old English Grammatical Terminology' (PhD diss., Harvard University 1939), 67-70.
[29] Specifically the Brown, Freiburg-Brown, LOB and Freiburg-LOB corpora in Knut Hofland et al., *ICAME Collection of English Language Corpora*, 2nd edn (Bergen 1999).
[30] Freiburg-Brown corpus (J J63:14).

mixture or consists of multiple parts. The process of combining that produced the compound is not as important in the sense as the resultant state.

In noting that the medieval terms *compositum* / *figura* and *gefēged* / *gefēgedness* also had a general sense of 'to build, fashion or form,' I am not claiming that the general sense would have been primary in the grammatical use of the terms. It is not likely that an Anglo-Saxon would have thought of the more general senses when encountering every instance of *compositum* or *figura* in a grammar; both words were technical terms with specialized senses when used in grammars. But it is possible that the general senses of *compositum* and *figura* could have leaked into the grammars so that the notion of a compound word would not be too far removed from the notion of a word that has been formed in some way. In contrast, if any more general sense leaks into modern English grammatical terminology, it would be that a compound word contains two or more parts. The Latin terminology places compounding within a larger framework of building or making things in ways that our term *compound* does not.

The medieval grammarians certainly saw the connection between compounding and the more general activity of creating. They commonly cite the etymology of *figura*, and point out that the category therefore has something to do with making or creating. A passage, very much like the gloss in the Harley Glossary cited above, is often repeated among Insular and Carolingian grammars, in which the sense of creating in *figura* is explicitly noted and then linked to the same sense in *compono*:

> Dicta uero est figura a fingendo, id est a componendo, quia antiqui fingebant imagines in parietibus uel etiam in lapidibus; unde modo compositores luti figulos uocamus.[31]

---

[31] Sedulius Scottus, *In Donati Artem maiorem*, ed. Bengt Löfstedt, CCCM 40B (Turnhout 1977), 137, ll. 34-6; see the *apparatus fontium* of Sedulius for similar passages elsewhere, as well as *Ars Laureshamensis: expositio in Donatum maiorem*, ed. Bengt Löfstedt, CCCM 40A (Turnhout 1977), 46, ll. 30-3; and Murethach, *In Donati artem maiorem*, ed. Louis Holtz, CCCM 40 (Turnhout 1977), 92, ll. 86-8. The passage is also found in a homily by Gregory the Great: 'Fingere namque componere dicimus; unde et compositores luti figulos uocamus' (*Homiliae in Evangelia*, ed. Raymond Étaix, CCSL 141 [Turnhout 1999], 194, ll. 17-19). Gregory was probably the source for both the grammars and the glossary.

Moreover, *figura* is thus called from *fingendo*, that is from *componendo*, since the ancients fashioned images on walls or in stone; thus we call those who work in clay '*figuli*.'

For the medieval *grammatici*, forming compounds could be seen as a creative activity similar to creating other artefacts, like paintings, sculptures or pottery. Commentaries on Donatus commonly regarded compounds as artefacts, while simplexes were held to be natural. An early description of compounds as artefacts comes from Pompeius, who compiled his commentary in north Africa in the fifth or sixth century.

> Figura aut naturalis est, aut ex arte descendit. quae est naturalis, simplex vocatur; quae ex arte descendit, conposita. nam quando dicimus doctus, hic nihil ars valet, sed ipsa positio simplex est constituta; quando autem dicimus indoctus, ex arte descendit. (GL 5 169.1-5)

> *Figura* is either natural or comes from craft. That which is natural is called simple; that which comes from craft is called composed. For when we say *doctus*, craft plays no part, but the simple form itself is set down. When we say *indoctus*, however, it comes from craft.

Pompeius does not elaborate on how simplexes are natural, except that they do not come 'ex arte,' which probably means human craft, intervention, or manipulation in this passage, though *ars* derives from an older sense meaning 'skill in joining.'[32] There is no human hand involved in the word *doctus*, for example, but there is in the word *indoctus*.

Pompeius's grammar was well known among the early grammarians in Anglo-Saxon England: Tatwine, Bede, Boniface, and Aldhelm all used it in their grammatical and paragrammatical works,[33] and so his remarks on compounds could well have been known in England. They were certainly known by Irish grammarians — like Murethach, Sedulius, and the anonymous writers of the *Ars Laureshamensis*, *Ars Bernensis*, and *ad Cuimnanum* — who elaborated on them in their commentaries. These eighth- and ninth-century

---

[32] Lewis, *Latin Dictionary*, and Latham, *Medieval Latin Dictionary*, s. *ars*.
[33] Vivien Law, *The Insular Latin Grammarians* (Woodbridge 1982), 16.

writers, working mainly on the continent, amplify the sense of craft or human creation present in compounds. One frequently repeated line states that the category *figura* involves artifice:

> Figura dicitur res artificialis, quae aut ex una parte constat et simplex dicitur aut ex pluribus et composita uocatur.[14]

> *Figura* is said to be a category involving craft, which is either made up of one part and is called simple or made up of many parts and is called composed.

And an oft-repeated definition of *figura* is:

> Figura est habitus uocum, per quas corpora aut res significantur, utrum sua natura an per artem enuntientur.[15]

> *Figura* is a characteristic of words through which solid objects or concepts are signified, whether they are expressed according to their own nature or by craft.

It is clear that the *grammatici* saw compounds as more artificial than simplexes, mainly because compounds are obviously formed while simplexes are not. How much more the phrase 'utrum sua natura' suggests is difficult to say. If 'sua' refers to 'corpora' and 'res,' the definition seems to border upon a statement about signification, almost as if simplexes could directly represent the natural state of the referents, while compounds are removed because of human intervention in creating them. The *Ars Bernensis* even links simplexes with the beginning of the world.

> Interrogandum est, quid naturalior est in uocibus, utrum simplicitas an conpositio. Naturalior est in uocibus simplicitatis ostensio, quia, quando mundi elementa facta sunt, primitus simplicibus nominibus usi sunt, postea autem per artem uoces conpositae factae sunt. (GL 8 85.20-4)

---

[14] Sedulius, *In Donati*, 137, ll. 37-8.
[15] *Ibid.*, 137, ll. 31-3.

It must be asked which is more natural in words, simplicity or composition. The manifestation of simplicity is more natural in words, because when the elements of the world were made, people first used simple nouns; afterwards, however, composed words were made through craft.

The passage suggests a golden age in which names for objects were naturally connected with them. In the beginning was the simplex; only later did less natural names arise through human intervention.

The *Ars Bernensis* may be more extreme on this point, but the idea that simplexes are more natural and compounds more contrived is well established in a number of commentaries. For these *grammatici* a simplex is natural insofar as it is not created as a label, whereas the compound is manifestly manufactured. We can recognize the origins of compounds, but not of simplexes, and since we cannot see their origins, simplexes presumably invite less reflection on them. In that sense, simplexes are more natural. Compounds, on the other hand, are created and their created status is always recognizable; consequently they would be less natural.

Perhaps compounds were also considered a less stable part of the lexicon. Of course, compounds often become lexicalized in a language, as they undoubtedly were in Old English and Latin, so that speakers lose track of their internal composition; for most speakers today, for example, blackboards do not have to be black.[16] But medieval grammarians, at least, would have recognized the composed nature of the compounds. Perhaps these grammarians would have viewed compounds not so much as a (natural?) part of a lexicon but rather as creations that could be formed where necessary. So even if compounds were still regarded as words (which they were), perhaps they were seen as less permanent, while simplexes were seen as more reified.

A view that emphasizes a process of combining rather than a static structure would fit in the combinatory view of language that Priscian presents in Book 17 of his *Institutiones grammaticae*. Priscian notes that letters combine to form syllables, syllables to form words, and words to form sentences. He sees all levels as essentially performing the same activities — combining to make larger units. So in that respect compounds would be seen as arising from a process similar to those that give us syllables and sentences. Combining

---

[16] Laurie Bauer, *English Word-Formation* (Cambridge 1983), 48–61.

words into a composed word is essentially the same as combining words into a sentence; in fact Priscian admits as much when discussing the effects of deleted elements in structures. He first notes deletion of letters (sounds) and syllables and then of words. Most of his examples of deleted words are from sentences, but then he also includes deleted words from compounds.

> In compositis quoque idem solet fieri, ut:
> Incubuere mari, totumque a sedibus imis
> Vna Eurusque Notusque ruunt
> pro 'errunt'; deest enim praepositio ad perfectionem plenae orationis.[37]

> In composed words the same thing also often happens, as in:
> East wind and south wind together falling prone on the sea,
> stir it up from its lowest chambers,
> *ruunt* is used in place of *errunt*; a preposition is missing for the completion of the whole sentence.[38]

The implication of his efforts to involve sounds, syllables, and words in the same process of combining is that words can combine to form two structures — sentences and other words — and the two processes for creating them are similar.[39] Even the results of such combination seem to make compounds more similar to sentences, or at least phrases, than we are accustomed to acknowledge. When working out the operation of metathesis and insertion on all levels (syllables, words, sentences), Priscian has to turn to compounds for examples of those operations on words. For metathesis, he proffers *publica res* instead of *res publica*, and for insertion he offers the example of *res felix est publica* (GL 3 113.6-7 and 114.5). Such examples would argue against *res publica* as a compound in modern terms, since indivisibility is a crucial characteristic for modern notions of a word.[40] The medieval notion of compounds may not

---

[37] Priscian, *Institutiones grammaticae*, GL 3 110.24-7.
[38] *Aeneid*, bk. I, ll. 84-5; trans. J.W. Mackail, *Virgil's Works* (New York 1934), 5.
[39] In current linguistic theory, generative processes for producing compounds are nearly universally held to be separate from processes generating clauses and sentences. See Stekauer, *English Word-Formation*, 99-101 n. 3. A few, such as Richard Leiber, have argued for a unified approach to word formation and syntax (*Deconstructing Morphology* [Chicago 1992]).
[40] The spelling of *res publica* with an intervening space would not disqualify it as a compound today, however, provided some other criterion, such as stress pattern, distinguished the combination of

have been as firm; possibly *compositum* really fits a looser notion of combining. Perhaps that is why collocations could be included as compounds. In the end, the difference between emphasizing the structures of compounds or emphasizing the processes that created them would not be great, but where the process is emphasized perhaps the compounds are seen as less reified, less stable, less permanent. Elements in the compounds should be readily recognized and we ought to see analysis of compounds like Ælfric's:

Participivm ys dæl nimend. he nymð anne dæl of naman and oðerne of worde. (ÆGram 9.18-19)

Participle is 'part-taker.' It takes one part from nouns and another from verbs.

Carpo ic totere oððe pluccige oððe tæse, carpsi, carptum and of ðam gefeged excerpo ic of apluccige. (ÆGram 170.12-14)

Carpo (I pull or pluck or rip), *carpsi, carptum* and from that is composed *excerpo* (I pluck out).

We also might expect frequent calques among glosses. If a word is regarded as a unit, no matter how many internal divisions, then when rendering it into a target language, the best approach would be to choose a word that is closest in sense and purpose to the word in the source language. But if the source word is recognized as being internally composed and the internal composition is held to be an important property of the word, then the target word should perhaps reflect the same division; thus a glossator would be motivated to render each part of the source word. Perhaps that is one reason for the relatively high incidence of calques in glosses.[4]

---

words from a syntactic phrase. Cf. Hans Marchand, *The Categories and Types of Present-Day English Word-Formation*, 2nd edn (München 1969), 20-30.

[4] A calque is a literal morpheme-for-morpheme rendition of a complex word from a source language, such as OE *ūpstīgend* as a rendition of Latin *ascensor*. The fullest treatment of OE calques and other loan formations remains Helmut Gneuss, *Lehnbildungen und Lehnbedeutungen im Altenglischen* (Berlin 1955). Such loan formations show up frequently in OE glosses of Latin texts: Gneuss (156) found that among the glosses of the Vespasian Psalter (PsGlA [Kuhn]), about 10 per cent of the words were loan formations.

It would still be nice to have a poetics or rhetoric to tell us the explicit attitudes of educated Anglo-Saxons towards the suitability and effectiveness of creating new words. In the absence of those, however, the medieval grammars can give us some idea. Presumably Anglo-Saxons who knew how to read Latin would have been trained to identify and distinguish compounds from simplexes. The grammatical terminology and commentary suggest that literate Anglo-Saxons would have recognized compounds as results of combining words, and as such the combinations would have been felt to be less natural and perhaps less permanent than simplexes. What they would have thought of poetic or creative compounds in particular is hard to tell, but the forming of compounds as such should not have seemed unusual to them. They had the tools to analyse and discuss compounds, and indeed they used those tools in exegesis, as we have seen in Bede's remarks on *hosanna* quoted above. If a literate Anglo-Saxon, like a Snorri, had been inclined to analyse the effects of new words, we can imagine that he would have used the notions of compounding from the grammars.

3

Cennan, 'to cause to be born'/ 'to cause to know': Incarnation as Revelation in Old English Literature

PAULINE HEAD

> Word biŏ wisdomes geswutelung, & þæt word þæt is
> se wisdom is acenned of ŏam ælmihtigum fæder butan anginne.
> For ŏan þe he wæs æfre god of gode, wisdom of ŏam wisan fæder ...'

> The word is the manifestation of wisdom, and that word that is
> wisdom is born from the almighty Father without beginning.
> For the reason that he was ever God of God, wisdom of the wise father ...

The Old English verb *cennan* embraces two quite distinct meanings. Several of its senses gather around the idea of generation: *cennan* signifies begetting or giving birth to a child, or the production of organic or inorganic matter. Its other senses share the basic meaning 'to cause to know.' These two areas of signification are sufficiently disparate that *cennan* is defined as two words by several dictionaries;² the morphological development of the verb, however, does not seem to indicate that it grew out of two distinct words with historically different forms and meanings.

Ācennan can almost always be translated 'to conceive' or 'to give birth (to),' yet many passages which include *ācennan* imply, in a less literal way, the other meaning, 'to make known.' Frequently, as in Ælfric's homily on the Nativity cited above, this wordplay has theological implications; Christ is

---

' Ælfric, 'Nativitas Domini,' ed. Peter Clemoes, *Ælfric's Catholic Homilies: The First Series*, EETS, ss 17 (Oxford 1997), sermon 2, ll. 167-9.
² *Cennan* is defined as two words by the *OED*, *MED*, and Julius Pokorny, *Indogermanisches Etymologisches Wörterbuch* (Bern and Munich 1959). It is treated as one word by the *DOE*, *BT*, and F. Holthausen, *Altenglisches Etymologisches Wörterbuch* (Heidelberg 1963). See also Javier e. Díaz Vera, '"On sarnesse þu acenst cild": *Being Born* in the History of English, with Special Reference to the Old and Middle English Periods,' *Estudios Ingleses de la Universidad Complutense* 8 (2000): 79-96, at 89.

born and thus makes known the wisdom of God. God, the wise father, begets
Christ in his 'godcundnes' (divinity) — Christ who is at once the 'word,' the
geswutelung (manifestation) of wisdom, and wisdom itself. Just as the Father
and Son are inseparable, neither can wisdom be considered apart from its
manifestation. In a very literal sense, *acenned* here means 'is born,' but within
such a context and especially in such a close relationship with *geswutelung*, the
meaning 'is made known' is strongly present. Elsewhere, *ācennan* often
describes, in an equally provocative way, Christ's *mennisce* (human) birth or
incarnation from Mary. This essay concerns the semantic ranges of *cennan* and
ācennan, and the way Old English Christian poetry and prose delighted in an
interplay of meanings that expressed the theological relationship between
incarnation and revelation.

In its entries for *ken*, the *Oxford English Dictionary* compares the Old High
German forms (*ir-, in-, pi-*) *chennan* for the meaning 'to make known,' and
(*ki-*) *chennan* for 'to generate'; in Old Saxon, the prefix *ant-* may be added to
kennan in its sense of making known, but is not added if the sense is
generation. This suggests that OHG and OS may have distinguished between
the two meanings by the addition of a prefix. All of these forms have a
cognate in Gothic *kannjan*, which, like them, derives from Germanic **kannjan*.
The *Oxford Etymological Dictionary*[3] gives **kann-*, 'I know, can,' as the root
of **kannjan*, and the *OED* describes this root as 'the second ablaut grade of the
series *kin-, kan-, kun-*'; this origin applies to both meanings of *ken*. Since the
Germanic period, the histories of *cennan*, 'to generate,' and *cennan*, 'to cause to
know,' seem to have been identical.

The Germanic ablaut series *kin-, kan-, kun-* is also the root of Gothic
*knaian (OE *cnawan*), Gothic *kunnan* (OE *cunnan*), and Germanic **kunþian*
(OE *cȳþan*), all of which are verbs of knowing. This sense can be traced back
further to the Indo-Germanic *gen-, gon-, gn-* roots that signify 'to produce,
engender, beget' (*OED*) and that give rise to such Latin words as *genus*, 'race,'
'lineage,' and *gignare*, 'to beget, cause, create.' Such a similarity in roots
indicates a possible historical connection between the two basic concepts
contained in *cennan*. In his *cennan* entry, Holthausen gives Sanskrit *jāyē*, 'to be
born,' and *janayāmi*, 'to generate, produce,' as collateral ancestors of *cennan*, 'to

---

[3] *Oxford Etymological Dictionary*, ed. C.T. Onions (Oxford 1966).

give birth.'⁴ Falk and Torp cite the Sanskrit word *jânāmi*, 'I know,' as cognate with OE *cunnan*, *cunnian*, and *cnāwan*.⁵ The identity of the roots of verbs of knowing and generating, however, is not universally agreed upon. Interestingly, Pokorny has two entries for the roots *ĝen-*, *ĝenǝ-*, *ĝne-*, *ĝno-*. The first gives words related in meaning to 'to generate, produce' (*erzeugen*): Latin *gignare*, *nascor*, *cognatus*, *agnatus*; OE *cennan*, *heofoncund*, *cnōsl*. The second includes words of knowing (*erkennen*, *kennen*): Latin *noscere*, *gnoscere*; OE *cennan*, *cnāwan*. This division suggests that Pokorny sees the two groups of verbs as similar in form but distinct in meaning; *cennan* is treated as two words, one belonging to each group. Falk and Torp do not attempt to resolve the question, but conclude their entry for *kunne*: 'The basic meaning of these words [with roots deriving from *ĝenǝ-*, *ĝne-*, *ĝno-*] is 'to get to know, to know'; to what extent there is a connection with the root "ĝen-," "to give birth, to generate" is uncertain ...'⁶ While a very similar (perhaps identical) historical development for the two groups of verbs can be traced, the precise nature of their relationship is difficult to define.

The *Dictionary of Old English* includes in the range of meanings of *ācennan* many senses and sub-senses of 'to generate,' among them: 'to bear or bring forth, give birth (to)'; 'to become pregnant, conceive; to be pregnant'; 'to beget'; also *(beon) ācenned* '(to be) begotten'; 'to grow, produce, generate.' Only one example is cited of *ācennan* denoting 'to make known, declare,' and yet the root *cennan* carries this sense and wordplay frequently derives from its lingering presence. In usage the meanings of *cennan* are not distinct or absent from occurrences of *ācennan*. Although the *ā*- prefix in Old English usually acts as an intensifier or indicates motion away, sometimes it has no meaning at all; this prefix does not alter the basic meaning of a word. The *MED* has two entries for *aken(ne*, the first meaning 'to recognise, reconnoitre.' This is said 'probably' to have an OE source. Since *cennan*, 'to cause to know,' develops into *ken*, 'to know,' perhaps *aken(ne*, 'to recognise,' has *ācennan*, 'to cause to know, to cause to recognise' as its source. Such speculation suggests that, despite the predominant attested meaning of 'to generate,' *ācennan* also denoted 'to cause to know' in Anglo-Saxon usage.

---

⁴ Holthausen, *Altenglisches Etymologisches Wörterbuch*, s.v.
⁵ H.S. Falk and Alf Torp, *Norwegisch-Dänisches Etymologisches Wörterbuch* (Heidelberg 1960).
⁶ 'Die grundbedeutung des wortes ist, wie man sieht, "kennen lernen, kennen"; wieweit zusammenhang mit der wurzel "ĝen-," – "gebären, erzeugen" ... besteht, ist unsicher ...'

Wordplay drawing on the two meanings of the verb to describe the incarnation of Christ involves the form *ācennan* much more frequently than *cennan*. Such use of *(ā-)cennan* occurs in OE homilies and Christian poetry, as well as in hymns. Theologically, the concept of Christ's birth as a revelation of God's presence derives from the opening verses of the Gospel of John:

> In principio erat Verbum, et Verbum erat apud Deum, et Deus erat Verbum ... Et Verbum caro factum est, et habitavit in nobis; et vidimus gloriam eius ... (John 1:1 & 14)

> In the beginning was the Word, and the Word was with God, and the Word was God ... And the Word was made flesh, and dwelt among us; and we saw his glory ...

Ælfric renders this:

> On angynne wæs Word, & þæt Word wæs mid Gode, & þæt Word wæs God ... And þæt Word is geworht flæsc [& hit wunode] on us. And we sylfe gesawon soðlice his wuldor ... (ÆHom 1 28-52)[7]

In the early Christian period and throughout the early Middle Ages, the opening of John's Gospel was explored exegetically, primarily under the influence of the writings of Augustine. Old English wordplay on *(a-)cennan* refers to this tradition but develops it in a way that is uniquely possible to this vernacular. Words are manifestations. The OE verb *(ā-)cennan* not only conveys either 'giving birth' or 'making known' but is able to make manifest the connection between the two actions in the event of Christ's incarnation.

My opening quotation from Ælfric is taken from the Nativity homily in his first series of Catholic homilies; following Luke 2:1-20, and drawing on sources including Bede, Gregory, and Augustine,[8] he tells the story of the birth of Christ ('gereccan þæs hælendes acenednysse' [ÆCHom I, 2 1-2]) in

---

[7] 'Nativitas Domini,' in John C. Pope, ed., *Homilies of Ælfric: A Supplementary Collection*, 2 vols EETS, os 259 and 260 (London and New York 1967), 1:198.
[8] See Malcolm Godden, *Ælfric's Catholic Homilies: Introduction, Commentary and Glossary*, EETS, ss 18 (Oxford 2000), 13-21.

order to strengthen his listeners' faith ('to trymminge eowres geleafan' [1]). Forms of *ācennan* describe the child's birth, while forms of *cennan* relate to 'declaring' (as when all people, by Roman decree, must declare their descent). There is one exception to this practice when *cynnan* denotes 'giving birth' in the clause: 'hire tima wæs gefulled þæt hio cynnan sceolde' (17) (the time had arrived when she must give birth). Possibly, even in this introductory section of the homily, the revelatory purpose of Christ's birth is being suggested through *cynnan*. Only one sentence separates the statement about Mary's giving birth from the clause: 'Ælc man oferheafod sceolde cennan his gebyrde' (11-12), (In every case each man had to make known his parentage). Mary's giving birth may possibly be considered a necessary (in the sense of 'preordained') proclamation of the word of God in light of the similar language used to describe the necessary (i.e., compulsory) declarations called forth by the census.

'An engel bodade þam hyrdum þæs heofenlican cyninges acennydnesse' (132-3; trans. Luke 2:8-15) (An angel announced to the shepherds the heavenly king's birth). In his exegesis of the angels' appearance to the shepherds, Ælfric (through direct statement and linguistically through paronomasia) links birth with kingship ('cyninges acennydnesse'), and word with revelation ('ðas word geswuteliað'), being ('þæt word þe geworden is'), and wisdom ('word bið wisdomes geswutelung'). The alliterative and, even more so, the paronomastic associations imply a necessary, preordained relationship between the word pairs: the king of heaven will inevitably have a human birth, and the word of God will come into being, thereby making wisdom manifest. In her essay 'Some Uses of Paronomasia in Old English Scriptural Verse,' Roberta Frank draws attention to a form of 'poetic imagination' wherein 'an etymological or pseudo-etymological relationship between two or more words' becomes a method of exploring and playing with meaning. She considers the implications of such wordplay in Cynewulf's pairing of *rōd*, 'cross,' with *rodera*, 'the heavens':

> This repeated formula succeeds as persuasive rhetoric by implying that the convergence of heaven (*rodor*) and earth (*rod*) was predestined by God from the beginning, the link foreshadowed and made manifest in these two English words.[9]

9 *Speculum* 47 (1972): 207-26, at 210-11.

Ælfric provides a version of the song of the angels ('Sy wuldor gode on heannyssum & on eorðan sib mannum þam ðe beoð godes willan' [139-40], [Glory to God in the highest and on earth peace to men who are of good will]) and comments: 'Ðas word geswuteliað þæt ðær wunað godes sib þær se goda willa bið' (140-1) (These words make manifest that where God's peace exists there will be good will). This overt statement expresses an Anglo-Saxon attitude about the revelatory power of words. For Ælfric, in Peter Clemoes's view, 'Words were not merely useful labels for things; they expressed ultimate meaning.'[10] The angels' song to the shepherds revealed divine truth about the coexistence of God's peace and good will; similarly, Ælfric's sermon depends on the precise choice of words to attempt to express the ultimate meaning of Christ's incarnation.

Ælfric renders Luke 2:15b ('Transeamus usque Bethleem et videamus hoc verbum quod factum est, quod fecit Dominus et ostendit nobis' [Let us go over to Bethlehem, and let us see this word that is come to pass, which the Lord has made and showed to us]): 'Uton gefaran to bethleem & geseon þæt word þe geworden is & god us geswutelode' (164-5). Again word and revelation are linked, but here it is the word of God that is being revealed by God through the nativity of Christ. 'Geswutelode' is found in 'ostendit,' but there is no parallel in the Latin for the OE wordplay of 'word/geworden.' Ælfric's words make manifest the Word's, Christ's, coming into being. Giving examples such as 'mane gemenged' (mingled with sin) and 'foldan befolen' (entrusted to the earth)' found in *Daniel*, Frank speculates:

> These past participles which contain within them the sound of an adjacent key noun must have seemed to the poet to epitomize the inevitable completion of God's plan, the working out of structures imbedded in language from the very beginning.[11]

The past participle 'geworden' contains 'word' as a seed that must inevitably come into being. Several sentences later, Ælfric insists that the Word was 'na geworht' (not made). Although, or perhaps because, 'geworden' and 'geworht'

[10] Peter Clemoes, 'Ælfric,' in Eric G. Stanley, ed., *Continuations and Beginnings: Studies in Old English Literature* (London 1966), 176-209, at 188.
[11] Frank, 'Some Uses of Paronomasia,' 219. Frank also draws attention to Ælfric's 'Word wæs geworden flæsc' as an example of the putting into practice of his principle: 'Englisc hæbbe his agene wisan' (English has its own style), 211.

are similar in sound, a theological distinction must be understood. The word *became* flesh so that we might see him ('þæt we hine geseon mihton' [174]); he was not *made* because he is God and not creature ('for ðan he is god ond na gesceaft' [170]).[12]

Falling between these two balanced statements about how the Word did and did not become flesh is a brief reflection on the Prologue to John's Gospel, a topic Ælfric takes up in more detail in his later 'Nativitas Domini' homily (ÆHom 1).[13] Augustine and Bede influenced Ælfric's thinking about John's Prologue. As is apparent from the quotation which opens this paper, the relationships between speaker and speech, wisdom and its expression, interested Ælfric as they did Augustine and Bede. Bede writes in a Nativity homily:

Ipsa lux inuisibilis ipsa Dei sapientia carne in qua uideri posset induta est quae in hominis habitu apparens et loquens hominibus paulatim fide purificata eorum corda ad cognotionem suae diuinae uisionis proueheret.[14]

The very Light invisible, the very Wisdom of God, put on flesh in which he could be seen. Appearing in the condition of a human being and speaking to human beings, he gradually brought hearts purified by faith to the recognition of his divine image.[15]

Through the incarnation of Christ, the wisdom of God put on flesh so that he could be seen and heard by human beings, bringing their hearts to a recognition of his divine image. Augustine had explored in depth the process and the results of an idea taking shape:

---

[12] Again, the Anglo-Saxon language helps Ælfric to make a theological point that his Latin source seems not to have made so clearly. Bede writes in his Homily 1.7: 'Hoc verbum natum ex patre non factum est, quia creatura Deus non est,' explaining that although the word was made ('videamus ... hoc verbum quod factum est'), it was born from, not made by, the father (Homily 1.7, in *Homiliarum Evangelii*, ed. D. Hurst, CCSL 122 [Turnhout 1955], 47).

[13] In Pope, ed., *Homilies of Ælfric*, 1.196-225.

[14] Homily 1.8 in Hurst, ed., *Homiliarum Evangelii*, 55.108-12.

[15] L.T. Martin and D. Hurst, trans., *Bede the Venerable: Homilies on the Gospels*, 2 vols, Cistercian Studies 110-11 (Kalamazoo 1991), 1:77.

Prius enim cor generat consilium, ut aliquam fabricam construas, aliquid amplum in terra moliaris; iam natum est consilium, et opus nondum completum est; uides tu, quid facturus es, sed alius non miratur, nisi cum feceris et construxeris molem, et fabricam illam ad exsculptionem perfectionemque perduxeris: adtendunt homines mirabilem fabricam, et mirantur consilium fabricantis; stupent quod uident, et amant quod non uident; quis est qui potest uidere consilium? Si ergo ex magna aliqua fabrica laudatur humanum consilium, uis uidere quale consilium Dei est Dominus Iesus Christus, id est, Verbum Dei? (AUG. Tract.evang.Ioan. 1.9)[16]

For first thy heart brings forth a design to construct some fabric, to set up something great on the earth; already the design is conceived, and the work is not yet finished: thou seest what thou wilt make; but another does not admire, until thou hast made and constructed the pile, and brought that fabric into shape and to completion; then men regard the admirable fabric, and admire the design of the architect; they are astonished at what they see, and are pleased with what they do not see: who is there who can see a design? If, then, on account of some great building a human design receives praise, do you wish to see what a design of God is the Lord Jesus Christ, that is, the Word of God?[17]

Once materialized, or fabricated, the previously private and imperceptible idea is shared with others. Admiring the product, observers come to admire its designer as well. This is true whether the product be cloth, a building, or a word. It is particularly true of the corporeal Word of God who astonishes and pleases humankind by allowing us to see the design of God.

Augustine's 'quale consilium Dei est Dominus Iesus Christus, id est, Verbum Dei' (what a design of God is the Lord Jesus Christ, that is, the Word of God), Bede's 'Dei sapientia carne in qua videri posset induta est' (the very Wisdom of God put on flesh in which he could be seen), and Ælfric's

---

[16] Augustine of Hippo, *In Iohannis evangelium tractatus cxxiv*, ed. R. Willems, CCSL 36 (Turnhout 1954).
[17] John Gibb and James Innes, trans., *St. Augustine: Lectures or Tractates on the Gospel According to St. John*, Nicene and Post-Nicene Fathers, ed. Philip Schaff, vol. 7 (New York, 1888; repr. Peabody, MA 1995), 10.

'word biŏ wisdomes geswutelung' (the word is the manifestation of wisdom) all draw on metaphors of birth and speech to describe the bond of equality between Father and Son. As Lynne Grundy writes: 'Since God's power can never be without its expression, the Son is necessarily co-eternal with the Father.'[18] These two ways of speaking of Christ's incarnation — as birth and as speech — converge in *(ā-)cennan.* Within the theological framework shaped by Augustine and Bede, many of Ælfric's uses of this verb that literally say 'Christ was born,' even in such a simple statement as 'nu todæg is eow acenned hælend crist' (120-1) (now today the Saviour Christ is born to you) can be understood as connoting the defining, the embodying, the making manifest of the Word of God.

Augustine writes of the difficulty of understanding anything as complex and elusive as the co-eternity of God and his Word without the capacity to comprehend figurative language:

> Cogitans, in hac praesenti turba Caritatis uestrae necesse esse ut multi sint animales, qui adhuc secundum carnem sapiant, nondumque se possint ad spiritualem intellectum erigere, haesito uehementer, quomodo, ut Dominus dederit, possim dicere, uel pro modulo meo explicare quod lectum est ex euangelio. (AUG. Tract.evang.Ioan. 1.1)

> When I consider that in the present assembly, my beloved, there must of necessity be among you many natural men, who know only according to the flesh, and cannot yet raise themselves to spiritual understanding, I am in great difficulty how, as the Lord shall grant, I may be able to express, or in my small measure to explain, what has been read from the Gospel. (Gibb and Innes, *St Augustine*, 7)

Since his listeners also include those who are able to perceive the things 'quae sunt spiritus Dei' (which are of the Spirit of God) (I Cor 2:14), and since 'aderit misericordia Dei' (there will be present the compassion of God) he will proceed to explain this difficult passage hoping 'fortasse ut omnibus satis fiat, et capiat quisque quod potest' (1.1) (perchance there may be enough for all, and each may receive what he is able) (1.1). Ælfric, as a Christian teacher and

---

[18] Lynne Grundy, *Books and Grace: Ælfric's Theology*, King's College Medieval Studies (London 1991), 54.

pastor, was also very aware of the strengths and limitations of his audiences and of his responsibility to convey to them (often difficult) spiritual truths. He knew, from his reading of Pseudo-Augustine's *Adversus quinque hæreses* (ch. 3), that 'mannes muð ne mæg his [Christ's] naman fullcyðan' (ÆHom I 131), (man's mouth may not fully make known Christ's name) that 'He is wisdomes spræc us unasecgendlic' (132) (he is the speech of wisdom unutterable for us). Ælfric's use of language that could be understood both literally or physically (the Son was born) and figuratively or spiritually (the Word of God was made known) would allow him to provide 'enough for all, and each may receive what he is able.'[19] Wordplay elsewhere in his writings indicates his awareness of the potential for the various levels of meaning of *cennan*:

Oncnawað nu þurh þisum wordum soðne mann acennedne of mædenlicum lichaman. (ÆCHom I, 13 112-13)[20]

Know now, through these words, true man born of a virgin body.

Hwæt ða ure Hælend, þæs heofonlican Godes sunu, cydde his mycclan lufe þe he to us mannum hæfde, swa ðæt he wearð acenned of anum clænan mædene butan weres gemanan. (ÆLS [Mem of Saints] 107-9)[21]

Truly our Lord, the son of the heavenly God, made known his great love he had for us men, in that he became born of a pure maiden without intercourse with a man.

Although forms of *(ā-)cennan*, here and elsewhere, can almost always be read literally, their proximity to the semantically related words *oncnāwan* and *cȳðan* opens up a second meaning to readers who perceive the alliterative reference and explore the semantic relationship. Ælfric carefully moulds language to

[19] Sara Maitland argues: 'We should extend ourselves, from the place where we find ourselves, towards the unlimited God, not reduce that God to the level of our experience ... The language of analogy is a limited language. It happens that, except in the Incarnation of Christ, it is the only language that we have to speak about the unnameable, to speak about God' (*A Big-Enough God* [New York 1995], 113).
[20] 'Adnuntiatio Sanctae Mariae,' in Clemoes, ed., *Ælfric's Catholic Homilies*, 285.
[21] 'Sermo de Memoria Sanctorum,' in W.W. Skeat, ed., *Ælfric's Lives of Saints*, 2 vols, EETS, os 76 and 82 (London 1881; repr. 1966), 1:344.

communicate Christian theology; in his writings on the Nativity, *cennan* works to convey the profound meaning of Christ's incarnation as revelation.

In *Christ A*, a series of antiphons based on the Latin petitions that traditionally accompanied the Magnificat at Advent,[22] *(ā-)cennan* has meaning in relation to the anticipated illumination of darkness, opening of locked doors, loosening of bonds, and uncovering of the hidden. Forms of *in-*, *on-līhtan*, 'to illuminate, enlighten' occur four times in the poem (43b, 108b, 115a, 204a), each occurrence combining the physical sense of bringing light into darkness with the conceptual meaning of conveying knowledge. God is implored:

> Ond þe sylf cyme
> þæt ðu inleohte þa þe longe ær
> þrosme beþeahte ond in þeostrum her
> sæton sinneahtes. (*Christ A* 114b-17a)

And come yourself so that you may illuminate those who for a long time have sat here in eternal night, covered by smoke and in darkness.

As the antiphon proceeds, the darkness comes to represent sin, despair, and grief, all of which will be dispelled by Christ, the Dayspring ('earendel'). Source of illumination, Christ is both sun and son, through wordplay that further mingles the physical and the conceptual:

> Sunu soþan fæder ...
> ... þec nu for þearfum þin agen geweorc
> bideð þurh byldo, þæt þu þa beorhtan us
> sunnan onsende. (110a-14a)

Son of the true father ... your own creation prays in confidence that now, because of our neediness, you send us the bright sun.

---

[22] Robert B. Burlin provides a history of the use of the 'Antiphonae Majores' or 'Great O's' in the early church and into the early Middle Ages (*The Old English Advent: A Typological Commentary* [New Haven and London 1968], 40-5). See also Susan Rankin, 'The Liturgical Background of the OE Advent Lyrics: A Reappraisal,' in Michael Lapidge and Helmut Gneuss, eds, *Learning and Literature in Anglo-Saxon England* (Cambridge 1985), 317-40.

As subject of the sentence, Christ is the Son, identified with and through the Father. He is petitioned to send the sun (the sentence's object), which symbolizes through its redemptive brightness Himself, the Son. Through this multilayered signification, the vivid and comprehensible image of the sun overlaps in meaning with the child — whose birth is both manifestation and mystery — and with God, absolutely beyond comprehension yet somehow made known, illuminated, through Christ.

The vocabulary that expresses an awaited 'opening,' 'loosening,' and 'unlocking' includes the verbs ontȳnan (19b, 27b, 253b), onlīesan (68b), and onlūcan (314b); this language develops the image, central to one of the Magnificat antiphons, of Christ as 'clavis David,' the key that will unlock knowledge contained but obscured in divine law and prophecy.[23] When the doors enclosing God's wisdom have been unlocked — when Christ is born — the hidden will be revealed; the verb onwrēon, 'to uncover, unfold, explain,' is repeatedly (95b, 316a, 384a) used to describe this process: 'Nu us hælend god / wærfæst onwrah þæt we hine witan motan' (383b-4) (Now, true to his word, God has revealed the Saviour to us so that we may know him).

Illumination, revelation, and the growth of new life all convey the heightened understanding that results from Christ's birth:

Eal giofu gæstlic   grundsceat geondspreot;
þær wisna fela   wearð inlihted,
lare longsume,   þurh lifes fruman
þe ær under hoðman   biholen lægon,
witgena woðsong,   þa se waldend cwom ...   (42-6)

Every spiritual gift sprouted through the earth's covering; then many a shoot became illumined by the creator of life — ancient knowledge, the songs of prophets, that previously lay concealed in darkness — when the Ruler came ...[24]

<hr>

[23] See Burlin, The Old English Advent, 70-2 and 75-6, for discussion of interpretations of 'clavis David' available to the Christ A poet.
[24] Burlin says that line 42 'is doubtless dependent upon the plant image of the famous prophecy in Isaiah 11:1, "the sprout [virga] from the root of Jesse," which is followed immediately by a catalogue of what become known as the "Gifts of the Holy Spirit." He argues that the Advent poet is also

The learning latent in the Old Testament is a seed that germinates, pushing through the dark earth into the light when Christ is born. Birth (of child or plant) is a coming out of darkness, a revelation of a once hidden presence, and so an effective metaphor to describe intellectual discovery and comprehension. The word *hoðma*, translated above as 'darkness,' also means 'grave,' so there is a suggestion in this passage of resurrection, as the dormant seed, apparently dead, bursts into new life.

Although the birth of Christ is the event signified through these images of enlightenment and disclosure, the incarnation itself will always remain an unfathomable revelation:

Wæs seo fæmne geong,
mægð manes leas,   þe he him to meder geceas;
þæt wæs geworden   butan weres frigum,
þæt þurh bearnes gebyrd   bryd eacen wearð.
Nænig efenlic þam,   ær ne siþþan,
in worlde gewearð   wifes gearnung;
þæt degol wæs,   dryhtnes geryne. (*Christ A*, ll. 35b-41)

The maiden, whom he chose as his mother, was young, a virgin free of sin; it came to pass without a man's embrace that through the bearing of a child the bride became great. Never in the world, before or since, has a woman's merit been equal; that was hidden, the Lord's mystery.

This passage is full of paradox and almost invites rephrasing as a riddle.[25] 'Ic gefrægn wundorlice wyrd': a virgin became a mother without a man's embrace. Bearing a child, she became large. No desire will ever compare with hers.[26] It is as if the poem were asking: 'Saga hwæt degol wæs, dryhtnes

---

indebted to Is 55:10-11, which compares the word of God, accomplishing God's purpose, to rain and snow which cause the earth to sprout (ibib., 73-4).

[25] George Hardin Brown observes that '[t]he richly complex lines 35b-38 exemplify well the facility Old English verse possesses to express Christian mystery' ('Old English Verse as a Medium for Christian Theology,' in Phyllis R. Brown, Georgia R. Crampton, and Fred C. Robinson, eds, *Modes of Interpretation in Old English Literature* [Toronto 1986], 15-28, at 24). In this essay, Brown describes the propensity of Germanic verse — with its paronomasia and its half-lines linked through alliteration — for reflecting the paradoxes affirmed by Christian faith.

[26] 'Gearnung' is frequently emended to 'geacnung,' 'pregnancy,' but the manuscript reading contributes to the paradoxical quality of the passage.

geryne.' The Advent poem, a hymn about expectation, frequently takes on the manner of a riddle, through which all expectations are turned upside down. 'Frigað þurh fyrwet' (ask inquisitively), Mary invites us, about her virgin birth (92-4); we are told that no one under the sky is wise enough to explain accurately how the ruler of heaven took to himself a noble son (219-23); in language specific to Old English riddles, the merciful Creator's receiving of flesh from a virgin is described as a 'wræclic wrixl' (extraordinary exchange) (416-21). Forms and compounds of *gerȳne*, 'mystery,' occur seven times in the poem (41b, 47b, 74b, 134a, 196a, 247a, 423a).

Christ's incarnation is 'wræclic' and 'wundorlic'; *(ā-)cennan*, the verb that describes this event, does not reduce it to a one-dimensional signification. In the passage evoking Christ as 'earendel engla beorhtast' (104) (dayspring, brightest of angels) — a passage filled with such references to Christ as enlightening light — he is also described as truly or entirely 'acenned':

> Swa þu, god of gode   gearo acenned,
> sunu soþan fæder,   swegles in wuldre
> butan anginne   æfre wære. (109-11)

So you, God of God truly begotten, son of the true father, were ever in the glory of heaven without beginning.

'Acenned' can meaningfully be translated as 'begotten' here, yet the vocabulary of the passage (104 29) hints that the language in the hymn — like the language of a riddle — should be examined thoughtfully. As discussed above, Christ is described as son (110a) and sun (106b and 114a), a wordplay, as Brown says, that is only available in Germanic languages.[27] As son, he is begotten of the father ('God of God truly begotten') but as sun he illuminates and thereby causes the father to be known ('God of God entirely made known').

This use of *cennan* is also a specifically Germanic wordplay. In a passage replete with images of light and enlightenment (*inlīhtan* occurs twice here) this alternative meaning, this other dimension, is strongly present. Christ is also addressed in language that echoes the opening verses of the Gospel of John:

---

[27] Brown, 'Old English Verse as a Medium,' 23.

... word godes ...

þe on frymðe wæs   fæder ælmihtigum

efenece mid god,   ond nu eft gewearð

flæsc firena leas ...

.... God wæs mid us

gesewen butan synnum.   (120-5)

The word of God ... which in the beginning was coeternal with God the Father Almighty, and now, afterwards, has become flesh without transgression ... God with us was seen without sins.

As Word Christ is heard, as flesh he is seen; God is thus made perceptible, made known, through the birth of Christ — an abundantly meaningful event signified by 'acenned.'

'Acenned' describes Christ as a child born through the craft and might of the Father of Glory (218a). 'Cende' shortly afterwards (232b) designates each person who will be born through the ages, and through its proximity suggests that 'acenned' simply means 'born,' but within the context of this antiphon, which refers to the 'O Sapientia' evocation, the meaning cannot be so simply pinned down. Lines 224-35 tell of God's division of darkness and light and his creation of the sun, and the poem goes on to speak of the mystery of the Son's cohabitation and co-creation with the Father (236-45a). The Son is identified as wisdom ('snyttro,' 239a), perhaps in reference to Prov 8:22-30.[28] In the context of God's creating, begetting, and making known, and of Christ's identity as wisdom, 'cild acenned' suggests 'child revealed' as well as 'child born.'

In lines 297a-8b, *cennan* occurs in close proximity to *cȳðan*, the OE word most closely related to it in meaning. *Cennan* and *cȳðan* can function in such similar ways that their substitution in a sentence would cause no change at all to the meaning.[29] In Ælfric's 'Sermo de Memoria Sanctorum,' *ācennan*

---

[28] Burlin explains that the *Glossa ordinaria* (CXIII.1091) links this passage with the prologue to John's Gospel, thereby associating Christ and Wisdom; he points out that Augustine develops this identification (XLII.936) (*The Old English Advent*, 133-4).

[29] Both verbs are causative and the two are associated etymologically. In BT, *cȳðan* is defined: 'To make known, tell, relate; to declare, reveal ... perform, confess, ...testify, prove.' As an example of their similar usage, both can take 'wisdom' as their object: 'he us cenneð wisdom' (HomS 39 [Verc 12] 80) (He makes wisdom known to us) and 'Wisdom sceoldon, / weras Ebrea, wordum cyðan' (Dan 95b-6) (The Hebrew men had to make wisdom known in words.)

and *cȳðan* are found in parallel grammatical constructions with the result that the two meanings of *cennan* are brought into play (as discussed above).[10] In the address to Holy Jerusalem in *Christ A*, *cȳðan* takes as its object the birth of Christ:

> ... þec heofones cyning
> siðe geseceð, ond sylf cymeð,
> nimeð eard in þe, swa hit ær gefyrn
> witgan wisfæste wordum sægdon,
> cyðdon Cristes gebyrd ... (61b-5a)

> ... Heaven's King seeks you on his journey, and He himself comes, takes up a home in you, just as long ago wise prophets described it in words, made known the birth of Christ ...

Jerusalem has many exegetical significations — the city itself, the Church, the soul, the Heavenly City — and here, in addition to all of these meanings, refers to Mary, sought by the King of Heaven to be the abode of Christ.[11] The relationship between *cȳðan* and *gebyrd* suggests that the prophets' 'making known' Christ's birth anticipates the way the birth itself will make known Heaven's King, illuminating divine prophecy.

In *Christ A*, the juxtaposition of the two verbs occurs in the following passage:

> Forðon heht sigores fruma
> his heahbodan hider gefleogan
> of his mægenþrymme ond þe meahta sped
> snude cyðan, þæt þu sunu dryhtnes
> þurh clæne gebyrd cennan sceolde

---

[10] ÆLS (Memory of Saints) 107-9.

[11] There is a vast bibliography on this topic. See, for example, Evelyn Berriot-Salvadore, ed., *Le myth de Jérusalem: du moyen age à la renaissance* (Saint-Etienne 1995); Thomas Renna, *Jerusalem in Medieval Thought, 400-1300* (Lewiston, NY, 2002); Gedaliahu Stroúsma, *Kanon und Kultur: Zwei Studien zur Hermeneutik des antiken Christentums* (Berlin 1999); Peter W.L. Walker, *Holy City, Holy Places: Christian Attitudes to Jerusalem and the Holy Land in the Fourth Century* (Oxford 1990); and Peter W.L. Walker, *Jesus and the Holy City: New Testament Perspectives on Jerusalem* (Grand Rapids, MI, 1996). In *Trinity and Incarnation in Anglo-Saxon Thought* (CSASE 21 [Cambridge 1997]), Barbara Raw discusses the significance of Jerusalem as a 'vision of peace.'

monnum to miltse,   ond þe, Maria, forð,
efne unwemme   a gehealdan.   (294b-300)

Therefore, the king of victory commanded his messenger to fly here
from his great majesty, and make known to you at once the abundance
of his powers, so that you, through a pure birth, should bring forth the
Son of the Lord in mercy for humankind, and you, Mary, from then
on should always be held unstained.

Just as the messenger must make known ('cyðan') God's power, Mary must
bring forth ('cennan') God's Son. The sense of revelation explicitly at work in
'cyðan' is also echoed in 'cennan,' found in a parallel construction. 'Cennan'
bridges the gap in signification between the very literal meanings of 'cyðan'
and 'gebyrd': through a pure birth, Mary will reveal God's Son.

Ælfric, following Augustine and Bede, explored the implications of
Christ as an expression of God. In the Advent poem, the idea of Christ being
the perceptible manifestation of God is emphasised by the verb *íewan*, 'to
show, display, reveal, disclose, point out.' Imperative forms of the verb occur
twice in *Christ A*:

> Cum, nu, sigores weard,
> meotod moncynnes,   ond þine miltse her
> arfæst ywe!   (243b-5a)

Come now, guardian of victory, Lord of humankind, and reveal here
your compassionate mercy!

> Iowa us nu þa are   þe se engel þe,
> godes spelboda,   Gabriel brohte.
> Huru þæs biddað   burgsittende
> þæt ðu þa frofre   folcum cyðe,
> þinre sylfre sunu.   Siþþan we motan
> anmodlice   ealle hyhtan,
> nu we on þæt bearn foran   breostum stariað.   (335-41)

Show us now the grace that the angel Gabriel, the messenger of God,
brought to you. Truly, people on earth pray for this — that you make

known to folk that Comfort, your own Son. Hereafter, all with one heart, we will be able to hope, now that we look upon the child at your breast.

'Þine miltse her arfæst ywe' and 'Iowa us nu þa are' both implore that blessings that are imperceptible be made visible and each of these Advent petitions prays for immediacy — that the gifts be shown 'her' and 'nu.' In the second of the passages, 'iowa' is parallel in function with 'cyðe': Mary is asked to show us grace and to make known to us Comfort / her Son. Making known is equated with showing, Christ with Comfort, and the awaited revelatory event is the birth of Christ. God, who is imperceptible and ineffable, and his blessings — mercy, grace, and comfort — which are incorporeal, are made visible and immediately present through the incarnation of Christ. Therefore, as they look upon the child ('stariað'), all people are offered hope.[32]

Such concepts are condensed and given visual form in the St John initial page of the Grimbald Gospels, which plays with the idea of making the word visible (see fig. 1 at the end of this essay).[33] The gilded letters of the opening of John's prologue comprise the text: 'In prin[cipio erat] verbum et verbum erat apud Deum et Deus erat verbum,' thus making visible the evangelist's words. The style of the words' inscription — their formal, gold lettering — is meant to be visually impressive in order to celebrate the Word and John's message about the Word's presence at creation. These words have substance, especially the introductory 'I' with its width, the texture provided by its interlace and acanthus decoration, the animation suggested by the animal's muzzle at its base, and the solidity shown by allowing it to support an angel. Surrounding the text is a thick, decorative frame, embellished with medallions

---

[32] Similarly, Christ is described as God made visible in lines 124b-5a: 'God wæs mid us / gesewen butan synnum' (God was seen with us, without sins).

[33] London, BL, Additional MS 34890, fol. 115r. This manuscript dates from the early 11th c. and was produced at either Canterbury or Winchester, where Grimbald was abbot. For further discussion of the history of the manuscript and its illumination see R. Gameson, 'Manuscript Art at Christ Church, Canterbury, in the Generation after St Dunstan,' in N. Ramsay, M. Sparks, and T. Tatton-Brown, eds, *St. Dunstan: His Life, Times and Cult* (Woodbridge 1992), 187-220; and E. Temple, *Anglo-Saxon Manuscripts 900-1066*, A Survey of Manuscripts Illuminated in the British Isles 2 (London 1976), no. 67.

and inhabited by 'the various choirs of the blessed'[34] and two seraphs (in its upper corner medallions). All of these figures look — 'stariað' — towards an upper central medallion containing the Virgin and Child.

This image embodies the meaning of *verbum*: Christ is the Word made visible to us (we who look upon the page), as he is to the figures in the frame turned towards him, and as he was to those who witnessed his nativity, ministry, passion, and resurrection. In fact, the two moments of the Word's birth are depicted, and thus conflated, on this page. In the text we read of his eternal, timeless birth from the Father, while the image celebrates Jesus' birth from Mary. In Ælfric's words:

He is tuwa acenned and ægðer acennednys is wundorlic, and unasecgendlic. He wæs æfre of ðam fæder acenned for ðan þe he is þæs fæder wisdom þurh ðone he geworhte and gesceop ealle gesceafta. Nu is ðeos acennednys buton anginne for ðan þe se fæder wæs æfre god ond his wisdom þæt is his sunu wæs æfre of him acenned buton ælcere meder. Þeos acennednys þe we nu todæg wurðiað wæs of eorðlicere meder buton ælcum eorðlicum fæder. (ÆCHom II, 1 5-12)[35]

He is twice born and each birth is wonderful and ineffable. He was ever born of the Father because he is the wisdom of the Father through whom he made and shaped all creation. Now this birth is without beginning because the Father was always God and his wisdom, that is his Son, was always born of him without any mother. This birth which we now today celebrate was of an earthly mother without any earthly father.

Barbara Raw writes: 'Through material images of Christ, who is himself the true image of God, man, created in God's image, learns to know God, rather than merely knowing about him.'[36] The Grimbald St John initial page offers two visual, material representations of Christ that reinforce and provide meaning for each other, and suggest a connection between the birth of Christ

---

[34] Janet Backhouse, D.H. Turner, and Leslie Webster, eds, *The Golden Age of Anglo-Saxon Art: 966-1066* (London 1984), 72.
[35] 'De Natale Domini,' in M. Godden, ed., *Ælfric's Catholic Homilies, The Second Series*, EETS, ss 5 (London 1979).
[36] Raw, *Trinity and Incarnation*, 6.

and the making known of God's Word. Together, text and illumination illustrate the theological framework within which *ācennan* has meaning. The uncertain relationship between the two meanings of *cennan* provided Anglo-Saxon Christian writers a fertile ground for exploring the revelatory meanings of Christ's incarnation. As Roberta Frank discovers through her reading of *Solomon and Saturn*, composers of Old English literature enjoyed conveying 'how Christian learning — operating through God-given words — can fathom the secret significances of things.'[37] Ælfric knew that Christ is 'wisdomes spræc us unasecgendlic' (ÆHom 1 132), (wisdom's speech unutterable for us). The *Christ A* poet meditated about the significance of Advent in language that puzzles at its strangeness. The use of *cennan* in Old English literature is an instance of complex, enigmatic language expressing a complex, enigmatic theology. In Anglo-Saxon thinking about language and in Christian theology the W/word makes ultimate meaning manifest; *cennan*, a word whose meaning cannot be pinned down, reveals an event — Christ's incarnation — whose ultimate meaning always eludes us.

---

[37] Frank, 'Some Uses of Paronomasia,' 208.

Fig 1. London, BL, Additional MS 34890, fol. 115r
(reproduced with permission)

4

Pride, Courage, and Anger: The Polysemousness of Old English *Mōd*[1]

SOON-AI LOW

In Anglo-Saxon depictions of personal experience, the interior principle denoted by *mōd* was a salient component. *Mōd* features prominently in many narrative depictions of inward experience: the notion of building Heorot, for instance, occurs to Hrothgar in his *mōd* (Beo 67: 'him on mod bearn'), and in *The Seafarer,* hunger gnaws away at the sea-weary *mōd* (ll. 11-12: 'hungor innan slat / merewerges mod'). In prose, the use of *mōd* to portray the inner life is well exemplified by citations such as LS 23 (Mary of Egypt) 424: 'Þa onhran soðlice min mod ... hælo andgit' (Then, truly, the understanding of salvation touched my mind). King Alfred's substitution of *Mōd* for Boethius in his translation of *De consolatione philosophiae* serves to underscore further the importance of this entity in the Anglo-Saxon world view.

Mōd is only one of a number of Old English words that denoted the inner part of man, alongside *hyge, sefa, ferhð,* and others.[2] But *mōd* survives in nearly 3000 occurrences, compared to *ingehygd* at 205 occurrences and *hyge* at about 170, and it was the main gloss for Latin *mens* and *animus*.[3] It was, without a doubt, the superordinate term for 'mind' in Old English.

---

[1] An earlier version of this essay was delivered at the International Society of Anglo-Saxonists Conference at the University of Notre Dame, Indiana, in August 1999. I would like to thank Ian C. McDougall for his advice on the present version.

[2] The scholar and teacher to whom this volume is dedicated has contributed a valuable discussion of the attestations of *hyge, ferhþ,* and *sefa* in 'Poetic Words in Late Old English Prose,' in Malcolm Godden, Douglas Gray, and Terry Hoad, eds, *From Anglo-Saxon to Early Middle English* (Oxford 1994), 87-107.

[3] The task of glossing *mens* was one that *mōd* shared with *geþanc* and *þōht;* that of glossing *animus,* with *geþanc* and *sāwol.* Because individual texts may exist in multiple manuscripts, absolute frequencies are only a rough guide to a word's currency in Anglo-Saxon usage and glosses are naturally less reliable as witnesses than prose or verse, but as a matter of interest *mōd, geþanc,* and

A curious fact about *mōd*, however, is that it denotes not only 'mind' or 'heart' or 'spirit' but also 'courage' and the darker qualities of 'pride' and 'anger.' A well-known example of *mōd* used to denote 'courage' occurs in Mald 312-13: 'Heorte sceal þe cenre, / mod sceal þe mare' (Heart shall be the keener, courage the greater). *Mōd* also appears unequivocally to mean 'pride' at GenA 53, where the about-to-be-fallen angels are characterized as being unworthy of sharing God's power, as they aspire to do: 'Ac him se mæra mod getwæfde, / bælc forbigde' (But the glorious One took pride from them, abased their arrogance). The 'anger' sense appears perhaps most clearly in the following two examples where *mōd* is applied (figuratively?) to nonhuman subjects: at Beo 549, 'wæs merefixa mod onhrered' (the anger of the sea-fish was aroused) and Ex 489, when Pharaoh's men are unable to withstand the 'anger' of the Red Sea, as expressed in the phrase 'merestreames mod.'

That the primary word for 'mind' in Old English should possess such secondary senses is a matter that requires explanation, especially as interest in the area of Anglo-Saxon psychology is growing.[4] But it is worth asking, at the outset, to what extent *mōd* may be considered polysemous at all. In some places where *mōd* is traditionally translated by 'pride' or 'courage,' the gloss 'mind' is equally plausible, and the sense of the passage is made clear in context by metaphor or some other means. The line from *Maldon,* for instance, could easily be rendered 'heart shall be the keener, mind the more expansive,' where 'mod,' modified by the metaphor implicit in 'mare,' indicates courage but need not strictly denote it. Compare with this Beo 1167: 'he hæfde mod micel' (he had great spirit/courage). The occurrence of *mōd* in Or6 30.147.16 presents a similar case: 'Æfter þæm þe his mod wæs mid þæm

---

þōht gloss *mens* in the ratio 40:14:2; *mentis* 45:12:25; and *mente* 39:24:9. *Mōd, geþanc* and *sāwol* gloss *animus* in the ratio 31:2:1; *animi* 14:1:0; *animo* 30:3:1. *Gehygde* glosses *animo* once.
[4] The seminal work is M.R. Godden, 'Anglo-Saxons on the Mind,' in Michael Lapidge and Helmut Gneuss, eds, *Learning and Literature in Anglo-Saxon England* (Cambridge 1985), 271-98. See also the dissertations by Margrit Soland, 'Altenglische Ausdrücke für Leib und Seele' (University of Zürich 1979), and Michael J. Phillips, 'Heart, Mind and Soul in Old English: A Semantic Study' (University of Illinois at Urbana-Champaign 1985). Three recent doctoral dissertations on the topic are J.A. Highfield, 'Old English *mōd* in the Context of Religious Change' (University of Manchester 1998); S.A. Low, 'The Anglo-Saxon Mind: Metaphor and Common Sense Psychology in Old English Literature' (University of Toronto 1998); Michael Matto, 'Containing Minds: Mind, Metaphor and Cognition in Old English Literature' (New York University 1998). See also Antonina Harbus, *The Life of the Mind in Old English Poetry* (Amsterdam and New York 2002).

bismre ahwet, he for eft on Perse & hie gefliemde.' BT glosses this instance of *mōd* as 'courage, high spirit,' and translates the sentence, 'after his courage had been sharpened by this disgrace, he once more marched against the Persians and put them to flight.' But *mōd* here could again be rendered 'mind' and the metaphorical process of sharpening understood to produce a mind more pointed in its purpose; in other words, more courageous.

BT also cites GenA 2237 'hire mod astah' with the translation 'her (Hagar's) pride mounted up.' Though the notion of pride is obviously expressed here, it seems less clear that assigning the sense 'pride' to *mōd* is strictly necessary. The metaphor implicit in the verb *āstīgan* 'to ascend' depicts a mind inappropriately exalted; an analogy might be made with the occurrence of *heorte* in LS 34 (Seven Sleepers) 24: 'He ða his heortan hof swa upp ofer his mæðe, swilce he God wære' (He then raised up his heart over his proper measure, as though he were God).[5] Hagar's pride in the line from *Genesis A* is more clearly expressed through the metaphor of exaltation than by *mōd*'s capacity to mean 'pride.'

The polysemousness of *mōd* must be more narrowly established than has been the case in BT's entry. In particular, the senses 'pride,' 'courage,' and 'anger' may only be assigned to *mōd* if there are places where 'mind' or 'spirit' is not a possible gloss. In fact, there *are* instances of *mōd*'s use which appear to resist the reading 'mind,' and which would seem to establish the word's polysemy. BT cites ChristC 1428 'Næs me for mode, ac ic on magugeoguðe / yrmþu geæfnde' (It was not from pride in me, but in youth I suffered hardship), where the reading 'mind' would fail to make sense, and we must instead substitute a quality of mind or soul such as 'pride.' The same analysis may be made of the line cited above from *Genesis A*, where God deprived ('getwæfde') the rebel angels of their 'mod.' The sundering action implied by the verb would rather strain a reading of *mōd* as 'mind' and, again, 'pride' appears to be the best reading. What these two citations have in common is a use of *mōd* which implies a temporal quality of character — an attitude or emotion — that is different in kind from the more durable and innate entity of mind. It is this dichotomy between the temporal and the enduring which marks these off as separate senses.

The two examples cited above where *mōd* is used of fish and flood respectively are slightly more complex, and may be considered together. Beo

---

[5] The Latin source has 'exaltatum est cor eius' (Sept.dorm. 8) (his heart was raised up).

549, 'wæs merefixa mod onhrered,' could be read as 'the mind of the sea-fish was agitated,' taking the stirring-up metaphor implied by *onhrēran* as one which indicates anger or arousal. The outcome would be to disqualify this example (by the criterion put forward in the previous paragraph) in establishing *mōd*'s polysemy. On the other hand, if the reader prefers not to think that the *merefiscas* might possess a 'mind,' then the translation 'the anger of the sea-fish was aroused' obviates this particular problem. (Of possibly figurative uses of *mōd,* more later.) The line from *Exodus* establishes more clearly the sense 'anger,' as the Egyptians are unable to 'forhabban merestreames mod.' The metaphor implicit in 'forhabban,' 'to contain or withstand,' clearly demands that 'merestreames mod' be understood as 'the fury of the sea,' since a force is envisioned. Violence is temporal in kind, and so this line might be taken to be an unequivocal reading of *mōd* as meaning 'anger' or 'fury.'

The fact, however, that there are cases inhabiting the borderline between the primary reading of *mōd* as 'mind' and the secondary readings of 'pride,' 'anger,' and 'courage' suggests that there is a close connection (naturally) among these things. It has been suggested above that temporality may be a criterion in sorting between *mōd*'s primary and secondary senses, but the actual process of polysemization is worth pursuing further, to see what light might be shed on the concept of *mōd* and on the nature of lexical meaning. Just how we are to understand *mōd*'s polysemy is what the rest of this essay explores, first by examining the word's genealogy and then by considering a number of other words that appear to show a similar semantic profile to *mōd.*

Pokorny lists *mōd* as the Anglo-Saxon offspring of Indo-European *mē, mō, ma-*, which also gave rise to, among others, Latin *mos, moris,* Old Icelandic *móðr,* and Modern German *Mut.*[6] These cognate words possess complex semantic profiles similar to that of *mōd.* The senses of Old Icelandic *móðr,* for

---

[6] Julius Pokorny, *Indogermanisches etymologisches Wörterbuch* (Bern 1959) 704–5; the relation of Lat. *mos* to OE *mōd* is confirmed by Walde-Hofmann, *Lateinisches etymologisches Wörterbuch,* 4th edn (Heidelberg 1965), s. *mos,* but Kluge and Seebold call the relationship into question, declaring the ultimate origin of *Mut* to be 'unklar' and only perhaps related to *mos* (*Etymologisches Wörterbuch der deutschen Sprache,* 23rd edn [Berlin and New York 1995], s. *Mut*). Winfred P. Lehmann rejects the relation of the Germanic root to Lat. *mos,* declaring the etymology of the Gothic reflex 'problematic' (*A Gothic Etymological Dictionary* [Leiden 1986], s. **mōþs*). The argument developed in this essay does not depend on *mōd* and *mos* being cognate.

instance, are listed as 'agitation' or 'emotion' in prose and 'mind,' 'soul,' 'passion,' 'courage,' 'high spirits,' and 'grief' in poetry.[7] Modern German *Mut* is listed as meaning 'courage,' 'heart,' 'fortitude,' 'humour' and 'mood.'[8] (Latin *mos* is treated in the next paragraph.) Pokorny's definition of the reconstructed Indo-European root is 'heftigen und kraftigen Willens sein, heftig streben' (to be of violent and powerful will, to strive violently), which suggests that the 'anger' and 'courage' senses of *mōd* may have been prior to all else.

This was also the conclusion reached by E.M. Meyer, whose 1926 monograph is still cited as an authority by Kluge and Seebold.[9] Meyer's hypothesis was that Primitive Germanic **mōða-* must have had as its semantic base the meaning of 'Macht' or power, from the evidence of the various reflexes and their derivatives and also from the propensity of words such as *mōd* to collocate with other words such as *mægen* and *miht*. In order to explain the development of the sense 'mind' for *mōd* and some of its cognates, Meyer hypothesized that the 'Macht' denoted by **mōða-* was a sort of animistic force believed by the early Germanic peoples to inhabit things and creatures (hence, presumably, 'merefixa mod' should not be regarded as a figurative usage). From there the reflexes of **mōða-* were extended, by analogy, to refer to 'mind' or the inner 'Macht.' As Meyer noted, this extension can be understood only 'vom Standpunkt der primitiven Psychologie,' with its preference for concrete rather than abstract phenomena.[10] Incidentally, the notion that the semantic developments of this Germanic root reflected something in the Germanic spirit was also suggested by Grimm, who wrote in his entry for *Mut* (1854) that the alternations between 'mind' and 'anger' shown by the various cognate lexemes indicated 'eine eigenthümliche noch nicht aufgehellte äuszerung des germanischen geistes, sei es nach der kriegerischen oder nach der religiösen

---

[7] Johan Fritzner, *Ordbog over det gamle Norske Sprog,* 2nd edn, 3 vols (Kristiania 1886-96; rpt. 1954); vol. 4 *Rettelser og Tillegg,* ed. Finn Hødnebø (Oslo 1972); Finnur Jónsson, *Lexicon poeticum antiquæ linguæ septentrionalis: Ordbog over det Norsk-Islandske Skjaldesprog, oprindelig forfattet af Sveinbjörn Egilsson,* 2nd edn (Copenhagen 1931; rpt. 1966); s. *móðr*.

[8] See, for example, Günther Drosdowski, ed., *Das grosse Wörterbuch der deutschen Sprache* (Mannheim, Leipzig, Vienna, and Zürich 1993); s. *Mut*.

[9] E.M. Meyer, 'Die Bedeutungsentwicklung von germanischen **mōða-*,' (diss. University of Leipzig 1926), 62.

[10] Ibid., 42.

seite hin' (a peculiar, as yet unclarified expression of the Germanic spirit, tending in either a martial or a religious direction)."

Be this as it may, it is possible to theorize about the semantic development of *mōða- without resorting to such constructions of 'the Germanic spirit.' To begin, we may look at mōd's supposed Latin cognate mos, whose semantic range offers some insight into the nature of mōd's polysemy. According to Lewis and Short, mos means, among other things, 'humour,' 'self-will,' 'caprice,' 'manner,' 'fashion,' 'habit,' 'conduct,' 'behaviour,' 'manners,' 'morals,' 'character,' 'quality,' 'nature,' 'precept,' 'law,' and 'rule.' In this bewildering array of senses, it is possible to isolate the senses 'caprice' and 'law' as the semantic poles belonging to an axis of temporality, since the one denotes a sudden turn of fancy and the other a custom written in stone. Between these two poles of temporal and enduring, the notions of 'character' and 'nature' might be considered to lie. For if we take Pokorny's word on the meaning of the Indo-European root of mos and mōd, then we might see how the sense 'to be of violent and powerful will' could very naturally give rise to meanings such as 'caprice,' 'humour,' and 'self-will.' Because qualities such as caprice and wilfulness are inherent features of conscious, intelligent life, meanings such as 'nature' and 'character' were possible, perhaps by the mechanism of metonymy, whereby the word denoting the phenomenon of caprice is extended to the entity exhibiting the capriciousness. If we replace Meyer's notion of 'Macht' with one such as 'lively principle,' we may see how the continuous and very human expression of whims and fancies and turns of mood became the basis for the stable and enduring notions of 'nature' and 'character.' By this process, a word that originally denoted a temporal state could come to denote an enduring principle. From a word meaning 'passing mood,' mos becomes a word that means 'personality basis for passing moods' — a different kind of thing altogether.

It is possible that a movement analogous to the one just sketched out for mos may have operated for Germanic *mōða-. If we accept Meyer's idea that the earliest meanings for this proto-Germanic root were those of 'anger,' 'courage,' and 'pride' and think of these as personal· experiences of an

---

" Deutsches Wörterbuch von Jacob Grimm und Wilhelm Grimm. Hrsg. von der Deutschen Akademie der Wissenschaften zu Berlin in Zusammenarbeit mit der Akademie der Wissenschaft zu Göttingen (Leipzig 1965-) s. Mut.

occasional nature, then the same progress from temporal state to enduring principle may have occurred, in that the name for these emotions was extended metonymically to the entity that underwent these experiences.

The history of another Anglo-Saxon 'mind' word, *hyge,* shows that these postulations are not entirely implausible. *Hyge* was a predominantly poetic word in Old English that survived as a rarely attested term in Middle English and then passed out of standard usage altogether. Interestingly, Meyer suggests that the word's demise in English stemmed from its omission from the Christian terminology for 'soul' and its related concepts (unlike in other Germanic languages, where the cognates of *hyge* — ON *hugr,* for instance — rather than those of *mōd* were co-opted into the Christian idiom).[12] While the *Middle English Dictionary* records only a tiny survival for *hige,* the *English Dialect Dictionary* shows it to have survived dialectally in the Midlands and the North (perhaps as the result of Norse reinforcement?) as *hig,* in a manner congenial to the theory put forward here. *Hig* is listed as meaning 'a fit of passion; a petulant, offended state of mind, a "huff"; an attack of illness,' such that the adjectives *higged* and *higly* were coined to mean 'angered, offended,' and 'passionate' respectively. *To take the hig* was to take offence or, as Wright has it, 'be in a pet.'[13] But most intriguingly of all, *hig* developed the meaning 'a temporary hurricane; a short shower of wind or rain,' such that in Yorkshire it was and perhaps still is customary to refer to the 'March igs.' The later history of *hyge* appears to be that of *mōd* in reverse: from the sense 'mind,' *hyge* comes to refer to temporary fits of passion, which are then figuratively extended to refer to the changeable English sky.

The semantic history of *hyge,* oscillating between weather and personal disposition, is surely analogous to that of *temper* (fit of passion), commonly supposed to share the same etymological origin as *tempest* (storm of limited duration), except that, as the *OED* cautiously has it, 'the sense history of both words [*temper* and *tempus*] is prehistoric and obscure.'[14] Embedded in this semantic oscillation is again that alternation between temporary passion and enduring principle, illustrated also by several other words.

The Latin loan *animus,* for instance, is listed in the *OED* as meaning originally '(1) soul, (2) mind, (3) mental impulse, disposition, passion.' Its

[12] Meyer, *Die Bedeutungsentwicklung,* 64.
[13] Joseph Wright, *English Dialect Dictionary* (London 1898-1905), s. *hig.*
[14] *OED,* s. *temper,* vb.

meaning in English is defined as 'actuating feeling, disposition in a particular direction ... usually of a hostile character; hence, animosity.'[15] The *Oxford Latin Dictionary* lists as sense 1 of *ingenium*, 'natural disposition, temperament. b (meton.) one having a specified disposition. c temporary disposition, mood.' The entry for *self* in the *OED* likewise lists in addition to sense 3, 'that which in a person is really and intrinsically *he* ... a permanent subject of successive and varying states of consciousness,' 'selfishness' as sense 5, citing in support this speech from *Adam Bede:* 'She's better than I am — there's less o' self in her, and pride.'[16]

The polysemousness exhibited by *mōd* obviously has something in common with that shown by *mos, hyge, temper, animus, ingenium,* and *self.* The semantic connections that *mōd* effects between the notion of 'mind' on the one hand and those of 'anger,' 'pride,' and 'courage' on the other are therefore not peculiar to Germanic **mōða-,* but are manifested in languages disparate in time and space. A primitive psychology is unlikely to be reflected, at least in the modern English developments of *animus* and *self,* and it is suggested here that Meyer's hypothesis that the semantic ramification of **mōða-* reflects the primitive Germanic world view be discarded in favour of an explanation more parsimonious as well as less patronizing.

This claim for a certain universality in the type of polysemy shown by *mōd* is relevant to recent scholarship, because the idea that it reflects some peculiarity of the Germanic disposition has not disappeared. For instance, based on his understanding of the polysemy of *mōd* and the meanings of its morphological derivations, Malcolm Godden has written that '*mōd* seems to convey to many Anglo-Saxon writers not so much the intellectual, rational faculty but something more like an inner passion or wilfulness, an intensification of the self that can be dangerous.'[17] In a similar vein, Michael J. Phillips, in his doctoral study of *mōd*'s collocations, concluded that 'an unrestrained *mōd* or *hyge* is dangerous.'[18] Incidentally, both scholars find support for these conclusions in the frequency with which *mōd* is called on in

---

[15] *OED*, s. *animus.*
[16] *OED*, s. *self.*
[17] Godden, 'Anglo-Saxons on the Mind,' 287. In support of the statement just quoted, Godden writes, 'In Anglo-Saxon generally ... *mōd* also carries the meaning "courage" and "pride," and its derivatives all point in the direction of these latter meanings: *mōdig,* "brave", "proud", *mōdignes* and *ofermōd,* "pride", "arrogance", *mōdigian,* "to be arrogant", *ormōd,* "devoid of spirit", "hopeless".'
[18] Phillips, 'Heart, Mind and Soul,' 221.

the literature to be restrained, as at Sea 109: 'Stieran mon sceal strongum mode' (One must control a strong mind). It may be, however, that these aphorisms say more about the religious didactic idiom than about the culturally specific notion of *mōd*. In Latin as well as Anglo-Saxon religious writing, the mind is often pictured as something rather flighty and unstable, which must be held firm in prayer and meditation.[19]

In the traditional lexical studies I have cited, the genealogy of *mōd*, its polysemous configuration and the semantics of its derivatives, such as *mōdig* 'brave' and *mōdigian* 'to be arrogant,' are all irresistibly taken to mean that the qualities of pride, anger, and courage were somehow essentially inherent in the concept of *mōd*. But it is worth remembering that a central tenet of modern linguistic theory is the arbitrariness of the sign. Words do not have fixed and essential meanings, and this is no less true from a historical perspective than from a synchronic one.

As Dirk Geeraerts has recently observed, 'polysemy is, roughly, the synchronic reflection of diachronic semantic change.'[20] The importance of this remark lies in its emphasis on the ultimate sameness of history's long march and the time-slice: that in order to understand a word's synchronic semantic profile we must be aware of its history, but equally, to know what to make of a word's semantic history, we must be aware of how lexical meaning operates synchronically. In the same way, a word's etymology and the meanings of its cognates are the synchronic reflection of diachronic semantic change; that is, polysemy writ large within the history of a language family rather than in that of a single language.

There are only a handful of ways in which a word extends its meaning — metaphor, metonymy, specialization, and generalization[21] — and these processes are only possible because of the arbitrariness of the sign. Let us return to the case of *self* as treated above, where the attested sense of this word as

---

[19] For instance, Gregory the Great remarks: 'Sed studendum nobis est ut etiam post orationis tempora, in quantum Deo largiente possumus, in ipso animum suo pondere et uigore seruemus, ne post cogitatio fluxa dissoluat, ne vana menti laetitia subrepat, et lucrum conpunctionis anima per incuriam fluxae cogitationis perdat' (But we should endeavour even after times of prayer, as far as we are able, with God granting, to keep the mind in its same weight and vigour, lest the fluid thought dissolve afterwards, lest vain pleasure steal upon the mind, and the soul lose the profit of remorsefulness through the negligence of fluctuating thought) (GREG.MAG.Dial. 4.61.2.).

[20] Dirk Geeraerts, *Diachronic Prototype Semantics* (Oxford 1997), 6.

[21] Ibid., 95.

'selfishness' is elaborated by the *OED* as 'one's personal welfare and interests as an object of concern.'[22] Observe the extension by metonymy that has taken place: the word that refers to the subject 'self' is extended to refer to the object 'interests of self,' and in the very moment of functional shift the pejoration of the word is made possible. The dichotomy of the temporal and the enduring, now found in the contrasting senses of *self*, reflects the mechanical process of metonymy, rather than the expression of cultural essence.

The polysemousness of *mōd* reflects a similar circumstance. The process by which the meaning 'mind' was derived from the meanings 'pride,' 'courage,' and 'anger' may also be understood as metonymy: the word denoting a passion is extended to refer to the site of that passion and thereby acquires a meaning different in kind from that whence it was derived. *Mos, hyge, animus, ingenium* and *temper* can be shown to have undergone identical developments. The fact that *mōd* means 'anger' and 'courage' as well as 'mind' need have no bearing on our interpretation of the Anglo-Saxon mind and its nature, because the various meanings of a word do not extrapolate to some larger picture of what the word 'really' means.[23] Lexical meaning is a process, not a thing, and it is a mistake to view the reconstruction of a word's meaning as though it were like the reconstruction of pottery from shards.[24] As the linguist E.M. Uhlenbeck has suggested, lexical meaning must be understood as 'cognitive potential at the disposal of the speaker' and '*knowledge* relative to linguistic forms which speakers use in the act of speech in various ways.'[25] Lexical items are extended to suit the individual context, according to the speaker's needs, and sometimes these usages are catching, whereupon they become part of the semantic profile of a word, and sometimes they are not catching, whereupon

---

[22] *OED*, s. *self*, sense 5.

[23] It is possible that *mōd*'s polysemousness influenced the way in which some Anglo-Saxons thought about what they called their *mōd*, but I believe that this would consist in idiosyncratic instances of 'folk-semanticizing' and be trivial in its implications for the present argument. Anglo-Saxonists are probably more aware of the polysemousness of Old English words than actual Anglo-Saxons were, because we are constantly looking these words up in dictionaries, of which they had none.

[24] See Dirk Geeraerts, 'Vagueness's Puzzles, Polysemy's Vagaries,' *Cognitive Linguistics* 4 (1993): 223-72, at 260.

[25] E.M. Uhlenbeck, 'Some Remarks on Homonymy and Polysemy,' in Barbara Partee and Petr Sgall, eds, *Discourse and Meaning: Papers in Honor of Eva Hajičová* (Amsterdam and Philadelphia 1996), 119-26, at 121.

they leave no trace.[26] The meaning of a word is only actualized by the speaker in the instant of usage: it has no continuous existence and should not be thought of as residing in every instance of the word's use. Polysemy is therefore not a collection of various meanings that a word possesses but a set of established directions in which its semantics may be extended.

The manner in which languages disparate in time and space will show the same semantic shifts over and over again is something that C.S. Lewis observed in *Studies in Words:*

> We find in the history, say, of *phusis, natura,* and *kind,* or again in that of *eleutherios, liberalis, free* and *frank,* similar or even identical semantic operations being performed quite independently. The speakers who achieved them belonged to different stocks and lived in different countries at different periods, and they started with different linguistic tools ... There is something either in the structure of the mind or in the things it thinks about, which can produce the same results under very different conditions.[27]

Exactly thirty years later, the cognitive linguist Eve Sweetser echoes these observations, but is able to go further than Lewis's intuition that 'there is something ... in the structure of the mind':

> Certain semantic changes occur over and over again throughout the course of Indo-European and independently in different branches across an area of thousands of miles and a time depth of thousands of years. I will show that a cognitive semantics that allows for metaphorical mapping within a conceptual system can explain such facts straightforwardly ...[28]

---

[26] Note that because semantic extension is limited to associational mechanisms such as metaphor and metonymy, there is a control placed upon the semantic flexibility of words. As Geeraerts observes, 'the constraint that new meanings be linked to existing ones prevents the semantic flexibility of lexical items from deteriorating into communicatively inefficient arbitrariness' (*Diachronic Prototype Semantics,* 114).

[27] C.S. Lewis, *Studies in Words* (Cambridge 1960), 5-6.

[28] Eve Sweetser, *From Etymology to Pragmatics: Metaphorical and Cultural Aspects of Semantic Structure* (Cambridge 1990), 9.

The semantic changes occurring with words such as *mōd, mos, hyge, animus, ingenium, temper,* and *self* are — as with *phusis, natura,* and *kind* – changes that reflect, as Lewis has it, something in the structure of the mind or in the things it thinks about. We learn relatively little from these changes about the concept of 'mind' in Anglo-Saxon culture but a great deal about the nature of lexical meaning.

A further implication of the process of polysemization as described here is that the resultant semantic changes do not reflect meaning that was latent in previous usage. As word historians, we find it is easy to assume latency because we have the benefit of hindsight. But the semantic history of a word is possible to reconstruct precisely because semantic extension takes place only in a very limited number of ways — generalization, specialization, metaphor, and metonymy. The fact that we can tell a story in hindsight does not mean that the events were latent in the situation, in the manner that a chicken is latent in an egg, but merely that they were explicable and to a certain extent predictable, in the manner that a chess game in progress (to use Saussure's familiar yet vivid metaphor) is explicable and to a certain extent predictable, from its configuration of pieces and the rules of their movement.

The fact that OE *mōd* means not only 'mind' but also 'pride,' 'courage,' and 'anger' is of interest for reasons not anthropological but lexicological. That the semantic histories of *mōd, mos, hyge, animus, ingenium, temper,* and *self* are so similar reflects nothing more nor less than the pragmatically prolific but typologically limited nature of semantic extension. If these histories reflect anything about the nature of 'mind' at all, it is that conscious intelligent life is inherently wilful and capricious. The polysemousness of *mōd* does not enjoin us to believe, as some scholars insist, that the Anglo-Saxons differed from us because their word for the 'mind' could also mean 'pride,' 'courage,' and 'anger.' What it does have us believe is that, like all human beings everywhere and at every point of history, they were intermittently proud, brave, and *higly,* just like ourselves.

Part II — On Anglo-Latin and Old
English Prose

5

Desipere in loco: Style, Memory, and the Teachable Moment

CARIN RUFF

> Interiectio est pars orationis interiecta aliis partibus orationis ad exprimendos animi adfectus: aut metuentis, ut ei; aut optantis, ut o; aut dolentis, ut heu; aut laetantis, ut euax. (Donatus, *Ars maior*)[1]

> An interjection is a part of speech thrown between other parts of speech to express an emotional state: either of one who fears, as in 'yikes!'; or of one who hopes, as in 'oh!'; or of one who grieves, as in 'alas!'; or of one who is happy, as in 'yippee!'

> Franco: Interiectio quid est?
> Saxo: Heu! Quid interrogas de interiectione? (Alcuin, *De grammatica*)[2]

> Frank: What is an interjection?
> Saxon: Oh, no! Why are you asking about the interjection?

Let me propose a false taxonomy of grammarians. All grammarians may be classified into two types: those who possess a sense of humour, and those who do not. Donatus, if not the *fons et origo* of the humourless type, would certainly be the type's chief exemplar for the Middle Ages, as he characterizes the spare, technical style: categorize, list, define, exemplify, move on. Alcuin, as in the example above, has a strong claim to speak for the humorous group: while ordinarily sober of style and purpose, he recognizes the value of a well-placed joke. The exchange on the interjection quoted above is the final item in Alcuin's treatment in dialogue form of Donatus's parts-of-speech inventory. Employing the dialogue form is, already, a nod to the pedagogical occasion.

---

[1] Louis Holtz, ed., *Donat et la tradition de l'enseignement grammatical: Étude sur l'Ars Donati et sa diffusion (IVe - IXe siècle)* (Paris 1981), 2.17, 652.5-7.
[2] PL 101, 849-902, at 901B.

The student-student variation on the dialogue form of some ancient grammars, where *Magister* catechizes *Discipulus* on the subject at hand, enhances the material's accessibility for its proximate audience.' To allow the students to joke with one another adds a further element of literary realism to a form that must draw as much from real-life classroom practice as from the conventions of genre. Most importantly, the end-of-dialogue joke clarifies the meaning of *interiectio* at the same time that it summons the student-audience's attention, which may have been flagging by the time it reached the eighth part of speech.

Another early medieval grammarian who allows himself the literary licence to inject humour into the school dialogue form is Aldhelm. In his *De metris*, Aldhelm follows the form and content of Audax, his chief source, but embellishes the dialogue to the benefit of its dramatic situation, humour quotient, and explanatory value. Aldhelm's main innovation is to allow the student to question the master, an innovation that has several repercussions for the way the dialogue proceeds. The student is allowed to ask for clarification when the master is being more than usually opaque. More than that, the student, not confined to providing memorized answers as in a schoolroom drill, is allowed to display his smart-alecky personality. Consider this exchange, in which the master is trying to explain the possible combinations of feet in a hexameter line containing fourteen syllables.

> D[iscipulus]: Versus .XIV. sillabarum quot scemata habet?
> M[agister]: Certissima definitione .X. scematibus constat.
> D: Da per ordinem earundem specierum rationem!
> M: Aut enim primo et secundo loco dactilus ponitur aut primo et
>   tertio aut primo et quarto [etc.] ...
> D: Da exemplis horum probationem!

> D: How many schemata does the verse of fourteen syllables have?
> M: By the most specific description it consists of ten schemata.
> D: Give an account of these same types in order!
> M: A dactyl is put in the first and second position, or the first and
>   third, or the first and fourth [etc.] ...

D: Give proof of these with examples!
(The master gives six verses from Juvencus, Sedulius, Juvenal, and Lucan as examples of three of the schemata.)

D: Versibus istis, quos exempli gratia protulisse visus es, nequaquam omnes .X. scematum regulae liquido patuerunt, sed tantum tres formulae id est dactilus loco primo et quinto, item loco secundo et quinto, item loco tertio et quinto; residua vero .VII. scemata necdum prolata delitescunt. Quamobrem operae pretium reor, ut id, quod passiva definitionis generalitate non ad integrum promulgaveras, nunc per ordinem eorundem scematum recapitulando nequaquam semiplena specialitate examusim enucleare studeas. (ALDH. Metr. 10.85.24-30)[4]

D: In no way are all the rules of the ten schemata perfectly clear from these verses, which you seemed to have brought out for the sake of example, but only three formulae, that is a dactyl in first and fifth place, in second and fifth place and in third and fifth place; but the seven remaining schemata are hiding unexplained. For this reason I think it would be worthwhile for you to set out in detail what you had promulgated incompletely and with a passive generalizing definition, by reviewing these same schemata in order and not with a partial picking and choosing.

The dialogue gains in vividness and clarity by Aldhelm's invention, and the literary form becomes a frame for the stitching-together and authorial glossing that medieval grammarians invariably bring to bear on their sources. Moreover, the dialogue form allows Aldhelm to poke fun at his own manner, when he implicitly enters the dialogue as Magister. Treating a technical subject as the occasion for literary elaboration thus allows the grammarian to teach and to comment at once, to gloss his text in order both to explain it and (gently) deflate the seriousness of the discourse.

The same licence allows Aldhelm to deploy exuberantly figurative language in technical parts of the Letter to Heahfrith outside the dialogic parts of the De metris. There is, for example, the famous passage in the De

---

[4] R. Ehwald, ed., *Aldhelmi opera*, MGH AA 15 (Berlin 1919).

metris in which Aldhelm introduces the importance of syllabic quantity for a proper understanding of versification:

> Neque enim in tam densa totius latinitatis silva et nemorosis sillabarum saltibus, ubi de singulis verborum radicibus multiplices regularum ramusculos pululasse antiqua veterum traditio declarat, rudibus facile negotium deprehenditur et praesertim metricae artis disciplina carentibus et nescientibus, qualiter vel quo pacto longae et breves sillabae vel etiam communes utrubi competentes, quas Graeci dichronas dicunt, sagaciter discriminentur. (ALDH. Metr. 8.78.4-9)

> For, in so dense a wood of the whole of Latinity and amid bushy groves of syllables, where from each root of words the venerable tradition of the ancients declares that many branchlets of rules have sprouted, this matter is not easily grasped by the untrained and especially by those lacking the discipline of the metrical art who do not know how or by what method long and short syllables, or even neutral ones compatible in either way, which the Greeks call two-timers, are expertly to be distinguished.

If syllables here are a kind of shrubbery pullulating with scannable words, they soon become slippery footsteps:

> Quibus (sc. enigmatibus) indesinenter secundum poeticae traditionis disciplinam cola vel commata seu pentimemerin et eptimemerin annectere progressis binis aut ternis pedibus procuravi; alioquin dactylici exametri regulae legitima aequitatis lance carentes lubricis sillabarum gressibus vacillarent. (ALDH. Metr. 6.76.11-15)

> To these (that is, the riddles) according to the discipline of poetic tradition I have taken care to join consistently cola and commata or pentimemerical and heptimemerical caesurae with progressions of double and triple feet; otherwise, lacking the correct scale of balance, the rules of dactylic hexameter would have wobbled on slippery footsteps of syllables.

Walking and climbing, it soon develops, are among Aldhelm's favourite metaphors for describing versification and scansion. Metrical elision (a metaplasm in Aldhelm's system) becomes a potential stumbling block for the inexperienced reader walking or climbing (scanning or scaling) the verse. By the end of the section, the path through the verse has become a path the eye travels.

> Propterea namque has duas metaplasmorum species ... indagare et explanare nisus sum, quia ... nisi sagaci subtilitate praecognitae fuerint, diversa impedimentorum obstacula et errorum offendicula scandentibus velut iter carpentibus generare solent. Idcirco diversos versus metrorum ad sinaliphae metaplasmum congruentes catervatim congessimus, quatenus his perspectis nullum deinceps explosae collisionis chaos et latebrosum confractae sinaliphae baratrum lucem scandentis confundat aciemque legentis obtundat. (ALDH. Metr. 9.81.1-8)

> For these reasons I have striven to explain these two varieties of metaplasm, since ... unless they are recognized in advance with sagacious subtlety, they tend to generate various obstacles of impediments and small stumbling blocks of errors for those scanners (or 'climbers') as it were picking their way. Therefore we have gathered together in groups various verses of metres pertaining to the metaplasm of synaloepha, so that when these have been looked over, no confusion of ejected elision or hidden pit of irregular synaloepha might henceforth confound the eye of the scanner or blunt the gaze of the reader.

Both the metaphor of walking through the verse and the conversion of walking to a figurative travelling of the eye are revealing as to the Anglo-Saxon perception of what it means to process quantitative verse in a foreign language. The movement is linear or sequential, but the experience — even, strikingly, the experience of a figure of sound like elision — is visual.

I suggested at the outset that a taxonomy of grammarians (+/- funny bone) was untenable. Perhaps I should rather say unprovable, for I doubt my ability reliably to diagnose the presence or absence of intentional humour in an Anglo-Saxon author. What is funny, after all, about the 'densa silva latinitatis' is not just the mismatch between syllables and shrubbery, but the dissonance (to modern taste) between the whole apparatus of the hermeneutic style — the long sentences, the crowds of adverbs, the supererogatory diminutives, the alliteration — and the extreme dryness of the subject matter. Vivien Law addressed this same modern discomfort with medieval notions of the appropriate stylistic vehicles for technical subjects in her 1998 O'Donnell Lecture, 'Why Write A Verse Grammar?'[5] Acknowledging the ludicrousness to modern readers of using verse to convey technical information clearly and succinctly, she demonstrates that, for medieval audiences, verse carried precisely those expectations of clarity and succinctness that we associate with technical prose.

While we seem to have the same disjunction between modern and medieval expectations concerning the appropriate uses of verse and of the more elaborate prose styles, the analogy is not complete. There is little evidence to suggest that anybody thought the hermeneutic style was valuable for its clarity. Indeed, there is some evidence that even Aldhelm's countrymen and contemporaries were uncomfortable with the application of highly wrought prose styles to technical subjects. After all, it was not Aldhelm but Bede, with his humane technical style (and complete absence of jokes) who became the master of Latin metrics to the next millennium. Even more tellingly, Boniface, one of Aldhelm's most accomplished imitators, backs off from applying the full-blown hermeneutic style to technical description in his grammar. Boniface borrows Aldhelm's 'densa silua' in his Letter to Sigibert that prefaces his grammar but he reserves the image to the more conventional trope of the compiler gathering cuttings from the auctores for his own use. He acknowledges the mandate from Sigibert:

> ... ut antiquam perplexae siluam densitatis grammaticorum ingrederer ad colligendum tibi diuersorum optima quaeque genera pomorum et uariorum odoramenta florum diffusa, quae passim dispersa per saltum grammaticorum inueniuntur ....[6]

---

[5] Printed in *The Journal of Medieval Latin* 9 (1999): 46-76.
[6] Boniface, *Ars grammatica*, ed. G.J. Gebauer and B. Löfstedt, CCSL 133B (Turnhout 1980), 9, ll. 16-20.

... that I should go into the ancient wood of the baffling density of the grammarians to collect for you each of the best kinds of diverse fruits and the diffuse aromatics of various flowers which are found scattered around the grove of the grammarians ...

While Anglo-Saxon notions of stylistic decorum in Latin remain an unresolved question, we can perhaps propose an alternative taxonomy of grammarians. Writers on grammar (and other technical subjects) could be arrayed on a continuum according to the extent to which they admit figurative language into technical description or analysis. When we admit the presence or absence of figurative language as a criterion of style, it becomes apparent that even the strictest technical prose is not without ornament. Consider the definition of the interjection that I quoted from the *Ars maior* at the beginning of this essay: 'Interiectio est pars orationis interiecta aliis partibus orationis.' Even Donatus admits an etymology in the very scarce real estate of his definitional paradigm: and interjection is something interjected. It is not especially funny, it is not especially clever, but it is explanatory. Isidore notes the explanatory function of etymology:

Nam dum uideris unde ortum est nomen, citius uim eius intellegis. Omnis enim rei inspectio etymologia cognita planior est. (ISID. Etym. 1.29.2)[7]

For when you see where a name has come from, you understand its force more quickly. For the inspection of every thing is clearer when the etymology is known.

Not only does etymology have an explanatory function, it also provides a mnemonic hook for the student faced with learning yet another technical term and the functions of the thing it signifies. The etymological 'tag' provided in the definition makes the unfamiliar term rational, so that it can be incorporated into the world of knowledge the reader already possesses. The etymology also suggests an image — of the interjection being 'tossed in' among other words, as the first translation I gave suggested — that makes the very abstract relatively concrete. This kind of mnemonic function of

---

[7] Isidore of Seville, *Etymologiae sive origines*, ed. W.M. Lindsay (Oxford 1911).

etymology and etymological paronomasia has been explored at length by Mary Carruthers as part of her ongoing work on medieval memory systems.[8] Etymological punning, she suggests, is a way of modelling the creation of mnemonic chains that learners will be able to invent anew as they ingest and ruminate on new terms and texts. In this model, any etymology given by a grammarian would not necessarily be definitive but would be suggestive, would be a site for rumination and further invention. Punning, the close cousin of etymology, would likewise be a way of 'playing around with' technical terms until they became comprehensible, useable, and memorable.[9]

Carruthers's argument that we should think of etymologies and puns as contributing to memory work suggests new ways of looking at some of the more eccentric texts in the Anglo-Saxon canon of technical treatises. Alcuin's innovation in his *Dialogue of a Frank and a Saxon*, quoted above, of expanding the dialogue form to admit jokes, uses a kind of realized paronomasia: the Saxon 'puns' on what he and the Frank both know to be the definition of 'interjection' (because they have both memorized Donatus), letting us know that he is fed up with the game but also reminding us that he knows Donatus's list of examples and how to use them. Alcuin's pun is to make 'interjection' both the subject and the method of the dialogue — both its content and its style.

Far more eccentric and mnemonically complex is Byrhtferth's *Enchiridion*. Byrhtferth is certainly a technical writer — what could be more technical than a manual of computus? — but he touches on grammar only in passing. The way he makes that pass, however, is revealing. Byrhtferth is prompted to extended grammatical free association by a coincidence of terminology between computus and Latin metrics. He has been discussing the *saltus lunae*, the day omitted in the 'leap month' in the nineteen-year cycle used in computus to correlate the lunar and solar calendars. The *saltus lunae*, 'moon's leap,' reminds him that Bede had described metrical elision, synaloepha, as a kind of *saltus*:

---

[8] Mary Carruthers, 'Inventional Mnemonics and the Ornaments of Style: The Case of Etymology,' *Connotations: A Journal for Critical Debate* 2, no. 2 (1992): 103-14.
[9] See also Roberta Frank, 'Some Uses of Paronomasia in Old English Scriptural Verse,' *Speculum* 47 (1972): 207-26, and particularly her example of the story of Pope Gregory and the slave boys as an 'event made memorable through puns' (207). In grammatical paronomasia, we have metalanguage made memorable through puns.

We cwædon herbufan hwanon se bissextus cymð, and manega þing we cyddon ymbe his fare, and þæræfter we geswutelodon ymbe þæs saltus hlyp, and hwanon he cymð and hu he byð and to hwan he gewyrð binnan nigontyne wintrum we amearkodon. We wæron atende grimlice swyðe ær we mihton þas gerena aspyrian, ac us com hrædlice fultum, we gelyfað of heofenum, swa hyt ræd ys þæt ælc æðele gife nyðerastihð fram þam fæder ealra leohta. Eac me com stiðlice to mode hu þa getyddusta boceras gewyrceað sinelimpha on heora uersum. Hwæt, hig ærest apinsiað wærlicum mode þa naman and þa binaman and heora declinunga and gymað hwylce naman geendiað on .a. oððe on .e. and eac hwylce on .i. oððe on .o. oððe on .u. ... Syððan hig þa word aginnað to aweganne mid þam biwordum, swylce ic þus cweðe:

nomen	pronomen	uerbum	aduerbium	iterum	uerbum	pronomen	iterum	nomen
Byrhtferthus ipse		scripsit	bene,	beneque	docet	ille	suis	discipulis.

Ðærto hig gewriðað þæne nymendan dæl and gesamniað oððe geendebyrdiað þa gefegnyssa and forsettað þæne dæl þære spræce þærtoeacan ... Hig eac deoplice þa stefna þæs lyftes swege gesleað and mid þære tungan clypole þæne sweg gewynsumiað and on feower wisan todælað, þæt he beo cuð þam þe hig gehyrað. Hig eac tosceadað þæt stæfgefeg on þrym wisan geaplice swyðe. (ByrM 1 2.1.425-8)[10]

We said above where the leap year comes from, and we made known many things about its course, and after that we explained about the leap of the *saltus*, and where it comes from and how it is, and we wrote down what it comes to over nineteen years. We were inflamed most painfully before we could investigate these mysteries, but aid soon came to us — we believe from heaven — as we read that every noble gift descends from the Father of all light. It also came forcibly to my mind how the most learned scholars produce synaloepha in their verses. Lo, they first examine with careful mind the nouns, the pronouns and their declensions, and they note which nouns end with *a*, with *e*, with *i*, with *o*, or with *u* ... Then they proceed to consider the verbs with the adverbs, as if I were to speak thus:

---

[10] *Byrhtferth's Enchiridion*, ed. Peter S. Baker and Michael Lapidge, EETS, ss 15 (Oxford 1995). Translations are the editors' except as noted.

noun	pronoun	verb	adverb	ditto	verb	pronoun	ditto	noun
Byrhtferth	himself	wrote	well, and well		teaches	he	his	students.[11]

To that they add the participle and they gather or order the conjunctions and they also set the part of speech [the preposition] in front ... They also strike deeply with noise the voices of the air, and with the tongue's voice they make the sound pleasing, and they divide the voice in four ways, so that it will be known to those who hear it. They also very cleverly classify the syllable in three ways.

This piece of text has struck readers — myself included — as at best disorganized and at worst bizarre, an intrusion into or a digression from the matter at hand. But if we see it as a teacher modelling the construction of a mnemonic chain for his students, it acquires a degree of shape and purpose. Byrhtferth's free association is useful as well: it exemplifies a way of integrating one set of recondite technical terms (those of metre and grammar) with another (those of computus). For the teacher, who is already in control of both vocabularies, the association comes 'stiðlice to mode': the coincidence of computistical leap and metrical leap launches as if inevitably a chain that runs from elision to nouns that end in vowels (and are thus susceptible to elision), to other parts of speech and their ordering, to a paraphrase of the opening sentence of Priscian's *Institutiones grammaticae*, and back to the classification of the syllable, which is of immediate relevance to elision. The fact that he crafts the chain in Old English for his students, while presumably making associations in Latin on the basis of a less familiar Greek term (*synaloepha*), makes the whole exercise even more impressive. Byrhtferth shows in several places in the *Enchiridion* that he is capable of free-associating, punning and etymologizing in three languages at once.

Byrhtferth's mnemonic riff (Carruthers's term) was prompted by a comparison by Bede of synaloepha — elision — to a leap. Bede says:

> Synalipharum quoque commemoranda ratio est, quia nonnumquam ultima uerbi syllaba uel particula syllabae uidetur absumi. Vnde

---

synalipha Graece dicitur quasi quodam saltu transmittens. (BEDA. Art.metr. 13.2-5)[12]

One must also remember the ratio of the elisions, because sometimes the final syllable or part of the final syllable of the word appears to be reduced. Whence it is called synaloepha in Greek, as if passing over in a kind of leap.

The 'quasi' marks the second sentence as an etymology (although not an accurate one, since *synaloepha* means 'smearing together'). I wonder whether Bede was influenced by the homophonic association of *-lipha* with *hlȳp*. If so — and Byrhtferth's rendering of *saltus* as *hlȳp* suggests the association was possible — Bede's etymology functions particularly well for speakers of Old English as a mnemonic explanation of the unfamiliar Greek term. But it also functions as a simile: the scanner, who would presumably wish to avoid being tripped up as in Aldhelm's cautionary tale, would do well to take a 'leap' over the elided syllable. The line that divides simile from etymology is not so fine as the one that divides etymology from paronomasia but the effect may be similar. An etymology or a pun or a simile vivid enough to create in the reader's mind a real-life image to associate with a new term or concept has both explanatory and mnemonic force.

The early medieval definition of simile emphasizes its explanatory utility as much as its ornamental value. Bede, following Donatus, defines simile — *homoeosis* — in his *De schematibus et tropis* as follows:

Homoeosis est minus notae rei per similitudinem eius quae magis nota est demonstratio. (BEDA.Schem.trop. 2.284-5)[13]

Homoeosis is the explanation of something less known by comparison to something more familiar.

This is a sound basis for understanding the mechanism of simile in scripture or literature, but it also suggests a locus of invention for the didactic writer. Simile works as a mechanism for introducing and clarifying unfamiliar terms

---

[12] Bede, *De arte metrica*, ed. C.B. Kendall, CCSL 123A (Turnhout 1975), 81-141.
[13] Bede, *De schematibus et tropis*, ed. C.B. Kendall, CCSL 123A (Turnhout 1975), 142-71, at 169.

with reference to familiar objects and experiences. The appeal of simile as a strategy is apparent in perhaps the most popular grammatical simile of the early medieval grammar.[14] Isidore, in surveying the parts of speech in Book 1 of the *Etymologiae*, compared the conjunction to 'a kind of glue':

> Coniunctio dicta quod sensus sententiasque coniungat. Haec enim per se nihil valet, sed in copulatione sermonum quasi quoddam exhibet glutinum. Aut enim nomina sociat, ut 'Augustinus et Hieronymus'; aut verba, ut 'scribit et legit.' (ISID.Etym. 1.12.1)

> The conjunction is so called because it joins senses and sentences. For it has no power in itself, but in joining discourse it acts like a kind of glue. For it either joins nouns, as in 'Augustine and Jerome,' or verbs, as in 'he writes and reads.'

The figurative intervention is timely, since the conjunction is notoriously difficult to account for adequately within the descriptive parameters of ancient grammar.[15] Isidore takes the simile no further, and is quoted verbatim by many later grammarians. But the comparison captured Ælfric's imagination and he turns it into an extended comparison to bookbinding:

> Coniunctio est pars orationis indeclinabilis adnectens ordinansque sententiam. Coniunctio mæg beon gecweden geþeodnys. Se is an dæl ledenspræce undeclinigendlic gefæstniende and endebyrdigende ælcne cwyde. Swaswa lim gefæstnað fel to sumum brede, swa getigð seo coniunctio þa word togædere. Þæs dæl gefæstnað and gefrætwað ledenspræce and hwilon tosceat and hwilon geendebyrt ... Næfð þes dæl nane mihte ne nan andgit, gif he ana stent, ac on endebyrdnysse ledenspræce he gelimað þa word, ne he bið naht on englisc awend butan oðrum wordum. (ÆGram 257.16-258.13)[16]

---

[14] Admittedly, there is not much competition for the distinction.

[15] On the problem of the description of the conjunction in the Roman tradition, see Marc Baratin, *La naissance de la syntaxe à Rome* (Paris 1989).

[16] *Ælfrics Grammatik und Glossar*, ed. Julius Zupitza (Berlin 1880), 257-8.

A conjunction is an indeclinable part of speech joining and ordering a statement. 'Conjunction' may be called 'geþeodnys,' 'joining.' It is an indeclinable part of Latin speech joining and ordering each statement. Just as glue fastens leather to a board, so the conjunction ties words together. This part fastens and adorns Latin speech and at times distinguishes, at times places in sequence ... It has no force or meaning if it stands alone, but in the sequence of Latin speech it glues the words, nor can it be translated into English without other words.

Ælfric's expansion of the simile goes beyond the two-term comparison to create an image of a concrete (and complex) familiar object. One can picture Ælfric in the classroom, holding up a book (a copy of the *Excerptiones de Prisciano*?) and showing how the glue works, how it both binds and articulates the whole. His students and his readers might be prompted to think of Ælfric's explanation (and Priscian's) of how words and *cwydas* — *sententiae* — are related to whole books.[17] Every time they pick up a book, they will be reminded of the uses of the conjunction, just as Alcuin's students will chuckle to themselves and congratulate themselves on their grammatical acumen every time they utter an interjection.

Isidore, Aldhelm, Bede, Alcuin, Ælfric, and Byrhtferth share a role as interpreters to new audiences of a tradition whose orthodox texts left little room for explanation, much less jokes.[18] All of them, to greater or lesser degrees, play with the explanatory, imaginative, mnemonic, and dramatic possibilities of figurative language. Their experimental attitude towards stylistic decorum is as much a part of the postclassical project of expounding the authoritative grammarians as are the supplements and commentaries offered by the new Insular grammatical genres. These early medieval adventures in technical writing are varied and original, often inspired responses to their rhetorical situations. They deserve to have their modes of expression taken seriously. But not too seriously.

---

[17] 'We todælað þa boc to cwydum and syððan ða cwydas to dælum, eft ða dælas to stæfgefegum and syððan þa stæfgefegu to stafum: þonne beoð ða stafas untodæledlice, forðan ðe nan stæf ne byð naht, gif he gæð on twa' (ÆlGram 4.19-5.4) (We divide books into statements and statements into parts of speech, and then parts of speech into syllables and syllables into letters: then letters are indivisible, since no letter is anything if it splits in two).

[18] I cannot recall seeing a single joke in 974 pages of Priscian, but I would be happy to be corrected.

6

Courtroom Drama and the Homiletic Monologues of *The Vercelli Book*

DOROTHY HAINES

In her essay 'Poetic Words in Late Old English Prose,' Roberta Frank examines the occasional use in prose of words otherwise found only in poetry. A majority of these occur in the homiletic literature, and in discussing the most common contexts for this heightened use of language, she notes that 'poetic words apparently prefer direct or reported speech to straight narrative' and that 'homilists in oral performance may have found it easier to put poetic words in the mouths of others.'[1] We already knew that certain homilists were given to rhetorical embellishment according to their abilities and inclination; the named authors Ælfric and Wulfstan are known for employing rhythmical prose and drawing upon oral rhetorical traditions, respectively.[2] The homilies of unknown authorship are not so easily examined from a stylistic point of view since they were composed by many individuals, possibly representing widely differing origins in place and time. Nonetheless, they too had the same aim of presenting their didactic material as attractively as possible, and a well-crafted speech spoken by an authoritative persona would suit such an aim well.

Old English verse shows that Anglo-Saxons found such speeches appealing. There we often find characters holding forth at length as they expound on their own experiences and knowledge, while the audience patiently listens. The voices of the Wanderer and the Seafarer and the speakers in *The Wife's Lament* and *The Husband's Message* all speak of inner turmoil

---

[1] Roberta Frank, 'Poetic Words in Late Old English Prose,' in Malcolm Godden et al., eds, *From Anglo-Saxon to Early Middle English: Studies Presented to E.G. Stanley* (Oxford 1994), 87-107, at 91.
[2] Ælfric's rhythmical prose is discussed in the introduction of John Pope, ed., *Homilies of Ælfric: A Supplementary Collection*, vol. 1, EETS, os 259 (Oxford 1967), 105-36. Andy Orchard lists compounding, doublets featuring rhyme and alliteration, and the repetition of formulas and structures as features of Wulfstan's oral style ('Crying Wolf: Oral Style and the *Sermones Lupi*,' *ASE* 21 [1992]: 239-64).

and a struggle with the hand that fate has dealt them. Apparently audiences could be counted on to creatively imagine the personas which were being conjured up by the poet-performer. Likewise, among *The Vercelli Book*'s poetic pieces, we find the speech of the Rood, narrating the tale of its part in the Passion, and the speech of the Soul to the Body.

We should not be surprised, therefore, to find that the sermon literature which the *Vercelli Book* compiler selected also makes effective use of the longer speech. When particular care has been taken to create a setting for these speeches, and some effort at character development has been made, I like to see these as early forms of the dramatic monologue. Nevertheless, though it is not so difficult to imagine a poet-performer assuming the varied personas of his creations as he declaims his poems, to suggest that the preacher-performer did the same gives us pause and perhaps even strikes us as unseemly.[3] Drama in the pulpit? Is it possible that the staid Anglo-Saxons engaged in such artifice?

To judge by *The Vercelli Book*, it at least seems possible that they did, though we will never know with what abandon they took up their role as performing artists nor how their acting skills affected the reception of the speech by their audiences. What can be shown is that they deliberately selected dramatic speeches from Latin sources, then prepared the audience with all the elements of setting that would be needed to fully imagine the dramatic moment, and finally often reworked their sources to heighten the rhetoric, at times by elevating the language through the use of rhetorical patterning, or by taking full advantage of the emotional effect of the persona's position.

Before I examine three of these monologues in *The Vercelli Book* (in homilies IV, VIII, and X), however, I would like to suggest a further reason why, especially for the sermon, the monologue was attractive. The purpose of much of the homiletic material of this period — particularly that coming from sources other than Ælfric — was to urge amendment of life in order that the listener might be prepared for the day of judgment. There are, of course, a

---

[3] For the most part, the performance aspects of the sermon literature have received little attention, and scholars are understandably reticent to speculate on the possibilities of oral delivery. Those most familiar with the literature, however, have often remarked on what may have been quite effective productions, 'especially if heard with appropriate declamation,' as, for example, J.E. Cross suggests ('Vernacular Sermons in Old English,' in Beverly Mayne Kienzle, ed., *The Sermon*, Typologie des sources du moyen âge occidental, fasc. 81-3 [Turnhout 2000], 561-96, at 576). For the later medieval period, cf. G.R. Owst, *Literature and Pulpit in Medieval England*, 2nd edn (Oxford, 1961), esp. 471-547.

variety of expressions of this theme, some focusing on the sins to be avoided or to be confessed once committed, but an extraordinary amount of the literature focuses on the Last Day itself. To the Anglo-Saxon, Judgment Day was certainly all-important in the sense that it is the day on which all prior activity will be assessed and either rewarded or punished. Since it lies in the future, the goal was to make its events seem familiar and palpably real; the picture had to be painted as vividly and colourfully as possible. The monologues I am about to discuss are all part of the imaginative creation of that future day. As will be seen, they not only serve to portray Judgment Day as a coming reality but are particularly effective in drawing forth the emotional responses likely to be felt by the participants. They invite members of the audience to be moved by the speakers, whether it is to identify with them or to imagine how it would feel should a particular speech be directed at them.

The three monologues I have chosen represent three players in that great final drama. We already know who will be in attendance: certainly all humankind will be there, good and evil; Christ the Judge will preside and both the heavenly and hellish hosts will be there to observe the proceedings, the latter led by Satan himself. The roles of these participants are also well-known: human beings will be the defendants, called to give an account of their earthly behaviour; Christ, the Judge, will divide good from evil; while Satan, the accuser, will claim the latter as his own. It is, of course, a trial, in fact the culmination of all trials, and the language and themes used to recreate the event make good use of legal imagery and rhetoric, along with the spectacles of fear and suspense attending any good drama of the type.[4] Grandstanding, outrage and accusation, emotional expressions of relief or despair — even the Anglo-Saxons were not immune to the allure of courtroom drama.[5]

---

[4] The use of legal rhetoric and drama in the literature of the later Middle Ages has been more thoroughly explored than for that of the Anglo-Saxons; see John Alford, 'Literature and Law in Medieval England,' *PMLA* 92 (1977): 941-51, and Jody Enders, *Rhetoric and the Origins of Medieval Drama* (Ithaca 1992).

[5] How much these representations parallel Anglo-Saxon legal proceedings remains an open question and is perhaps immaterial, given the otherworldly context of the following examples. Patrick Wormald maintains that '[t]here is no such thing as a typical Anglo-Saxon lawsuit' (145), though some idea of the procedure may be obtained through records found in charters, *notitiae*, Domesday Book, cartulary-Chronicles, and other sources (*The Making of English Law: King Alfred to the Twelfth Century*, vol. 1. Legislation and Its Limits [Oxford 1999], 143-61, 507-10). Cf. Wormald, 'A Handlist of Anglo-Saxon Lawsuits,' *ASE* 17 (1986): 247-81.

Let us begin with the defendant. In medieval theology Judgment Day is also the day when those long dead will be reunited with their bodies in order to face judgment together. In the introduction to *Vercelli IV*, long antithetical lists are used to contrast the short suffering of living rightly in this world with the enduring pain otherwise experienced in the next. This prepares the audience for the upcoming speeches of the good and evil souls to their bodies. The homilist underscores feelings of fear and complete isolation:

> & mid ure sawle anre we sculon riht agyldan on þam myclan dome. Wa is hyre þonne earmre, gif hio ana stent, ealra godra dæda wana, on domes dæge beforan Gode. Þær þonne ne mæg se fæder helpan þam suna, ne [se] sunu þam fæder, ne nan mæg oðrum. (HomU 9 [Verc 4] 66-70)

> And with our soul alone we must pay what is due at that great judgment. Woe to it then, the wretched [soul], if it stands alone, lacking in all good deeds, on Doomsday before God. There the father may not help the son, nor the son the father, nor anyone another.

What follows is a scene of a grand assembly that describes each person standing before all mankind, the hosts of hell, the angels and archangels, and, of course, God.[6] All of these have speaking parts, though the souls will take centre-stage in this production. The setting is developed with some care by the homilist, using visual cues and what might be seen as 'stage directions' that indicate tone of voice. God praises the good soul and the angels turn to it and say that they have sighted its body ('hus'). From the outset, the demeanour and emotions of the good soul are indicated in tone of voice ('bliðheortre stefne,' 'joyful-hearted voice'), and in the loving looks she throws in the direction of her body: 'Besyhð þonne sio sawl swiðe bliðum eagum to hire lichoman' (133) (Then the soul looks at its body with very joyful eyes). Direct speech is carefully separated from the narrative with introductory phrases and the

---

[6] HomU 9 (Verc 4) 96-102.

unmistakable return to the preacher persona with the appellation 'Men þa leofestan' in line 153.[7]

A contrasting scene confronts the listener in the prelude to the speech of the evil soul. Visual cues help one move from the blissful reunion to an atmosphere of fear and repulsion. Later we catch sight of the crowd of evildoers:

> And þonne standað forhte & afærede þa þe ær wirigdon & unriht worhton, & swið[e] betwyh him heofað & wepað, hwylcne dom him dryhten deman wille be ðam dome þe he ðam halgum demed hæfð, & cwacigende on anbide standað, hwanne ær hie þæs reðan cyninges word gehyren. (HomU 9 [Verc 4] 194-8)

> And then they will stand afraid and frightened, those who before committed evil and worked wickedness, and among themselves they will greatly lament and bewail whichever sentence the Lord Judge may decree for them according to the judgment with which he has judged the saints. And quaking they will stand in anticipation of [the time] when they will at last hear the words of the fierce king.

The Judge is now a 'fierce king,' 'terrible in appearance' (on swiðe ongryslicum hiwe) and his tone is indicated by the 'very terrible voice' (swiðe egeslicre stefne) as he calls these souls to account.[8] The evil soul's mental anguish is known from its voice, too; it speaks with 'swiðe unrotre stefne & unbealdre & heofendre' (203) (with a very unhappy and fearful and lamenting voice), and in line 221 again with 'swiðe geomre stefne' (with a very troubled voice). After its diatribe, the preacher-performer again breaks character with a 'Men þa leofestan' (288). He therefore not only acts out the emotions of the various personas but also reinforces these feelings in his narrative transitions.

---

[7] HomU 9 (Verc 4): 'Þonne cwyð dryhten be þisse sawle to his englum' (117-18) (Then the lord said to his angels concerning this soul); 'þyssum wor[d]um þonne onfoð þa englas þære sawle 7 hire to cweðað' (120-1) (then the angels received the soul and spoke to it in these words); 'Cwið þonne sio sawl to þam englum' (124) (the soul said to the angels); and 'sio sawl ... cwyð to him' (133-4) (the soul ... said to him).

[8] HomU 9 (Verc 4) 198-200.

These emotions could not be developed as effectively were it not for another aspect of these speeches: that of an intimate relationship.[9] Thus, as the good soul expresses its extreme pleasure at being reunited with the body, the homilist has it praise its body in a personal tone that suggests a love relationship and plays with the grammatical gender of soul and body in Old English. For instance, the angels lead the soul 'to ðam þe ðu ær lufodest' (123) (the one you before loved); as soon as she sees her body, she cries out, 'Ic gesio hwær min lichama stent on midre þisse menigo. Lætaþ hine to me' (124-5) (I see where my body stands in the middle of this crowd! Allow him to come to me). She asks God not to keep them apart, and especially to preserve her body from the horror of decay: 'Ne sie he næfre wyrma mete, ne to grimmum geolstre mote wyrðan' (126) (May he never be food for worms, nor may he become horribly decayed). The soul includes herself as being responsible for any sin when she says: 'Uncra synna he sworette & uncra scylda' (131-2) (He bemoaned our sins and our errors). The wicked soul, on the other hand, dissociates itself from its body and its corruption. Instead of the good soul's delight in its body, we have here the sense of a relationship that was never destined to be harmonious, especially made clear in the following complaints:

Wa me þæt ic þin æfre owiht cuðe, swa unsofte swa ic on þe eardude! (206-7)

Woe to me, that I ever knew you at all, as uncomfortably as I dwelled in you!

Næs ic næfre in þe aret, ac a me þuhte þæt wyt wæron to lange ætgædere. (214-15)

I was never made happy in you, but always it seemed to me that the two of us were together too long.

Æghwæt þæs ðæs ðu [hyðgodest] mid þinum flæsce, æghwæt me wæs þæs earfoðlices. Eall þæt þu lufodest, eall þæt ic feode. Næron wyt

---

[9] Cf. the use of the word *sinhiwan* 'married couple' to describe body and soul in Guth 968b and Jul 698b. C.L. Smetana first noticed this aspect of the Soul's Address in the poetic version in his 'Second Thoughts on "Soul and Body I,"' *Mediaeval Studies* 29 (1967): 193-205, at 199.

næfre ane tid on anum willan, for þan þu hyrwdest Godes beboda & his haligra lare. (284-7)

Each thing with which you [comforted] your flesh, each was full of hardship to me. All that you loved, all that I hated. We were never at any time of one mind, because you despised God's commandments and his holy doctrine.

From a didactic point of view it is clear that the good soul is meant to represent — in a highly personal and moving way — the eventual bliss obtained through a life lived in conformity with Christian belief, and the evil soul the disastrous consequences of the opposite choice.

Verbal ornamentation and visually emblematic transformations underscore this theme. The homilist uses embellishments such as *blīðheort* 'happy of heart, glad-spirited' for the good soul's voice, a compound which occurs only in this homily and another four times in poetry.[10] The address itself, short as it is, contains uncommon compounds such as *ēaðbilge* (139) and *līðwyrde* (151); rhyming doublets, such as 'geomrode & sorgode' (129) and 'gytsere ne strudere' (140); and alliteration, such as 'grimmum geolstre' (126) and 'strang & staðolfæst' (137). It seems that sound and rhythm are designed to parallel the attractiveness of the soul's piety as well as to fix the address in the memory of each listener. The preacher-performer himself interjects his own opinion that the good soul spoke 'glædlice ... wynsumlice ... fægre & ... mildlice' (153-4) (gladly ... joyfully ... beautifully and ... kindly).

The same, of course, cannot be said of the evil soul, whose speech is clearly meant to repel the listener. It distances itself from its evil-doing body, drawing attention to what distinguishes the flesh from itself, namely the process of putrefaction that it, the soul, does not participate in and can therefore point out with repulsion and loathing. This is not to say that the wicked soul does not have its own memorable eloquence. Choice words, though hardly pleasing, are to be found here, too: 'La, ðu eorðan lamb & dust & wyrma gifel, & þu wambscyldiga fætels & gealstor & fulnes & hræw, hwig forgeate ðu me & þa toweardan tide?' (207-9) (Lo, you clay and dust of the earth and food of worms, and you sinful sack and decay and foulness and

[10] *DOE* s. *blīþheort* lists Beo 1802, And 660, 1262, and GenA 192; another instance in HomU 9 (Verc 4) occurs in line 239.

carrion, why did you forget me and the future time?). And, to a lesser extent — given that its speech is twice as long as that of its counterpart — the evil soul also uses language that seems heightened: a rhyming doublet in 'swenctest ... wlenctest' (205); alliteration in 'arfæst ... elþeodigum' (239-40), 'glædmod ... Gode' (240), and 'rihtwis ... rummod ... rihtra' (241); unique or poetic compounds in *tesoword* (261) and *gramhīdig* (274); and even an otherwise exclusively poetic word, *andsaca* (267).[11] A centrally placed apostrophe provides the opportunity to broaden the direction of the discourse, now directing a complaint about the body to a third party, Death, which is accused of not freeing the soul from its body soon enough (221-87).

As noted, both the good and evil souls frame their complaint in antithetical lists which, though they at times may seem mind-numbingly redundant to the modern reader, effectively drive home the message of opposing choices.[12] The good soul uses such lists to draw attention to its body's accomplishments, following the rhetorical pattern 'he did this in order that I may do that.' An instance is: 'He sealde þam geswenctum mannum reste & are, þæt he wolde þæt ic ne swunce on þysse langan worulde' (149-51) (He gave rest and comfort to those weighed down by toil, because he wished that I might not toil in this long-lasting world). Such result clauses make each good deed of the body seem a kindness done on behalf of its mate, the soul, and personalize the enumeration of desirable Christian acts. The damned soul simply presents a mirror image of these with its own antithetical statements throughout the speech. Again, earthly pleasure is shown to result in eternal suffering and earthly restraint in eternal bliss, epitomized in the metaphor: 'Nolde he mid þam lænan drynce gebycgan þone þæs ecan wines' (226-7) (He did not wish to buy with that transitory drink that of eternal wine). Here, using the comparison of the alleged deeds of the two bodies, the homilist develops the metaphor of a careful tending to the needs of the soul, so

---

[11] Cf. *DOE*, s. *and-saca*: '19 occ. (all but IX in poetry).'
[12] Lists of antithetical clauses serve the twofold purpose of rhetorical ornament and mnemonic device, which explains their frequent use in OE sermons. A third function has been noted by Eugene Green (in a discussion of Wulfstan's sermon output) — that of encouraging listeners to focus on the moral choice before them ('On Syntactic and Pragmatic Features of Speech Acts in Wulfstan's Homilies,' in Irmengard Rauch and Gerald F. Carr, eds, *Insights in Germanic Linguistics I. Methodology in Transition*, Trends in Linguistics, Studies and Monographs 83 [Berlin and New York 1995], 109-25, at 123-5).

representing a focus on one's eternal destiny, and its opposite, a preoccupation with the needs of the body, the transitory life of this world.

If tone, language, and rhetorical patterning all work together to underscore this opposition, the narrative interludes, which show in a visually stimulating way the destinies of our two speakers, contribute a further theatrical element to the drama. Following its speech, the homilist presents the spectacular transformation of the good soul's body, which involves mutations from bursts of colour in the shape of a lovely human being to something more like a beautiful flower, then gold or precious stones, and finally the moon and the sun (155-61). The audience is meant to long for such a reward for itself. In contrast, the evil soul's body 'swæt swiðe laðlicum swate, & him feallað of unfægere dropan, & bryt on manig hiw' (289-92) (sweats a loathsome sweat, and ugly drops fall from it and it changes into many colours), darkening until it is 'collsweart' (coal-black).

It is surely conceivable that a skilled preacher, following these clues provided in the text, might well have been able to take each part in turn and thereby create a minidrama. The advantage of choosing lengthy first-person monologues instead of simple narrative or reported speech is the audience's participation in the varying emotions of the speakers. Though both the good and evil souls have come to this trial to be judged by God, they are, in effect, already self-judged. So also the audience must judge itself in preparation for the great day of doom, and the Soul's Address to the Body provides the listener with both specific content and emotional impetus to do so. The contrast of joy and relief versus repulsion and shame, if capably acted out by the preacher-performer, can be vicariously experienced as in any dramatic production, providing not just a glimpse into the events of the Last Day but also the emotional experience of some of its participants.

The same is true for *Vercelli VIII*, where an address by Christ to a condemned man is the focus of the Judgment Day scene. The setting is elaborately prepared with the author introducing the Doomsday themes early in the sermon, including the topos that it is better to confess now before one person than on Judgment Day before the angels and all the inhabitants of heaven, when Christ comes in the clouds and nothing will be concealed."¹³ A translation of Matt. 16:27 provides elements of the setting here:

> Mannes sunu cymeð in heannysse wolcnum & in his wlite wundorlice & in his þrymme to [us mid] englum & mid heahenglum & mid ealle þy heofoncundan mægene. (HomS 3 [Verc 8] 21-3)

> The son of man will come in clouds of majesty and wonderfully in his beauty and in his glory to [us with] angels and with archangels and with all the heavenly host.

Further details that paint the scene follow: 'Þonne arisað ealle þa þe fram frymþe middangeardes hira eagan in deað betyndon & rihtum ge[leafan] onfengon; þa bioð to þam dome gelaðode' (37-9) (Then all will arise, all those who from the beginning of the world closed their eyes in death and received the right belief; those will be led to that judgment). The audience is invited to experience the fear and dread when 'we hyne mid his mægenþrymme cumendne gesioð, in ðam dome mid his englum' (33) (we see him coming with his retinue, [coming] to the Judgment with his angels); angels blow their trumpets from the four corners of the earth and all human beings who ever lived arise to face their doom.'¹⁴ The earth is stirred with fire, and 'þa scyldegan him hearde ondrædað' (44) (the guilty will greatly fear him), when in a harsh voice (mid his heardlican stemne [45]), Christ begins to speak and the individual listener is directed to the personal application of the address with the reminder that it will feel 'gelicost þe he to anum men sprece' (46) (most like he spoke to one man).

In the midst of this introduction, the homilist pauses to insert an appropriate preparatory remark which invites the audience to imaginatively recreate its own role of defendant-debtor in the dramatic events to follow:

> Uton we nu geþencan hwylce we nu syn & hu us þonne lysteð. Hwæt, we siððan ne magon nane lade gedon, ac we sculon gehwyl[c]ra þinga

¹³ HomS 3 (Verc 8) 9-23. The relationship of this motif to other occurrences has been examined by Malcolm Godden in 'An Old English Penitential Motif,' *ASE* 2 (1973): 221-39, at 231-2. See also Joseph Trahern, 'Caesarius of Arles and Old English Literature,' *ASE* 5 (1976): 105-9, at 109-11.
¹⁴ HomS 3 (Verc 8) 34-9.

Gode riht ongyldan on urum sylfra sawlum, ealles þæs ðe we him on anegum þi[n]gum abulgon, butan we ær eaðmodlice beten. (HomS 3 [Verc 8] 28-32)

Let us now consider what we now are and what we will then desire to be. Alas, afterward we will not be able to make any defence, but we must for everything pay what is due to God with our own souls, for all that in which we have angered him in any respect, unless we should have humbly done penance beforehand.

After all, the goal of the sermon, though it deals with future events, is to emphasize an obligation to reform in the present.

The Soul's Address to the Body has no formal function within the Judgment Day trial except perhaps to confirm the justice of the final verdict. However, in Christ's address, a piece drawn from the sermons of Caesarius of Arles,[15] the Lord takes the dual role of judge and plaintiff, making his case for the consummate guilt of mankind and his own long history of patience with its rejection. It may have echoed Anglo-Saxon judicial procedure, which seems to have involved a claim spoken by the plaintiff and directed at the accused, a custom unlike that of the present in which parties tend to rely on intermediaries.[16] Its effectiveness lies in its design as a moving and yet incontrovertible reproach: beginning with mankind's creation, Christ narrates his close and personal involvement with the fate of man. His arguments are irrefutable and the failure and guilt of the doomed are evident. The emotional appeal of such an address is obvious; what may be less clear at first glance is the rhetorical structure which in fact consists of a reasoned forensic argument exhibiting the classical divisions of *exordium, narratio, argumentatio,* and *peroratio.*[17] Though these divisions may not have been a part of contemporary judicial oratory, nor necessarily recognized by the translator or his audience,

---

[15] CAES.ARELAT. Serm 57.4. The source was first discovered in reference to the poetic version by A.S. Cook, *The Christ of Cynewulf. A Poem in Three Parts: The Advent, the Ascension, and the Last Judgment* (Boston 1900), 210. ChristC 1379-523 also contains this speech.
[16] F. Liebermann notes the following regarding the legal procedure of Anglo-Saxon England: 'Der Kläger spricht zuerst, redet den Angeklagten als seinen Gegner mit Du an ... und fordert ihn zur Antwort auf ... bittet ihn um Recht, vor ... dem Richter aber nicht durch diesen' (*Die Gesetze der Angelsachsen* [Halle 1903-16; repr. Aalen 1960], 2:626.
[17] The corresponding English terms are introduction, exposition or narrative, evidence, and close.

their clarity and logic nonetheless made a favourable impression, since this speech was quite popular, to judge from the many extant versions (see below).[18]

Two purposes of the *exordium* in judicial oratory are to establish the speaker's credibility and to provide a link to the audience.[19] Both of these are accomplished admirably in the first few phrases of the address:

> Eala man, hwæt, ic þe geworhte of eorþan lame mid minum handum, & þinum ðam eorðlicum limum ic sealde mine sawle, & ic þe hiwode to mines sylfes anlicnesse, & þa þe gestaðelode on neorxnawonges gefean & þe bead mine bebodu to healdanne. (HomS 3 [Verc 8] 46-50)

> Alas, man, lo, I made you from the clay of the earth with my hands, and to your earthly limbs I gave my soul, and I formed you in my own likeness, and established you in the joy of paradise and asked you to keep my commandments.

The intimate relationship of Creator and creature is repeatedly underlined in the speech so that mankind's fall is established as an outrage against the divine benefactor to whom it owes its origin and continued existence.

In the sparse and straightforward narration (*narratio*)[20] of Christ's Incarnation and Passion, the personal is consistently underlined, as in mankind's rejection of the Creator ('ðu forhogodest mine bebodu & me sylfne' [50-1] [you despised my commandments and myself]) and the 'cildlican teonan' (53-4) (childish indignities) Christ underwent in order to take on human form. A close connection is made with the benefits for mankind in result clauses like that seen in the following sentence: 'Mine sawle ic sende betweoh þa wælgrimman helle tintregan, to þan þæt ic þa þine sawle þanon generede' (58-9) (I sent my soul among the slaughter-grim torments of hell, so that I saved your soul from there). In the *Vercelli* version, the homilist has added 'for þe' (for you) at several points where the Latin does not, as if to

---

[18] Gabriele Knappe has cautioned against assuming a knowledge of classical forensic rhetoric in Anglo-Saxon England (*Traditionen der klassischen Rhetorik im angelsächsischen England* [Heidelberg 1994], 422-3).
[19] Clemens Ottmers, *Rhetorik*, Sammlung Metzler 283 (Stuttgart 1996), 54-5.
[20] Ottmers, *Rhetorik*, 56-7.

underscore the personal obligation which these actions have created.[21] The section ends with a rhetorical question in which this link is made explicit: '& ic þis eal fremede for ðe. Hwæt gedydest ðu for me?' (59-60) (And I performed all this for you. What did you do for me?).

The *argumentatio* begins with a presentation of the incontrovertible evidence.[22] The audience is invited to view the signs of Christ's sacrifice, and they are produced in the mind's eye as indisputable witnesses to his sacrifice: 'Loca nu & sceawa þa dolg on minum handum & on minum fotum, & gesioh ðas mine sidan þe wæs spere þurhstungen' (60-2) (Look and examine the wounds on my hands and on my feet, and see this my side which was pierced through with a spear). More rhetorical questions then begin the *peroratio* by forcefully reiterating the cause of complaint, aiming to establish the guilt of the sinner and draw an emotional response of both sympathy and guilt in the final sentence: 'For hwan, la man, forlur ðu þis eal, þe ic for þe þrowode? For hwan wær ðu swa unþancul þinre onlysnesse?' (64-5) (Why, O man, did you forfeit all this, which I suffered for you? Why were you so ungrateful for your redemption?).

Most of the Old English versions here proceed to the final crescendo of the dismissal to hell, but *Vercelli VIII*, perhaps prefiguring the affective piety of the later Middle Ages, extends the personal pathos:

> For hwan forwyrndest ðu me þæs mines agenan yrfes? Ic wæs þin fæder & þin dryhten & emne eallinga þin freond geworden, and ðu hit þa sealdest þinum ehtere, þam awyrgedan & þam beswicendan diofle ... And þu me mid ealle forhogodest. & ic þe laðode to minum þam ecan life to ðam uplycan rice, þæt ðu agymeleasodost. (HomS 3 [Verc 8] 68-75)

> Why have you denied me my own inheritance? I was your father and your Lord, and even became your friend entirely, and you gave it then to your persecutor, to the accursed and deceiving devil ... And you despised me utterly. And I invited you to my eternal life in the celestial kingdom which you neglected.

---

21 HomS 3 (Verc 8) 54-7, 60.
22 *Probationes inartificiales* (Ottmers, *Rhetorik*, 58).

The relationship of father, lord, and friend and the images of a squandered inheritance and a rejected invitation all personalize the appeal in this surprisingly emotional addition.[23]

One can easily see that this plea to the individual is much more effective delivered in the first person as a monologue than it would be otherwise. In Christ's own voice the case of the aggrieved party is made eloquently and irrefutably, and the notion of a sacrifice that was never compensated undoubtedly resonated with the Anglo-Saxon legal practice of compensation.[24] The homilist wisely does not end with this pessimistic picture. Following the dismissal, the preacher-performer, signalling the end of the drama with the usual 'Men ða leofestan' (88), offers an alternative to the listener: the welcome that may be heard by those who responded appropriately to Christ's sacrifice. The sermon ends with this positive vision, urging the audience to amend their lives so that the reproof just heard will not be directed at them.

And yet the trial would not be complete without the third player in this final drama. The figure of a haughty and almost heroic Satan is well-known to Anglo-Saxonists, and so, even in a sermon and even at the moment of his final doom, he does not disappoint. *Vercelli X* has often been described as an exceptionally well-crafted exhortation.[25] In it, the Devil is not only

---

[23] Scragg, ed., *The Vercelli Homilies and Related Texts*, EETS, os 300 (Oxford 1992), makes note of the addition in his Latin apparatus to lines 44-68, calling it 'an extended legal image' (146).

[24] In OE sermons, the Passion very often has built into it the idea of compensation. The anonymous homilies often follow the descriptions of Christ's sufferings with a mention of repayment, whether it is to call for a consideration of repayment or the realization that such a sacrifice is beyond compensation (cf. HomS 8 [BlHom 2] 169-79; HomS 26 [BlHom 7] 132-52; HomM 13 [Verc 21] 96-8; HomU 32 [Nap 40] 132-6). Charles Wright also has discussed several homilies that mention the payment or pledge of the soul as required on Judgment Day ('The Pledge of the Soul: A Judgment Day Theme in Old English Homiletic Literature and Cynewulf's *Elene*,' *NM* 91 [1990]: 23-30). See also Margaret Bridges, 'The Economics of Salvation: The Beginnings of an English Vocabulary of Reckoning,' in A.M. Simon-Vanderbergen, ed., *Studies in Honour of René Derolez* (Ghent 1987), 44-62.

[25] Again, a Latin source — a passage from Paulinus of Aquileia's *Liber exhortationis ad Henricum comitem* — has been used, but has been rearranged and expanded so that 'the brief demand of Satan for the damned in the original becomes a long, powerful and dramatic speech with good homiletic effect' (Scragg, ed., *The Vercelli Homilies*, 191). Paul Szarmach has called the homily a 'seamless *tour de force* in its structure' ('The Vercelli Homilies: Style and Structure,' in Szarmach and Bernhard F. Huppé, eds, *The Old English Homily and Its Backgrounds* [Albany, NY 1978], 241-67, at 244); Jonathan Wilcox notes its 'strikingly heightened prose style' ('Variant Texts of an Old English Homily: Vercelli X and Stylistic Readers,' in Paul E. Szarmach and Joel T. Rosenthal, eds, *The*

allowed to make his own legal claim but tells us how he led sinners astray and gloats over his own success.[26] However, before he does so, the homilist underscores the danger that the Devil poses: 'Ne gelette us þæs siðes se frecna feond, ne us ðæs wilweges ne forwyrne, ne us þa gatu betyne þe us opene standaþ' (HomS 40.3 [Verc 10] 40-1) (May the savage fiend not prevent us from that journey, nor oppose us in that desired path, nor shut to us those gates that stand open to us). Immediately prior to the Doomsday scene, the author reminds the listener that we can 'þone awyrigedan gast aflymen ... þurh ða heahmyhte ures dryhtnes' (HomS 40.3 [Verc 10] 53-4) (put to flight the accursed spirit through the high power of the Lord), as though the vigour of the speech might cause some to forget this important fact.

The setting this time involves negatives which prefigure the introduction of a miserly rich man in the second half of the homily: it will not be possible to use royal status and earthly wealth to affect the outcome of *this* trial, but good deeds alone will be brought forth as evidence. Then, as our speaker enters the scene, we observe a healthy dose of attitude even before he begins his oration:

> Gif ðær þænne bið þara misdædena ma & þæs godes to lyt, þonne wynsumaþ se wiðerwearda feond & se awirigeda gæst on gesyhðe þæs reðan cyninges. & he ðonne bealdlice cliopaþ to þam hean deman. (HomS 40.3 [Verc 10] 63-6)

> If then more of those misdeeds will be there, and too few of good, then the hostile fiend and the accursed spirit will exult in the sight of the fierce King, and he will then boldly cry out to the high judge.

Satan, apparently relishing his triumph, allows himself mock magnanimity as he invites God to judge the sinners in a grandiose thrice-

---

Preservation and Transmission of Anglo-Saxon Culture [Kalamazoo 1997], 335-51); and Lynn McCabe says it is 'unusually vigorous and poetic, marked by alliterating doublets, strong rhythmical patterns, and poetic formulas' ('An Edition and Translation of a Tenth-Century Anglo-Saxon Homily, Vercelli X [Codex CXVII]' [PhD diss., University of Minnesota, 1968], 6).
[26] Similar, though later, depictions of the struggle between Christ and Satan in terms of legal claims and rights have been examined by C.W. Marx, *The Devil's Rights and the Redemption in the Literature of Medieval England* (Cambridge 1995).

repeated 'Dem, la ...'[27] (Judge, lo ...). These divide the speech into a three-part structure in which the speaker becomes increasingly audacious. He begins with statements that are inoffensive, even complimentary. Drawing attention to the three hosts that are present — and thereby completing the setting for our audience — he notes the indisputable wickedness of those before him. The righteousness and justness of the judge are also affirmed.[28]

However, in the second section we see that Satan was merely laying the foundation for his true objective: God's just verdict must mean that Satan will get what is his due. He offers significant proof that the sinners present indeed belong to him, noting that they 'þine hyrnesse forhogodon' (78-9) (neglected obedience to you); 'hie scyrpton minum reafum' (79) (dressed themselves in my garments); and 'wæron ungemetfæste eallum tidum & oferhidum to fulle & mines willan to georne' (80-1) (were excessive at all times and too full of pride and too eager for my will). Growing more insolent, Satan dwells on the ease with which he obtained his devotees, which is best shown in this well-known musical metaphor:[29]

> Þonn[e] hie gehyrdon þine bec rædan & þin godspel secgan & hira lif rihtan & him ecne weg cyðan, hy symle hiera earan dytton & hit gehyran noldon. Ac ðonne ic mine hearpan genam & mine strengas styrian ongan, hie ðæt lustlice gehyrdon, & fram þe cyrdon & to me urnon. (HomS 40.3 [Verc 10] 81-5)

> When they heard your books read and your gospel told and their life set straight and the eternal way revealed to them, they always closed their ears and would not hear it. But when I took up my harp and began to stir my strings, they heard that gladly, and turned from you and hastened to me.

Emboldened by this account of his success, he lastly even turns to Christ's efforts, which apparently came to naught for these sinners, and here his

---

[27] HomS 40.3 (Verc 10) 67, 76, 92.

[28] HomS 40.3 (Verc 10) 67-75.

[29] This image is not in the Latin source. Christina Heckman has drawn attention to 'the dangerous power of music to surpass and subvert spoken sacred text' implied in this image ('The Sweet Song of Satan: Music and Resistance in the Vercelli Book,' *Essays in Medieval Studies* 15 [1999]: 57-70, at 66).

speech in fact resembles Christ's Address to the Sinner in *Vercelli VIII*, narrating the good things done on mankind's behalf. Coming from the mouth of Satan, however, the narrative becomes blasphemous mockery. The speech ends on this note, with the result that the focus is not so much on the Devil's own seductive powers as on the foolishness of those who do not recognize their true benefactor. And again the Anglo-Saxon practice of compensation may be reflected, since the legal obligation to repay a favour is clearly alluded to by the devil in the clause '& hie þe þæs leanes ealles forgeaton' (HomS 40.3 [Verc 10] 97) (and they entirely forgot your recompense). The sinners in the drama are justly condemned for their neglect to repay with life and soul the good things done on their behalf, and the listener should give thought to avoiding their fate.

There is a certain irony in finding in this carefully crafted speech the comment on the presumably dull Christian teaching that caused some to close their ears and turn to the sweet music that is the devil's seduction.[30] Perhaps the homily itself represents an effort to make Christian instruction somewhat more enticing, possibly by taking a page from the competition's playbook. Apart from the dramatic rhetoric just mentioned, the author heightens the language with rarities such as *þrymdōm* (71), which is only found here,[31] and *scondword* (89), which has only one other occurrence; with semipoetic compounds such as *hordcofa* (88); and with the use of *swat* to mean blood (96). Finally, alliteration can be seen in 'strengas styrian' (84) and 'leahtras lærde' (85), which, again, makes the speech more striking.

From the perspective of the audience, there is a certain amount of shock value to Satan's speech. It develops his character well, exposing his insolence in inviting God to judge justly and his brazen confidence in his legal right to retain those who have followed him. His deceit and trickery and, most disturbing, the ease with which he was able to induce conformity to his will are designed to heighten the contrast between God's loving care and Satan's cynical corruption.

The process of conjuring up a dramatic persona in these sermons, unlike in later dramatic monologues, is never really about the character as

---

[30] Szarmach has made a similar observation in relation to the 'music that leads men to the Lord, namely, the kind of rhythmical prose the homilist has used to relate the Incarnation earlier in the homily' ('The Vercelli Homilies,' 245).

[31] *Þrymdōm* is actually in a short section omitted by the Vercelli scribe but supplied by Scragg from another copy of the homily in CCCC MS 302.

such, but about the audience's response to what these figures have to say. It may be that it is easier to exhort and reproach using another's voice, and so it is not surprising that the anonymous homilists sought out these entertaining vehicles for their pedagogical needs. The affective aspect of these speeches may be more unexpected for this period, especially in a sermon context, but it clearly was meant to move the audience towards difficult changes in behaviour.[32]

All of these examples of Judgment Day drama are found in *The Vercelli Book*. Is there a pattern here? Did the compiler deliberately seek out speeches that were dramatic and that simultaneously urged amendment of life? Had he heard these compelling sermons himself and requested copies for his collection? One way of approaching this question is to see whether his contemporaries and those coming after him found these speeches just as attractive and useful as he did, particularly in the face of the material provided by a certain prolific homilist called Ælfric. A look at their continued use will confirm their popularity. The Soul's Address to the Body appears in its *Vercelli* form written in the margin of an eleventh-century Bede and in fragmentary form in another twelfth-century manuscript.[33] Similar speeches of the soul are to be found in six more places, three in eleventh-century and three in twelfth-century manuscripts; four of these are in predominantly Ælfrician collections.[34] Christ's Address to the Sinner is found in five eleventh-century versions and three twelfth-century manuscripts, all of which are made up of mostly Ælfrician material.[35] And finally, the speech of Satan is found in two manuscripts besides *The Vercelli Book*, one eleventh-century and one twelfth but both, again, mainly Ælfrician.[36]

---

[32] Szarmach comments on the Vercelli collection as a whole that it is the product of someone who was 'primarily interested in evoking an emotional response from his audience' ('The Vercelli Homilies,' 255).
[33] CCCC MS 41 (s. xi') and CCCC MS 367 pt. II (s. xii).
[34] Oxford, Bodleian Library, MS Junius 85/86 (s. xi^{med}); CCCC MS 201 (s. xi^{med}); Oxford, Bodleian Library, MS Hatton 113 (s. xi$^{3rd\ qtr}$); CCCC MS 302 (s. xi/xii); London, British Library, MS Cotton Faustina A.ix (s. xii'); Cambridge, University Library, MS Ii.1.33 (s. xii²).
[35] Oxford, Bodleian Library, MS Bodley 340 (s. xi^{in}); twice in Oxford, Bodleian Library, MS Hatton 114 (s. xi$^{3rd\ qtr}$); CCCC MS 198 (s. xi'); CCCC MS 41 (s. xi'); CCCC MS 303 (s. xii'); London, British Library, MS Cotton Faustina A.ix (s. xii'); CCCC MS 302 (s. xi/xii).
[36] CCCC MS 302 (s. xi/xii) and CCCC MS 421 (s. xi').

It has been said that *The Vercelli Book* represents a homiletic tradition inferior in quality to that of Ælfric, but perhaps it all depends on what the measure of a successful sermon is. The fact that these sermons were recopied well into the twelfth century argues that for some they held a merit sought by speakers everywhere, that of keeping the audience engaged and able to recall what was said once the speech was finished.

Part III — On Old English Poetry

7

'Him þæs grim lean becom': The Theme of Infertility in *Genesis A*

KARIN OLSEN

Although it is now generally agreed that the *Genesis A* poet did not slavishly paraphrase the Book of Genesis 1:1 to 22:1, his poetic technique has not always received sufficient attention. The reason for this relative neglect is readily discernible. By reproducing and interpreting the biblical text as traditional patristic and exegetical commentary required, the poet certainly did not take the poetic liberties that can be found in *Exodus* or even *Daniel*. Paul Remley, for example, has recently called *Genesis A* 'a *tour-de-force* of bilingual (Latin–Old English) lexical negotiation,' which 'reproduces nearly all of the episodic contents and most of the Latin diction of Genesis I-XXII in a proficient and only occasionally pedestrian versification.'[1] Yet the poet could certainly be creative within these bounds, as Roberta Frank's examination of paronomasia in the poem has amply illustrated.[2] Frank suggests that the poet's play on OE *word* represents 'a deliberate and specifically Christian attempt to show the same Word of God at work, shaping the course of history, at the beginning of time.'[3] In a similar vein, Peter Lucas in his examination of the themes of loyalty and obedience in *Genesis A* identifies the noun *ar* 'favour, honour, grace' as a 'keyword in the conceptualization of God's reward' for the faithful.[4]

---

[1] Paul G. Remley, *Old English Biblical Verse: Studies in* Genesis, Exodus, *and* Daniel, CSASE 16 (Cambridge 1996), 96. For an analysis of the poet's use of the Vulgate and the *Vetus Latina*, see also Remley, 'The Latin Textual Basis of *Genesis A*,' *ASE* 17 (1988): 163-89.

[2] Roberta Frank, 'Some Uses of Paronomasia in Old English Scriptural Verse,' *Speculum* 47 (1972): 207-26, at 211-15.

[3] Ibid., 213.

[4] Peter Lucas, 'Loyalty and Obedience in the Old English *Genesis* and the Interpolation of *Genesis B* into *Genesis A*,' *Neo* 76 (1992): 121-35, at 128. A thematic approach to *Genesis A* is also provided by Paul Battles ('*Genesis A* and the Anglo-Saxon Migration Myth,' *ASE* 29 [2000], 43-66), who suggests that a traditional 'migration' theme underlies the migration passages in the poem. See below.

Those lacking *ar* because they have broken the *wær* 'covenant' with God are, on the other hand, severely punished.[5]

The following discussion will examine God's punishment of the wicked from a different angle. It will illustrate how the poet uses recurrent images of infertility in order to recall with each transgression and punishment on earth Lucifer's rebellion and fall in heaven. While the faithful are allowed to increase and multiply, and enjoy the fecund earth, God unleashes the powers of chaos so as to torture and destroy those who, like Satan, have forgotten their true Creator and shamefully commit sin.

In *Genesis A*, God's creative power manifests itself in the divine bestowal of prosperity on the virtuous, while the wicked are excluded from such favours. Both themes are biblical, but the *Genesis A* poet gives them special emphasis by introducing them in the nonbiblical opening of his narrative, with its vivid depiction of the joyful community in heaven and the subsequent exclusion of the rebel angels from this ideal existence. Before the rebellion, the 'engla þreatas' (132a) 'host of angels,' experiences the 'gleam and dream' (12b) (revelry and joy), and the 'beorhte blisse' (14a) (bright bliss) of their 'ordfruman' (13a) (creator) and the poet comments: 'Wæs heora blæd micel' (14b) (their glory/prosperity was great). But once Lucifer and his followers disrupt the unity of the celestial body with their arrogant behaviour,[6] God cuts them off from this heavenly *blæd*, responding to their spiritual alienation with their physical removal from heaven. They have to abandon the 'wlite and wuldre' (36a) (radiance and glory), and face infertility and torment in hell:

> Sceop þam werlogan
> wræclicne ham   weorce to leane,
> helleheafas,   hearde niðas.
> Heht þæt witehus   wræcna bidan,
> deop, dreama leas,   drihten ure,
> gasta weardas,   þa he hit geare wiste,
> synnihte beseald,   susle geinnod,

[5] Lucas, 'Loyalty and Obedience,' 125, 128.
[6] Alvin A. Lee has called this disruption the 'primal crime'; see his *The Guest-Hall of Eden* (New Haven and London 1972), 19. A detailed discussion of the theme of separation in *Genesis A* is provided by Constance Hieatt, 'Divisions: Theme and Structure of *Genesis A*,' *NM* 81 (1980): 243-51.

geondfolen fyre   and færcyle,
rece and reade lege.   Heht þa geond þæt rædlease hof
weaxan witebrogan.   Hæfdon hie wrohtgeteme
grimme wið god gesomnod;   him þæs grim lean becom! (36b-46)[7]

He created for the faith-breakers a wretched home as reward for their
deed, hell-wailings, severe humiliations. He, our Lord, commanded
the guardians of souls to endure that punishment-house of exiles, deep,
without joys, when he knew it ready, surrounded by eternal night,
filled with torment, filled completely with fire and intense cold,
smoke and red flame. He ordered then the tormenting terrors to grow
throughout that damned building. They had gathered fiercely a crime-
troop[8] against God; a grim reward befell them for that!

Having created a 'wræclicne ham' for the 'werlogan,' God orders the 'gasta
weardas' to endure 'þæt witehus wræcna.' Alliteration and vowel repetition
make this new hall indeed the inescapable destination for the exiles,[9] just as
vowel repetition has made the 'engla þreatas' perfect recipients for the 'gleam
and dream' in heaven. The spiritually barren rebels have found their natural
surroundings in the sterile landscape of hell. Engulfed in 'synnihte,' they are at
God's command tortured by the 'witebrogan,' that is, the 'fyre and færcyle'
and the 'rece and reade lege.' Furthermore, the radiant appearance of the fallen
angels, once it is 'þystrum beþeahte' (76a) (covered with darkness) soon
becomes better suited to the dark new habitat. They hover 'swearte' (72a)
(black) in the depths of hell, having merged with the powers of destruction in
both mind and body.[10]

---

[7] The edition of *Genesis A* used in this essay is that by George Philipp Krapp, in *The Junius
Manuscript*, ASPR 1 (New York and London 1931), 3-87. All translations of the Old English text
are my own.
[8] For the rendering of *wrohtgeteme* as 'crime-troop,' see Karin Olsen, 'OE *wrohtgeteme*: "crime-
troop", not "series of crimes,"' *NQ*, n.s. 38 (1991): 438-42.
[9] The motif of the anti-hall also occurs in *Genesis B* and in *Christ and Satan*. See further Kathryn
Hume's discussion of the concept of the hall motif in 'The Concept of the Hall in Old English
Poetry,' *ASE* 3 (1974): 63-74.
[10] In her recent analysis of the illustrations in MS Junius 11, Catherine E. Karkov (*Text and
Picture in Anglo-Saxon England*, CSASE 31 [Cambridge 2001], 50) notes the artist's change of
colours (from red to brown) to indicate Lucifer's fall from light into darkness.

The dichotomy between prosperity and joylessness first illustrated in the heaven-hell complex continues to play a prominent role in the poet's rendering of God's creation of the fertile earth from formless, dark and purposeless chaos (Genesis 1:1-5):[11]

> Ne wæs her þa giet   nymþe heolstersceado
> wiht geworden,   ac þes wida grund
> stod deop and dim,   drihtne fremde,
> idel and unnyt.   On þone eagum wlat
> stiðfrihþ cining,   and þa stowe beheold,
> dreama lease,   geseah deorc gesweorc
> semian sinnihte   sweart under roderum,
> wonn and weste,   oðþæt þeos woruldgesceaft
> þurh word gewearð   wuldorcyninges. (103-11)

Not anything except for darkness-shade had arisen here yet, but this wide ground stood deep and dark, alien to the Lord, idle and useless. With his eyes the resolute King gazed at that and beheld the place, without joys, saw the murky darkness hover black in eternal night under the skies, bleak and desolate, until this created world arose through the word of the King of glory.

The significant verbal correspondences are noted by Constance Hieatt:

> One biblical verse, Genesis 1:2, is expanded to over twenty lines, describing the first state of the earth in terms which clearly suggest Section I's description of hell: it is shadowy (103b), 'dreama leas' and dark (108); God viewed it 'semian sinnihte sweart' just as He saw hell 'synnihte beseald' and the fallen angels found it a place where they 'seomodon swearte' (72a).[12]

Hieatt concludes that the use of verbal repetition reinforces 'the contrast between the darkness of hell and the light which graces the newly created

---

[11] Hugh Magennis, *Images of Community in Old English Poetry*, CSASE 18 (Cambridge 1996), 150.
[12] Hieatt, 'Divisions,' 246.

earth.'³ But the poet's use of identical diction also reminds us of the more comprehensive concept of *blæd* from which the fallen angels were excluded, and which is now reinstated on earth. The poet explicitly refers to the earth before the creation as 'idel and unnyt,' 'wonn and weste,' and later as a 'westen' covered by the dark flood:

> Folde wæs þa gyta
> græs ungrene;   garsecg þeahte
> sweart synnihte,   side and wide,
> wonne wægas.   Þa wæs wuldortorht
> heofonweardes gast   ofer holm boren
> miclum spedum. (116b-21a)

The earth was yet ungreen grass;'⁴ the black eternal night covered the ocean, dark waves, far and wide. Then the gloriously bright spirit of the Guardian of heaven was carried across the sea with great speed.

Rendering the Latin 'abyssi' of Genesis 1:2 as 'garsecg' and 'wonne wægas,' the poet evidently identifies the sea with the primeval void.'⁵ The reference to the gloomy colour of the waves, furthermore, makes sea and perpetual night (109, 118a) companions,'⁶ while associating both with Lucifer's gloomy dwelling. The absence of light and dry land results in the conception of the earth as 'græs ungrene,''⁷ barren and devoid of God's creative principle.'⁸ However,

---

¹³ Ibid.

¹⁴ For the translation, see Alfred Bammesberger, 'Old English *Græs Ungrene* in *Genesis A*, line 117a,' *NQ* n.s. 46 (1999): 427-8. Bammesberger's claim that the earth was grass without growth and therefore of no use for animal husbandry is, however, somewhat odd, as the earth was still covered by the flood (cf. ll. 155b-7a).

¹⁵ For the identification of sea and abyss in Eustathius, *In Hexaemeron S. Basilii*, see A.N. Doane, *Genesis A: A New Edition* (Madison 1978), 233, note on ll. 117b-19a.

¹⁶ Bernard Huppé (*Doctrine and Poetry: Augustine's Influence on Old English Poetry* [New York 1959], 145) distinguishes between the darkness of the perpetual night covering the uncreated world and the colourlessness of the 'wonne wægas,' which signify 'the wan void, which is to take form and become the visible world.' Still, since the *Genesis A* poet uses both *wonn* and *sweart* for the colour of the flood (see below), Huppé's argument fails to convince.

¹⁷ See Scott Norsworthy, 'The Un-green Earth in *Genesis A*, *NQ* n.s. 46 (1999): 171-3, for the Yahwist version as source of the phrase.

¹⁸ See also A.N. Doane, 'The Green Street of Paradise,' *NM* 74 (1973): 456-65, at 463; Magennis, *Images of Community*, 150.

whereas God gave darkness free rein in hell to withhold physical and spiritual prosperity from the rebel angels, He now ensures such prosperity on earth by confining darkness to night and shade[19] and by separating water from land.

Blæd was the privilege that God bestowed on the angels in heaven before their fall and that Lucifer and his followers forfeited forever. In contrast, *blæd* can be lost and regained on the newly created earth. Adam and Eve's disobedience causes them to be expelled from Paradise and seek a 'sorgfulre land' (961b) (more sorrowful land), but because of their repentance God still commands sea and earth to yield their produce to the couple (952a-60b) and their faithful descendants. According to Hugh Magennis, Paradise is the archetypal 'good landscape,' which, though irrecoverable for mankind after Adam and Eve's transgression, becomes in the poem the pattern for other fertile and green landscapes enjoyed by those faithful to God.[20] Conversely, no such divine mercy is shown to the wicked, whose spiritual infertility is punished with physical sterility and even death. Thus Cain is exiled from the green landscape.[21] God says to Cain:

> 'Þu þæs cwealmes scealt
> wite winnan   and on wræc hweorfan,
> awyrged to widan aldre.   Ne seleð þe wæstmas eorðe
> wlitige to woruldnytte,   ac heo wældreore swealh
> halge of handum þinum;   forþon heo þe hroðra oftihð,
> glæmes grene folde.   þu scealt geomor hweorfan,
> arleas of earde þinum,   swa þu Abele wurde
> to feorhbanan;   forþon þu flema scealt
> widlast wrecan,   winemagum lað.' (1013b-21)

---

[19] Cf. Karkov, *Text and Picture*, 51.

[20] Magennis, *Images of Community*, 145-54. See also Lee (*The Guest-Hall of Eden*, 40), who identifies paradise as 'an extension of heaven' which recurs in form of the 'green-earth' motif to indicate God's reward to the faithful. Greenness as a sign of spiritual and physical growth occurs fourteen times in *Genesis A*. See Antonette di Paolo Healey et al., eds, *The Complete Corpus of Old English in Electronic Form*, CD-ROM (Toronto 2000), s. *grene*.

[21] Cf. Gen. 4:11-12: 'Nunc igitur maledictus eris super terram quae aperuit os suum et suscepit sanguinem fratris tui de manu tua. Cum operatus fueris eam non dabit tibi fructus suos. Vagus et profugus eris super terram' (Therefore you are now accursed on the earth, which opened its mouth and received your brother's blood from your hand. When you have tilled it, it will not yield you its fruits. You will be a vagrant and exile on earth). For the Vulgate text, see *Biblica sacra iuxta vulgatam versionen*, ed. R. Weber, 4th edn (Stuttgart 1994), 8 (my punctuation and translation).

'For the killing you must suffer punishment and go in exile, forever accursed. The earth shall not give you bright fruits for your worldly benefit, but she swallowed holy battle-blood from your hands; therefore she, the green earth, shall withhold her benefits, splendour. You shall depart from your homestead, sad, without honour, as you became Abel's slayer; therefore you must travel a distant path as an exile, hostile to dear kinsmen.'

The poet stresses the gravity of Cain's deed with his introduction of the compound 'winemagum' (1021b) and its reference to the natural bond between family members. Kinsmen (*magas*) are friends (*wine*) by nature, yet Cain has proven to be his brother's mortal enemy and has therefore become hateful to his other kinsmen as well.[22] In fact, Cain's transgression of one of the most elementary laws of nature makes it impossible for him to enjoy the goodness of God's creation ever again. His violation of the divine principle of procreation while enjoying the fertile soil of his land highlights the discrepancy between spiritual and physical growth, a discrepancy that can only be solved by restricting or even reversing the physical growth. Just as God restored the balance between physical and spiritual prosperity in heaven by banishing the degenerate rebel angels, He now separates Cain from his kinsmen, from his 'eard' (1019a) (native land), and from the fruits of the 'grene folde' (1010a) 'green earth.'[23] Still, Cain's spiritual drought gives rise to a new perverse growth, a sprouting tree of crime and sorrow that already foreshadows later transgressions in human history:

Æfter wælswenge   wea wæs aræred,
tregena tuddor.   Of ðam twige siððan
ludon laðwende   leng swa swiðor
reðe wæstme.   Ræhton wide

---

[22] Bennett A Brockmann ('"Heroic" and "Christian" in *Genesis A*: The Evidence of the Cain and Abel Episode,' *Modern Language Quarterly* 35 [1974]: 115-28) has argued that the poet understood Cain's fratricide as much in social as in spiritual terms. According to Brockman, the poet was particularly moved by Cain's fate as a human damned to eternal exile for violating 'one of the most basic Germanic laws' (117). Given the poet's elaborate treatment of the tree of sin and the spread of vice from Cain's transgression, however, it is more likely that the poet simply expands on the familiar concepts of kin slaying and exile as a means to highlight the gravity of Cain's spiritual offence and its consequences.

[23] Karkov, *Text and Picture*, 158-9.

geond werþeoda   wrohtes telgan,
hrinon hearmtanas   heardes and sare
drihta bearnum,   (doð gieta swa)
of þam brad blado   bealwa gehwilces
sprytan ongunnon. (987-95a)

After the deadly blow sorrow was raised up, the fruit of pains. From that branch hateful angry fruit grew afterwards, the longer the more intensively. Branches of crime extended widely through the nations, hard and painful shoots of sorrow reached the children of multitudes (they still do so), from which broad leaves of each harm began to sprout.

Cain's initial crime, like a thornbush,[24] grows and spreads, quelling all beneficent forces with its branches. This negative force is manifested early in the narrative. Although Seth is blessed with abundant descendants for 807 years (1138a-40a), the descendants can only thrive as long as they remain uncontaminated by Cain's transgression. When the sons of Seth take the daughters of Cain as their wives and bring forth the giants, divine punishment awaits this evil offspring.[25] As they are 'wærlogan' (1266a) (faith-breakers) just like the fallen angels,[26] God announces that the perpetrators will be drowned by the 'sweart wæter' (1300b) (black water) and 'wonne wælstreamas' (1301a)

---

[24] Charles D. Wright ('The Blood of Abel and the Branches of Sin: *Genesis A*, *Maxims I* and Aldhelm's *Carmen de virginitate*,' *ASE* 25 [1996]: 7-19, at 14-16) postulates Aldhelm's *Carmen de uirginitate* as source for the nonbiblical tree metaphor. In Aldhelm's *Carmen*, brambles spring up from Abel's blood. For an alternative interpretation of the tree metaphor, see Nina Boyd, 'A Revaluation of "Genesis A,"' *NM* 83 (1982): 230-8, at 231-2. Boyd claims that the tree image describes the loss of Abel.

[25] Hieatt ('Divisions,' 249) argues that Seth's descendants have violated the divine division of the two races and are duly punished for that. For a discussion of the origin and development of the tradition that identifies *filii Dei* with the sons of Seth and *filiae hominum* with the daughters of Cain, see Ruth Melinkoff, 'Cain's Monstrous Progeny in *Beowulf*: Part I, Noachic Tradition,' *ASE* 8 (1979): 143-62, at 145-8; see further Andy Orchard, *Pride and Prodigies: Studies in the Monsters of the Beowulf-Manuscript* (Cambridge 1995), 74-9.

[26] *Wærloga* occurs 12 times outside *Genesis A* (*The Complete Corpus of Old English*, s.v.). The references to devils as *wærlogan* can be found in GuthA 298 and 623, GuthB 911, Jul 455, and in And 613 and 1297. In Whale 37, the whale is a *wærloga* in its allegorical signification as the Devil. Very evil people are also called *wærlogan* in And 71 and 108 (the Mermedonians), in Jud 71 (Holofernus) and in Wid 9 (Ermanaric). Only in ChristC 1561 does the compound refer to the damned soul in general, making it akin to the inhabitants of hell.

(dark waves), expressions that not only echo the 'sweart synnihte' and the 'wonne wægas' before the creation of light and dry land but also point back to the abode of the first 'troth-breakers,' the 'sweart synnihte' of hell. He then angrily unleashes the watery expanse that He had so powerfully checked at the creation of the earth:

> Strang wæs and reðe
> se ðe wætrum weold;   wreah and þeahte
> manfæhðu bearn   middangeardes
> wonnan wæge,   wera eðelland. (1376b-9)

Strong and fierce was He who ruled the waters; a wicked strife covered and hid the children of the middle-earth, the homeland of men, with a dark wave.

Submerged in the murky waters, the earth has reverted to its primordial state.

After His destruction of the earth with its wicked inhabitants, God restores the fertile earth to the virtuous. Noah finds a new prosperous living space, where he can be fruitful and multiply by enjoying the produce of the 'ælgrene' (1517a) (all-green) earth. And yet the restoration of peace and tranquillity proves to be temporary. Although the faithful Noah may indeed work in perfect harmony with nature at this point,[27] the poet already foreshadows future offences against God's creation in his long description of Noah's release of the raven and its failure to return to its master. His repeated references to its naturally 'sweart' (1441b, 1449b) (black) colour and its unsavoury habit of feeding on corpses associate this beast of battle not only with sterility and death (as opposed to the greenness of the fertile earth), as may be expected from its traditional role, but also with spiritual darkness. This underlying association may also explain the use of the word *feond* to refer to the bird, a designation that has puzzled critics. The raven is certainly not a figure of Satan nor does it, as Bernard Huppé suggests, specifically represent

---

[27] Magennis, *Images of Community*, 153. However, Noah's drunkenness in the vineyard illustrates that even the virtuous can submit to *luxuria*. Although Noah is a faithful man, his exposure of his genitals indicates excess that will play a prominent role in the future generations descending from him. Cf. Magennis, *Images of Community*, 91-2; Doane, *Genesis A*, 277-8, note on ll. 1562-96a.

the inhabitants of Babylonia even in an allegorical sense.[28] Instead, it functions
as a reminder of the fallen human and angelic world.

It is through Noah's descendants that sinful human nature continues to
misuse God's gift of prosperity after the Flood. As 'rofe rincas' (1651a) (brave
men) and 'æðelinga bearn' (1654a) (sons of princes), they are given the 'grene
wongas' (1657b) (green plains) of Shinar, where they can enjoy 'wilna
gehwilces weaxende sped' (1660) (growing prosperity in respect to each of their
desires).[29] But the settlers soon forget God's favour. Instead of responding with
deep gratitude to it, they attempt to promote their own worldly fame with the
building of a glorious city and a tower reaching up to heaven:

> Þæs þe hie sohton   Sennera feld,
> swa þa foremeahtige   folces ræswan,
> þa yldestan   oft and gelome
> liðsum gewunedon;   larum sohton
> weras to weorce   and to wrohtscipe,
> oðþæt for wlence   and for wonhygdum
> cyðdon cræft heora,   ceastre worhton
> and to heofnum up   hlædræ rærdon,
> strengum stepton   stænenne weall
> ofer monna gemet,   mærða georne,
> hæleð mid honda. (1668-78a)

For they sought the plain of Shinar, as the mightiest leaders of the
people, the oldest ones, were accustomed to pleasures often and
frequently; cunningly they sought men for the work and for the crime,
until they showed forth their skill because of pride and recklessness,
built the city and raised a ladder up to heaven; the men, eager for

---

[28] Huppé, *Doctrine and Poetry*, 174-5. Cf. Milton McC. Gatch ('Noah's Raven in *Genesis A* and the Illustrated Old English Hexateuch,' *Gesta* 14, no. 2 [1975]: 3-15, at 7), who interprets the carrion bird as a representative of a sinful Christian.

[29] Following Bede's and Gregory the Great's commentaries on the symbolic meaning of Shinar, Huppé (*Doctrine and Poetry*, 184-5) points out that its greenness is deceptive, as it represents earthly glory. No allusion to such an interpretation can be found in *Genesis A*; on the contrary, greenness is a positive attribute representing spiritual fecundity not only in this but also in all other Old English biblical poems in which it occurs. See also Doane, 'The Green Street of Paradise.'

glory, erected a stone wall with their hands powerfully beyond human measure.

Paul Battles has suggested that the poet condemns only the foolish deed of the tower-builders, while otherwise giving a sympathetic description of Noah's migrating descendants both before Babel and after the confusion of tongues.[10] According to Battles, 'migration, like sea voyages and battle, constitutes heroic action, and as such is generally depicted in approving terms.'[11] But even though the poet endows the settlers with a heroic determination to which the Anglo-Saxon audience could relate, he also illustrates — even if temporarily — how such determination can be misapplied. Driven by 'wlence' and 'wonhygdum,' the builders and their employers wish to emulate God by raising the tower into the sky (1675). Significantly, the poet condemns this act as 'wrohtscipe,' reminding us of the fallen angels' 'wrohtgeteme' in heaven.

In fact, the parallel is not coincidental. The poet has already introduced Ham's grandson Nimrod in lines 1633a-6b, which render Gen. 10:9 'robustus venator coram Domino' (mighty hunter before the Lord), traditionally exemplifying pride:[12]

Se wæs Babylones   bregorices fruma,
ærest æðelinga;   eðelðrym onhof,
rymde and rærde.   Reord wæs þa gieta
eorðbuendum   an gemæne.

He was the leader of the kingdom of Babylon, the first of princes; he increased the glory of his own land, enlarged it and raised it up. The earth-dwellers still had one language in common then.

[10] Battles, '*Genesis A* and the Anglo-Saxon Migration Myth,' 48-9.
[11] Ibid., 59.
[12] See, for example, Jerome, *Commentarii in Naum* 3.1-4, ed. M Adriaen, CCSL 76A (Turnhout 1970), 556; Augustine, *De civitate Dei* XVI.4, CCSL 48 (Turnhout 1955), reproduction of text by B. Dombart and A. Kalb (Leipzig 1928-9), 505; Bede, *In Genesim* III, x.9, ed. C.W. Jones, CCSL 118A (Turnhout 1967), 144-5. For Isidore's and later Alfred's descriptions of Nimrod as proud giant warrior and tyrant, see Orchard, *Pride and Prodigies*, 81-2.

By inserting Gen 11:1 ('erat autem terra labii unius et sermonum eorundem,' [however, the earth had one tongue and the same speech]) after the reference to Nimrod's rulership of Babylon in Gen 10:10 ('fuit autem principium regni eius Babylon ... ' [but the beginning of his kingdom was Babylon ...]), the poet reinforces the connection between Nimrod and the building of city and tower made in the various commentaries.[33] Nimrod is 'Babylones bregorices fruma' (the leader of the kingdom of Babylon) (1633) before the confusion of tongues (in Babel) and consequently the leader of both the allegorical Babylon, that is, the City of the World, and its representative, Babel.[34] Nimrod and his subjects' pride is duly punished with exile. When they finally attempt to commit the 'wrohtscipe,' they are deprived of the prosperity of their home and consequently follow in Satan's and his followers' footsteps.[35] While Satan's band lost the heavenly *blæd*, the tower-builders are now cut off from the 'grene wongas' (1657b) (green plains), and, as a result, from the 'wilna gehwilces weaxende sped' (1660) (growing prosperity of each desire) as well.

Even more important, however, are the parallels between the punishments of Noah's posterity and of Cain, who was blessed with fertile land but after Abel's murder had to leave his homeland. The settlers thrive on the Plain of Shinar, but when they offend God with their pride and vanity

---

[33] Doane, *Genesis A*, 280-1, note on ll. 1628b-36.

[34] This identification is also made by Augustine (*De civitate Dei*, XVI.4) and Bede (*In Genesim*, III, 10.10, 145-6; cf. Doane, *Genesis A*, 282-3, note on ll. 1649-1701. Battles ('*Genesis A* and the Anglo Saxon Migration Myth,' 48 n. 24) rejects any connection between Nimrod and Babel, but the last sentence in the citation given above suggests otherwise.

[35] According to Karkov (*Text and Picture*, 96), the traditional association between Nimrod and the devil is strengthened in the illustrations. Karkov observes that 'the crenellated wall of the town in which Nimrod and his men stand gazing upwards also echoes the crenellated walls of hell from which Satan and his demons gaze upwards (pls VIII, IX), indicating that Satan's attempt to establish his greatness in heaven was as futile as Nimrod's attempt to establish a kingdom on earth.' Nimrod is also seen as devil by Bede in *In Genesim* III, 10.10 (CCSL 118A, 145-6): 'Quia uero Babylon cum ciuitatibus quarum caput est, superbam huius mundi gloriam, quae confusioni obnoxia est, designat; Babel enim confusio dicitur. Recte conditor eius ipsum malorum omnium caput diabolum figurate denuntiat; cui etiam Nemrod uocabulum, quod tyrannum uel profugum uel transgressorem sonat, apte congruit.'

(Verily, therefore, Babylon with its cities [i.e., the other cities on the Plain of Shinar] of which it is the head betokens the proud glory of this world, which is subject to confusion; for Babel is called 'confusion'. In a figurative way, its founder correctly designates the head of all evils, the devil; to him the word 'Nimrod' aptly corresponds, which means either 'tyrant,' or 'exile,' or 'transgressor'.) I would like to thank Alasdair MacDonald for his helpful comments on the exegetical source material used in this paper.

their earthly prosperity becomes as short-lived as Cain's. In fact, by adding 'ða gieta' (still) to 'reord wæs / eorðbuendum an gemæne' (1635b-6b) (the earth-dwellers had one language in common), the poet leaves no doubt that Nimrod's people will enjoy the divine gift of common speech and the resulting worldly *sped* only for a limited time. Without 'þære spæce sped' (1686) (prosperity of speech) confusion arises in the community (as the names 'Babel' and 'Babylon' indicate), forcing the city-dwellers to leave the unfinished 'stiðlic stantor' (1700a) (strong tower of stone) as a sign both of their failed blasphemous aspirations and of their own spiritual barrenness.

Still, Battles is correct to point out that the poet distinguishes between the builders of city and tower, on the one hand, and the fallen angels, Cain, the giants, and finally the inhabitants of Sodom and Gomorrah, on the other.[36] Although the builders cannot expect 'wilna gehwilces weaxende sped' on the Plain of Shinar after their dispersion, they are allowed to migrate to new regions and to settle and procreate. In contrast, the citizens of Sodom and Gomorrah prove to be beyond redemption. Not only do they, like their ancestors, put the '(æl)grene' land (1751, 1787, 1921) — in this case the prosperous Plain of the Five Cities — to ill use, but their offences are so severe that they face total extinction, leaving nothing but a wasteland behind them. These unredeemable crimes have been explained in the patristic commentary as pride, luxury, blasphemy, and, more specifically, sexual transgressions.[37] Jerome, for example, identifies pride, abundance in all things, and their resulting blasphemous *oblivio Dei* as the Sodomites' major sins.[38] The poet links precisely these sins with God's punishment:

---

[36] Battles, '*Genesis A* and the Anglo-Saxon Migration Myth,' 48.

[37] For a brief analysis of the various commentaries on the sin of Sodom, see Mark D. Jordan, *The Invention of Sodomy in Christian Theology* (Chicago and London 1997), 32-40.

[38] Jerome, *Commentarii in Hiezechielem* V, 16.48-51, ed. F. Glorie, CCSL 75 (Turnhout 1964), 206: 'Superbia, saturitas, rerum omnium abundantia, otium et deliciae, peccatum sodomiticum est, et propter hoc sequitur Dei obliuio, quae praesentia bona putat esse perpetua et numquam sibi necessariis indigendum' (The sodomitic sin is pride, satiety, abundance of all things, inactivity and pleasures; and because of it there follows the forgetting of God, which believes all present good things to be everlasting, and that there ought never to be a lack of necessities). For the identification of luxury as the main sin, see Ambrose of Milan, *De Abraham* I, 3.14, ed. Karl Schenkl, CSEL 32/1 (Vienna 1897), 512. For a discussion of Jerome's evaluation of public and shameless blasphemy as 'sodomiticum peccatum' in his commentary on Isaiah 3:8-9, see Richard Kay, *Dante's Swift and Strong: Essays on the Inferno XV* (Lawrence 1978), 243. Blasphemy is also a common sin of the people of Sodom and Gomorrah in Jerome's *Commentarii in Sophoniam* 2.8-11, ed. M. Adriaen, CCSL 76A (Turnhout 1970), 687: 'Sicut Sodoma et Gomorrah erunt, uidentur

Hie þæs wlenco onwod   and wingedrync
þæt hie firendæda   to frece wurdon,
synna þriste,   soð ofergeaton,
drihtnes domas,   and hwa him dugeða forgeaf,
blæd on burgum.   Forþon him brego engla
wylmhatne lig   to wræce sende. (2581-6)

Pride and wine-drinking pervaded them so much that they were too greedy for wicked deeds, daring in sins, forgot the truth, the decrees of the Lord, and [they forgot] who granted them favours, prosperity in the cities. The Prince of angels sent them the rushing hot flame as punishment for that.

The Sodomites openly defy God's command to be fruitful and multiply when instead of heeding Lot's obligations towards his guests they propose to 'hæman' (2460b) (have sexual intercourse) with the strangers.[19] Yet both the Sodomites' homosexual practices and their drunkenness are in the end a mere

quidem sibi in eo quod gentiles non sunt, exisse de Sodomis et Gomorrhis, sed quia blasphemant populum Dei, et contra Israel faciunt, in Sodomam reputabuntur et Gomorrahm; et ita delebuntur ut illae deletae sunt ante, nullum in se habentes uestigium uiroris et uitae' (Like Sodom and Gomorrah will they [i.e., Moab and Ammon] be; indeed, they believe themselves not to be gentiles, but to have proceeded from the Sodomites and the Gomorrahns; but because they blaspheme the people of God and act against Israel, they will be reputed with Sodom and Gomorrah; and they will be destroyed even as those were destroyed before, leaving in them no trace of greenness and of life).

[19] In the given line, the *Genesis A* poet has perhaps incorporated a tradition based on Gen. 19:5 in the *Vetus Latina*, where the Sodomites wish to have intercourse with them 'duc illos ad nos coitum faciamus cum eis,' while in the Vulgate, they wish to know them 'educ illos huc ut cognoscamus eos.' See Remley's table in 'The Latin Textual Basis of *Genesis A*,' 189. Jerome does not mention the homosexual practices in his commentary, but, as Jordan points out (*The Invention of Sodomy*, 34) they are discussed in Augustine's *De mendacio* VII, 10 (ed. Joseph Zycha, CSEL 41 [Vienna 1900], 429, and *Confessiones* III, 8.15 (ed. M. Skutella and L. Verheijen, CCSL 27 [Turnhout 1981], 35). The poet's explicitness on this issue becomes especially noticeable when compared with Bede's interpretation of the passage. Bede refers to the Sodomites' sin as 'infando' (unspeakable), but it is not entirely clear that this unspeakable sin refers to any homosexual act. Kay (*Dante's Swift and Strong*, 229-31) argues that Bede's 'infando' is a more general allusion to the Sodomites' 'impiety,' which includes their misuse of the gifts of nature, a lack of gratitude, and incorrigibility, as well as aberrant sexual practices. Although Kay's argument has recently been attacked by Allen J. Frantzen, who sees a clear reference to the Sodomites' homosexuality in the allusion (*Before the Closet: Same Sex Love from* Beowulf *to Angels in America* [Chicago and London 1998], 194-5), Bede's restraint remains indisputable.

manifestation of their moral depravity. Having become oblivious to the 'soð' (2583b) (truth) that God gave them 'duguða' and 'blæd in burgum,' they commit their sins openly and without shame.

By making pride and *oblivio Dei* the chief crimes of Sodom and Gomorrah, the *Genesis A* poet continues to link those who have transgressed against God's creative principle with the fallen angels. He calls the city-dwellers 'wærlogan' (2411b; also 2505b, 2532a) (faith-breakers), an epithet, which, as illustrated above, he has already used for both the antediluvian giants and the truant angels. Furthermore, the inhabitants of Sodom and Gomorrah and the devils both wilfully refuse to repent. According to Bede, Abraham's surprising victory over the superior five kings of the North should have taught the proud city-dwellers that God is most powerful and can change any event.[40] Bede, however, makes the connection between the fiery destruction of Sodom and the fire awaiting all sinful souls at the Last Judgment,[41] whereas the *Genesis A* poet stresses the punishment common to city-dwellers and the devils for their wrongful use of God's *blæd*:

Þa ic sendan gefrægn swegles aldor
swefl of heofnum and sweartne lig
werum to wite, weallende fyr,
þæs hie on ærdagum drihten tyndon
lange þrage. Him þæs lean forgeald
gasta waldend! ...
 ...
  Lig eall fornam
þæt he grenes fond goldburgum in,
swylce þær ymbutan unlytel dæl
sidre foldan geondsended wæs
bryne and brogan. Bearwas wurdon

---

[40] Bede, *In Genesim* III, 14.1-2, CCSL 118A, 182-3, summarized in Kay, *Dante's Swift and Strong*, 230-1.

[41] Bede, *In Genesim* IV, 19.17: 'Generaliter quidem incendium et perditio Sodomorum, de qua ereptus est Loth, poenam ultimae districtionis designat, quando, completa in fine seculi summa electorum, omnes impii aeternum rapiuntur in ignem ...' (In a general way, the fiery destruction of the Sodomites, from which Lot was rescued, indeed betokens the punishment of the Last Judgment, when, at the end of time the number of the elect having being fulfilled, all the impious are carried off into the eternal fire ...), CCSL 11A, 223, quoted in Kay, *Dante's Swift and Strong*, 285 n. 45, discussed in the same work, 231; see further *In Genesim* IV, 19.23-5, CCSL 118A, 226.

to axan and to yslan,   eorðan wæstma,
efne swa wide   swa ða witelac
reðe geræhton   rum land wera. (2542-57a)

Then I heard of the Lord of the sky send sulphur from heaven, and the black flame, surging fire, for men's punishment, because they had formerly provoked the Lord for a long time. The Ruler of souls gave retribution for that ... The flame carried off everything green that it [the flame] found in the rich cities, so that not a small part of the spacious earth around that place was covered by fire and terror. The groves, the produce of the earth, turned to ashes and to cinders, even as far as the angry punishments reached the spacious land of men.

The lines 'him þæs lean forgeald / gasta wealdend' immediately remind us of the poet's conclusion concerning Lucifer's fate: 'him þæs grim lean becom.'[42] Everything inside and outside the 'goldburgum' is swallowed up by the ferocious 'sweartne lig' (see also 1926b, 2417a, 2507b),[43] a composite of the darkness and the 'reade lige' (44a) to which Lucifer and his troop are exposed. Not surprisingly, nothing is left behind, as even the green surroundings are reduced to dark ashes and cinders. The moral sterility of the doomed people has led to the sterilization of everything fertile once associated with them, making the Plain of the Jordan hell on earth.

The *Genesis A* poet took a special interest in God's punishment of the evil who suffer from pride and *oblivio Dei*.[44] The sinners are excluded from His creative principle: the green earth promised to Adam and Noah is soon taken away from Cain and the inhabitants of Babel; it is temporarily submerged in the Flood and finally eradicated on the Plain of the Jordan. Earthly fertility can only be enjoyed by the pious; pride, blasphemy and luxury cause exile and even death. The link between propagation and man's moral behaviour is of

---

[42] Cf. Lucas, 'Loyalty and Obedience,' 125.

[43] The phrase *sweart lig* also occurs in *Christ C* where it refers once to the fire in hell, but three times to the fire at Judgment Day (*The Complete Corpus of Old English*, s. *lig*). It may therefore be argued that in *Christ C* the connection between the punishment of the fallen angels and the punishment of all sinful men at the end of salvation history, including the evil inhabitants of the two cities, is made.

[44] The story of Abilmelech and God's affliction of him and his nation with sterility is not discussed in this essay, as the poet keeps his references to the king's plight short and simple.

course made in the biblical source,[45] but, as has been argued in this essay, the consistent portrayal of human transgression and its subsequent punishment in terms of the first rebellion in heaven and the subsequent fall springs from the poet's own imagination. We are constantly reminded of the fact that God unleashed the powers of chaos against the first sinners and will repeat this process when human nature sins openly and without repentance. Even when, in the last scene, the poet presents the sacrifice of Isaac as an act prefiguring Christ's passion,[46] the dire consequences of *oblivio Dei* are not forgotten. Abraham, to whom God has already promised an 'ælgrene' land (1551a, 1787b) and a multitude of descendants in Canaan, is now commanded to hand Isaac over to the 'sweartan lige' (2858b). Only his unfaltering obedience to God's command releases him from his obligation and earns him 'ginfæstum gifum' (2920a) (liberal gifts) and 'lissum' (2921a) (joys). In the end, Abraham, unlike the devils and the inhabitants of Sodom and Gomorrah, can give thanks to God for the 'leana' (2934b) and 'sælða' (2935a) (blessings), granted him, his descendants, and, in a figurative sense, all the faithful. The extant poem therefore finishes with the clear message that the nature of the final *lean*, everlasting prosperity or eternal damnation, will always depend on the sincerity of man's belief in God.

---

[45] For a discussion of the theme of propagation and survival in the biblical Genesis, see Robert Alter, 'Sodom as Nexus: The Web of Design in Biblical Narrative,' in Jonathan Goldberg, ed., *Reclaiming Sodom* (New York and London 1994), 28-42.

[46] J.R. Hall, 'The Old English Epic of Redemption: The Theological Unity of MS Junius 11,' *Traditio* 32 (1976): 185-208, at 196. Both Hall and Doane (*Genesis A*, 324-5, note on l. 2936) argue that Genesis 22 with its emphasis on redemption provides an appropriate ending and in fact is a common stopping place in Genesis commentaries.

8

Odd Characters: Runes in Old English Poetry

ROBERT DiNAPOLI

The use of runes in some Old English poems offers hints as to how the poets regarded this strange and limited inheritance of pre-Christian literacy. To Christian authors such as Ælfric and Cynewulf, runes must have felt both familiar and uncanny. The conventions of scribal shorthand, whereby the scribe could use the runic characters *dæg* or *man*, for example, in place of the words themselves, point to two likelihoods: first, that the runic alphabet was familiar enough for a scribe to use it in what seems an almost offhand way, just as a modern writer might use an ampersand with no consciousness of its being a compressed form of the Latin word *et*;[1] second, that a knowledge of these runic characters and their names was sufficiently widespread to allow such scribal practices to develop in the first place.

For scribes raised in a tradition of Christian literacy as dominant as it was among the Anglo-Saxons after their conversion, such recourse to these other letters that had not come across the sea from Rome with Augustine and his missionaries demands further consideration. The Germanic tribes that occupied Britain in the wake of Rome's collapse had brought with them the practice of runic inscription, and no one can say with any certainty how much earlier still they had first taken it up. It is surely the case that runes in Anglo-Saxon England would have sported the patina of antiquity that the Anglo-Saxon imagination tended to cast over any artefact it saw as a relic of the deep past.

To consider how runes may have been used by pre-Christian Anglo-Saxons raises the oft-mooted and vexed questions of rune magic and Anglo-Saxon paganism. While virtually no direct evidence exists, Scandinavian

---

[1] We can also note in this context the very common scribal adaptation of the w- and th-runes in Anglo-Saxon manuscripts to represent sounds for which no equivalent in the Roman alphabet then existed, or the use of runes in manuscripts as reference marks. See R.I. Page, *An Introduction to English Runes* (London 1973), 213.

literary tradition does point to some intriguing possibilities. In the *Poetic Edda*, for example, *Hávamál* narrates how Óðinn acquired both the mead of poetry and mastery over the forces of nature through the occult manipulation of runes. Human characters in sagas, such as Egill Skallagrímsson, practise a species of rune magic as well. On the one hand, these literary treatments of the runic alphabet's occult power are too prevalent to have been wholly invented, but on the other hand, they appear in late medieval texts. Any attempt to reconstruct early Anglo-Saxon rune practice by inference from Scandinavian texts runs the double risk of, first, assuming too much about the possible similarities between those related but far from identical cultures and, second, of mistaking later literary imaginings for much older anthropological fact.

All of this would leave us in an apparently hopeless cul-de-sac, were it not for the possibility that our uncertainties about ancient rune practice may in fact be matched by those of the Anglo-Saxon poets whose own use of runes I wish to discuss. Apart from the commemorative inscriptions on stones and wrought artefacts, little direct evidence exists for the use of runes in Anglo-Saxon England outside the manuscript tradition. Whatever the early Anglo-Saxons might have done with their runes, the memory of their practice appears not to have survived the swift rise of Christian belief and ideology.

The Old English word *rūn* itself almost never denotes runic characters, for which the compound *rūnstæf* tends to be used instead. The most common meanings of *rūn* cover a broad semantic range, which includes 'a mystery,' 'a secret,' 'counsel,' or 'private counsel.'[2] These meanings are reflected by the Middle English verb *rownen*, 'to whisper,' often in a secretive or conspiratorial fashion. It is highly suggestive that the simple Old English noun that looks, from a modern vantage-point, as though it ought to mean 'runic character,'[3] actually possesses a range of meanings that could easily be associated with the esoteric lore and occult power that some have thought characteristic of early Germanic rune practice.

Thus we can at least say that the runic alphabet would have been familiar enough to become an unremarkable minor element of monastic scribal practice, yet by its mere presence it was also a reminder of past ages in

---

[2] BT, s. *rūn*, first gives 'a whisper (v. *rūnian*), hence speech not intended to be overheard, confidence, counsel, consultation.' Subsequent definitions under the same entry include 'a mystery' and 'a secret' (804). For *rūnstæf*, it simply offers 'a runic letter, a rune' (805).
[3] Though at first glance it looks as if it ought to be the ancestor of the modern English word for 'runic character,' it is not. Modern English *rune* was borrowed later from Old Norse.

which things were done differently. It is precisely this hazy association of runes with old pagan practice that Bede exploits in the fourth book of his *Ecclesiastical History.*[4] Bede relates a dramatic story about Ymma, a Northumbrian nobleman captured by his enemies in battle; his brother believes he has been killed and so has masses performed for the release of his soul from purgatory. As these masses are sung, the manacles binding the still-living Ymma fall away of their own accord, to the consternation of his captors, who then ask Ymma whether he has any 'litteras solutorias' (releasing letters) on his person. Bede's later Old English translators assume he is referring to some sort of small artefact on which runes with magical powers to unbind have been inscribed. In his discussion of this episode, Lerer points out how Bede draws an instructive contrast between pagan and Christian notions about the efficacy of language.[5] Pagan magic uses letters and words as manipulable counters of a power occult in its operations but worldly in its ends, while Christian doctrine uses language as a pointer to a higher reality whose spiritual powers are invoked through the words of liturgy and prayer.

A key element of Lerer's discussion is that, whatever the historical facts of pre-Christian rune use may have been, they have little or no bearing on how Bede and other Anglo-Saxon authors conceived them. Writers such as Bede display a generalized awareness that runes were somehow employed in pagan ritual magic, but they remain hazy on the specifics, interested as they are in making a strong and simple contrast between pagan past and Christian present.

The Rune Poem occupies a curious and ambiguous position among surviving Old English poetry.[6] Extant only in a seventeenth-century transcription by the antiquarian George Hickes, the poem consists of twenty-nine stanzas of usually three or four lines. Each stanza briefly explores aspects of one of the rune names and the sequence follows, with only a few displacements, the

---

[4] Bede, *Opera Historica,* ed. C. Plummer (Oxford 1896), 249-51. For a thorough discussion of this episode see Raymond Page, 'Anglo-Saxon Runes and Magic,' *Journal of the British Archaeological Association,* 3rd ser. 27 (1964): 14-31; repr. Page, *Runes and Runic Inscriptions: Collected Essays on Anglo-Saxon and Viking Runes* (Woodbridge 1995), 105-24.
[5] Seth Lerer, *Literacy and Power in Anglo-Saxon England* (Lincoln, NE 1991), esp. chap. 1, 'The Releasing Letters: Literate Authority in Bede's Story of Imma,' 30-60.
[6] Apart from the ASPR edition used here, see Margaret Halsall, *The Old English Rune Poem: A Critical Edition,* McMaster Old English Studies and Texts 2 (Toronto 1981).

traditional order of runes in the *futhorc*.[7] Key to each stanza is the 'X *bi∂* Y' formula that characterizes Anglo-Saxon wisdom poems such as *Precepts* and *Maxims*. Likewise, the propositions this formula predicates of the objects or concepts named by each rune often have a proverbial flavour.[8] A few of them speak with a cryptic indirectness that recalls the manner of Old English riddles.[9]

The Rune Poem has parallels in *The Icelandic Rune Poem* and *The Norwegian Rune Poem*.[10] These two poems appear to have served a mnemonic purpose. But while the Old English *Rune Poem* contains a few verses echoed in the Scandinavian poems, its lengthier treatment of each rune name may indicate that its author intended it to serve as more than just an aide-memoire. If the poet's intentions were more 'literary' in the modern sense, what might they have been? Among all the Anglo-Saxon poems that make use of runes, *The Rune Poem* is unique in its use of the traditional rune sequence as its overarching structural principle. Rather than using runes, the poem is generated by them, or, more precisely, by their names, which introduce a note of ambiguity from the outset, since each is the name of both a runic character on the page and an object, being, or concept in the world. In the first stanza the poet presses this ambiguity further:

·ᚠ· (feoh) byþ frofur   fira gehwylcum.
Sceal ðeah manna gehwylc   miclun hyt dælan
gif he wile for drihtne   domes hleotan. (*The Rune Poem* 1-3)

---

[7] The name *futhorc* (as well as the Scandinavian *futhark*) is derived from the first six characters in the traditional arrangement of the runes.

[8] Paul Cavill, *Maxims in Old English Poetry* (Cambridge 1999), points out that this characteristic 'X *bi∂* Y' formula links the Old English *Rune Poem* not only with Anglo-Saxon wisdom poetry but also with the Scandinavian rune poems, which, though they otherwise reflect traditions different from those that lie behind the Old English *Rune Poem*, make use of the same formula (152-4).

[9] See Paul Sorrell, 'Oaks, Ships, Riddles and the Old English Rune Poem,' *ASE* 19 (1990): 103-16.

[10] For a useful single-volume edition of Old English runic poetry that includes transcriptions and translations of the Icelandic and Norwegian poems, see *Anglo-Saxon Verse Runes*, ed. Louis J. Rodrigues (Felinfach 1992). See also Margaret Clunies Ross, 'The Anglo-Saxon and Norse Rune Poems: A Comparative Study,' *ASE* 19 (1990): 23-39. For a specific treatment of the Icelandic poem see R.I. Page, *The Icelandic Rune-Poem* (London 1999).

WEALTH (F)[11] is a comfort to every man, but nevertheless each must part with much if he wishes to play for his lord's good opinion.

While the opening line offers a fairly transparent observation about wealth in a proverbial manner, the next two complicate this notion of property as a comforting possession with the antithetical notion of parting with it. The underlying motive for such renunciation, a man's desire to 'play for his lord's good opinion,' opens up two familiarly divergent semantic possibilities. Is the poet referring to the heroic ideal's traditional insistence on liberality as a fundamental virtue in the mead hall? Or is the lord here God, and the parting with property an expression of the Church's diffident attitude towards worldly wealth? Neither possibility excludes the other, and if, as some believe, the verb *hleotan* carries further connotations of the kinds of sortilege that may have been practised with runes,[12] it is possible to see here a nuanced command of both Christian and pagan tradition broadly similar to that seen in *Beowulf*.[13]

A similar subtlety attends the poet's treatment of the o-rune. Its Old English name, *os* (god or divinity) occurs virtually nowhere else. Religious writers prefer the word *god* or traditional expressions for 'lord' (*dryhten*, *frea*, etc.), and *os* otherwise appears only in a metrical charm, which attributes a shooting pain to 'esa gescot' (*Metrical Charms* 4.23) (the shooting of the gods), alongside 'ylfa gescot' (4.23) (the shooting of the elves), and 'hægtessan gescot' (4.23-4) (the shooting of witches). Clearly the word fell into some disuse after the conversion, left to keep unsavoury company with the elves and witches of folk superstition. The author of *The Rune Poem*, however, executes a neat linguistic sidestep here, turning to the unrelated Latin homonym *os* (mouth) to create a multilayered conceptual pun:[14]

---

[11] In my translations, rune names appear in small capitals, followed by their roman letter equivalent in parentheses; words derived from runic characters appear in italics.

[12] See, for example, Marijane Osborn, '*Hleotan* and the Purpose of the Old English *Rune-Poem*,' *Folklore* 92 (1981): 168-73. The related noun *hlyt* gives us the modern English 'lot' (as in 'to cast lots').

[13] Roberta Frank, 'The *Beowulf* Poet's Sense of History,' in L.D. Benson and S. Wenzel, eds, *The Wisdom of Poetry: Essays in Early English Literature in Honor of Morton Bloomfield* (Kalamazoo 1982), 53-65, 271-7.

[14] Cf. Eric P. Hamp, 'On the Importance of *os* in the Structure of the Runic Poem,' *Studia Germanica Gandensia* 17 (1976): 143-51.

· ᚩ· (os) byþ ordfruma   ælcre spræce,
wisdomes wraþu   and witena frofur,
and eorla gehwam   eadnys and tohiht. (10-12)

The *mouth* is the origin of every speech, wisdom's prop and the
comfort of the wise, a blessing and a hope for every man.

These lines play a remarkable double game, first with the mouth as the
physical organ of speech and hence its source, but second with the older
resonance of the Anglo-Saxon word *os*, since the chief god of the Germanic
pantheon, Óðinn or Woden, like his Roman counterpart Mercury, was an
inspirer of poetry and eloquence.[15] At the same time, the God of Christianity
was characterized as the transcendent logos or Word named at the beginning
of John's Gospel. Roberta Frank has pointed out how some Old English
scriptural poets pun compulsively on *word* in ways that suggest precisely this
dimension of its meaning.[16] Christ as the Word was routinely imagined as the
inspirer of the written word (that is, Scripture), which forms the sole
foundation of wisdom in medieval Christian tradition, yet to read this pious
meaning into the text of *The Rune Poem* one has to look past the tidy
substitution of the Latin *os* for the Old English *os* and back to the original
meaning of the rune name with its banished pagan associations. The poet has
exploited the runic character as a point of fruitful overlap between his pagan
past and his Christian present.

Another notable exception to the poem's predominantly naturalistic and
secular mode is seen in the stanza on the m-rune:

·ᛗ· (man) byþ on myrgþe   his magan leof;
sceal þeah anra gehwylc   oðrum swican,
for ðam dryhten wyle   dome sine
þæt earme flæsc   eorþan betæcan. (59-62)

---

[15] See, for example, Snorri Sturluson's account in *Skáldskaparmál* (*Edda*, trans. Anthony Faulkes
[London 1987], 62-4) of Óðinn's theft of the mead of poetry, which he subsequently bestows upon
human poets.
[16] Roberta Frank, 'Some Uses of Paronomasia in Old English Scriptural Verse,' *Speculum* 47
(1972): 207-26, at 211-15.

A joyful MAN (**M**) is dear to his kinsman, but each is bound to betray the other, since the Lord desires, through his own decree, to consign the wretched flesh to the earth.

Here the poet appears to be voicing a Christian commonplace about human mortality and the transience of earthly comforts, presumably in the orthodox context of death's entry into the world as a consequence of Adam and Eve's fall, yet the explicit context is one of treason among kinsmen, not only the central motif of the story of Cain and Abel but also a staple villainy in the mead hall melodramas of the heroic tradition. Once again the perspectives of secular literary tradition and Christian reflection overlap in a fashion that leaves unclear which is the literal matter and which the figural.

To summarize, the runes in this poem act as triggers for verses which, while turning primarily to the world of human knowledge and experience, also hint at profound depths both before and behind. I find nothing in *The Rune Poem* to suggest that the poet's design comprised any deeply coded subtext, either Christian or pagan.[17] If these strange marks surviving from out of the murky mental hinterland of a pagan past meant anything specific to him, they indicated that particular focusing of imagination and thought that produces poetry.

The poets who composed the Old English riddles similarly depended on both the familiarity and the strangeness of runes to their audience. A simple example occurs in *Riddle 19*:[18]

Ic on siþe seah ·ᛋᚱᚠ
ᚾ· hygewloncne, heafodbeorhtne,
swiftne ofer sælwong swiþe þrægan.
Hæfde him on hrycge hildeþryþe —
·ᚻᚠᛗ· Nægledne rad
·ᚠᚷᛗᚦ· Widlæst ferede
rynestrong on rade rofne ·ᚻᚠ

[17] Cf. René Derolez, 'Runes and Magic,' *ANQ* 24 (1986): 96-102. For a contradictory opinion see Karl Schneider, *Die germanischen Runennamen: Versuch einer Gesamtdeutung. Ein Beitrag zur idg./germ. Kultur- und Religionsgeschichte* (Meisenheim-am-Glan 1956).
[18] For the texts of the riddles, I follow Craig Williamson's edition, *The Old English Riddles of the Exeter Book* (Chapel Hill 1977), though where Williamson's numbering differs from Krapp and Dobbie's I retain the latter.

ᚠᚫᚠᚾ· For wæs þy beorhtre,
swylcra siþfæt.   Saga hwæt hit hatte.

I saw a proud *horse*, bright of head, travel swift and strong across the
seal-plain. On its back it bore a mighty one in battle, a *man*. The
warrior[19] rode on a nailed creature. Swiftly flowing, the broad path
conveyed a valiant *hawk* on its road. Their journey was all the more
splendid, the voyaging of such as these. Say what it is called.

Here the runes serve as the first of several layers of encryption. Their angular
forms stand out against the curvilinear backdrop of the late tenth-century
minuscule hand of the *Exeter Book* scribe. He has set them off further with
pointing which, as Williamson notes (8-19), is used to distinguish runes used
individually (that is, with their names to be read as separate words) from runes
used as letters in word groups. The reader must first recognize the rune forms,
translate them into their Roman equivalents, and then realize that they must
be read backwards to produce words that fit both the metre and sense of the
lines.[20] To this the runes themselves provide a clue, since in traditional
practice, as seen on the Frank's Casket, rune rows can be read from right to
left as well as from left to right.[21]

    To reach the solution favoured by most editors, 'ship,' the reader must
apply conventions out of both the heroic tradition — where compounds for
ship involving an element that means 'horse' are common (for example,
brimhengest, sæmearh, yðhengest) — and, apparently, the riddle tradition itself,
where the convention of using the image of a hawk as camouflage for a ship's
sail may have been common (see my discussion of *Riddle 64* below). Even in
this fairly simple example, the runes function as much more than mere
alternatives to letters from the Roman alphabet, requiring their own distinct
species of interpretation and handling.

    Riddle 64, also commonly solved as 'ship,' uses a similar but slightly
more complex mode of runic encryption:

---

[19] I take the reversed WEGA indicated by the rune sequence in line 6a as a variant form of *wiga*
(warrior), following Williamson (190-1).
[20] On this aspect of *Riddles 19* and *64*, see Arthur G. Brodeur and Archer Taylor, 'The Man, The
Horse, and the Canary,' *California Folklore Quarterly* 2 (1943): 271-8.
[21] See, for instance, Alfred Becker, *Frank's Casket. Zum Runenkästchen von Auzon* (Regensberg
1973).

Ic seah · ᚹ· ond ·ᛁ·   ofer wong faran,
beran · ᛒ· and · ᛖ·   Bæm wæs on siþþe
hæbbendes hyht   · ᚻ· and · ᚪ·
swylce þryþa dæl.   · ᚦ· ond · ᛖ·
gefeah, · ᚠ· ond · ᚫ·   fleah ofer ·ᛠ
ᛋ· ond ·ᛈ·   sylfes þæs folces.

The pointing in the manuscript indicates that each rune is to be taken singly, either as its name or as the first letter of its name. For the riddle to work at all as verse, the full rune names are necessary, though they result in a few irregular lines.[22] To translate the poem in this fashion, however, leads to difficulties:

> I saw JOY (**W**) and ICE (**I**) travelling across a plain, carrying BIRCH (**B**) and a HORSE (**E**). For both on that journey the HAIL (**H**) and the OAK (**A**) were the owner's delight, and likewise a part of his power. The THORN (**TH**) and the HORSE (**E**) rejoiced; WEALTH (**F**) and the ASH (**Æ**) flew over the EARTH (**EA**), the SUN (**S**) and GAME (**P**)[23] of the whole company.

Cryptic, indeed. A correct reading requires the runes to be taken at their letter value in pairs, each pair providing the first two letters of the words they actually signify: WIcg (horse), BEorn (man/warrior), HAfoc (hawk), THEgn (retainer), FÆlcu (hawk), and EASpor (water-track or wak[24]). A translation along these lines would be:

> I saw a *horse* crossing a plain, bearing a *man*. For both of them on that voyage the *hawk* was the holder's joy, sharing its *power*. The *retainer* rejoiced; the *hawk* flew above the *wake* of all that company.

To solve the riddle is therefore to shatter the poem as a metrical construct, an extreme form of 'code breaking,' and the runic characters map out the

---

[22] Williamson, *Old English Riddles*, 188.
[23] I have followed the guess of most editors and runologists that the name of the p-rune, given in *The Rune Poem* as peorð (an otherwise unattested word), refers to a game or gaming piece. See Halsall, *Rune Poem*, 128, for a summary of critical discussion of this rune.
[24] I have followed Williamson's suggestion (326) that the EA-S pairing of runes represents the unattested compound *easpor*.

conceptual and linguistic (and almost visual) fault line along which this fracture must occur.[25] The runes can thus be said to signal a pressure point at which the demands of two competing necessities meet. *Riddle 64* ought to work as both a riddle and a poem, but it cannot do both at the same time, and we can probably discern in this unresolvable uncertainty some reflection of the runic alphabet's ambiguous status on the larger stage of Anglo-Saxon literacy and literature.

Yet another play of ambiguous multivalency attends the appearance of runes in *Riddle 24*, which all editors agree depicts a jay. It is the only riddle using runes whose solution speaks in the first person:

> Ic eom wunderlicu wiht — wræsne mine stefne:
> hwilum beorce swa hund,   hwilum blæte swa gat,
> hwilum græde swa gos,   hwilum gielle swa hafoc.
> Hwilum ic onhyrge   þone haswan earn,
> guðfugles hleoþor;   hwilum glidan reorde
> muþe gemæne,   hwilum mæwes song,
> þær ic glado sitte.   ·X· mec nemnað
> swylce ·Ᵽ· ond ·R· Ᵽ· fullesteð,
> ·N· ond ·l· Nu ic haten eom
> swa þa siex stafas   sweotule becnaþ.

I am a wondrous creature — I alter my voice: sometimes I bark like a dog, at times I bleat like a goat, at times I honk like a goose, at times I scream like a hawk. Sometimes I imitate the dusky eagle, the voice of the bird of war. Sometimes my mouth will counterfeit the voice of the kite, sometimes the seamew's song, where I sit rejoicing. A GIFT (**G**) names me, likewise the ASH (**Æ**) and the ROAD (**R**), the MOUTH (**O**), lends support, HAIL (**H**) and ICE (**I**). Now I am named, as these six letters clearly betoken.

The runes in this riddle supply the letters that spell out *higoræ*, the feminine form of the Old English word *higora* (jay). Unlike the runes in the two cryptic

---

[25] To an extent this is true of all the runic riddles, but in *Riddle 64* it is given extra prominence both by the pointing of the runes in the manuscript and by their evenly dense distribution across the poem's syntactic and metrical structures.

ship riddles these runes actually encode the answer, which thus lies in plain view.[26] But like the jay itself, they declare themselves in an oblique and disguised fashion that eludes instant identification. The riddle leaves open the question of *why* the jay sings in so many different voices: the quick rattle of clauses suggests sheer exuberance, but the jay's frequent and sudden shape- (or sound-) shifting might also hint at evasiveness and camouflage. Might this not also hint at the cultural circumstances of the Anglo-Saxon poet himself?[27] Like the runes he inhabits a *mearclond* or debatable ground between two antithetical traditions, and like the jay he sings in a voice not wholly his own, in that the structures and vocabulary of the poet's native tradition were of course ultimately co-opted to sing a new song in the manner of Bede's archetypal Christian poet Caedmon. In a previous article[28] I have discussed a number of riddles that appear to explore and celebrate the peculiar visionary powers that the poet's craft confers, quite independently of the scriptural and patristic foundations from which such powers would otherwise have to draw their authority. If such an interpretation of this riddle is possible, it is the poet's use of runes that brings the issue into sharp focus.

Nowhere does the sense of restless multiple ambiguities associated with runes stand out more vividly than in the runic 'signatures' that occur in the closing lines of the four poems attributed to Cynewulf. It must be acknowledged from the start that a strict interpretation of the manuscript evidence offers no absolute assurance that they are the signatures of a poet named Cynewulf or that the person or persons who composed them actually wrote the poems in which they occur. On the other hand, the runes and the passages enclosing them display sufficient similarities of treatment, content, and tone to leave those who would question their authenticity with more explaining to do than those who would accept them as miniature self-portraits by the poems' author.[29] Beyond this, it will not matter greatly to my argument whether the

---

[26] Some scholars, however, solve as 'woodpecker': e.g., Richard Wells, 'The Old English Riddles and Their Ornithological Content,' *Lore and Language* 2, no. 9 (1978): 57-67.

[27] Cf. Emma Sonke, 'Zu dem 25. Rätsel des Exeterbuchs,' *Englische Studien* 37 (1907): 313-18.

[28] 'In the Kingdom of the Blind, the One-Eyed Man Is a Seller of Garlic: Depth-Perception and the Poet's Perspective in the Exeter Book Riddles,' *ES* 81 (2000): 422-55.

[29] For a good summary of the issues raised by modern critics concerning the identity of Cynewulf and his status as author of the poems that bear his name, see Jacqueline A. Stodnick, 'Cynewulf as Author: Medieval Reality or Modern Myth?' *Bulletin of the John Rylands University Library of Manchester* 79 (1997): 25-39.

Cynewulf who names himself at the end of *Elene* is the poem's actual author or a fiction.

Cynewulf's self-presentation appears to be a unique phenomenon. Most Anglo-Saxon literature is anonymous, and where it is not there are usually other motives at play than those that lie behind our sense of an author's proprietorial relationship to his or her own work. The homilists Ælfric and Wulfstan, for example, attach their names to collections of their works as an assurance to their readers of sound doctrine and authority. Other poets who name themselves are patent fictions (Widsith) or likely ones (Deor).

Cynewulf's reasons for adding his signatures remain far from clear. In the signature passages to *Juliana* and *The Fates of the Apostles* he asks for his readers' 'help' in the face of impending divine judgment, in *Juliana* asking specifically for their prayers for his soul. It is widely assumed that all four signature passages, each of which addresses the theme of divine judgment, are requests for such prayer, either explicit or implicit. But this assumption begs the question of why, if he wished to identify himself to his audience for so urgent a purpose, Cynewulf would have concealed his name in runic acrostics that, as many critics have noted, recall the deployment of runic elements in the riddles. Some Anglo-Saxon scribes occasionally signed their work in runic colophons,[10] but their signatures appear utterly transparent alongside the sometimes baffling complexity of Cynewulf's. On the one hand, his runic characters cause the letters of his name to stand out from the text, both visually on the page and syntactically/semantically in the challenges they pose for any straightforward reading of the passages where they appear. Yet on the other hand, they resist easy analysis: usually out of sequence, sometimes in idiosyncratically arranged groups, they disintegrate and rearrange Cynewulf's name in a fashion that, on the face of it, suggests evasion as much as self-display.

Scholars have taken various views of this question. Frese and Elliott suggest that Cynewulf was aiming for specific literary effects, most specifically verbal and thematic echoes from the main body of the poems.[11] Lass suggests the possibility that Cynewulf made it hard for his hearers/listeners so that only

---

[10] René Derolez, *Runica Manuscripta* (Bruges 1954), 402ff.
[11] Dolores Warwick Frese, 'The Art of Cynewulf's Runic Signatures,' in Lewis E. Nicholson and Dolores Warwick Frese, eds, *Anglo-Saxon Poetry: Essays in Appreciation for John C. McGalliard* (Notre Dame 1975), 312-34, at 314. Ralph W.V. Elliott, 'Cynewulf's Runes in *Christ II* and *Elene*,' *ES* 34 (1953): 49-57, at 56-7.

those who could pray the most effectively — those with the diligence and concentration to crack his code — would be able to pray for him.[32] But the sheer verbal ingenuity Cynewulf displays in weaving the letters of his name into the fabric of his texts — greater, I would argue, than any analogous display in the riddles — seems to call greater attention to itself than either of these approaches allows. Cynewulf appears to be playing a double game, in ways that say as much about the status of runes and the native poetic tradition as they do about the poet's pious dread of imminent judgment.

I shall take as my example the passage that concludes *Elene*. Based on a lost earlier Latin text of the *Acta Quiriaci*,[33] the poem is narrated largely from the viewpoint of Judas, a wise Jewish resident of Jerusalem. Helena coerces him into revealing where the Cross was hidden and converting to Christianity, after which he takes the narrative lead, performing several miracles, debating with an enraged devil, and ultimately being ordained a bishop. Certain details Cynewulf has added to his source place extra emphasis on the role of Judas and his family as custodians of ancient and esoteric lore concerning a crucial juncture in their people's history. Cynewulf's treatment of the story confers on this lore a quasi-poetic character, handed down orally from generation to generation.[34]

The autobiographical opening of this concluding passage offers a telling glimpse of the Anglo-Saxon poet's mind at work and communicates the desperate effort demanded by the poet's craft:

Þus ic frod and fus   þurh þæt fæcne hus
wordcræftum wæf   ond wundrum læs,
þragum þreodude   ond geþanc reodode
nihtes nearwe. (1236-9)

---

[32] Roger Lass, 'Cyn(e)wulf Revisited: the Problem of the Runic Signatures,' in Graham Nixon and John Honey, eds, *An Historic Tongue: Studies in English Linguistics in Memory of Barbara Strang* (London and New York 1988), 17-30, at 26-7.

[33] *Acta Apocrypha Sancti Judae Quiriaci*, from AASS, Mai I, 445-8. This version is translated as the major source of *Elene* by M.J.B. Allen and Daniel G. Calder, *Sources and Analogues of Old English Poetry: The Major Latin Texts in Translation* (Cambridge 1976), 60-8.

[34] For a tentative analogy between Judas and Anglo-Saxon poets in the aftermath of the conversion, see Robert DiNapoli, 'Poesis and Authority: Some Traces of Anglo-Saxon *Agon* in Cynewulf's *Elene*,' *Neo* 82 (1998): 619-30.

Thus, old and eager, because of this treacherous body, I gathered and wove marvellously with the craft of words, pondered long and sifted my thoughts painstakingly at night.

His testimony is reminiscent of a passage in *The Order of the World* in which the poet, giving his counsel and example to an imagined would-be poet, issues a stern caution about the daunting rigours of the poetic enterprise:

> Forþon scyle ascian,   se þe on elne leofað,
> deophydig mon,   dygelra gesceafta,
> bewritan in gewitte   wordhordes cræft
> fæstnian ferðsefan,   þencan forð teala;
> ne sceal þæs aþreotan   þegn modigne,
> þæt he wislice   woruld fulgonge. (OrW 17-22)

Thus he who lives boldly, a man of subtle thought, must investigate mysterious creations, inscribe into his thoughts the power of language, secure it in his heart, ponder it endlessly. Nor must it exhaust the man of spirit that he wisely carry out his role on earth.

Cynewulf's first three and a half lines seem to embody this injunction. His account of his labours involves the cultivation not only of his craft but also of his own soul, in roughly equal proportions:

> Ic wæs weorcum fah,
> synnum asæled,   sorgum gewæled,
> bitrum gebunden,   bisgum beþrungen ... (*Elene* 1242-4)

I was tainted by my deeds, chained by my sins, immersed in sorrows, cuttingly bound and oppressed by cares ...

The poet achieves his work ultimately through God's grace, which enters him through a mind and a soul prepared by his preliminary struggle with words. This lonely and solitary endeavour is imaged in the nocturnal setting Cynewulf gives his labours. It is most certainly not the image of a scholar like Bede browsing peacefully through a garden of Latin sources. Rather, the language is that of the visionary. What divine guidance leads him to is not an

appropriate source but 'rumran geþeaht' (more spacious thought), expanded by
a personified wisdom.

> ... me lare onlag þurh leohtne had
> gamelum to geoce, gife unscynde
> mægencyning amæt ond on gemynd begeat,
> torht ontynde, tidum gerymde,
> bancofan onband, breostlocan onwand,
> leoðucræft onleac. (1245-50a)

... the mighty king bestowed lore on me in a luminous form as succour
to an old man, measured out an uncorrupted gift and implanted it in
my mind, unveiled it in its brilliance, enlarged it from time to time,
released my body, unwrapped my heart, and unlocked the craft of song.

For all the note of triumph in Cynewulf's account of how he came to
compose his poem, the note struck by the autobiographical passage as a whole
is distinctly valedictory. Certainly the lines incorporating his runic signature
sound a note of exhaustion.

> A wæs secg oð ðæt
> cnyssed cearwelmum, ·ᚳ· drusende,
> þeah he in medohealle maðmas þege,
> æplede gold. ·ᛁ· gnornode
> ·ᚾ· gefera, nearusorge dreah,
> enge rune, ær him · ᛗ· fore
> milpaðas mæt, modige þrægde
> wirum gewlenced. ·ᚹ· is geswiðrad,
> gomen æfter gearum, geogoð is gecyrred,
> ald onmedla. ·ᚢ· wæs geara
> geogoðhades glæm. Nu synt geardagas
> æfter fyrstmearce forð gewitene,
> lifwynne geliden, swa ·ᛚ· toglideð,
> flodas gefysde. · ᚠ· æghwam bið
> læne under lyfte. (1256-70a)

Always until then the man was pounded by waves of care, a guttering TORCH (C), even if he received gold-dappled treasures in the mead hall. The HORN (Y) lamented, his companion in NEED (N), enduring strangling sorrow, a desperate secret, while before him his HORSE (E) traversed the military roads,[35] raced proudly, tricked out with wires. JOY (W) has withered, amusement, with the years. Youth is altered, the old magnificence. Once the splendor of youth was OURS (U).[36] Now, after the allotted span, the days of yore are all completely spent, the gladness of life departed as WATER (L) flows away, floods driven on. To all beneath the sky WEALTH (F) is fleeting.

Cynewulf recreates his remembered younger self using the language and imagery of the heroic mode, but drained of its vital energies: he likens himself to a guttering torch, a horn that laments and shares the warrior's 'need' or 'necessity.' The horse's headlong gallop and the rushing water both dramatize the poet's swift loss of his youth. Cynewulf goes on in the following lines to associate these images of transitoriness with the theme of the failing world's headlong rush to Doomsday, and ends the poem with an anxious summary of the judgment God will then execute on humankind.

Somewhat as in *The Wanderer*, Cynewulf's sense of his own impending death leads him to contemplate the world's looming end and the day of judgment that will follow. But he engages in this contemplation with none of the frantic anxiety about his sins that attends his meditation on final judgment in *Juliana*. Despite whatever motives of penitence and pious humility he may have acted on when he recorded his name in this fashion, it is hard to imagine a more bravura act of poetic self-affirmation, a dramatic staking of the poet's claim to his own identity and powers. By using runic characters, Cynewulf also affirms the esoteric lore of his native Germanic heritage even as he bids it farewell. He uses the cultural associations of the

---

[35] For this translation see Andrew Breeze, '*Exodus, Elene*, and *The Rune Poem*: *milpæþ* "Army Road, Highway,"' *NQ* 236 (1991): 436-8.

[36] The u-rune, ᚢ, normally has the name *ur*, which refers to the aurochs. But since *ur* is virtually a homonym of *ure*, the Old English possessive pronoun 'ours,' I prefer to read this rune as the latter, especially as the context virtually demands it. Perhaps Cynewulf intended a pun on the two possibilities, since the aurochs could symbolize the kind of physical vigour and virility that characterize the youth whose passing Cynewulf marks here.

runic alphabet here to locate himself with a poignant exactitude on the mental watershed that divides the Anglo-Saxon poet's pagan past from his Christian present and future.

The common thread running through the poetic uses of runes I have discussed is ambiguity: the careful orchestration of antithetical elements in *The Rune Poem*; the use of runes in the Exeter Book Riddles to set up unresolvable tensions between the demands of grammar, metre, and semantics; and Cynewulf's psychologically charged use of runes to craft a double portrait of himself, both as a stricken penitent and as an accomplished poet. In all these instances of runic verse, the runic characters themselves function as focal points on a number of levels: the visual, the lexical, the metrical, and the thematic. The runes, for Anglo-Saxon poets at least, are ambiguity incarnate. However much assimilated to scribal and authorial practice in a monastic setting, their angular forms continue to point to their origins outside the cloister and outside the grand edifice of Christian literacy erected in Anglo-Saxon England by the Church. With only vague and scant knowledge of what the runes may have meant to their pagan forebears in the poetic craft, the poets who use them in surviving texts make them very much their own, emblems of an ancient and venerable verbal art whose authority they continued to honour alongside that of the institutional authorities of Scripture and the Church Fathers.

9

The Education of Beowulf and the Affair of the Leisure Class[1]

HARUKO MOMMA

1. A Prince of Peace in the Heroic Age

In the region of Anglo-Saxon studies *Beowulf* is a heavily ploughed field
where, after almost two hundred years of rich harvesting, the labourers are
often caught in the exasperating feeling that they have already gathered
everything to be yielded from the poem's 3182 lines, that they are now left
with little prospect for a new crop. In writing yet another essay on *Beowulf*, I
hope to draw inspiration from Roberta Frank's comment that 'there is always
the chance that one's own peculiar perspective may suggest new lines of
inquiry, add something ... to the small kernel of evidence that is safe to regard
as the established fact of *Beowulf* scholarship.'[2] It is now more than twenty
years ago that Frank shed new light on the character of Beowulf: while the
poet has made his champion 'authentically representative of the culture and
traditions of central Scandinavia,' this prototypical Northman is
simultaneously an anti-Odinic hero who, unlike characters in Old Norse
literature, values peace over fighting and 'insists on making friends of potential
foes.'[3]

An Odinic warrior would, for example, strike up a skirmish with a
coastguard who confronts him at the end of his journey, whereas Beowulf
almost immediately convinces the Danish lookout of the honourable intention
of his voyage and wins safe passage to the king's residence. At Heorot,

---

[1] I would like to thank Heide Estes for her comments and editorial assistance with this essay. I am
also grateful to Michael Matto for his valuable suggestions on the subject.
[2] Roberta Frank, 'Skaldic Verse and the Date of *Beowulf*,' in Colin Chase, ed., *The Dating of
Beowulf* (Toronto 1981), 123-39, at 123. This passage refers to the question of the date of
composition for the poem, but her statement may be applied, I believe, to the whole of *Beowulf*
scholarship.
[3] Ibid., 129 and 132.

Beowulf is verbally challenged by the king's *þyle*, but unlike his Scandinavian counterparts, he manages not only to win the flyting but also to secure Unferth's friendship — a course of events that puzzled one Scandinavianist as involving 'a sudden, unmotivated, and unexplained character change away from the prototypical evil Germanic counsellor.'[4] The Anglo-Saxon poet's presentation of his protagonist as a 'prince of peace,' Frank tells us, is 'perhaps the boldest manipulation of Scandinavian poetic convention in *Beowulf*.'[5]

The Scandinavian society depicted by the *Beowulf* poet is so realistic that it is often taken for an authentic reconstruction of the northern heroic age. But Frank has demonstrated that the world of *Beowulf*, despite its historical depth and geographical breadth, is no more than a verisimilitude crafted by the poet with his 'chronological acrobatics and fascination with cultural diversity.'[6] The protagonist in this historical fiction is characterized as a *novus homo* who, not unlike Deor or Widsith, guides us through the legendary North by letting us observe how 'he meets and mingles with the heroes of past time.'[7] This is how we learn about the famous 'breaker' or Breca, because the poet makes Beowulf compete with him as a boy. We also have a glimpse of Hrothulf, one of the most well-known heroes of the Scylding cycle, because the poet places him next to his uncle Hrothgar at the banquet held to celebrate Beowulf's victory over Grendel. In this sense *Beowulf* resembles the *Aeneid*, because it, too, reads like a period novel that is 'mythically presented, philosophically committed, and focused on the adventures of a new hero.'[8]

That observation, however, points to an apparent paradox in the historical framework of this Anglo-Saxon poem. On the one hand, *Beowulf* takes place in a sixth-century Scandinavia inhabited by warlike champions. On the other, its protagonist is a conflict-averting prince of peace whose prototype apparently does not exist in legends of the northern heroic age. This curious gap between character and setting seems to provide the impetus for the

---

[4] Ibid., 133; Peter A. Jorgensen, 'Beowulf's Swimming Contest with Breca: Old Norse Parallels,' *Folklore* 89 (1978): 52–9, at 52.

[5] Frank, 'Skaldic Verse,' 133.

[6] Roberta Frank, 'The *Beowulf* Poet's Sense of History,' in Larry D. Benson and Siegfried Wenzel, eds, *The Wisdom of Poetry: Essays in Early English Literature in Honor of Morton W. Bloomfield* (Kalamazoo, MI 1982), 53–65, at 56.

[7] Roberta Frank, 'Germanic Legend in Old English Literature,' in Malcolm Godden and Michael Lapidge, eds, *The Cambridge Companion to Old English Literature* (Cambridge 1991), 88–106, at 98.

[8] Frank, 'Sense of History,' 64.

unfolding of the poem, whose social and historical complexity has kept readers fascinated and confounded simultaneously since the dawn of *Beowulf* scholarship almost two centuries ago. The following is an attempt to interpret in a sociological light the subtle tension that seems to exist between the hero and his world.

2. A 'Barbarian' Hero and an 'Archaic' Hero

In considering the social structure of *Beowulf*, we have often relied on studies conducted in the realm of anthropology. While many of these studies have provided insight into the poem, such an approach tends to employ models, like gift exchange and potlatch, that are derived from 'stateless societies' and may therefore explain only partially the complexity of the society depicted in the poem.[9] Instead, I will refer to a socio-economic model that may have better applicability to medieval literature: namely, the theory of the leisure class proposed by the American economist Thorstein Veblen.[10] Despite its lasting influence on modern sociology, this theory is historical in perspective and is best used for the analysis of social phenomena as diachronic processes. According to Veblen, the institution of the leisure class rose and developed in 'barbarian' society, by which he means the form of communities immediately preceding the industrial era. In the theory of the leisure class, therefore, the whole of medieval Europe falls under the category of barbarism, although it exhibits various degrees of socio-economic evolution within itself.

Veblen explains that the leisure class emerged with the rise of social elites who have acquired 'a predatory habit of life' and become 'habituated to the infliction of injury by force and stratagem' (7-8). While the leisure class values prowess at all states of its evolution, those belonging to the early stage are particularly keen on demonstrating it in the aggressive acquisition of booty and other trophies, thus constantly appealing to an 'assertion of the strong hand' and approving the contest as an 'accredited, worthy form of self-assertion' (17). Through repeated predation, they will build a mechanism of strife in which 'the killing of formidable competitors' receives the highest

---

[9] Ross Samson, 'Economic Anthropology and Vikings,' in Ross Samson, ed., *Social Approaches to Viking Studies* (Glasgow 1991), 87-96, at 96.
[10] Thorstein Veblen, *The Theory of the Leisure Class: An Economic Study of Institutions* (New York 1899). Henceforward, references to this book will be given in the main text.

degree of honour and hence 'casts a glamour of worth over every act of slaughter and over all the tools and accessories of the act' (18). Having a tendency to equate 'honourable' with 'formidable,' they often employ honorific epithets in addressing a person with superior power, because these appellations 'very commonly impute a propensity for overbearing violence and an irresistible devastating force to the person who is to be propitiated' (18).

The leisure class gradually comes out of the 'predatory stage proper' when it makes improvements in productivity and other aspects of the economy. During this transitional period, the social elites are said to become less dependent on exploits, because they now derive more of their capital from new forms of industry such as 'an established chattel slavery, herds of cattle, and a servile class of herdsman and shepherds' (40). In order to gain maximum benefits from these new institutions of economy, members of the leisure class will try to develop a more stable society by making a 'formal observance of peace and order' (63). According to Veblen, the leisure class in pre-industrial culture reaches its evolutionary apex with the establishment of feudalism (1) But even this most advanced form of medieval society, he adds, cannot hope to reach beyond the level of 'quasi-peaceable' culture, because 'life at this stage ... has too much of coercion and class antagonism to be called peaceable in the full sense of the word' (63-4).

We may assume that the world of *Beowulf* falls somewhere between the 'predatory stage proper' and the most advanced stage of pre-industrial culture. On the one hand, it seems to have gone beyond the exclusively predatory level, because we recognize in it a certain degree of development in obtaining a land-based economy. On the other hand, it probably has not reached a stage that may comfortably be called feudal or quasi-peaceable, because the kings in the poem seem to have less sovereignty than liege lords in the High Middle Ages and are often unable to sustain stability despite their repeated efforts to promote peace by arranging political marriages or making treaties after inconclusive battles.[11] If the sixth-century Scandinavia of *Beowulf* is still far distanced from the quasi-peaceable stage of feudalism, we may wonder where the poet found a model for his peaceable character.

The choice made by the *Beowulf* poet marks an anomaly in Old English poetry, at least as we now have it, since he has brought in his

---

[11] The Finn episode, for example, offers a case against both strategies. See further John M. Hill, *The Cultural World in* Beowulf (Toronto 1995), 28-9.

protagonist from the land of folk tale. It has been suggested that certain incidents in the first half of *Beowulf* — such as the hero's fight with Grendel, his tearing off of his arm, and his descent into the monsters' lair — derive ultimately from the 'Bear's Son,' a story of a semi-animal character who is endowed with superhuman strength.[12] In the realm of medieval studies, folk tale is often treated as a (poor) neighbour of the heroic legend, but these two genres seem to differ in their socio-cultural outlook: the heroic ethos, as we have seen, may best be located in an intermediate stage of pre-industrial or 'barbarian' culture with lingering habits of predation; folk tale, in contrast, shows traits that seem to hearken back to a 'pre-barbarian,' archaic culture. According to Veblen, archaic society typically comprises small communities whose members are poor — and uniformly so, because 'individual ownership is not a dominant feature of their economic system.' People in archaic society are said to be 'commonly peaceable and sedentary' and demonstrate 'a certain amiable inefficiency when confronted with force or fraud' (7). Whether such a genuinely peaceable culture actually existed before the rise of the leisure class in northern Europe or was merely a product of human imagination that wished to see a golden age in an unretrievable past, folk tale is often set in a corner of the world where the only discord is caused by monsters and other nonhuman beings, and where even a king and his men are helpless in the face of aggression and wait for a powerful man to remove the threats so that everyone can live happily ever after. A hero in a peaceable culture, in other words, is a saviour of the people.

---

[12] The 'Bear's Son' thesis was first proposed by Friedrich Panzer in his *Studien zur germanischen Sagengeschichte*, vol. 1, *Beowulf* (Munich 1910). It has been pointed out that many motifs related to Grendel and his mother in *Beowulf* have their analogues in *Grettis saga* and several other Old Norse sagas: see, for example, G.N. Garmonsway, Jacqueline Simpson, and Hilda Ellis Davidson, Beowulf *and Its Analogues* (London 1980), 302-31. A consensus has yet to be reached on the exact relationship between the Anglo-Saxon poem and the Scandinavian prose narratives. For some of the theories on the relationship between *Beowulf* on the one hand and the Scandinavian sagas and the Bear's Son story on the other, see, among others, G.V. Smithers, *The Making of* Beowulf (Durham 1961), esp. 6-12, and Magnús Fjalldal, *The Long Arm of Coincidence: the Frustrated Connection between* Beowulf *and* Grettis saga (Toronto 1998). Another theory associates *Beowulf* with an Irish folk tale known as 'the Hand and the Child': on this, see R. Mark Scowcroft, 'The Irish Analogues to *Beowulf*,' *Speculum* 74 (1999): 22-64. The rivalry between the Germanic and Irish origins of the Grendel narrative does not affect our discussion here, since both stories belong to folk tale tradition.

3. The Hero's Inglorious Youth

Although both are historical narratives about the adventure of a new hero, the *Aeneid* and *Beowulf* are different in the way the authors chose their protagonists. Virgil drew his main character from long-established epic tradition, and particularly from the *Iliad*, where Aeneas already had a place in a royal house, a reputation as a good warrior, cultural sophistication, and even a glorious future prophesied by a god. This is not the case with Beowulf, however, for his name is virtually unknown in heroic legends set during the migration period.[13] In recruiting his protagonist from a different narrative tradition, the *Beowulf* poet has provided him with a noble lineage which would make him more than qualified for an 'archetypal Northman.'[14] But a closer look at his parentage reveals vestiges of his former life as a monster slayer. Beowulf, we are told, was born of a sister of the Geatish king, Hygelac. The presence of Hygelac in Beowulf's family tree may seem to us to add a touch of realism, because he has been identified as a historical figure — Chlochilaichus in Gregory of Tours's *History of the Franks* — who died in a raid on the continent in the early sixth century. For an Anglo-Saxon audience, however, Hygelac might have been yet another fabulous element in the poem, because this king was so famous for his extraordinary size that he was counted among the wonders of the world in the *Liber monstrorum*.[15] We all know that Beowulf's father was named Ecgtheow, thanks to the formula used to introduce the hero's speeches: 'Beowulf maþelode, bearn Ecgþeowes.'[16] But this recurrent long line also reminds us that Beowulf's name does not alliterate with his father's and hence underlines the hero's genealogical anomaly in comparison with many other characters in the poem, such as Hrothgar, son of Healfdene, or Wiglaf, son of Weohstan.[17]

---

[13] See, for example, Garmonsway et al., Beowulf *and its Analogues*, 91-112.

[14] Frank, 'Sense of History,' 64.

[15] For medieval references to Hygelac, including the *History of the Franks* and the *Liber monstrorum*, see Garmonsway et al., Beowulf *and its Analogues*, 112-15.

[16] The formula ('Beowulf, son of Ecgtheow, spoke') appears in lines 529, 631, 957, 1383, 1473, 1651, 1817, 1999, and 2425, with a few spelling variations. All the citations from *Beowulf* are taken from Elliott van Kirk Dobbie, *Beowulf and Judith*, ASPR 4 (New York 1953). All the translations are mine unless otherwise noted.

[17] It has been suggested that 'Beowulf' may etymologically mean 'bee-wolf,' and hence 'bear.' If so, the name might point to the character's old association with the animal. See, for example, Friedrich Klaeber, *Beowulf and the Fight at Finnsburg*, 3rd ed. (Lexington, MA 1950), xxv. See now R.D.

If Beowulf is a character taken from the land of folk tale and planted in the heroic world, he may have to be adjusted to the new climate and take roots in the new soil before playing his role as an *æþeling* who is to protect his people from adjacent tribes for half a century. In what follows, I will argue that the young Beowulf whom we encounter at the beginning of the poem is rather desperately in need of guidance to make the transition from a monster-fighting saviour to a warrior in the leisure class. A reading of the first half of *Beowulf* as a story of the development of a young hero — an evolutionary *Bildungsroman*, if you like — will add an extra layer of complexity, I believe, to a poem in which emphasis is often placed on the transformation of its main character in terms of age, namely from a young hero to an old king.

There is a passage in the text of *Beowulf* that seems to support such an interpretation. After Beowulf's triumphant homecoming, the narrator explicitly states that the hero endured a long period of abjection,

> swa hyne Geata bearn   godne ne tealdon,
> ne hyne on medobence   micles wyrðne
> [drih]ten Wedera   gedon wolde;
> swyðe [wen]don   þæt he sleac wære,
> æðeling unfrom.   (2184-8a)

since the sons of Geats did not consider him to be good, nor would the Geatish lord show him great honour on the mead bench: they were convinced that the prince was idle and listless.

The reference to the hero's inglorious youth has baffled *Beowulf* scholars for a long time. Some have questioned its very existence and offered alternative readings of the passage by rethinking its syntax or its grammatical tense.[18] Others have acknowledged the reference but expressed their reservations about its credibility. Even Klaeber contends that the 'introduction of the commonplace story of the sluggish youth is not very convincing' and surmises that the poet has added this motif to his narrative, despite its awkwardness,

---

Fulk and Joseph Harris, 'Beowulf's Name,' in David Donoghue, ed. and Seamus Heaney, trans., *Beowulf: A Verse Translation. Authoritative Text, Contexts, Criticism* (New York 2002), 98-100.
[18] For the former interpretation, see Norman E. Eliason, 'Beowulf's Inglorious Youth,' *Studies in Philology* 76 (1979): 101-8. For the latter, see Raymond P. Tripp, 'Did Beowulf Have an "Inglorious Youth"?' *Studia Neophilologica* 61 (1989): 129-43.

because it was a convention.[19] Klaeber supports his argument by citing Beowulf's self-assertion, made to Hrothgar at their first meeting, that he has accomplished many acts of bravery in his youth ('hæbbe ic mærða fela / ongunnen on geogoþe,' 408b-9a). While Klaeber praises Beowulf's claim as a 'proud self-introduction [which] is in line with the best epic usage' found in the *Aeneid* and the *Odyssey*,[20] an examination of the speech in question will reveal that the champion's boasting is slightly off the mark in the economic and cultural setting of the poem.

4. Beowulf's Resumé

In his first address to the Danish king, Beowulf focuses on two points. One is the magnitude of his physical strength ('mægenes cræft' 418a)[21] — a claim which conforms not only to the narrator's earlier remark that Beowulf is the strongest man alive on earth ('se wæs moncynnes mægenes strengest / on þæm dæge þysses lifes' 196-7), but also to the rumour brought to Hrothgar by seafarers that the son of Ecgtheow has the strength of thirty men in his hand grip.[22] The other point is his credentials in monster fighting: at one time, says Beowulf, he battled against the giant race and bound five of them; at another, he slew water-monsters in billows at night ('þær ic fife geband, / yðde eotena cyn ond on yðum slog / niceras nihtes' 420b-2a). Beowulf's self-introductory speech seems to suggest that our hero has spent much of his youth applying his physical strength to combatting monsters and other breeds of unfriendly creatures. He does not make any claim to have won fame by fighting enemies on behalf of his lord Hygelac. Nor does the narrator inform us about the protagonist's achievements in warfare, including the Geatish-Swedish conflict that erupted after the death of his grandfather Hrethel. In the decisive battle of this conflict, Eofor killed the Swedish king Ongentheow, and this Geatish thegn was given, in return for Ongentheow's war equipment, precious ornaments, land, and even Hygelac's only daughter in marriage (2484-9, 2961-

---

[19] Klaeber, *Beowulf*, 207 and xxvii n. 6.
[20] Ibid., 142.
[21] For the semantic range of *cræft*, see *DOE*, s.v.
[22] 'þonne sægdon þæt sæliþende ... þæt he XXXiges / manna mægencræft on his mundgripe / heaþorof hæbbe' (377-81a). The use of subjunctive for the verb *hæbbe* may imply that the seamen's account is more hearsay than a reliable report.

98). Regardless of the part he played in this war, Beowulf loses the only chance to become the king's son-in-law.

But the young Beowulf apparently takes little interest in such issues as contest, booty, and royal recognition. Even when he responds to Unferth's calumny concerning the competition he once had with Breca at sea, he dismisses the contest itself as a juvenile adventure and quickly moves on to his subsequent combat with the sea creatures that tried to feast on him at the bottom of the sea. It seems that Beowulf is less concerned with the outcome of the match than with the ramifications of his self-defence: by putting his assailants to sleep with sword edge, he was able, so he pronounces with a touch of pride, to eliminate water menaces from the area and to guarantee safe navigation for everyone. There is little wonder that seafaring men admire Beowulf and spread positive rumours about him.[23]

Beowulf's self-introduction also gives us the impression that the youth has built his reputation mainly on the popular level. According to Veblen, exploit is one of the most estimable virtues in the eyes of the populace at all stages of socio-cultural evolution (29-30). The leisure class, on the other hand, shares this sentiment only in its formative period but will come to place more emphasis on an effective application of exploit than on exploit itself when it begins to measure the 'basis of commonplace reputability' by the 'possession of wealth' (29). Beowulf explains to Hrothgar that in his homeland he was urged to undertake the expedition by 'my people, the best ones, the wise men' who were all eye-witnesses to his prowess (leode mine / þa selestan, snotere ceorlas 415b-6). This claim, again, agrees with the narrator's earlier statement that 'snotere ceorlas' (202b) are the ones who supported Beowulf's plan to fight Grendel despite their love of the prince. By using the appellation ceorl ('free man, churl'), however, the poet may imply that these men do not belong to the upper crust of Geatish nobility. He also seems to suggest that the wisdom of the Geatish sages pertains to such an unsophisticated and old-fashioned practice as watching omens.[24]

---

[23] Beowulf, in turn, seems to be partial to his reputation spread by the seafarers. At his death he requests that his barrow be built on a headland so that seafarers will thenceforward call the place Beowulf's cliff ('þæt hit sæliðend syððan hatan / Biowulfes biorh,' 2806-7b).

[24] *Snotere ceorlas* misjudge events elsewhere in the poem, as well: at the beginning of Heremod's reign, many a wise man held great expectations for the new king (907-13a); at the sight of blood in Grendel's mere, Hrothgar's sages assume that Beowulf has been killed by Grendel's mother and return to Heorot (1591-9).

It is even possible that the highest-ranking men in the Geatish kingdom did not show much favour to Beowulf's cause, which, because of its altruistic nature, was not likely to advance his social standing. There was, indeed, at least one Geat who openly objected to Beowulf's plan to visit Denmark: the king himself. Upon seeing his nephew alive and back from the expedition, the overjoyed Hygelac reveals the fact that he had repeatedly tried to dissuade his nephew from taking the journey because he did not have faith in such an enterprise. It would have been better, he thought, if the Danes had been left to solve the problem on their own (1992b-7a). Hygelac may have a point. After all, Hrothgar has managed to sustain his kingdom for twelve years despite a decrease in his retinue resulting from Grendel's assaults. All this while, the Danes had shared their living space with the monster in a daily rotation: 'during dark nights' (sweartum nihtum 167b), Grendel had been the sole occupant of Heorot excluding its *gifstol* (168a), and he would remove any violators (usually beer-emboldened warriors) by consuming them on the spot; at dawn he would leave the hall so that the king and his thegns could issue forth from the private quarters in the *burh* and resume their courtly life.

As this bizarre *Wohngemeinschaft* indicates, the monster from a primitive landscape cannot be incorporated into the Danish leisure class, because he refuses to engage in its socio-economic activities. He does not, for example, agree to pay *wergild*, even though his lair — no mean residence — is filled with precious objects. Unlike a *bana* who would strip the armour from his combatant and take it home as a trophy with which to enhance his prestige among his peers, Grendel shows no interest in war equipment or other man-made objects, because his loot is the body itself. Grendel's alienation in economic terms may explain why he is ultimately incapable of inflicting a fatal blow on the Danish throne. The real threat to Hrothgar is not the nightly marauder but his own nephew, who has partaken of his mead and received gifts from his hand.

From a socio-economic point of view, Beowulf's expedition has no set value at the time of his arrival in Denmark. The narrator is silent about the motivation of the fourteen *cempan* who have accompanied Beowulf on the dangerous mission, even though these 'keenest' (cenoste 206b) of Geatish warriors may well have regarded the expedition as being comparable to a war opportunity where they could expect to gain reward and win fame. But the poet allows Beowulf to lay out the reason for his journey: he has come to 'cleanse Heorot' (Heorot fælsian 432b), because he has learned that the 'affair of Grendel' (Grendles þing 409b) has forced the best of halls to stand 'idle and useless for every man' (rinca gehwylcum / idel ond unnyt 412b-13a) once the world becomes bereft of light.

Hrothgar responds to Beowulf's offer of selfless service with a factual statement that may at first sound irrelevant or even ungrateful: Beowulf's father Ecgtheow once visited his court as a friendless exile who had killed a Wulfing warrior and incurred the fear of war among his own people; he settled the feud by sending ancient treasure (ealde madmas 472a) to the Wulfings; and Ecgtheow swore him oaths (aþas swor 472b), presumably in response to the financial settlement. What Hrothgar seems to intend here, however, is to reinterpret the hero's rescue mission in the light of socio-economic reciprocity: the youth has come to repay his father's debt.[25] In his subsequent fights with the Grendel kin, Beowulf wins trophies but they have little market value: a gory arm of Grendel and the gory head of Grendel.[26] It is Hrothgar who places a price tag on these organic trophies by rewarding the champion with magnificent gifts.

5. A Lesson in Conspicuous Consumption

The expedition to Denmark turns out to be a stroke of luck for Beowulf's career plan, thanks largely to the king who takes an immense liking to this other-worldly youth. Upon receiving the news of Beowulf's arrival, Hrothgar proclaims his friendship with him and expresses his intention to award treasure for the hero's bravery. As soon as he exchanges salutatory speeches with the Geatish visitor, he invites him to a feast and seats him between his sons. After Beowulf's fight with Grendel, he even offers to honour him as a son in spirit ('on ferhþe' 948a). The admonition that he gives against pride after Beowulf's victory over Grendel's mother sounds as sincere as the tears he sheds at the hero's departure seem gneuine. While the ambiguous nature of Hrothgar's

---

[25] See, for example, John M. Hill, 'Hrothgar's Noble Rule: Love and the Great Legislator,' in Ross Samson, ed., *Social Approaches to Viking Studies* (Glasgow 1991), 169-78, at 172.

[26] Warriors in the heroic age apparently do not share intellectual curiosity with natural historians: after Beowulf's death, the Geats push the body of the fire dragon over the cliff into the sea (3131b-3). For the implications of Beowulf's trophies, see Rolf H. Bremmer, 'Grendel's Arm and the Law,' in M.J. Toswell and E.M. Tyler, eds, *Doubt Wisely: Papers in Honour of E.G. Stanley* (London and New York 1996), 121-32.

'spiritual adoption'[27] will be discussed in the next section, this self-appointed father-in-spirit of Beowulf does at least one thing which neither Ecgtheow, the hero's biological father, nor Hygelac, his de-facto foster father, managed: namely, to teach the youth how to become a respectable member of the leisure class.

For a young *æþeling* who has yet to figure out how to use his enormous potential for his own good, Heorot serves as a finishing school which offers pleasure and education in one package. In the poem, Denmark is a centre of civilization where pathways are paved with stones and the royal hall is adorned with gables. The Danish court even shows traits that are characteristic of an advanced stage of the pre-industrial leisure class. To begin with, the royal household makes a consistent effort to promote an orderly and peaceable ambience by emphasizing, to use Veblen's expression, 'manners and breeding, polite usage, decorum, and formal and ceremonial observances' (45-6). Hence, the official Wulfgar delivers a message after placing himself in front of the king ('for eaxlum' 358b) according to the custom of the court ('duguðe þeaw' 359b). During his sojourn, Beowulf is served by a hall thegn ('seleþegn,' 1794a) whose duty is to attend to the royal guest's personal needs for the sake of proprieties ('for andrysnum' 1796a). At banquets, seating seems to follow a strict hierarchical order (e.g., 491-2, 620-4, 1188-91, 2011-13). Entertainment is provided not only by the court poet (*scop*) but also by the king himself, who would from time to time recite wondrous stories in measured language, as he reminisces about his old exploits and bemoans the passing of his youth. If the Danish leisure class is an epitome of heroic culture in the poem, the grey-haired king may be seen as an embodiment of what Veblen calls 'the gentleman of leisure,' a man who has not only cultivated a good 'manner of life' by savouring 'qualitative excellence in eating, drinking, etc.' but also undergone proper 'training and intellectual activity' so that he is 'no longer simply the successful, aggressive male.'[28] The manner in which the Danish

---

[27] John M. Hill, 'Beowulf and the Danish Succession: Gift Giving as an Occasion for Complex Gesture,' *Medievalia et Humanistica* 11 (1982): 177-97, at 183.

[28] Veblen, *Leisure Class*, 74. In the poem, Hrothgar falls in the fourth generation of the Scylding dynasty. This royal house has been developed by a succession of monarchs who fulfilled obligations in their own generations: the eponymous king Scyld was a destitute child with no known parentage but he eventually made himself an overlord in the region by aggressively plundering neighbouring tribes; his son Beow took advantage of his father's reputation and wealth in his cultivation of the warriors' loyalty with generous gifts during his father's lifetime; his son Healfdene, in turn, begot

courtiers conduct feasting clearly makes a lasting impression on Beowulf. Upon his return to his uncle's court, he gives an enthusiastic account of the first feast he attended at Heorot:

'Werod wæs on wynne; ne seah ic widan feorh
under heofones hwealf healsittendra
medudream maran.' (2014-16a)

'The company was in bliss. Never in my entire life, under the vault of heaven, have I seen greater joy of mead among people seated in the hall.'

Feasting also provides the Danish leisure class with an opportunity to exercise conspicuous consumption, an economic activity that consists of the extravagant expenditure of material goods and leisure time in order to demonstrate the privileged status of the spenders. In an early stage of its development, Veblen explains, the leisure class focuses on the quantitative aspect of conspicuous consumption by squandering goods 'without stint' and 'in excess of the subsistence minimum.'[19] With the advancement of the economy, however, greater attention will be paid to the quality of goods to be consumed. By the time the institution of the leisure class reaches the quasi-peaceable level, its members have become accustomed to consuming both 'freely and of the best, in food, drink ... shelter, services, ornaments, apparel, weapons and accoutrements, amusements,' and more (73). It is evident that the Danish leisure class has gone beyond the simple, quantity-based level of conspicuous consumption: for example, while the king's residence seems to be

---

three sons and one daughter so as to secure his bloodline and promote friendship with an adjacent super power through political marriage.

[19] Ibid., 73. Men of substance at this stage may, however, already show some preference for 'better grades of goods' (ibid.). Veblen argues that alcoholic beverages are favoured for conspicuous consumption at all stages of economic development, because their costliness bestows honour and prestige on their consumers. The leisure class often considers drunkenness to be 'honorific, as being a mark, at the second remove, of the superior status of those who are able to afford the indulgence' (70). In the flyting scene, Beowulf subtly reprimands Unferth for the excessive consumption of beer: 'Hwæt! þu worn fela, wine min Unferð, / beore druncen ymb Brecan spræce' (530-1) (Well, my friend Unferth, you spoke a great deal about Breca after drinking beer). But the Danes apparently condone Unferth's inebriation. On drinking in *Beowulf*, see, for example, Hugh Magennis, 'The *Beowulf* Poet and His *druncne dryhtguman*,' *NM* 86 (1985): 159-64; and David Gould, 'Euphemistic Renderings of the Word *druncen* in *Beowulf*,' *NQ* 44 (1997): 443-50.

stocked with an endless supply of mead, wine, and beer, these alcoholic beverages are served by royal cupbearers ('byrelas' 1161b). In fact, many of the items ascribed to the advanced level of conspicuous consumption seem already familiar to the Danish aristocrats: Heorot is constructed with the latest technology and adorned with golden tapestries (771-5a, 994b-6); wine is poured 'from marvellous vessels' ('of wunderfatum' 1162a); weapons and precious ornaments are freely bestowed as gifts by the king and the queen on whomever they please.[10]

6. A Lesson in Dynasty Management

Hrothgar makes the offer of adoption while he stands on the doorsteps of Heorot and gazes at Grendel's severed hand:

> 'Nu ic, Beowulf, þec,
> secg betsta,   me for sunu wylle
> freogan on ferhþe.' (946b-8a)

> 'Now, Beowulf, I want to honour you, the best warrior, as a son in spirit.'

Hrothgar prefaces his proposal with contemplation of God's favour given to Beowulf's mother in childbirth (942a-6a) and concludes it with encouragement for Beowulf to embrace the new relationship ('heald forð tela / niwe sibbe' 948b-9a). Despite his enthusiastic tenor, Hrothgar does not explain the stipulations of his offer other than the tentative promise that he will grant the hero anything he desires, as long as it lies within his authority ('Ne bið þe nænigre gad / worolde wilna, þe ic geweald hæbbe' 949b-50).[11] The provisional nature of Hrothgar's promise should come as a surprise, since his kingdom does not lie in the land of folk tale where monster slayers are routinely awarded royal kinship through marriage. Hrothgar does have a

---

[10] Cf. Veblen, *Leisure Class*, 75.
[11] The narrator explains that Hrothgar built Heorot in order to dispense all kinds of gifts other than public land and people's lives (71-3). The importance of land and people — two major ingredients for an advanced stage of pre-industrial society — is confirmed by Wealhtheow in her address to Hrothgar quoted below.

daughter at a marriageable age, but he has already betrothed her to the Heathobard prince Ingeld in order to promote peace between the two tribes.

Hrothgar's announcement must be startling for the Danish court in general and for the queen in particular, since it may well be taken as a promise of the Danish throne to a foreigner. Rich, powerful, and determined to guard the property of her offspring (a sign of a competent member of the leisure class), Wealhtheow takes the next opportunity to remove any fear of having Beowulf replace her eldest son. With the queen's interference, the education of Beowulf becomes a family issue, and our hero catches glimpses of conflict at the heart of the Danish royal house. He is now enrolled in an elective course, entitled 'Dynastic Management 101,' which does count towards a degree in leisure-class sociology. During the celebration banquet held in honour of Beowulf, Wealhtheow announces her opinion of Hrothgar's proposal in front of the entire court. The elegant but forthright words in her 'wassailing' are worth quoting in full:

'Onfoh þissum fulle,   freodrihten min,
sinces brytta!   Þu on sælum wes,
goldwine gumena,   ond to Geatum spræc
mildum wordum,   swa sceal man don.
Beo wið Geatas glæd,   geofena gemyndig,
nean ond feorran   þu nu hafast.
Me man sægde,   þæt þu ðe for sunu wolde
hererinc habban.   Heorot is gefælsod,
beahsele beorhta;   bruc þenden þu mote
manigra medo,   ond þinum magum læf
folc ond rice,   þonne ðu forð scyle
metodsceaft seon.'   (1169-80a)

'Take this cup, my noble lord, dispenser of treasure! Be glad at heart, generous friend of men, and speak to the Geats with kind words in the way one must. Be courteous to the Geats; remember to bestow gifts which you now have from far and near. I was told that you wished to consider the warrior as a son. Heorot, the bright ring hall, is cleansed. Grant many rewards while you can, but leave the people and the kingdom for your kinsmen when you must depart to face the decree of fate.'

By using the phrase 'me man sægde' (someone told me), Wealhtheow subtly conveys the message that Hrothgar had not properly consulted her about the adoption in advance, since everyone knows that she accompanied her husband when the offer was made.[32] The queen also seizes the opportunity to make a reference to her nephew-in-law, Hrothulf, who is seated right next to Hrothgar, to the effect that she expects him to support her sons even after the king's death and, by implication, never to claim the throne. Finally, Wealhtheow offers a cup to Beowulf and grants him splendid gifts. While this action conforms to the queen's customary conduct, her 'wassailing' at this time has a different connotation, because it closely follows the procedure she has just prescribed to Hrothgar: speak to the Geat with kind words and reward him with precious objects, but nothing more. In her address to Beowulf, the queen acknowledges his now-established fame, wishes for his prosperity, and asks him to support her young sons. Her gracious words flow ceaselessly until her concluding remark:

'Her is æghwylc eorl oþrum getrywe,
modes milde,   mandrihtne hold;
þegnas syndon geþwære,   þeod ealgearo,
druncne dryhtguman   doð swa ic bidde.' (1228-31)

'Here every nobleman is faithful to others, gentle at heart, and loyal to his lord. The thegns are obedient, the people duty-bound; the feasting retainers will do what I ask.'

The poet makes no mention of Beowulf's response to the speech of the queen, his stepmother-in-spirit, but ends the scene with three laconic sentences: she went back to her seat; it was the most exquisite feast; and the men were drinking wine (1232-3a). Although the narrator never spells out Beowulf's expectations about Hrothgar's offer of adoption anywhere in the poem, it is likely that the prince correctly interprets Wealhtheow's speech as a deportation notice: he has completed his project towards the fulfilment of his degree, his student visa is about to expire, and she has a hall full of immigration officers

---

[32] Cf. Klaeber, *Beowulf*, 177, and Hill, 'Beowulf and the Danish Succession,' 186-7. In addition, Hrothgar may show some lack of tact when he praises Beowulf's mother in front of the queen, who has borne him two sons.

consisting of Danish courtiers who have been symbolically nourished with her wine. There is one place in the poem where Beowulf asks Hrothgar to take his father's position ('on fæder stæle' 1479b). But this request would take effect only if the hero lost his life fighting Grendel's mother, and even then the king's obligations would involve only the handling of movable property. Beowulf would be a son to Hrothgar only in death. Having survived the fight, he leaves Denmark at the next sunrise.

7. 'Þæt Wæs God Cyning'[33]

Beowulf returns home with a deeper understanding of his place in the Geatish leisure class. For Hygelac and his courtiers, Beowulf's report on his voyage, the longest speech in the poem,[34] must be a clear indication that this is not the idle youth they knew, but a prince with an impressive record behind him and enormous promise ahead. Beowulf's account of the Danish court shows that he has acquired a sophisticated sense of politics. For instance, he mildly censures Hrothgar for expecting lasting friendship with the Heathobards through the promise of his daughter's hand to Ingeld. A glance at Freawaru during the banquet seems sufficient for Beowulf to predict that this peace arrangement will be shattered at the wedding banquet by one of the bridegroom's thegns, who will reopen the old wound of feud at the sight of his father's sword carried by one of the bride's attendants. This is the first of several comments Beowulf makes to demonstrate, to use Roberta Frank's words, his 'remarkable sense of the past and of the future'; decades later, the old Beowulf traces the 'origins of the feud between the Swedes and Geats' by looking back two generations.[35] In addition, the royal house of Denmark seems to have taught the value of kinship to a Geatish prince who had earlier left his country without his uncle's endorsement. In his address to Hygelac, Beowulf never

---

[33] The formula 'þæt wæs god cyning' (that was a good king) occurs three times in the poem. In 11b, it is used as unconditional praise for Scyld. In 863b, the formula seems to function as somewhat qualified praise for Hrothgar. The third example, 2390b, is unconditional praise, but its referent may be ambiguous: does it refer to Beowulf, who is about to ascend, or has just ascended, to the Geatish throne, or to King Onela, who returned to Sweden after killing Heardred, so that Beowulf might rule the Geats?

[34] For the function of this and other speeches in *Beowulf*, see Robert E. Bjork, 'Speech as Gift in *Beowulf*,' *Speculum* 69 (1994): 993–1022.

[35] Frank, 'Germanic Legend,' 100.

mentions Hrothgar's offer of adoption but commends the Danish king on his conformity to customs ('þeawum' 2144b) in granting ample rewards for the service rendered by the hero. Even this restrained encomium is used by Beowulf as a prologue to the presentation of Hrothgar's gifts and the declaration of a pledge of loyalty to his uncle:

'Ða ic ðe, beorncyning,   bringan wylle,
estum geywan.   Gen is eall æt ðe
lissa gelong;   ic lyt hafo
heafodmaga   nefne, Hygelac, ðec.'   (2148-51)

'I want to bring them in and present them to you in good will,   lord of heroes. After all, my happiness depends entirely on you. I have few close kinsmen other than you, Hygelac.'

The treasure brought to Hygelac is already familiar to the audience, since it consists of the four gifts which the Danish king granted Beowulf after his fight with Grendel: a golden banner with a boar figure, a high battle-helmet, a grey corselet, and an adorned sword. But we learn something new about the war-dress ('hildesceorp' 2155a)[36] when Beowulf delivers a message from Hrothgar: the king of the Danes wants to inform the king of the Geats that these accoutrements of battle were long in the possession of the former king of Denmark, Heorogar, who did not, however, wish to bequeath them to his own son, Heoroweard.[37] Wrought in a coded language, this message echoes with the prediction Hrothgar made at Beowulf's departure: should Hygelac die of a battle wound or illness, the seafaring Geats would not have a better king to choose than Beowulf for the protection of their treasure (1845b-53a). At this point in the poem, Hrothgar's projection may sound more wistful than realistic: the premature death of Hygelac aside, how could the king of Denmark be certain that the Geats would favour Beowulf over the son of the deceased king? But Hrothgar's prophecy is supported by his political manoeuvres, both material and verbal. The endowment of treasure alone

---

[36] Hill argues that *hildesceorp* in 2155a refers not just to the corselet but to all the four gifts ('Beowulf and the Danish Succession,' 184). The exact reference of *hildesceorp* here does not, however, affect the following discussion.
[37] 2158-62a. For the poet's reference to Heoroweard, see Frank, 'Germanic Legend,' 103.

should elevate Beowulf's prestige in Geatish society significantly, since, to quote Veblen one last time, 'wealth acquired passively by transmission from ancestors or other antecedents ... becomes even more honorific than wealth acquired by the possessor's own effort' (29). By making Beowulf rehearse the origin of the war-dress in front of Hygelac, moreover, Hrothgar hopes to impart the extraordinary nature of the friendship his nephew has won with the Scylding dynasty. Hygelac is quick to decipher Hrothgar's message: in exchange for the Danish dynastic treasure, he bestows Beowulf with his own father's heirloom, the best sword found among the Geats (2190-3). After the ceremonial placement of this dynastic treasure on Beowulf's lap, Hygelac grants him 7000 hides of land (the equivalent of North Mercia, according to one reckoning[38]), complete with its own hall and its own throne ('bold ond bregostol' 2196a). The monster slayer has become a protofeudal lord who enjoys the blessing of hereditary land ('eðelwyn' 2493a).

8. Conclusion

The rest is history. The poet tells us that Beowulf, once given treasure and land, set his mind to repaying his debts to his uncle by fighting on the front line of every war (2490-8a). Even in the doomed expedition in which Hygelac loses his life, Beowulf manages to win the sword Nægling from the Frankish standard-bearer Dayraven (possibly his uncle's *bana*) and return home with armour he plundered from thirty men (2354b-68, 2501-8a). He remains loyal to Hygelac even after the king's death, as he declines Queen Hygd's plea to rule the kingdom but, instead, insists on serving her son Heardred as a guardian during his minority. It seems that Beowulf has taken to heart Wealhtheow's admonition (which had been directed to her nephew-in-law Hrothulf, who was not, somewhat ironically, to heed her words): a royal kinsman should never usurp the throne of an underage heir.

When Beowulf finally accepts the throne, he maintains the kingdom in a state of peace and prosperity for fifty years. Aside from his involvement in a Swedish dynastic feud to avenge his lord and kinsman Heardred (2391-6), Beowulf seems to maintain stability by warding off the neighbouring tribes

---

[38] See Thomas Miller, *The Old English Version of Bede's Ecclesiastical History of the English People*, EETS, o.s. 96 (London 1891), 240.

through virtue of his sheer authority (2733b-6a). As an old monarch, he ponders his reign with contentment because he has never caused hostility among his people by killing his own kinsmen or swearing false oaths (2736b-43a). Any one of his thegns would attest that Beowulf is a generous lord who constantly offers feasts and gifts (2633-8a, 2865-70). So Beowulf rules his people as a good heroic-age king should — until the dragon comes and summons him back to the primeval battlefield, where he stands as a monster slayer for the last time, without succour, without offspring, and without hope of peace beyond that day.

10

Articulate Contact in *Juliana*

ANTONINA HARBUS

Cynewulf's *Juliana* is a poem alive with the power of words. As in many other Old English literary saint's lives, direct discourse drives the narrative, and the choice and deployment of words appears to be at the heart of the poetic enterprise. This poem exploits verbal encounters on both these textual levels. Spoken words seem also to be implicated in the notion of sanctity that informs this text and shapes its didactic agenda. In *Juliana*, holiness is manifest in verbal straight-forwardness, combined with a tendency in her adversaries to use the spoken word to cajole, attack, or deceive the heroine. In a poem dominated by threats, insults, perceived blasphemies, and verbal abuse, encoded in a rich poetic vocabulary, confrontational speech acts' are a matter of course. Their conventionality, however, should not obscure what they say about the poet's views on language. Even in a text considered by modern readers to have a more dominantly didactic than aesthetic agenda,[2] the very construal of verbal exchange is part of the message that the text speaks to the reader. Of particular interest is the implied relationship between what is thought and what is said, and how the speech of others is interpreted.

In this language-centred text, Cynewulf seems to imagine a close connection between thought and speech. Here, speech appears to be conceptualized as part of the thought process itself rather than as a mere communication of preformed ideas. Both of these models of the thought/language relationship are considered in contemporary research to be

---

[1] See Marie Nelson, '*The Battle of Maldon* and *Juliana*: The Language of Confrontation,' in P.R. Brown, G.R. Crampton, and F.C. Robinson, eds, *Modes of Interpretation in Old English Literature: Essays in Honour of Stanley B. Greenfield* (Toronto 1986), 137-50.

[2] Modern critics are generally unimpressed by this poem: see, e.g., Claes Schaar, *Critical Studies in the Cynewulf Group* (Lund 1949), 326: 'Has a certain epic meagreness'; Rosemary Woolf, ed., *Cynewulf's Juliana* (London 1955; rev. edn Exeter 1977), 19: 'Its smooth competence is achieved at the expense of a certain thinness and lack of vigour and variety'; and C.L. Wrenn, *A Study of Old English Literature* (London 1967), 125: 'Lack of poetic quality.'

theoretically possible. Modern-day philosophers and linguists continue to debate this relationship, those of the semiotic view arguing that words are essentially signs of already constituted thoughts, others maintaining that speech itself constitutes rather than represents conscious reality. St Augustine presented the semiotic position in his *De doctrina christiana* and other writings.[3] It has been developed by the influential early twentieth-century writers C.S. Peirce and Ferdinand de Saussure, along with later semioticians.[4] Among those who have argued the latter position are Martin Heidegger and Hans-Georg Gadamer;[5] recently it has been refined by John Stewart and others in an argument for language as 'constitutive articulate contact.'[6] In this post-semiotic scheme, language is viewed as an element of thought rather than a representation of it, an interpretive and communicative event rather than a system of signification.[7] The semiotic view may be challenged precisely on the grounds that to consider language as a surrogate for experienced reality requires that consciousness exist outside language, which itself would have to be viewed as a tool; but 'one cannot be in a subject-object relationship with the very feature that characterizes us as human.'[8]

---

[3] Augustine's views were influential in the development of medieval sign theory. See the discussions in John M. Rist, *Augustine: Ancient Though Baptized* (Cambridge 1994), 23-40; Jesse M. Gellrich, *The Idea of the Book in the Middle Ages* (Ithaca 1985), 112-22; and Brian Stock, *Augustine the Reader* (Cambridge, MA and London 1996), 7-9 and 138-45.

[4] On the development of the semiotic view, see the relevant entries in Roy Harris and Talbot J. Taylor, *Landmarks in Linguistic Thought: The Western Tradition from Socrates to Saussure* (London 1989); and Floyd Merrell, *Peirce, Signs, and Meaning* (Toronto 1997).

[5] Martin Heidegger's dictum 'language is the house of being' ('Letter on Humanism,' in D.F. Krell, ed., *Basic Writings* [New York 1977], 193) has become a central idea in the debate. See also Heidegger, *On the Way to Language*, trans. Peter D. Hertz (New York 1971); Hans-Georg Gadamer, *Truth and Method*, trans. Joel Weinsheimer and D.G. Marshall (New York 1989); and Lev Vygotsky, *Thought and Language*, trans. Alex Kozulin (Cambridge, MA and London 1986), 218: 'Thought is not merely expressed in words; it comes into existence through them.'

[6] John Stewart, *Language as Articulate Contact: Towards a Post-Semiotic Philosophy of Communication* (Albany, NY 1995); and *Beyond the Symbol Model: Reflections on the Representational Nature of Language* (Albany, NY 1996). The subject is also debated by philosophers, psychologists, anthropologists, and linguists in Peter Carruthers and Jill Boucher, eds, *Language and Thought: Interdisciplinary Themes* (Cambridge 1998), where the two models are labelled respectively the 'communicative conception of language' and the 'cognitive conception.'

[7] Although this theory is still controversial, it builds on the ideas of respected philosophers and has been debated and endorsed by several communication theorists. See the articles and editorial responses in Stewart, ed., *Beyond the Symbol Model*.

[8] Stewart, *Language as Articulate Contact*, 115. Stewart goes on to explain: 'To be human is to be an understander, which is to engage in processes of coherence building or sense making, processes

Stewart's notion of articulate contact provides a useful entry into vernacular narrative poetics and a way of understanding Cynewulf's verse account of a spoken drama, at least by freeing a discussion of language from the implications of the symbolic model. For, despite Augustine's acknowledged theological influence in Anglo-Saxon England, there is no reason to presume that Cynewulf was acquainted with or accepted his philosophy of language or specifically his theory of signs.[9] Other considerations might have been uppermost in the poet's mind. His presentation of direct discourse brings immediacy to the story of Juliana's martyrdom on the didactic level, but it also provides clues on how verbal communication between the saint and others is conceived of in the poem and how thought comes alive in words. In his departures from his Latin source text, Cynewulf creates a 'dialogic' interpretation of the original,[10] which situates speech and its reception by others in the foreground.

As a vernacular reinterpretation of a conventional Latin *passio*, *Juliana* encodes Cynewulf's construal of the hagiographic message, as well as his artistic choices and assumptions about language. Although the identification of Cynewulf's source text has been a fraught issue, Michael Lapidge has recently identified and published an edition of a Latin version of the *Vita Iulianae* very similar to *Juliana* or perhaps the same as that used by Cynewulf: Paris, BN, lat. 10861, fols 113v-121r (early-ninth century).[11] This version seems to be even

---

that occur communicatively and that enable humans to constitute, maintain, and develop the words we inhabit.'

[9] Joseph F. Kelly, 'The Knowledge and Use of Augustine among the Anglo-Saxons,' in Elizabeth A. Livingstone, ed., *Studia Patristica*, vol. 28 (Leuven 1993), 211-16, describes the selective use of Augustinian philosophies among the Anglo-Saxons. See also Stewart, *Language as Articulate Contact*, 47-52.

[10] See Martine Irvine, *The Making of Textual Culture: 'Grammatica' and Literary Theory, 350-1100* (Cambridge 1994), 422-3, on dialogic or hybrid textuality, 'an internal dialogue between the discursive systems that make up Old English and Latin literary discourse' (423).

[11] Michael Lapidge, 'Cynewulf and the *Passio S. Iulianae*,' in Mark C. Amodio and Katherine O'Brien O'Keefee, eds, *Unlocking the Wordhoard: Anglo-Saxon Studies in Memory of Edward B. Irving Jr* (Toronto, 2003), 147-71. Prior to this find, the AASS version had been used as the closest available Latin source (Feb. II, 873-7). This is the version reprinted in William Strunk, ed., *The Juliana of Cynewulf* (London and Boston 1904), 33-49; and Woolf, *Cynewulf's Juliana*, p. 17, cites this AASS version, which is translated in M.J.B. Allen and D.G. Calder, *Sources and Analogues of Old English Poetry: The Major Latin Texts in Translation* (Cambridge 1976), 122-33. In the following discussion all citations from *Juliana* will be drawn from the ASPR edition (6:113-33); quotations from the Latin source are from Lapidge's edition; translations are my own.

closer to the probable text used by Cynewulf than the Cotton-Corpus version, which has been suggested as a possible source.[12] Lapidge's edition of the Parisian manuscript is most welcome, not only for consultation and comparison with *Juliana*, but also for filling in lacunae in *The Exeter Book*, the sole extant manuscript witness to the OE text.[13] Cynewulf's narrative modifications to his Latin source have been well scrutinized,[14] including some aspects of his use of speech,[15] though not the dynamic trinity of thought, language, and sanctity. One way of interpreting Cynewulf's text is within the models provided by John Searle's version of speech act theory, as Marie Nelson has done with respect to the presentation of confrontational speech in *Juliana*.[16] Nelson traces the development from requests to demands and threats in the poem and investigates the mediation of discord through language. Within a different theoretical model, A.H. Olsen has argued that, in this poem in

---

[12] The late ninth-century version of the text found in the mid-eleventh-century Worcester manuscript known as the Cotton Corpus Legendary (London, British Library, Cotton Nero E. 1 pt 1, fols 154v–7r) is also very similar to that used by Cynewulf, though no thorough survey has yet been undertaken. My own reading of the Cotton Corpus text indicates very few major variations between this and the Strunk/AASS text, but see Michael Lapidge, 'The Saintly Life in Anglo-Saxon England,' in Malcolm Godden and Michael Lapidge, eds, *The Cambridge Companion to Anglo-Saxon England* (Cambridge, 1991), 243-63, at 260; and E. Gordon Whatley, 'Iuliana,' in ed. F.M. Biggs et al., eds, *Sources of Anglo-Saxon Literary Culture* (Kalamazoo 2001), 1:276-8, where a further MS of this legendary is cited (Salisbury, Cathedral Library, MS 222), along with three other MSS of English provenance containing the Juliana legend.

[13] It appears that two leaves, each containing about seventy lines of poetry, are missing from the codex in its current form, one after line 288 and the other after line 558 in modern editions (Woolf, *Cynewulf's Juliana*, 1).

[14] See O. Glöde, 'Cynewulf's *Juliana* und ihre Quelle,' *Anglia* 11 (1889): 146-58; James M. Garnett, 'The Latin and Anglo-Saxon *Juliana*,' *PMLA* 14 (1899): 279-98; Lenore MacGaffey Abraham, 'Cynewulf's *Juliana*: A Case at Law,' *Allegorica* 3 (1978): 172-89; repr. Robert E. Bjork, ed., *Cynewulf: Basic Readings* (New York and London 1996), 171-92; Daniel Calder, *Cynewulf* (Boston, 1981), 75-103; Earl R. Anderson, *Cynewulf: Structure, Style, and Theme in His Poetry* (Rutherford 1983), 84-102; and John P. Hermann, 'Language and Spirituality in Cynewulf's *Juliana*,' *Texas Studies in Literature and Language* 26 (1984): 263-81.

[15] A.H. Olsen, *Speech, Song, and Poetic Craft: The Artistry of the Cynewulf Canon* (New York 1984); Robert E. Bjork, *The Old English Verse Saints' Lives: A Study in Direct Discourse and the Iconography of Style* (Toronto 1985), 45-61; A.H. Olsen, 'Cynewulf's Autonomous Women: A Reconsideration of Elene and Juliana,' in H. Damico and A.H. Olsen, eds, *New Readings on Women in Old English Literature* (Bloomington 1990), 222-32; and Nelson, 'The Battle of Maldon and Juliana.'

[16] Nelson, 'The Battle of Maldon and Juliana.' Cf. Barrie Ruth Straus, 'Women's Words as Weapons: Speech as Action in *The Wife's Lament*,' *Texas Studies in Language and Literature* 23 (1981): 268-85; repr. in Katherine O'Brien O'Keeffe, ed., *Old English Shorter Poems: Basic Readings* (New York and London 1994), 335-56.

particular, characters reveal their thoughts through speech.[17] Moving forward from the work of Nelson and Olsen, it is possible to look more closely at the narrative strategies employed by Cynewulf in terms of the articulate contact model of communication described above.

Within his rendering of the story into Old English poetry, Cynewulf's characters attempt to 'negotiate understanding'[18] through speech, though this is usually unsuccessful because no one is willing to modify his or her position. There exists a basic misunderstanding or misinterpretation of Juliana's thought by her three adversaries: her father, Affricanus; her suitor, Eleusius; and the devil who visits her in her cell. Conversely, the saint acknowledges, understands, and rejects the ideas of these three, but does not change her position in response, so very little negotiation occurs. As a result of these cross-purposes, the specific verbal encounters in this poem are confrontational rather than conciliatory.

This narrative shape derives from the Latin source, but the expression of the subject matter in Old English incorporates a heightened interest in the power of the spoken exchanges and the implications of verbal discord. For example, in the Latin source, the initial exchanges between Juliana and her suitor, Eleusius, are conducted through messengers and written proposals ('Transactis paucis diebus denuo misit ad eam' [§1, 47-50] [After a few days had passed, he sent to her again], and Juliana gives her reply through messengers who carry words 'ei mandauerat' [§2, 80-1] [she had commissioned for him]). In the poem, there is no mention of the messengers, but Juliana's reply is humiliatingly public ('Ond þæt word acwæð on wera mengu' [45] [And spoke these words amidst a host of men]).

Later, Eleusius complains to Juliana's father about this perceived insult. His speech (at lines 68b-77) is original in the Old English poem;[19] in the Latin, the exchange is merely reported ('Dixit ei omnia uerba quae ei mandauerat Juliana' [§2, 60-1] [Reported to him all the words which Juliana had commissioned for him]). In this interpretation of his source, Cynewulf construes the nature of Juliana's affront to her suitor: her words are her

---

[17] Olsen, *Speech, Song*, 108.
[18] Naomi Quinn and Dorothy Holland, 'Culture and Cognition,' in Holland and Quinn, eds, *Cultural Models in Language and Thought* (Cambridge 1987), 3-40, at 9.
[19] Also noted in Michael D. Cherniss, *Ingeld and Christ: Heroic Concepts and Values in Old English Christian Poetry* (The Hague and Paris 1972), 202.

'orwyrðu' (69a) (dishonour). Eleusius says: 'Me þa fraceðu sind / on modsefan mæste weorce' (71b-72) (These insults are distressing to the mind in the greatest degree). Juliana's own words, not her religious beliefs or her behaviour, constitute her wrongdoing. Her chief crime has been to insult Eleusius publicly by asking him to praise her God, a double verbal crime of asking inappropriately for the wrong kind of speech:

> 'Heo mec swa torne   tæle gerahte
> fore þissum folce,   het me fremdne god,
> ofer þa oþre   þe we ær cuþon,
> welum weorþian,   wordum lofian.' (73-6)

> 'She cruelly spoke to me of blasphemy before these people, commanded me to praise in words and fully honour a foreign god over those ones that we already know.'

The source of the conflict and the reason for Juliana's death is configured elsewhere in the poem as speech-based. The saint is punished and killed not for her ideas or her behaviour but for her words, particularly the way they are interpreted by Affricanus and Eleusius as disobedience, blasphemy, deception, and insult. Affricanus threatens not to spare his daughter if what Eleusius reports is true: 'Gif þas word sind soþ ... þe þu me sagast' (83b-4) (If those words are true ... which you spoke to me). This is a fairly close rendering of the Latin: 'Quod si uera sunt haec verba' (§2, 83) (If these words are true), but Cynewulf later develops the idea that words are equivalent to thought. Affricanus warns Juliana:

> 'Onwend þec in gewitte,   ond þa word oncyr
> þe þu unsnyttrum   ær gespræce,
> þa þu goda ussa   gield forhogdest.' (144-6)

> 'Change your mind and retract those words which you unwisely spoke previously when you showed contempt for the worship of our gods.'

The Latin mentions only Juliana's speech: 'Quod si permanseris in his sermonibus' (§2, 125) (If you persist in these remarks).

Later, Eleusius threatens Juliana with the idea that she deserves to die for her foolish and disrespectful words:

> 'Gen ic feores þe
> unnan wille,   þeah þu ær fela
> unwærlicra   worda gespræce.' (191b-3)

'Yet I will spare your life, though you previously spoke many foolish words.'

For Eleusius, the threat posed by Juliana is a verbal one. He says he will be compelled to punish her opprobrious speeches ('leahtorcwidum' 199a), threatening that if she continues to talk as she has,

> 'þonne ic nyde sceal   niþa gebæded
> on þære grimmestan   godscyld wrecan,
> torne teoncwide.' (203a-5a)

'then I will be impelled by enmity out of necessity to punish the most cruel impiety of your attacks, your grievous blasphemy.'

Once articulated, the effect of Juliana's speech on Eleusius is to produce anger and violence:

> Ða se æþeling wearð   yrre gebolgen,
> firendædum fah,   gehyrde þære fæmnan word. (58-9)

Then the nobleman became provoked by rage, stained by wicked deeds, heard the words of the maiden.

Words are equated with deeds: Juliana's speech constitutes her insult and disobedience. When the exchange is related to him by Eleusius, Affricanus likewise 'sweor æfter worde, / þære fæmnan fæder' (78b-9a) (became angry after those words, the father of the maiden).

In this story, Cynewulf explores the filial and social contract as it is tested through speech. Juliana's father had expressed his disappointment at his daughter's speech and he repays her in kind. When thwarted, the wrathful

Affricanus gives an answer that is the verbal opposite of a promised gift of jewellery:

> Hyre þa þurh yrre   ageaf ondsware
> fæder feondlice,   nales frætwe onheht. (117-18)

> Then her father in his wrath gave her an answer in a hostile way, by no means promised her jewels.

There is no precedent for this remark in the Latin source. In the poem, the father's speech constitutes his hostility. Juliana, however, maintains her even tone and consistent, truthful position. A little later during this exchange, Juliana's comment in the Latin that 'vere dico et non mentior' (§2, 132-3) (I speak truly and do not lie) becomes a more generalized expression of her commitment to truth in speech:

> 'Ic þe to soðe   secgan wille,
> bi me lifgendre   nelle ic lyge fremman.' (132-3)

> 'I will tell you truthfully, during my lifetime I will not tell a lie.'

Juliana construes her own speech as a direct expression of her position, a straightforward communication of meaning. Her consistent ideology arises from her strong faith, which has a bearing on the manner of her speech. The narrator says she gave her father an answer 'þurh gæstgehygd' (148a) (by means of spiritual reflection) when she refused to sacrifice to his pagan gods. The preposition þurh is difficult to construe precisely in this sort of collocation, but the phrase seems to suggest that while Juliana's declaration is informed by her spiritual conviction, her position with respect to her father's wishes and her danger are realized through her speech. Her perceived disobedience and blasphemy are brought into being by her words, even though her religious beliefs are already long-held. We had been told earlier: 'Hio in gæst bær / halge treow' (28b-9a) (She bore in her spirit holy faith), but this position is unproblematic until her faith is tested by a marriage proposal.

In her own estimation, the enunciation of allegiance is binding. Juliana refuses to pay lip service to her father's demand to worship pagan gods and expresses her understanding of the implications of any spoken promise:

'Næfre þu gelærest   þæt ic leasingum,
dumbum ond deafum   deofolgieldum,
gæsta geniðlum   gaful onhate.' (149-51)

'You will never teach that I should promise a tribute hypocritically to
deaf and dumb images of the devil, enemies of the soul.'

Here, Juliana configures faith as a spoken oath and considers genuine divinity
to be a speaking and hearing entity. The Latin source contains a similar idea,
though the emphasis on speech is missing: 'Non credo, non adoro, non
sacrifico idolis surdis et mutis' (§2, 149-52) (I do not believe in, I do not
revere, I do not sacrifice to deaf and dumb idols).

    Given the importance of the oath and pledge in Anglo-Saxon law,[20]
along with the possibility that Cynewulf has reshaped the legend of Juliana's
passio to conform to his local expectations of legal proceedings,[21] it is
unsurprising to find such value placed on speech in the text. One change
wrought by Cynewulf that seems at odds with this focus, though, is his
omission of all but the last of Juliana's own public speeches contained in his
Latin source.[22] Perhaps this pruning is to bring the narrative development into
line with Anglo-Saxon legal practices, but it might also be true that Cynewulf
was interested in presenting dialogue, or articulate contact, rather than formal
speeches, and therefore cut down Juliana's public addresses and enlarged the
dialogue portions of the story accordingly. The addition of dialogue between
Affricanus and Juliana near the beginning of the poem seems to support this
idea. Section 2 of the Latin text (about 250 words) is expanded into a lengthy
verbal battle (78-160a) that includes cajolery, threats, abuse, and expressions of
disgust.

    Juliana's declarative statements are perceived by her father and suitor as
verbal affronts, as they are perhaps intended to be: we do not see Juliana
moderating her discourse; even though she is aware of her contentious
ideological position, she remains unconcerned about its implications. Her

---

[20] Patrick Wormald, *The Making of English Law: King Alfred to the Twelfth Century*, Vol. 1,
Legislation and Its Limits (Oxford 1999), 283; further discussion is expected in Vol. II
(forthcoming); Peter Clemoes, *Interactions of Thought and Language in Old English Poetry*
(Cambridge 1995), 159.
[21] Abraham, 'Cynewulf's *Juliana*.' Cf. John P. Hermann, 'Language and Spirituality.'
[22] Abraham, 'Cynewulf's *Juliana*,' 187.

apparently inappropriate speech causes so much trouble precisely because it constitutes her ideas and intentions, an interpretation of the situation made explicit in Cynewulf's handling of the narrative. Her declaration of defiance and expression of belief at lines 210-24 conflates and expands two shorter speeches in the Latin (§4).

Although the initial line of attack by Affricanus and Eleusius in the Latin source is verbal, physical punishment quickly follows as a direct result of Juliana's uncompromising verbal position. Cynewulf downplays the torture and gruesome details found in his exemplar, which is typical of the genre of the female virgin *passio*. For example, the scourging ordered by Eleusius (at the beginning of §4) is rolled in with another torture, mentioned briefly as a beating inflicted while the saint is suspended by her hair (228-9). The scalding torture is omitted altogether, though the molten lead bath is described, with greater emphasis on the destruction of heathen onlookers than in the original (577b-89b).[23] The torture is generally less significant in the Old English poem; Cynewulf seems to be more interested in speech-based conflict. Even Juliana's reaction to the news of her imminent death is changed in the poem to reflect the receipt of speech. In the Latin source, Juliana is delighted that the end is near ('Audiens autem haec sancta Iuliana gaudens ualde dum adpropinquasset finis certaminis eius' [§19, 610-12] [But, hearing this, St Juliana rejoic[ed] greatly, while her certain death drew near]). In the Old English poem, she is delighted 'siþþan heo gehyrde hæleð eahtian / inwitrune' (609-10a) (when she heard the men consider the evil decision).

While Juliana and her father and suitor are at complete ideological loggerheads, there is better understanding between Juliana and the devil, which is why the scenes featuring their verbal tussling are perhaps the most interesting.[24] Although the saint's speech is privileged in the poem, in that the narrative provides an ideal platform for Juliana's sermonizing and the expression of her dogmatic point of view, the devil's confession to Juliana in her cell is the dominant centre of the poem.[25] One of Cynewulf's many apparent modifications of his source is the enhancement of the rhetorical skill of the devil,[26] yet there are other changes which emphasize his reactions to

---

[23] A further torture, breaking the woman's body on a wheel, may have been related within the second lacuna prior to line 559b, as the flame miracle is recounted just after this.
[24] T.A. Shippey, *Old English Verse* (London 1972), 172; and Woolf, *Cynewulf's Juliana*, 15.
[25] Occupying 43 per cent of the extant text according to one calculation (Anderson, *Cynewulf*, 85).
[26] Calder, *Cynweulf*, 96.

Juliana's speeches, specifically his construal of them as insults. The Latin request 'Noli me iam amplius omnibus hominibus ridiculum facere' (§12, 541) (Do not now make me even more ridiculous to all men) becomes a plea 'þæt þu furþer me fraceþu ne wyrce,/ edwit for eorlum' (541-2a) (that you do not produce further insults for me, reproaches before men).

Later, there is a further reference to the subjective interpretation of speech as insult when the narrator reports that Juliana 'gehyrde ... hearm galan helle deofol' (629) (heard ... the devil of hell screaming insults), and the devil himself laments that the saint will again overcome him 'yflum yrmþum' (634a) (with evil insults). The Latin has no reference to insults, but only to the saint's torture of the devil ('cruciatus fuerat ab illa' [§19, 614-15] [he had been tortured by her]), which he refers to as 'multa ... mala' (many ... evils) suffered at her hands. The devil's stress in *Juliana* on the power of words to humiliate is similar to the remarks made earlier by Eleusius and Affricanus about the saint's apparently inappropriate words. All three are likewise frustrated that they have been unable to change her speech.

The devil's speech is in some respects the evil twin of Juliana's perfect match between thought and word, in that it constitutes his sin rather than recounts it, just as Juliana's saintly talk is her holy virtue.[27] Because the devil deludes by persuasion, speech is his main weapon of destruction. He corrupts by urging people to use words wrongly. He uses persuasion to ensure that John the Baptist 'wordum styrde' (296b) (urged [Herod] in words) to believe that his marriage was unrighteous; and later the devil brought it about that Simon 'þa halgan weras hospe gerahte' (300) (addressed the holy men blasphemously). The devil uses words of persuasion to corrupt peoples' minds: 'we soðfæstra/ þurh misgedwield mod oncyrren' (325b-7) (through perversion we change the minds of those steadfast in truth). Juliana extracts the devil's confession of his past sins, his evil conquests: 'Þu scealt ondettan yfeldæda ma' (456) (You must confess more evil deeds). In a statement that neatly expresses the articulate contact model of communication, the devil says he cannot resist her words:

'Nu ic þæt gehyre þurh þinne hleoþorcwide,
þæt ic nyde sceal   niþa gebæded
mod meldian.' (461-3a)

---

[27] Cf. Bjork, *The Old English Verse Saints' Lives*, 54: 'Her words ... constitute the icon that expresses her.'

'Now by means of your speaking I hear that I must reveal my mind, forced by your attacks.'

In the Latin (§10), the saint physically beats the devil but there is no comment about speech as in the vernacular poem, where he sees that he must 'onwreon' (467a) (reveal) his evil deeds through words. Similarly, in the latter, part of the devil's own punishment is the necessity to recount his defeat to his demonic colleagues and to his superior: 'Magum to secgan,/ susles þegnum, hu him on siðe gelomp' (557b-8) (He must tell of his torment to his kinsmen, what had befallen him on his journey). This reference to articulated failure is original in the poem.

The devil uses speech to hide reality; Juliana uses it to communicate her own spiritual reality. Like many saints, particularly those featured in Old English poetry, Juliana exhibits verbal mastery as a chief attribute of sanctity.[28] She represents an articulate rather than a reflective model of sanctity, whose speech can deflect evil. This skill is seen in her ability to wrest from the devil the 'power of interrogation' when she deflects his questions and imposes her own.[29] Conversely, the evil of Affricanus, Eleusius, and the devil is embodied rather than just expressed in their speech,[30] and it is on this articulation of evil and its management by Juliana that Cynewulf seems to focus.

Apart from the added emphasis on dialogue, there are further references to speech in the poem. For example, when the saint is brought before Eleusius for the last time, the Latin has: 'Iussit praefectus Iulianam de carcere accersiri ad se' (§12, 530-2) (The prefect ordered Juliana to be fetched to him from the prison).[31] Cynewulf renders this as a further opportunity for speech between Christian and heathen:

> Ða se gerefa het,
> gealgmod guma,   Iulianan

---

[28] Bjork, *The Old English Verse Saints' Lives*, 46-9. See also Antonina Harbus, *The Life of the Mind in Old English Poetry* (Amsterdam and New York 2002), 91-8.

[29] Hermann, 'Language and Spirituality,' 276.

[30] Bjork, *The Old English Verse Saints' Lives*, 57: 'Words do not metamorphose in the mouth of Juliana as they do in the mouths of Affricanus and Eleusius.'

[31] The Cotton-Corpus text differs at this point: 'Misit prefectus iulianam de carcere eici, ut si forte inuenirent ipsam uiuentem adducerent illam ante tribunal suum' (fol. 156r, col. B) (The prefect ordered her to be thrown out of the prison so that if by chance they found her alive they could bring her before his tribunal). Cf. Strunk's MS M, quoted at 42 n. 4 of his edition.

of þam engan hofe   ut gelædan
on hyge halge   hæþnum to spræce
to his domsetle. (530b-4a)

Then the steward, the angry man, commanded that Juliana be led out
of the narrow dwelling in a holy mind for speech with the heathen at
his judgment seat.

Numerous other references to speech occur throughout the poem and
many have no precedent in the Latin source. Cynewulf's choice of diction to
express these spoken interactions of his characters is of particular interest,
especially his use of the term *word* itself and the compound terms based on it.
Taken together, this semantic information, as well as narration through direct
discourse and references to speaking, expresses the place of speech in the
grammar of thought. Cynewulf uses *word* to refer to holy decree ('ofer word
godes' [23a]; 'his halig word' [560b]); speech ('unwærlicra worda gespræce'
[193]); and, even more interesting, attitude or thought ('onwend þec in
gewitte, ond þa word oncyr' [144]); and perhaps both speech and thought
('gehyrde þære fæmnan word' [59b]).

The connotation 'thought' or 'attitude' appears not to have been within
the usual scope of Old English *word*, which has a relatively well-defined
semantic range, quite similar to the connotations of its modern-day reflex. BT
typically lists the definitions of *word*:

> I. a word, a single part of speech, a. a verb, b. a written word; II a
> word, a group of words forming a phrase, clause, sentence or sentences
> ... (5) report ... (8) word, solemn statement (9) promise, oath ... (10) an
> (expressed) intention; IIIa. language, style, b. where speech is
> contrasted with act or thought, IV word of God.[32]

Definition IIIb. is of interest here, as collocation with *dæd* (deed), *weorc*
(work), *gewitte*, (thought), and *geþoht* (thought) strongly suggests that the
connotation 'thought' was not within the semantic range of *word*. For II (10),

---

[32] J.R. Clark Hall, *A Concise Anglo-Saxon Dictionary*, 4th edn (Toronto 1960) and Henry Sweet, *The Student's Dictionary of Anglo-Saxon* (Oxford 1896), provide similar definitions; and Jane Roberts and Christian Kay with Lynne Grundy, *A Thesaurus of Old English*, 2 vols (London 1995) defines the term likewise, though it does cite *word* as 'an (expressed) intention' (06.02.06, 1:392).

'an (expressed) intention,' BT (s.v.) cites a handful of prose examples which are of a different character to its use in *Juliana* in that they communicate an intention rather than an ideological position.[13] Cynewulf uses *word* to refer to thought or intention as a binding declaration in a way that draws a conceptual if not a semantic connection between the two.

In Anglo-Saxon royal decrees the spoken word was considered to be significant as law.[14] In the broader legal context, the idiomatic collocation 'word ond weorc' nicely separates speech and deed in oath swearing.[15] In *Juliana*, however, the word is the deed: *word* connotes a solemn, immutable pledge and an immovable ideological position. In the saint's mind, speech is resolution. She says: 'Næfre þu ... mec onwende worda þissa' (55-7) (You will never turn me from these words). Earlier, as noted, Eleusius told her to change her mind and retract her words. These exchanges suggest that speech is morally, socially, and legally binding.[16]

Cynewulf uses simple words, not 'formulaic phrases' that emphasize the type of speech act.[17] He also uses *word* pleonastically with verbs of speech as in 'þæt word acwæð' (spoke the word) (45a; cf. 92b, 'þa worde cwæð'). There is nothing idiosyncratic about this; it is so common that it is considered to be a typical stylistic feature of Old English poetry (BT, s.v.) and operates in verbal play with like-sounding words such as *weard*, *woruld*, and *wyrd*.[18] But taken in conjunction with his other uses of *word*, these instances in *Juliana* keep the focus on the verbal, and also connect speech with thought and action.

Two poetic compounds containing *word* have a bearing on the power of speech in this context and reflect the verbal variation on negative or aggressive speech acts. The narrator invites the reader or hearer of the text to

---

[13] E.g., 'Wæs Eþelwald ðæs wordes, ðæt he no ðes rihtes wiðsacan nolde' (BT ref. is Chart. Th. 140; *DOE* ref. is Ch 1441 [HarmD 14] 19): 'Ethelwald declared his intention of not opposing the right' (BT, s. *word*, II.10).

[14] Simon Keynes, 'Royal Government and the Written Word in Late Anglo-Saxon England,' in Rosamond McKitterick, ed., *The Uses of Literacy in Early Medieval Europe* (Cambridge 1990), 226-58, at 243.

[15] Wormald, *The Making of English Law*, 1:283.

[16] Cf. the binding force of the uttered promise in the heroic context. Beowulf, for example, is morally committed to action once Unferth successfully goads him to articulate his intentions to fight, in contrast to Unferth's own empty boast (Beo, 601b-03a). See Harbus, *Life of the Mind*, 172.

[17] Olsen, *Speech, Song*, 91-5

[18] Roberta Frank, 'Some Uses of Paranomasia in Old English Scriptural Verse,' *Speculum* 47 (1972): 207-26, at 211-15.

hear the wrong-headed aggression in Eleusius's address to Juliana when he 'beotwordum spræc' (185a) (spoke threatening words), and 'hospwordum spræc' (189b) (spoke abusive words).[19] Both *bēotword* and *hospword* are rare poetic compounds.[40]

Cynewulf's *Juliana* is rich in other words denoting insult, blasphemy, or abuse. Eleusius construes Juliana's words as 'fraceðu' (71b) (insults) and 'tæle' (73b) (blasphemy), and is offended by her 'unwærlicra worda' (193) (foolish words), 'leahtorcwidum' (199a) (opprobrious speeches), 'godscyld' (204b) (blasphemy), 'torne teoncwide' (205a) (grievous blasphemy), which he says are conducted 'tælnissum' (205b) (slanderously) (and later in exasperation, Eleusius even blasphemes his own gods, ['tælde,' 598b]); the devil tricks Simon into speaking 'hospe' (300b) (blasphemously) and construes Juliana's interrogations as 'fraceðu' (541b) (insults), 'edwit' (542a) (reproaches), 'yflum yrmþum' (634a), (evil insults); and 'galan' (629a) (insults). These expressions for the wrong sort of speech focus the narrative interest on verbal discourse and the spoken drama of the story. They also suggest a focus on how ideological position informs the interpretation of another's speech.

To return to the idea of articulate contact, it may be argued that the interest shown by the poet in speech, and the presentation of most of the narrative through direct discourse, places the drama of the story within spoken communication. We as readers may give the power of the spoken words in this text their full measure by interpreting this discourse as intentional reality rather than as a signifier of an already constituted reality, thought. Juliana's words are her experience of the world: they constitute her engagement in dispute, as well as her perceived shame, blasphemy, and wrongdoing as articulated by her adversaries. Her control of speech and its misinterpretation by others sets her

---

[19] Cf. the construal of *bēotword* in *Beowulf*: 'A publicly declaimed self-definition in the form of a verbal commitment'; the word is considered to have a ritualistic function, 'a powerful positive social significance' (Barbara Nolan and Morton W. Bloomfield, '*Bēotword, Gilpcwidas*, and the *Gilphlæden Scop* of *Beowulf*,' *JEGP* 79 [1980]: 499–516, at 504 and 499).

[40] *Bēotword* occurs only once elsewhere in the extant corpus (Beo 2510b), as does *hospword* (And 1315b); cf. *hospcwide* (El 523b) (*MC*).

apart from them ideologically,[41] though all the characters share a direct verbal engagement in their own reality. Their speech makes them what they are.[42]

Cynewulf's presentation of speech in *Juliana* invites our construal of a prime role for spoken discourse in constructing as well as representing a person's character and ideological position. The threatening and abusive speech of Eleusius makes him as mad as a wild beast (rather than just acting in a beastly way),[43] the devil's work is in speech, and Juliana's steadfast hold on her version of the truth makes her the saint she is. This role of communication in the formation of individual identity works in concert with the diction and narrative form of the poem to present a model of verbal contact that places speech as an element of thought, not just a signifier of it. The grammar of thought in this vernacular interpretation of a Latin story is closely implicated in the power of speech with respect to oneself as well as to others. There is a close identification between words and ideas in the text. Words are significant on a semantic level, but also as objects constituting the self or an individual's interiority. On another level, words are important in the way they appear to have been construed by the poet himself.

Cynewulf's personal colophon (695b-731) also contributes to the power of direct speech in his poem and constructs a key role for spoken words in personal development. He enjoins those reciting his poem to say a prayer for him, a triple-decker speech act with cosmic consequences:

> Bidde ic monna gehwone
> gumena cynnes, þe þis gied wræce,
> þæt he mec neodful bi noman minum
> gemyne modig, ond meotud bidde
> þæt me heofena helm helpe gefremme
> meahta waldend, on þam miclan dæge. (718b-23)

---

[41] Cf. Bjork's comments on her verbal powers, 'her control of language'; and 'the fusing of her words and deeds' (*Old English Verse Saints' Lives*, 47, 49).
[42] Cf. the specifically verbalized identity of the female prophets of the Icelandic tradition, recorded for example in *Vǫluspá*. On the existence of prophetesses in Northern Germanic cultures, see Jenny Jochens, *Old Norse Images of Women* (Philadelphia 1996), esp. 41-4.
[43] In the Latin, Eleusius 'fremebat contra ipsam quasi fera maligna' (§18, p. 46) (howled at her like an evil beast); in the poem, he tore his clothes, gnashed his teeth, and 'wedde on gewitte swa wilde deor' (597-8a) (became mad in his mind like a wild beast).

I ask each member of the human race who delivers this poem that he, earnest and magnanimous, will remember me by name and entreat the lord that heaven's guardian, the ruler of powers, afford me help on that great day.

This conventional request is invigorated by the focus on spoken words in the text. It activates the traditional and didactic saint's life just recounted as a spiritually enabling form of speech. If it is true, as the poem suggests, that the more straightforwardly speech enunciates core truths, the nearer towards perfection one aspires, then uttering the poem and the prayer provides a benediction to both author and recipient of the text. This understanding of the didactic dynamic of the text helps to explain the way that prayer is perceived to be useful, as it is suggested at the end of the narrative: articulation can be a means of training and refining thought, rather than just a purely ritualistic utterance.

If the work of a philologist is 'trying to read the past through words' to achieve 'the kind of truth we can get from an autopsy or arson report,'[44] then perhaps this interpretation of Cynewulf's textual design and verbal care offers some insight into the intended or perceived role of the verse saint's life in personal spiritual development. The precise role, or probably roles, of *vitae* in religious practice is still not clearly understood, and the place of vernacular poetic celebrations of foreign and temporally remote saints like Juliana is even more difficult to fathom. The verse context must have contributed something to the didactic message, or at least increased palatability or ease of memorization. Alcuin tells us in his Preface to his *Life of Willibrord* that poetry was more suitable than prose as a catalyst for private meditation. He explains why he has produced two versions of the narrative, one in prose (for public use) and one in poetry (for private meditation):

> Unam prosaico sermone gradientem, qui puplice fratribus in ecclesia, si dignum tuae videatur sapientiae, legi potuisset; alterum Piereo pede currentem, qui in secreto cubili inter scolasticos tuos tantummodo ruminare debuisset.[45]

---

[44] Roberta Frank, 'The Unbearable Lightness of Being a Philologist,' *JEGP* 96 (1997): 486-513, at 513. *Passio*, arson, and autopsy might seem like natural bedfellows.
[45] Ed. W. Levison, MGH, Scriptores rerum Merovingicarum (Hanover and Leipzig 1919), 7:81-141, at 113.

One walking along in prose can be read publicly by the brothers in church, if it seems worthy to your wisdom. The other, running with the muse of poetry, your pupils can read over and over again privately in their rooms.[46]

But perhaps *Juliana*, evidently produced for a community of nuns,[47] was designed for reading aloud in public veneration rather than for private contemplation. The dialogue in the poem and its vernacular verse format lend themselves to incantation or recitation, and the dramatic aspect of much of the dialogue makes it suitable for an engaging public delivery to a suitably inclined audience. It is likely that Cynewulf has adjusted the take-home message of his source (especially playing down the torture in favour of Juliana's verbal skills), and it is evident that he has provided a personal request in the form of his colophon. The invitation to prayer in this final section of the poem articulates a nascent purpose of the saint's life: to encourage or invite prayer to the saint. Public recitation of the vernacular poetic saint's life with this personal conclusion must also have brought a very different response from the articulation of a Latin prose version or even an Old English prose text like one of the sermons of Ælfric.

If you are what you utter, as the articulate model of speech maintains, and aspire to holiness, then enunciating saints' lives might appear to be an ideal occupation, all the more so if the *vita* under consideration features an articulate, argumentative interlocutor who says what she thinks. Threats, insults, and other forms of verbal aggression must have spiced up the refectory at meal times or invigorated personal reading in a way that sober prose or declarative speeches were unable to do. Perhaps the potential for dramatic performance in *Juliana* lies behind its selection for vernacular adaptation by Cynewulf and possibly also the transmission of this text amongst the elegies, riddles, and other more obviously entertaining texts of *The Exeter Book*.[48]

---

[46] English translation by C.H. Talbot, in T.F.X. Noble and T. Head, eds, *Soldiers of Christ: Saints and Saints' Lives from Late Antiquity and the Early Middle Ages* (University Park, PA 1995), 189-211, at 190-1.

[47] Rosemary Woolf, 'Saints' Lives,' in E.G. Stanley, ed., *Continuations and Beginnings: Studies in Old English Literature* (London 1966), 37-66, at 45; and Hermann, 'Language and Spirituality,' 277.

[48] I would like to thank Carol Percy and Andrew Gillett for their comments on an earlier version of this essay.

Part IV — On Old Norse Literature

11

The Refracted Beam: Einarr Skúlason's Liturgical Theology

MARTIN CHASE

Everyone who knows anything about the twelfth-century Icelandic skald Einarr Skúlason agrees that he was one of the most learned men of his age, an assessment which his contemporaries clearly also shared. Unfortunately, nothing is known of how and where he acquired his learning. Biographical information found in *Þinga saga*, *Morkinskinna*, and *Skáldatal* tells us that although Einarr spent much of his life in diplomatic service as a travelling skald, he was also a priest. In addition to his training as a skald, he must have had the typical clerical education of his day.[1] Evidence for precisely what this may have entailed is unfortunately vague and scant. Schools had been opened in Iceland at Skálaholt, Haukadalr, and Oddi, but whether Einarr studied in Iceland or abroad is unknown. And even if we knew where Einarr studied, there would remain the question of what he was taught.

No course catalogues, syllabuses, or lesson plans survive from the eleventh- and twelfth-century schools, but scholars are gradually piecing together an idea of the curriculum from the evidence that does exist. One of the more helpful conclusions they are coming to share is that, in the wake of the tenth-century monastic reforms, education in the monastic schools of western Europe and England was remarkably uniform. Furthermore, the parish and episcopal schools followed the pattern set in the monasteries.[2] Therefore, bits of information gleaned about a particular school can be applied (cautiously and tentatively) in general.

---

[1] Gustav Storm, *Sigurd Ranessöns Proces* (Kristiania 1877), 16; Finnur Jónsson, ed., *Morkinskinna* (Copenhagen 1932), 390-1; *Diplomatarium Islandicum* (Copenhagen 1857-76), 1:186.
[2] See, e.g., George Hardin Brown, 'The Dynamics of Literacy in Anglo-Saxon England,' *Bulletin of the John Rylands Universiy Library of Manchester* 77 (1995): 109-42.

The study of *grammatica* and its effect on skaldic poetry has received
increasing attention in recent years.[3] Studies have tended to focus on the use of
poetic manuals in the teaching of *grammatica*, but they have also shown that
the Psalter and the hymnary were equally significant. As I hope to show, the
apparent influence of the hymnary on Einarr Skúlason's major poem, *Geisli*,[4]
reveals his familiarity with the hymns and suggests a background for his
theology.[5] I am pleased to contribute this brief study in honour of Roberta
Frank. As my teacher she showed me how to unfold a skaldic verse like an
infinite Chinese box,[6] and her delight in the complex interplay of Latin and
vernacular, Christian and pagan, English and Nordic continues to be
contagious.[7]

Liturgical scholars like Helmut Gneuss,[8] Margot H. King,[9] George
Hardin Brown,[10] and Susan Boynton[11] have shown just how prominently the

---

[3] See especially Guðrún Nordal, *Tools of Literacy: The Role of Skaldic Verse in Icelandic Textual Culture of the Twelfth and Thirteenth Centuries* (Toronto 2001).

[4] Finnur Jónsson, ed., *Den Norsk-Islandske Skjaldedigtning, B: Rettet Tekst* (Copenhagen 1912-15, rpt. Copenhagen 1973), 1:427-45.

[5] Another aspect of Einarr's learning, also related to the study of *grammatica*, is even more difficult to assess. The evidence of a strong cultural relationship between Iceland and Denmark has long been acknowledged in prose texts from both sides, such as *Skjoldunga saga* and Saxo's *Gesta Danorum*, and Guðrún Nordal has recently suggested that there is evidence of this relationship in skaldic poetry as well (Nordal, *Tools of Literacy*, 310-11). In particular, she sees this in the gold-kennings of twelfth- and thirteenth-century skaldic verse: the kennings often allude to Danish mythological figures like Sigurðr, Helgi, Ragnar loðbrók, and Fróði (309-38). The close association of the poems with Danish texts suggests that they were composed in the context of the early textual culture in Iceland that used the Danish texts for inspiration (319). Kennings for gold figure prominently in *Geisli*, and this may be evidence that Einarr's education also included the antiquarian study of Danish myth: *Geisli*'s gold-kennings focus on the story of Sigurðr Fáfnisbani. In addition, *Geisli* contains a high proportion of *heiti* which are primarily associated with heroic and mythological poems.

[6] See Roberta Frank, *Old Norse Court Poetry: The Dróttkvætt Stanza*. Islandica 42 (Ithaca, NY 1978), 29.

[7] Despite the egalitarian undertones of Professor Frank's now-famous entomological metaphor of termite fecal pellets and the value of collective intelligence (see Frank, 'Skaldic Poetry,' in Carol J. Clover and John Lindow, eds, *Old Norse-Icelandic Literature* [Ithaca, NY 1985], 157-96, at 184), much of the collaborative progress in skaldic studies over the past many years is the direct result of her inspiration and leadership.

[8] Helmut Gneuss, *Hymnar und Hymnen im Englischen Mittelalter* (Tübingen 1968).

[9] Margot H. King, 'Grammatica Mystica: A Study of Bede's Grammatical Curriculum,' in Margot H. King and Wesley M. Stevens, eds, *Saints and Scholars* (Collegeville, MN 1979) 1:145-59.

[10] Brown, 'Dynamics of Literacy.'

[11] Susan Boynton, 'Glossed Hymns in Eleventh-Century Continental Hymnaries' (Diss., Brandeis

texts of the Divine Office figured in monastic education in England and on the continent, and evidence from *Jóns saga* suggests that this is true of Iceland, as well:

> Heilagr Jón byskup tók marga menn til læríngar ok fekk til góða meistara at kenna þeim: Gísla Finnason, er fyr gátum vér, at kenna grammaticam, en einn franzeis, Rikinna prest, kapulan sinn ok ástvin, at kenna söng eða versagerð, því at hann var ok hinn mesti lærdomsmáðr ... Ok þegar er til var ríngt tíða, þá kómu þeir þar allir ok fluttu fram tíðir sínar með miklum athuga. Var ekki at heyra í kórinn nema fagr söngr ok heilagt bænahald. Inir ellri menn kunnu sér at vera vel siðaðir, en smásveinar varu svá hirtir af meistörum sínum, at þeir skyldu eigi treystask með gáleysi at fara.

> The holy bishop Jón took many men as students, and he got good masters to teach them: Gísli Finnason, whom we mentioned earlier, to teach *grammatica*, and a Frenchman, the priest Rikini, his chaplain and close friend, to teach song or verse-making, because he was also a man of great learning ... And whenever the bell rang for choir, they all came and performed the office with great attention — nothing was to be heard in the choir but beautiful song and holy prayer. The older men were clearly well accustomed to it, and the boys were so well disciplined by their masters that there was no need to fear that they would not pay attention.[12]

The new pupil in a monastic or cathedral school typically began his education by committing the hymnary and the Psalter to memory. Participation in the liturgy was not the only goal: once these basic texts had been drummed in, they formed a ready frame of reference for the teaching of Latin vocabulary, grammar, rhetoric, metrics, poetic composition (it is not coincidental that Bishop Jón's students interrupted their study of poetics to sing hymns and psalms), and eventually, theology. Familiar texts like Bede's

---

University 1997); 'Latin Glosses on the Office Hymns in Eleventh-Century Continental Hymnaries,' *The Journal of Medieval Latin* 11 (2001): 1-26.

[12] *Biskupa Sögur*, ed. Sigurgeir Steingrímsson, Ólafur Halsórsson, and Peter Foote, ÍF 15 (Reykjavík 2003), 1-2. The English translations throughout are my own.

De schematibus et tropis[13] bear witness to the use of the Psalter in the teaching of poetics, but the office hymns were equally important. The contents of the hymnary were not as strictly defined as the 150 psalms of the canonical Psalter.

The 'New Hymnary' that emerged in the wake of tenth-century reforms varied somewhat from place to place according to local usage. Nevertheless, it is possible to speak of a core repertory, which we can assume that anyone who had studied at a European school would have known.[14] The New Hymnary in its Scandinavian and English forms was roughly the size of the Psalter, and contained about 150 hymns.[15] Since the hymns were used to teach theology, debates (notably the ninth-century Trinitarian controversies) about their contents had led to the establishment of a quasi-canonical list,[16] and, as with skaldic poetry, the demands of rhyme and metre helped to keep textual variants to a minimum. Thus, even though there is no hard evidence for what Einarr Skúlason studied or where, we are not too far out on a limb in assuming his familiarity with the hymns of the New Hymnary. Indeed, the existence of a specific body of verse that was deeply etched into the minds of all literate Europeans provides the background for one of the most significant (and least studied) verbal encounters of the central Middle Ages. It is hard to imagine that the Latin hymns are not in some way related to all the poetry, vernacular as well as Latin, written during this period.

The guiding metaphor of *Geisli* is the sunbeam, and much of the light imagery of the *drápa* reflects the influence of the Latin hymnary. Light is by far the most common image in the hymns — there are few indeed that do not contain some form of it. Not surprisingly, light imagery figures most prominently in the hymns for lauds and vespers, the offices sung at daybreak and sunset. Most of the light imagery of these hymns is associated with one or more of four themes: the theology of the Trinity, the struggle between forces of good and evil, the 'enlightenment' of the human mind or spirit, and the reflection of divine light in the lives of apostles and saints.

---

[13] *Bede, Opera Didascalica*, ed. C.B. Kendall, CCSL 123 (Turnholt 1975), 142-71.

[14] Boynton, 'Latin Glosses,' 1-2.

[15] Lilli Gjerløw, ed. *Ordo Nidrosiensis Ecclesiae (Orðbók)*, Libri Liturgici Provinciae Nidrosiensis Medii Aevi 2 (Oslo 1968), 494-6; Helmut Gneuss, 'Latin Hymns in Medieval England,' in Beryl Rowland, ed., *Chaucer and Middle English Studies in Honour of Rossell Hope Robbins* (Kent, OH 1974), 418-21; and Inge B. Milfull, *The Hymns of the Anglo-Saxon Church: A Study and Edition of the 'Durham Hymnal,'* CSASE 17 (Cambridge 1996).

[16] Boynton, 'Glossed Hymns,' 232-72.

The use of the sun as a symbol of the relationship between the Father, the Son, and the Holy Spirit in the Trinity goes back at least as far as the days of the Church Fathers. The First Council of Nicaea (325 A.D.) found it necessary to resort to the abstract 'light of light' ($\phi\hat{\omega}_S$ ἐκ $\phi\omega\tau\acute{o}_S$, *lumen de lumine*) in its attempt to explain that the Father and the Son are at the same time inseparably one and utterly distinct, like the sun and the light which emanates from it. This image subsequently became popular in homiletic literature,[17] but it would have been familiar most of all from its occurrence in so many hymns, as in 'Splendor paternae gloria,' the Ambrosian hymn for lauds:

> Splendor paternæ gloria,
> de luce lucem proferens,
> lux lucis et fons luminis,
> diem dies illuminans.[18]

Radiance of the Father's glory, light proceeding from light, light of light and fountain of light, day illuminating day.

It also occurs in the compline hymn, 'Christe, qui splendor et dies':

> Christe, qui splendor et dies,
> noctis tenebras detegis,
> lucisque lumen crederis,
> lumen beatis prædicans ... (10)

Christ, radiance and day, you lay bare the shadows of night, and you are believed to be light of light, proclaiming light to the blessed ...

the hymn for matins, 'Consors paterni luminis':

---

[17] For examples, and a discussion of the image in Ælfric's homilies and in the Old English Advent lyrics, see J.E. Cross, 'The "Coeternal Beam" in the Old English Advent Poem (Christ I) ll. 104-129,' *Neo* 48 (1964): 72-81.

[18] Anselmo Lentini, ed., *Te Decet Hymnus: L'Innario della 'Liturgia Horarum'* (Vatican 1984), 18. Henceforward, references to Lentini's edition will be in parentheses in the text.

Consors paterni luminis,
lux ipse lucis et dies ... (20)

Consort of fatherly light, light itself of light, and day ...

and the Christmas vesper hymn, 'Christe, redemptor omnium':

Tu lumen, tu splendor Patris,
tu spes perennis omnium ... (77)

You are light, you are the radiance of the Father, you are the eternal
hope of all ...

These last three date from the sixth century and are found in all the versions of
the New Hymnary.

A variation on this idea is the more focused image of Christ as a ray or
beam of light. In 'Nox et tenebræ et nubila,' one of the hymns of Prudentius's
Cathemerinon, Christ is 'solis spiculo' (26) (the ray [literally 'dart' or 'arrow']
of the sun) as he is in 'Aurora iam spargit polum,' an eighth-century hymn for
lauds (38). A Marian homily in the Norwegian Homily Book[19] uses the word
geisli for this image: 'Solen merkir guð-dóm ... en geislen droten várn Iesum
Crist,'[20] (The sun represents the Divinity, and the sunbeam, our Lord Jesus
Christ).

Many hymns assign a specific function to the sunbeam/Christ. The
beam that breaks through the clouds can symbolize a vigorous Christ breaking
the powers of sin and darkness (*spiculum* properly denotes a weapon — the
meaning 'sunbeam' is metaphorical), or the gracious Christ who glides gently
into the ignorant or confused human mind and enlightens it. Often these
functions are linked, as in 'Nox et tenebræ et nubila':

Nox et tenebræ et nubila,
confusa mundi et turbida,
lux intrat, albescit polus:
Christus venit; discedite.

---

[19] A collection of twelfth-century homilies in a manuscript produced c. 1200.
[20] Gustav Indrebø, ed., *Gamal norsk homiliebok, cod. am. 619, 4to*, Skrifter utg. for
Kjeldeskriftfondet 54 (Oslo 1931), 132.

Caligo terræ scinditur
percussa solis spiculo,
rebusque iam color redit
vultu nitentis sideris.

Sic nostra mox obscuritas
fraudisque pectus conscium,
ruptis retectum nubibus,
regnante pallescet Deo.

Night and shadows and clouds, the world's confusion and disorder, light enters, the sky grows pale: Christ is coming: be gone. Earth's dark shroud is torn, struck by the ray of the sun, and colour returns to things in the face of the flashing star. Soon may our darkness — the gloom of the guilty heart — be exposed as the clouds break and are dispelled under the rule of God (26).

or in 'Aurora iam spargit polum':

Aurora iam spargit polum
terris dies illabitur,
lucis resultat spiculum:
discedat omne lubricum.

Iam vana noctis decidant,
mentis reatus subruat,
quicquid tenebris horridum
nox attulit culpæ, cadat.

Ut mane illud ultimum,
quod præstolamur cernui,
in lucem nobis effluat,
dum hoc canore concrepat (38).

Now dawn streaks the sky, day slides in over the earth, the ray of light reverberates, slippery dangers slink away. Night's fantasies now depart, the mind's guilt is dispelled, whatever shadowy horrors night's guilt brought on fall away, so that the final morning, which we devoutly await, will flood us with light, while we sing this song.

The imagery becomes more combative in the tenth-century hymns, such as 'Verbum supernum prodiens,' for matins of Christmas:

Illumina nunc pectora
tuoque amore concrema;
audita per præconia
sint pulsa tandem lubrica (74).

Now enlighten our hearts, and burn them up with your love; may the herald's promise finally strike down evil and deceit.

and 'Iesu, redemptor sæculi,' for Easter compline:

Qui frangis ima tartara,
tu nos ab hoste libera,
ne valeat seducere
tuo redemptos sanguine.

You shatter the depths of hell, you free us from the enemy, lest he should be able to seduce those redeemed by your blood (120).

Hymns for the morning and evening offices typically follow a pattern whereby natural phenomena (the dawning or waning light) are given symbolic value. The hymns begin with a poetic description of daybreak or sunset: the coming morning light begins to dispel the darkness of night, or the light of day gives way to evening shadows. Next, the sunlight is metaphorically linked to Christ, and the darkness to chaos and sin, reminding the monks gathered for prayer at these liminal and potentially perilous times that Christ repels the assaults of the Prince of Darkness and restores life and order to the world. The morning hymns celebrate the return of light; the evening hymns anticipate it. Lenten and Easter hymns then go on to link this daily victory to the Resurrection, while Advent and Christmas hymns link it to the Incarnation. Finally, many hymns associate it with the apocalyptic dawning of a new age and the renewal of the world at the end of time.

Light imagery appears much less frequently in the hymns of the *sanctorale*. In 'Æterna Christi munera,' the classic Ambrosian hymn for the feasts of martyrs, the saints are called 'vera mundi lumina' (261) (true lights of the world) but the image does not recur in hymns on the saints until the seventh century and later. Peter and Paul are called 'vera mundi lumina' in the Carolingian 'Aurea luce et decore roseo' (177), and the epithet appears again in 'Exultet cælum laudibus,' the hymn for the feasts of apostles in the Easter season that dates from the same period (259). Paulinus of Aquileia refers to Peter and Paul as 'candelabra luce radiantia / praeclara caeli duo luminaria' (178) (candelabra radiant with light / two bright lights of heaven) in 'Felix per omnes festum mundi cardines'

Peter Damian uses the images 'mundi iubar atque caeli' (light of the world and of heaven), for St John the Evangelist in 'Virginis virgo venrande custos' and says in 'Excelsam Pauli gloriam' that St. Paul 'perfused the world with light like a shining lamp' (Micantis more lampadis / perfundit orbem radiis [149]). The twelfth-century hymn for the feast of St Augustine, 'Fulget in cælis celebris sacerdos,' calls Augustine the morning star that disperses the light of intact faith throughout the world ('stella doctorum rutilat corusca, / lumen intactum fidei per orbis / climata spargens' [206]), and in the later Middle Ages the image became increasingly more common.

There are homiletic texts that explicate in greater depth the image of the saints as reflected light. Bede's Christmas homily is cautiously precise:

Et sancti quidem homines lux sunt recte uocati dicente ad eos domino: *Vos estis lux mundi*; et apostolo Paulo: *Fuistis aliquando tenebrae nunc autem lux in domino.* Sed multum distat inter lucem quae inluminatur et lucem quae inluminat, inter eos qui participationem uerae lucis accipiunt ut luceant et ipsam lucem perpetuam quae non solum lucere in se ipsa sed sua praesentia quoscumque adtigerit inlustrare sufficit.[21]

It is right for the Lord to refer to holy men as 'light,' when he says, 'You are the light of the world'; and the apostle Paul says, 'Once you were in darkness, now you are light in the Lord.' But there is a great distance between the light that is illuminated and the light that illuminates, between those who accept participation in true light so

[21] D. Hurst, ed., *Bedae Venerabilis Opera*, CCSL 122 (Turnhout 1999), 267.

that they might give light, and that perpetual light itself that not only in itself gives light but by its presence suffuses whomever it touches with the power to shine.

Leo the Great, in a homily on the Transfiguration, echoes St Paul's idea that the saints shine with the glory of Christ as the result of participating in his suffering:

> Aperit ergo dominus coram electis testibus gloriam suam, et communem illam cum caeteris corporis formam tanto splendore clarificat, ut et *facies eius solis* fulgori similis ... Spes sanctae Ecclesiae fundabatur, ut totum Christi corpus agnosceret quali esset commutatione donandum, et eius sibi honoris consortium membra promitterent, qui in capite praefulsisset. De quo idem Dominus dixerat ... *Tunc iusti fulgebunt sicut sol in regno Patris sui,* protestante hoc ipsum beato Paulo apostolo atque dicente: *Existimo enim quod non sunt condignae passiones huius temporis ad futuram gloriam, quae reuelabitur in nobis,* et iterum: *Mortui enim estis, et uita uestra abscondita est cum Christo in Deo. Cum enim Christus apparuerit uita uestra, tunc et uos apparebitis cum ipso in gloria.* [22]

The Lord disclosed his glory before chosen witnesses and illuminated that form, common to other bodies, with such splendour that his face was like the brightness of the sun ... The hope of the church was made firm, so that it might know with what sort of exchange the whole body of Christ was to be given, and that the members might promise to themselves a sharing in the honour of the one who had shone as their head. The Lord himself had said ... 'The just will shine like the sun in the kingdom of their Father.' The apostle Paul assures us of the same thing when he says, 'I think that the sufferings of this time are not to be compared to the future glory that will be revealed in us,' and again, 'You have died, and your life is hidden with Christ in God. And when Christ your life appears, then you also will appear with him in glory.'

---

[22] Antonius Chavasse, ed., *Sancti Leonis Magna romani Pontificis Tractatus Septem et Nonaginta,* CCSL 138A (Turnhout 1973), 299.

The prologue to John's Gospel says that John 'was not the light, but was to give testimony of the light,'[23] and St John is commonly referred to as a mediator of the light of Christ. Augustine's imagery in a homily for the Birthday of John comes close to that of the Trinitarian hymns:

> Baptizat ergo, inquam, Joannes Christum, servus Dominum, vox Verbum, creatura Creatorem, lucerna solem; sed solem, qui fecit hunc solem; solem de quo dictum est, *Ortus est mihi sol justitiæ, et sanitas in pennis ejus.*[24]

> John, I say, baptizes Christ; the servant, the Lord; the voice, the Word; the creature, the creator; the lamp, the sun; but it is that sun that made the sun; the sun of whom it is said, 'The sun of righteousness is risen for me, with healing in his wings.'

The metaphors found in these hymns and homilies are the context for Einarr's kenning 'gunnoflugr geisli miskunnar sólar' (battle-strong beam of the sun of mercy), the metaphor which gave *Geisli* its name. Einarr's kenning combines the image of the saints as reflected light with the Trinitarian imagery of the morning and evening hymns. The imagery of the hymns expresses a complex theological doctrine (the relations within the Trinity), and Einarr Skúlason imitates it to make an analogous, equally complicated statement about St Olaf. The hymns use the images of the sun and its radiant light to symbolize, respectively, God the Father and God the Son. Einarr borrows this image and puts it to a new use: he uses the sun to symbolize the Son, and its beam as the symbol for St Olaf, moving things down a notch, as it were. In so doing he suggests that the relationship of Olaf and Christ is analogous to that of the divine Father and Son.

The typological association of the saints and Christ is a common motif in twelfth-century hagiography, but the sun/sunbeam image as a metaphor for it is not. It is remarkable, given the pervasiveness of the image in the hymnary as a Trinitarian metaphor, that no hymn writer appears to have adapted it, as Einarr did, for a poem about a saint. While we find the sun used as a

---

[23] John 1:7.
[24] *Sancti Aurelii Augustini Opera Omnia*, ed. Monachorum Ordinis Sancti Benedicti, 2nd edn (Paris 1888), vol. 5, pt. 2, col. 1720.

metaphor for God the Father throughout the hymnary, it is rare as a metaphor for Christ.[25] The only occurrence may be in 'Iam Christe, sol iustitiæ,' the popular sixth-century hymn for lauds in Lent. This designation, 'sun of righteousness,' for Christ is ultimately biblical (cf. Ps. 111:4 and Mal. 4:2), and it appears frequently in liturgical texts and homilies for Christmas. Einarr's kenning for Christ, 'réttlætis sunnu,' in stanza 2 of *Geisli* is a direct translation, and the analogous kenning in stanza 1, 'miskunnar sólar' (sun of mercy) is just a step away. The phrase 'lumen misericordiae' (light of mercy) occurs occasionally in Latin writings,[26] but never as a metaphor for Christ. A Christmas homily in the Norwegian *Homilíubók* also contains a verbal parallel in its reference to the annunciation to the shepherds:

> Skin því gnoglegar lios guðs miskunnar yfir þæim ... Maclega vittraðesc engil með liose þa er Cristr var boren. Þvi at hann er sialfr lios ret-latra þat er lysir hvern mann er kemr í hæim.[27]

Thus the light of God's mercy shone abundantly over them. It was fitting that the angel shone with light when Christ was born, because he was himself the righteous light that enlightens every man who comes into the world.

The opening stanzas of *Geisli* are ostensibly a summary of the life, death, and resurrection of Christ, but typological allusions to the story of Olaf lie just beneath the surface. The mention of Olaf by name in stanzas 1 and 7, which bracket this section of the *drápa*, makes this association explicit. Lest there

---

[25] Since the hymns were used to teach Christology and Trinitarian theology, there was great concern that their doctrine be unambiguous. The standardization of imagery may reflect this concern.

[26] As in Prosper of Aquitaine's commentary on Psalm 142: 'Oriatur inquit in me lux misericordiae tuae, fiatque quod credidi, ut spes, quae auditu concepta est, impleatur' (He says, 'May the light of your mercy arise in me, and may what I have believed come to pass, that the hope which your words have inspired in me may be fulfilled') (P. Callens, ed., *Prosperi Aquitani Expositio Psalmorum*, CCSL 68A [Turnhout 1972], 182); and in Gregory's *Moralia on Job*: 'Necesse est ut quaeramus ne lumen misericordiae dationis tarditate fuscauerit' (We must take care that the light of mercy not be darkened by our slowness to give) (Marcus Adriaen, ed., *S. Gregorii Magni Moralia in Iob*, CCSL 143A [Turnhout 1979], 1084).

[27] Indrebø, *Gamal norsk homiliebok*, 39–40. The homily is a translation of a homily by Gregory the Great, but these lines are an addition by the Norwegian author. Cf. Raymond Étaix, ed., *Gregorius Magnus Homiliae in Evangelia*, CCSL 141 (Turnhout 1999), 55.

should be any confusion about the 'gunnǫflugr geisli miskunnar sólar,' we are told that the reference is to 'ítrum Óláfi' (bright Olaf). The educated audience of Einarr's day, accustomed to the sun as a symbol for God the Father and the sunbeam or *geisli* as a symbol for God the Son,[28] would have been tipped off to a shift in imagery by the identification of the beam as Olaf. The implication is obvious: Olaf, like Christ, the heavenly king of the Latin hymns, has shattered the darkness of the world ('heims myrkrum brá'[29]) and enlightened his faithful subjects so they can reflect his glory. In stanza 43, Einarr shifts the image to another level in his description of Olaf's swordsmanship at the Battle of Stiklarstad, where Olaf's sword becomes a metaphor for the saint:

Þeim klauf þengill Rauma
þunnvaxin ský gunnar
(rekin bitu stǫl) á Stiklar-
stǫðum valbastar rǫðli. (4-8)

With that sun of the sword-hilt (sword) the king of the Raumar clove the clouds of battle (shields), grown thin, at Stiklarstad; driven steel bit.

In the opening stanzas of *Geisli*, Einarr adds layer upon layer of allusion. 'Ljósi sólar brá' (the sun's light failed) in stanza 3 refers metaphorically to the death of Christ, the light of the world ('heims ljós'), and literally to the solar eclipse that occurred at his crucifixion. But it also calls to mind the death of Olaf, the new sunbeam, which likewise was accompanied by an eclipse. The repetition of the verb *brá* in stanzas 2 and 3 emphasizes the give and take of the struggle between light and darkness. The account of the Resurrection in stanza 4, which describes how Christ, the 'sun of righteousness' (réttlætis sunna), 'arose' (rann upp), echoes the biblical *orietur sol iustitiae*.[30] As 'king of the sun-home' (dagbóls konungr), the risen Christ has become more sun than beam, no longer active in the world but rather, like God the Father, remotely enthroned above the angels ('ýfri englum' [stanza 5]). On this side of

---

[28] Cf. the citation from the Norwegian Homily Book, above and note 24.

[29] *Geisli*, stanza 2 (see note 4 above). Henceforward, stanza references will be given in the text.

[30] 'The sun of righteousness will arise' (Mal. 4:2), traditionally interpreted as a prophecy of the birth of Christ.

the 'hall of the heath' (und heiða sal) it is now Olaf who is the 'beam of God's hall' (geisla guðs hallar) that shines with miracles and reveals God's power in the world.[31] While the Latin hymns avoid this extension of the image by analogy to include saints as well as Christ, it appears in prose texts such as the Transfiguration homily of Leo the Great cited above.

Einarr's theme in *Geisli* is theologically subtle. By applying to Olaf the imagery the hymns use for Christ, he is attempting to illustrate the *commutatio* or exchange (cf. Leo) whereby the properties of Christ can be predicated of the saint who is 'in Christ.' St Paul was the first to articulate this idea, and it is found throughout Paul's writings. Leo quotes Paul[32] to underline his point that participation in the sufferings of Christ leads to participation in his glory, and this is precisely what *Geisli* wants to show: that Olaf's sufferings (never mind the details) were a participation in and a re-presentation of the sufferings of Christ, and that as a consequence Olaf now participates in Christ's glory and can re-present his miracles. One way in which Einarr attempts to communicate this idea in *Geisli* is through the use of kennings that force the audience to ponder the relationship between Olaf and Christ.

In the account of the Ascension in stanza 5, Christ is called 'sonr allsráðanda' (son of the all-ruler) in the first helming. Then, after 'ascending with ease from earth to the highest hall,' he becomes 'dagbóls konungr' (king of the sun-home) in the second. The change from 'son' to 'king' emphasizes the change in status (and function) brought about by Christ's ascension into heaven: suffering and death has led to exaltation, and this is the pattern that we are about to see repeated in Olaf's life. When Einarr turns his attention to Olaf after the seven introductory stanzas on Christ, he refers to Olaf as 'vin röðuls tyggja' (the friend of the king of the sun) in stanza 9. The kenning both reemphasizes Christ's new place in the cosmic order and associates Olaf with him. The 'king of the sun' formula turns up again in the recurring *stef* or refrain introduced in stanza 18, where Christ is called 'gram sólar.' The context ('brave Olaf gets all he desires from the king of the sun') makes it clear that the kenning refers to Christ and not to Olaf. Einarr wants to show that just as in the dynamics of the Trinity, there is a paradoxical congruence of equality and hierarchy in their relationship.

---

[31] Stanza 7. At another level there is the implied comparison of Olaf to the risen and ascended Christ.

[32] Rom. 8:18 and Col. 3:3-4.

After describing the death and many subsequent miracles of Olaf in the body of the *drápa*, Einarr introduces his conclusion with seven stanzas summarizing Olaf's career (stanzas 62-8), which together with the corresponding stanzas 1-7 frame the poem. The conclusion begins by restating the theme of the *stef*: Olaf, the 'witness of glory' (dyrðar váttr), the 'friend of the Redeemer' (vinr lausnara), and the 'ruler of men' (liðs valdr), 'gets from the Lord all kinds of blessedness.' Stanza 63 then speaks of Olaf's 'martyrdom' and exaltation in terms that call to mind the death, Resurrection, and Ascension of Christ: 'The king was taken young from here,' Einarr says, 'thus God usually tests his friends; now the strong misfortune-diminisher (fárskerðandi) of men lives in the heavenly ruler's highest vision of peace (friðar syn).' *Friðar syn* is a direct translation of *visio pacis*, familiar from the hymn 'Urbs beata Jerusalem.'[33] The kenning *fárskerðandi* is more interesting. It is the first in a series of potentially ambiguous kennings that, out of context, could refer to either Olaf or Christ. The context of this stanza leaves no doubt,[34] but the ambiguity of the kenning itself is an intentional reminder that Olaf now does what Christ does. The anonymous poem *Leiðarvísan*, which like many later Christian *drápur* shows the influence of *Geisli*, uses the analogous 'fárskerðir' to refer to Christ.[35]

Stanza 64 opens with an inexpressibility topos: 'Who is so wise that his tongue can tell the gifts of the prince of the bright path of the breeze' (ljóss byrjar vegs lofðung) in this life?' The poem has just recounted a list of Olaf's miracles: are we to presume that he is the prince of heaven referred to here? The heiti, *lofðungr* (prince) refers to Olaf ('lofðungr Þrœnda' [prince of the Trondheimers]) in stanza 13, but in stanza 46 it is used in a kenning for Christ ('vinar lofðungs tungla ranns' [friend of the prince of the hall of the stars]). Or is the 'king of heaven' formula still to be reserved for Christ? The second helming is likewise ambiguous:

Þær es heims ok himna
heitfastr jǫfurr veitir
(skreytt's of skatna dróttinn
skrín) dýrðar-vin sínum.

---

[33] Lentini, ed., *Te Decet Hymnus*, 251.

[34] And cf. the analogous kenning for Olaf, 'harmskerðandi,' in stanza 38.

[35] *Skjaldedigtning*, B II, p. 625 (*Leiðarvísan*, stanza 11).

Those (honours) that the oath-keeping king of heaven and earth gives to his glorious friend — it is the ornamented shrine of the lord of men.

There is no doubt that the 'king of heaven and earth' is Christ; Olaf is once again designated as his 'friend.' But who is the 'lord of men?' Einarr uses the epithet *dróttinn* for references to both Olaf and Christ. The term is used absolutely to refer to Christ in stanzas 10 and 62, and Christ is also designated by the kennings, 'dýrðar dróttinn' (Lord of glory) in stanza 6, and 'dróttinn harra' (Lord of kings) in stanza 25. But Olaf is called *dróttinn* in the parallel kennings 'dróttins Hǫrða' (lord of the Hordar) and 'Sygna dróttinn' (lord of Sogn) in stanzas 21 and 22. There have been enough references to the shrine of Olaf at Trondheim (stanzas 9, 6, and 41) to make it clear that this is what is meant, but here the shrine is not designated as Olaf's. And to add to the ambiguity, the following stanza draws attention to the relic of 'the torture-cross of the maker of heaven.' In addition to the shrines of Olaf and of the cross, the cathedral at Trondheim would almost certainly have had a eucharistic shrine, also richly ornamented. There is an overlapping of lords and shrines here, which is sorted out somewhat by the statement that the king of heaven and earth gives honours to his glorious friend.

Up to this point in the poem, the miracles at the shrine have been ascribed to Olaf, the benefactor of 'his' people. Now Einarr echoes the *stef* again and explains more precisely that Christ is the true author of the miracles, who honours Olaf by using him as the mediator. The phrase, 'snarr tyggi sólar bergr seggjum' (the quick king of the sun saves men) in stanza 65 continues the double-entendre. There is no doubt that 'Christ, the clever prince of the sun, saves men,' but the terms *snarr* and *bergr* tend to move the tone of the statement earthwards. *Snarr* means 'clever' or 'quick' — it is the word for a king who can think on his feet as he dashes about the battlefield. This stanza is the only known instance of its use in reference to Christ. *Bergr* (from *bjarga*) is likewise a strange choice. Perhaps most commonly used in connection with shipwreck, it means 'rescue' more than 'save' in the theological sense — it has more to do with pulling someone out of a physically dangerous situation than with redeeming the soul.

After predicating on Christ what might more properly be predicated on Olaf in stanza 65, Einarr does the opposite in stanza 66. 'Qld nýtr Óláfs mildi' the stanza begins, 'people benefit from Olaf's mercy.' *Mildi* can mean 'kindness' or 'generosity,' but it occurs most often in Christian contexts with the theological meaning 'mercy' or 'grace,' and almost always in reference to Christ or God the Father. The kenning for Olaf in the second helming reminds us how this can be his attribute as well: Olaf is 'lim salkonungs himna' (the limb of the king of the hall of heaven). The epithet echoes the biblical 'membrum Christi,' which St Paul uses in his theology of participation[16] and which became a commonplace in medieval hagiography. The stanza concludes:

> Sæll es hverr, es hollan
> hann gervir sér, manna.

> Happy is every man who makes him his friend.

Sæll is yet another slippery term: in stages of increasing intensity, it can mean 'prosperous,' 'happy,' or 'blessed.' This latter meaning is common in theological writings, where *sæll* is used to translate Latin *beatus* (cf. German *selig* and Danish *salig*). *Geisli* promises that Olaf's 'friends' will prosper with respect to health and wealth just like the beneficiaries of his miracles described in the poem. But it may not be reading too much into the term to see an intimation that they will also be blessed in the way Olaf is blessed — that by association with him they can participate in the life of Christ just as he does.

From the point of view of thematic unity, *Geisli* really concludes with stanza 68. The final three stanzas are a postscript apostrophe to Einarr's patron asking for payment. Stanzas 67 and 68 sum up and bring to a close the concluding section composed of stanzas 62-8. These final two stanzas restate and reemphasize the theme of the *drápa*. The second helming of stanza 67 reads:

> Bóls taki seggr hverr, 's sólar
> siklings, þess's goð miklar
> hilmis, ást ens hæsta
> heiðbjartrar, lof reiðir.

---

[16] Cf. 1 Cor:6 and 12.

Let every man who gives praise to the prince, the one whom God makes great, receive the highest love of the king of the home of the heaven-bright sun.

Einarr wants to shift the focus of the poem away from the list of sensational (and conventional) miracles worked by Olaf and back to the pious theme with which he began: the miracles are a means to a higher goal. By honouring Olaf, whose miracles are a manifestation of God's glory, one can come to participate in God's love.

Einarr repeats the key word, *ást*, in line 7 of stanza 68:

Svát lausnara leysi
langvinr frá kvǫl strangri
nýta þjóð of nauðum
nafnkuðr við trú jafnan,
víga skýs þars vísa
veljendr glaðir telja
ǫflugs Krists af ástum
alnennins brag þenna.

So that the renowned, long-time friend of the Liberator might always free good people from harsh torment and need on account of their faith, where the choosers of the clouds of battle ('men') happily proclaim this, the powerful king's poem about the love of all-efficacious Christ.

The poem has become a sermon, and not a bad one. The main section of the *drápa*, with its accounts of battles and miracles, leaves no doubt that Einarr Skúlason was accomplished in and relished the traditional art of skaldic poetry. *Geisli* was commissioned by a secular ruler whose primary concern was to celebrate the spectacular deeds of St Olaf and thereby strengthen his own reputation by association.[37] Einarr ably fulfils this assignment, but he takes the opportunity to promote his own agenda as well. He concludes the poem with an artfully pedagogical shift back to the theme he considers most important:

---

[37] Indeed, 'ǫflugs vísa' can at one level be an ironic reference to Eysteinn. After all, he paid for the poem.

Olaf is to be honoured, not for his own accomplishments, but because he is *langvinr lausnara*, and although *Geisli* is Olaf's poem, its true subject is *ǿst alnennins Krists*.

Einarr Skúlason is a pivotal figure, and *Geisli* is a pivotal poem, gracefully balanced between the cultures of the Viking age and the new age of European Christianity. Einarr was a skald but also a priest, an Icelandic nationalist as well as a representative of international culture. *Geisli* was commissioned by a king, but for performance in a church, not at court. It celebrates a national hero, but on the occasion of the establishment of a see of the Roman church in Norway. The form of the poem, with its series of anecdotes, recalls not only the traditional *drápur* composed to honour Viking princes but also the office of matins for a saint's day with its coda of biographical nocturns. Einarr uses intentionally ambiguous vocabulary, drawn from both the skaldic tradition and the Latin liturgy, to keep the imagery shifting: the poem's hero has the face now of Olaf the king, now of Olaf the saint, now of Christ.

12

Beardless Wonders: 'Gaman vas Sǫxu' (The Sex Was Great)[1]

OREN FALK

> WINCHESTER: Do what thou dar'st, I beard thee to thy face.
> GLOUCESTER: What! am I dared, and bearded to my face?
> Draw, men, for all this privileged place;
> Blue-coats to tawny-coats. — Priest, beware
> your beard;
> I mean to tug it and to cuff you soundly.
> Under my feet I stamp thy cardinal's hat.
> In spite of Pope or dignities of Church,
> Here by the cheeks I'll drag thee up and
> down.
> (Shakespeare, *I King Henry VI*, I.iii)

Since the 1960s, scholars of Old Norse literature have consistently been pricking holes in Snorri Sturluson's confident (and perhaps tongue in cheek) assertion that skaldic verse is historically truthful.[2] Gone now from the halls of historical veracity are the *berserkir*, gone is the blood eagle, even Kvasir has been reduced from authentic pagan myth to frothy antiquarian fantasy[3] — at

---

[1] I thank Kristin Kane, David McDougall, Ian McDougall, William Sayers, and the editors of this volume for their invaluable help with various aspects of this paper.

[2] See his prologue to *Heimskringla* (ÍF 26:5). To Snorri's explanation here of why skalds can be trusted (they would not dare lie to their addressee's face), contrast (Snorri's? account of) Egill's grumble when coerced to compose *Hǫfuðlausn*: 'Ekki hefi ek við því búizk, at yrkja lof um Eirík konung' (*Egils saga*, chap. 59, ÍF 2:182) (For that I hadn't prepared myself, to compose praise for King Eiríkr). I owe the apposition of these two passages to Matthew Vernon's insightful suggestion.

[3] See, respectively, Klaus von See, 'Exkurs zum Haraldskvæði: Berserker,' *Zeitschrift für deutsche Wortforschung* 17 (1961): 129-35; Roberta Frank, 'Viking Atrocity and Skaldic Verse: The Rite of the Blood-Eagle,' *English Historical Review* 99 (1984): 332-43 (and the ensuing debate with Bjarni Einarsson in *Saga-Book* 22, no. 1 [1986]: 79-82, 22, no. 5 [1988]: 287-9, and 23, no. 1 [1990]: 80-3); and Frank, 'Snorri and the Mead of Poetry,' in Ursula Dronke, Guðrún P. Helgadóttir, Gerd

least, such is the fate to which philological exorcists have consigned them, though many historians still stubbornly cling to their ghosts. The present paper, an historian's amateur pecking at some verse morsels from *Gísla saga Súrssonar* (and, I hope, more a tribute to our honorand's sensibilities than a travesty of her talents), seeks to extend this philological project by dissipating yet another dubious skaldic whiff, but at the same time also to raise hopes that we historians might still draw sustenance from insubstantial poetry.[4]

Like many other Family Sagas, *Gísla saga* opens with a 'prehistoric' section, a Norwegian prelude to the story of Gísli's family in Iceland. The prologue 'motivat[es] what happens later and [reproduces it in] microcosm' – all the more so here, where much of the 'prehistory' concerns not foreshadowing ancestors but the same heroes who will later star in the body of the saga.[5] In one complex episode, Gísli becomes entangled in a conflict with a certain Hólmgǫngu-Skeggi. The interim climax of this segment comes when Skeggi and Gísli face off in single combat:

> Ok ganga þeir á hólm ok berjask, ok heldr skildi hvárr fyrir sik. Skeggi hefir sverð þat, er Gunnlogi hét, ok hǫggr með því til Gísla, ok gall við hátt. Þá mælti Skeggi:
> Gall Gunnlogi,
> gaman vas Sǫxu.
> Gísli hjó í móti með hǫggspjóti ok af sporðinn skildinum ok af honum fótinn ok mælti:
> Hrǫkk hræfrakki,
> hjók til Skeggja.
> Skeggi leysti sik af hólmi ok gekk ávallt við tréfót síðan. (*Gísla saga*, chap. 2, ÍF 6:10-11)

They go into the ring and fight, and each holds his shield in front of himself. Skeggi has the sword which is called Gunnlogi, and he strikes

---

Wolfgang Weber, and Hans Bekker-Nielsen, eds, *Speculum Norroenum: Norse Studies in Memory of Gabriel Turville-Petre* (Odense 1981), 155-70.

[4] Already in her 'Skaldic Poetry' (in Carol J. Clover and John Lindow, eds, *Old Norse-Icelandic Literature: A Critical Guide*, Islandica 45 [Ithaca 1985], 157-96, at 170), Roberta Frank drew attention to the verses discussed here as an example of saga authors' misreading of embedded verse.

[5] Theodore M. Andersson, 'Some Ambiguities in *Gísla saga*: A Balance Sheet,' *BONIS* (1969, for 1968): 7-42, at 17.

at Gísli with it, and it rang out loudly. Then Skeggi declared: (verse couplet).

Gísli struck back with (his) halberd and (chopped) off the tip of the shield and his foot, and declared: (verse couplet).

Skeggi ransomed himself from the duel and ever after walked with a peg leg.

(Skeggi will be killed shortly thereafter in another round of hostilities.)

Traditionally, readings of the *kviðlingar* (verse snatches) with which Skeggi and Gísli punctuate their martial exchange have exhibited a tin-eared tendency to flatten the poetry and desiccate it. By rendering the verses as literally as possible (only tweaking the sense to harmonize their content with what is perceived to be going on), scholars have turned these couplets into a kind of running commentary on the combat, as moving and rhapsodic as a bus driver's narration of her daily route by calling out the stops over a PA system. 'Sværdet (el. Gunnloge, egennavn) gjalded; det var Saksas fryd' (The sword [or: Gunnlogi, a proper name] resounded; that was Saxa's joy), Finnur Jónsson has Skeggi say, and his Gísli responds: 'Sværdet fór frem, jeg huggede til Skegge' (The sword pressed ahead, I hewed at Skeggi).[6] Martin Regal's version is barely more musical: 'War-flame sings out / Saxo is entertained ... Halberd hovered / I struck down Skeggi.'[7] With such poetry to his (partial) credit, it is no wonder that Gísli is described as 'the strong *silent* type'[8] — hardly a serious competitor for an Egill or a Kormákr.

---

[6] *Skj* B1, 93, 96 nn. As Anne Holtsmark stresses in her *Studies in the Gísla saga*, Studia Norvegica 6 (Oslo 1951), 26-7, Finnur's translation of *hrøkkva* as 'fara frem,' indicating an (energetic) movement forward, is unparalleled elsewhere in ON literature. His German translation is essentially identical: 'Gunnlogi tönte laut; es war lustiges spiel für Saxa ... Die waffe bewegte sich schnell; ich richtete einen hieb gegen Skegge' (*Gísla saga Súrssonar*, Altnordische Saga-Bibliothek 10 [Halle a.S. 1903], 6-7 nn) (Gunnlogi rang loudly; it was fun play for Saxa ... The weapon moved quickly; I directed a blow against Skeggi).

[7] *Gisli Sursson's Saga*, trans. Martin S. Regal, in Viðar Hreinsson et al., eds, *The Complete Sagas of Icelanders, including 49 Tales*, 5 vols (Reykjavík 1997), 2:3-4.

[8] Andersson, 'Some Ambiguities,' 17 (my emphasis). Some translators have gone to greater lengths to preserve the poetic merit of the *kviðlingar*, though they still render the contents entirely blandly: see, e.g., George Webbe Dasent: 'Warflame fierce flickered, / Flaring on Saxa ... Grimly grinned Ogremaw, / Gaping at Skeggi' (*The Story of Gisli the Outlaw* [Edinburgh 1866], 14-15); Friedrich Ranke: 'Gellt' Gunnlogi: / Grimmig freut's Saxa ... Hüpft Hels Waffe: / Hackt' ich auf Skeggi' (*Die Geschichte von Gisli dem Geächteten*, in *Fünf Geschichten von Ächtern und Blutrache*, trans. Andreas Heusler and Friedrich Ranke, Thule: Altnordische Dichtung und Prosa 8 [Jena 1922],

More recently, however, Preben Meulengracht Sørensen (following in Anne Holtsmark's footsteps)[9] has offered an interpretation of the poetic exchange that rather rehabilitates Skeggi and Gísli's skaldic reputations. Sørensen locates the *kviðlingar* in the context of a reading in which *Gísla saga*'s entire 'prehistory' becomes suffused with sexual competition, innuendo, and insult. Bjǫrn inn blakki, the rapacious *berserkr* who sets the plot in motion, is (among other stereotyped vices) a sexual predator, seeking to rob Gísli's uncles of their womenfolk. Conversely, the defence that Ari Þorkelsson and (after his death) his brother Gísli put up is concerned not merely with protecting the fairer sex, as part of a general defence of their property rights, but also with vindicating their manhood:

> Bjǫrn gerir Ara tvá kosti, hvárt hann vill heldr berjask við hann í hólmi ... eða vill hann selja honum í hendr konu sína. Hann kaus skjótt, at hann vill heldr berjask en hvárttveggja yrði at skǫmm, hann ok kona hans ... Þá berjask þeir, ok lýkr svá, at Ari fellr ok lætr líf sitt. Þykkisk Bjǫrn hafa vegit til landa ok konu. Gísli segir, at hann vill heldr láta líf sitt en þetta gangi fram, vill hann ganga á hólm við Bjǫrn. (chap. 1, ÍF 6:4–5)

> Bjǫrn gives Ari two options, whether he would rather fight a duel with him ... or he would give over his wife to him. He chose quickly, that he would rather fight than bring calumny upon them both, himself and his wife ... Then they fight, and it ends thus: Ari falls and loses his life. It seems to Bjǫrn that he has won the land and the woman. Gísli says that he would rather lose his life than let this come about, (that) he wishes to fight a duel with Bjǫrn.

---

64) (Gunnlogi yelled: Saxa rejoiced grimly ... Hel's weapon sprang: I hacked at Skeggi); Jan de Vries: 'Luid klonk de Strijdvlam, / een lust om te hooren ... Snel sloeg mijn strijdspeer / een houw tegen Skeggi' (*De Saga van Gisli den Vogelvrijverklaarde* [Lochem 1925], 5) (Loud clanged the Battle-flame, a joy to hear ... Swift struck my battle-spear a blow against Skeggi); Ralph B. Allen: 'Screamed aloud Battle-flame; / Sport was on Saxi ... Slid off his harmless sword; / Then struck I back at Skeggi' (*The Saga of Gisli Son of Sour* [New York 1936], 8); and George Johnston: 'Warflame whistled, / Wild sport for Saxa ... Hack went the halberd, / Hewed down Skeggi' (*The Saga of Gisli*, with notes and an essay by Peter Foote [Toronto 1963], 4).
[9] Sørensen, *The Unmanly Man: Concepts of Sexual Defamation in Early Northern Society*, trans. Joan Turville-Petre, The Viking Collection 1 (Odense 1983), esp. 58–61; Holtsmark, *Studies*, esp. 20–8.

In the following generation, Gísli Súrsson kills one of his sister Þórdís's
suitors for the insolence of seeking her company without first securing her
male relatives' approval. Unaccountably, however, Gísli later sides with
Kolbjǫrn, another of his sister's boyfriends, against the advances of yet a third,
Skeggi (a kinsman of the first slain beau). Skeggi and his unfortunate relative
are resisted on the same grounds that the *berserkr* Bjǫrn had to be resisted: as
outsiders who prey on the family's female capital and male reputation. It is
unclear, then, why Kolbjǫrn, who fills the same functional slot ('Þat var talat,
at Kolbjǫrn væri í þingum við Þórdísi' [chap. 2, ÍF 6:9] [It was said that
Kolbjǫrn was intimate with Þórdís]),[10] fails to excite the same opposition.

To make matters worse, Kolbjǫrn's own manliness is soon called into
question: when challenged by Skeggi, he replies boldly but then fails to make
good on his bravado. Skeggi undertakes a ritual procedure aimed at
humiliating both Kolbjǫrn and Gísli, apparently by representing them as
homosexuals in a compromising position. In the nick of time, Gísli steps in
to accept the duelling challenge in Kolbjǫrn's stead. As Sørensen proceeds to
demonstrate, the versified quips Skeggi and Gísli then trade – pelting each
other with rounds of *níð* (defamatory poetry) – form another chapter in the
ongoing sexual hostilities. In the (presumably older) verse, *Saxa*, which the
saga prose glosses as a place name, probably denotes Gísli's blade; Skeggi
belittles it by choosing an appellation implying femininity: '*saxa* might have
signified a Saxon woman [or] a giant woman [as] in Snorri's *Edda*,' hence an
axe or some other chopping implement.[11] Opposing his own phallic weapon[12]

---

[10] For the erotic sense of *vera í þingum við* (which survives into modern Icelandic), see Peter Foote,
'Things in Early Norse Verse,' in Bjarne Fidjestøl et al., eds, *Festskrift til Ludvig Holm-Olsen: på
hans 70-årsdag den 9. juni 1984* (Bergen 1984), 74-83, at 75.
[11] Sørensen, *The Unmanly Man*, 59, alluding to Járnsaxa (Snorri Sturluson, *Edda*, ed. Finnur
Jónsson [Copenhagen 1900], 87, 186, 197; cf. Holtsmark, *Studies*, 25). As the name of a giantess,
Saxa might be a suitable *heiti* (appellation), or part of a kenning, for an axe: Snorri's claim that
'øxar kalla menn trǫllkvinna heitum' (*Skáldskaparmál*, chap. 46 [49], §155; in *Edda*, 115) (people
call axes by the names of trollwives) leads Rudolf Meissner to discern an entire group of battleaxe
kennings based on she-giants, trollwives, and witches (*Die Kenningar der Skalden. Ein Beitrag zur
skaldischen Poetik*, Rheinische Beiträge und Hülfsbücher zur germanischen Philologieund
Volkskunde 1 [Bonn and Leipzig 1921], 148). Sørensen assumes that *Saxa* denotes Gísli's weapon,
identified in the prose as a *hǫggspjót* (hacking spear) (cf. Cleasby-Vigfusson, s.v.), an acceptable
semantic extension of 'axe.' These points notwithstanding, the unavoidable association with *sax*
(gladius) argues in favour of imagining Gísli to be armed with a sword. Reference to a sword by a
giantess-*heiti* would be unusual, but not impossible: cf. such *heiti* for 'sword' as *skrýnir*, a (male)

to Gísli's feminized one allows Skeggi to configure the clang of arms as *gaman*, a specifically erotic 'pleasure,'[13] in which his sword performs the thrusting while Gísli's is (so to speak) penetrated:

> Gunnlogi banged,
> Saxa had sex.

There is no mistaking the utter lack of romanticism and tenderness in Skeggi's vision of gladiatorial coitus: the males in his metaphoric world of sexed swords conquer and rape, the females are used as passive vehicles, for whom intercourse can only equal violation. Both from Gunnlogi's aggressive macho perspective and from Saxa's feminized viewpoint, mutually passionate lovemaking is not an option; sex is strictly a masculine triumph and a feminine degradation.[14]

---

giant's name, and *gróa*, the name of a *vǫlva* and possibly a giantess, since her husband, Aurvandill, seems to be a giant: *Skáldskaparmál*, chap. 75 (Tillæg IX), in *Edda*, 202; cf. 46-8, 87-8. Hjalmar Falk, *Altnordische Waffenkunde* (Christiania 1914), 51, thinks, however, that *gróa* might be an axe *heiti* erroneously listed among the sword appellations.

[12] Sørensen relies largely on the strophes in *Grettis saga*, chap. 75 (ÍF 7:240-1; *Skj* B1, 290; B2, 474) for establishing that swords were accepted in Norse literature as phallic symbols (*The Unmanly Man*, 60; cf. Bo Almqvist, *Norrön Niddiktning. Traditionshistoriska studier i versmagi: 1. Nid mot furstar*, Nordiska texter och undersökningar 21 [Stockholm 1965], 176-7). If Gísli, too, is armed with a sword, Skeggi's choice of *heiti* might be a calculated insult on yet another level, degrading Gísli's *sax* from prestigious stabbing weapon to mere chopping implement. On the semiotic gap between utilitarian axes and honourable swords in Viking Age Scandinavia, see, e.g., Hákon Magnússon's instructions for arming freeman levies in the Norwegian *Nyere Lands-Lov* of the 1270s (*Landværnsbolk*, §11; NGL, 2:42): after specifying the weapons required of each level of property-holder ('En drengmaðr huer oc þeir menn er minna fé eigu en nu er sagt. þeirra huer skal eiga skiolld oc spiot oc suerð eða [v.l. ok] œxi' [But each bachelor, and those men who have less property than was just said, each of them shall have a shield and a spear and a sword or (*v.l.* and) an axe]), the legislator adds: 'En er verkmaðr gengr i fyrstu uist oc tekr fulla leigu, þa kaupi hann ser fyrsta sumar œxi. en annat skiolld. hitt þriðia spiot' (But when a labourer first takes lodging and receives full wages, let him buy himself the first summer an axe, the next a shield, the third a spear). Cf. Peter Foote and David M. Wilson, *The Viking Achievement: The Society and Culture of Early Medieval Scandinavia*, Great Civilizations Series (London 1970; repr. 1973), 272-7. The preference for stabbing over cleaving is evident also in Vegetius's instructions for training a Roman army (*Epitoma rei militaris* 1.12, ed. Alf Önnerfors, Bibliotheca scriptorum Graecorum et Romanorum Teubneriana [Stuttgart and Leipzig 1995], 25-6); cf. Dave Grossman, *On Killing: The Psychological Cost of Learning to Kill in War and Society* (Boston 1995), 120-1, 129-30.

[13] See Fritzner, s.v., sense 2; LP (1913-16), s.v., sense 2.

[14] Such a view of sex acts is consonant with the idiom of obscene provocation elsewhere in the saga; cf., e.g., Sørensen's interpretation of Gísli's versified statement *bǫllr á byrðar stalli brast* (chap. 15, ÍF

Sørensen's analysis of the first line of Gísli's rebuttal brings out the equally cutting wit with which the latter turns Skeggi's sexual defamation against its author. Gísli denies Skeggi's sword an appellation as flattering as *Gunnlogi* (flame of battle), christening it instead *Hræfrakki* (corpse-Frank).[15] He also claims that the blade *hrǫkk*, 'flinched,' 'recoiled,' or perhaps even 'retracted.' In Gísli's account, then, Skeggi's weapon loses its erection; capable of necrophilia, it is far from equal to the task of facing a vibrant parry or counter-thrust. But even Sørensen's spirited reading leaves the final line of verse lacklustre and limp. In contrast to the metaphoric acid Gísli found for degrading Skeggi's sword, he seems unable to transcend a laconic indicative when addressing its owner, telling him what he cannot have failed to notice on his own: that he is under attack.

This sudden loss of interpretative nerve at the very end of the versified duel seems embarrassing. Gísli's statement – 'hjók til skeggja' – ought to be just as laden with sexual innuendo as the previous lines had been. The tendency to take Gísli's last word as a straightforward reference to his adversary must be due to readers' enduring allegiance to the prose context of this verse. Yet, as Sørensen amply demonstrates, the prose saga is an unreliable guide through these lines, encumbering the poetry with an ad hoc island and possibly a gratuitous halberd in order to account for turns of phrase that the saga author found (or chose to make) impenetrable. Surely here, too, Gísli says more than he appears to.

6:50; *Skj* B1, 97) as 'the penis struck hard upon the laden (and supplied with a hole) mast-step' (*The Unmanly Man*, 67), a (figurative) homosexual rape. An identical sensibility towards heterosexual acts, including the linking of male martial and sexual prowess with an objectification of women, is apparent, e.g., in the *berserkr* Bjǫrn's designs on Gísli's aunt (chap. 1, ÍF 6:4-5), discussed above; and in those one of Eyjólfr's men has on Gísli's wife (chap. 35, ÍF 6:113).

[15] Like OE *franca*, ON *frakka* (of which *frakki* would appear to be a variant) seems to mean 'Frankish-made javelin' (but see Jan de Vries, *Altnordisches etymologisches Wörterbuch* [Leiden 1961], s.v.). Most previous readers evidently took *Hræfrakki* to be Gísli's weapon, despite its identification as a halberd (Meissner notes the difficulty in deciding whether *hræfrakki* should signify a sword or a spear [*Kenningar*, 145]; cf. Cleasby-Vigfusson, s. *frakka*). Holtsmark, who recognizes that the reference is to Skeggi's armament, assumes he must wield both a sword (viz. *Gunnlogi*) and a spear or axe (viz. *Hræfrakki*; see *Studies*, 25-7). Sørensen accepts Holtsmark's claim that Gísli talks about what his opponent brandishes but resists multiplying Skeggi's arsenal: a single sword makes better sense as the referent of both proper names. Holtsmark also notes a possible geo-political pun: where Skeggi speaks of Saxons, Gísli brings up Franks, perhaps 'alluding to the often unfriendly relation between the tribes' (*Studies*, 24 n. 31).

To begin with the verbal phrase, *hjók til* seems to mean simply 'I hewed towards' or 'struck at.' ON lexicographers note no other sense for *hǫggva + til*.[16] But comparison with an indirect modern derivative suggests at least one plausible alternative: Danish *tilhugge* can mean 'to trim' (a tree, for instance) or 'to dress, rough' (stone or timber).[17] If such a meaning might also be imputed to an assumed ON enclitic verb, Gísli's statement could conceivably be read as 'I cropped the beard,' taking *skeggja* as a gen. pl. of *skegg*, 'beard,' rather than the gen. sg. of *Skeggi*.[18] For Gísli to boast of having shorn his rival's jowls would be rather more scathing than to claim merely to have levelled a blow at him: such a reading patently recalls beard plucking (or worse), a humiliating gesture customary throughout medieval Europe and beyond. (The notorious images of Nazis savaging the beards of Orthodox Jews, for example, are still within living memory.)

Whereas Greco-Roman society from the time of Alexander had cultivated a clean-shaven standard of manly respectability, historians generally imagine early-medieval Germanic barbarians to have been *barbati*.[19] Modern

---

[16] The form *hǫggvask til* (+ dat.) deserves mention, however, especially given its *Grettis saga* context, where, in a satirical verse, it seems to mean 'to join, assemble' (or perhaps 'cause to collide'): 'Heldu Hlakkar tjalda / hefjendr saman nefjum, / Hildar veggs ok hjoggusk / hregg-Nirðir til skeggjum' (*Skj* B1, 290; chap. 72, ÍF 7:234-5) (The raisers of Hlǫkk's awnings [i.e. warriors] put their noses together, and the squall-Nirðir of Hildr's wall [i.e. warriors] thronged with their beards). Grettir's lampoon hinges on the contrast of hyperbolic martial diction with cowardly, indecisive action: instead of making sparks fly from steel, his warriors exchange whispers among whiskers. Thus, *hǫggvask til skeggjum* might properly denote an aggressive encounter, to which Gísli's verse, despite its different grammar, may allude. Cf. the Middle English idiom 'rennen in [the] berd' (to oppose [somebody] openly) (*MED* s. *berd*, sense 4a [c]).

[17] See Hermann Vinterberg and C.A. Bodelsen et al., *Dansk-Engelsk Ordbog*, 2 vols (Copenhagen 1956), s.v.; cf. Det Danske Sprog- og Litteraturselskab, *Ordbog over det danske Sprog*, 23 vols (Copenhagen 1918-46; repr. 1966-9), s. *til-holde: -hugge*, sense 2, 'hugge (noget) i (rette, passende) form' (to carve [something] into [a correct, fitting] form). This sense is not attested prior to the early modern period and may be a Middle Low German loan (see Karl Schiller and August Lübben, *Mittelniederdeutsches Wörterbuch*, 6 vols, 1875-89 [repr. Wiesbaden and Münster 1969], s. *tohouwen*); it is absent from Otto Kalkar's *Ordbog til det ældre danske Sprog (1300-1700)*, 5 vols (Copenhagen 1881-1918 [repr. with a 6th vol. 1976]), s. *tilhugge* (cf. *hugge*, sense 3, s. *Hug*).

[18] The use of a pl. form should not be regarded as anomalous, mandating emendation of *skeggja* to *skeggs* in order to have Skeggi wear a sg. 'beard': ON pl. nouns can at times denote sg. objects (e.g., *dyrr*, 'door') and pl. *skegg* could conceivably mean something like 'whiskers' or a collective 'facial hair.'

[19] See, e.g., Achim Leube, 'Grundzüge der materiellen und geistigen Kultur: Tracht und Schmuck,' in Bruno Krüger, ed., *Die Germanen: Ein Handbuch. Geschichte und Kultur der germanischen Stämme in Mitteleuropa*, 5th edn, 2 vols, Veröffentlichungen des Zentralinstituts für

opinion has venerable late antique antecedents, which lend support to the hypothesis that a cultural watershed separates facial fashions in antiquity from those in the Middle Ages (if not necessarily along ethnic lines).[20] Given the importance of hair and beard as cultural markers, it is no surprise that early medieval evidence points to involuntary depilation of scalp or cheek as a manifest gesture of degradation in Germanic societies.[21] Concomitantly, Christian injunctions for shaving and tonsuring clerics not only hark back to an older, Roman aesthetic but also honour the newer value system in the breach, attempting to transmute a mark of humility into a badge of virtue.[22]

Alte Geschichte und Archäologie der Akademie der Wissenschaften der DDR 4, no. 1 (Berlin 1988), 1:344: 'Auf den römischen Kunstwerken werden alle Germanen bärtig dargestellt' (All Germanic people are represented as bearded in Roman works of art). Leube is, of course, oblivious to the circularity of his argument: representations of 'Germans' in Roman art are picked out partly by their distinctive coiffure. On the shift from Greco-Roman to medieval hair fashions, see Giles Constable and R.B.C. Huygens, 'Introduction [to Burchard of Bellevaux's *Apologia de barbis*]: Beards in the Middle Ages,' in R.B.C. Huygens, ed., *Apologiae Duae*, CCCM 62 (Turnhout 1985), 47-150, at 58-9, 85-8.

[20] See discussion and references in Constable and Huygens, 'Introduction,' 88; cf. 51 n.14. The best known example of such late antique opinion is Isidore of Seville's etymology of 'Langobard,' tracing the ethnonym to the Lombards' long beards (*Etymologi[æ]*, ed. W.M. Lindsay, 2 vols, Scriptorum classicorum bibliotheca Oxoniensis [Oxford 1911], 9.2.95). Ammianus Marcellinus, who derides the Huns for their bare-featured, scarred ugliness ('senescunt imberbes absque ulla venustate,' [beardless, they age without any beauty]), may provide early testimony of a shift in fashions among Greco-Romans themselves; see his [*History*], 31.2.2.2 (ed. and trans John C. Rolfe, 3 vols, Loeb Classical Library [Cambridge, MA, and London 1935-9], 3.380).

[21] Numerous examples, ranging from the early sixth to the mid-eighth century, are collected in Jean Hoyoux, 'Reges criniti: Chevelures, tonsures et scalps chez les Mérovingiens,' *Revue belge de philologie et d'histoire* 26, no. 3 (1948): 479-508, at 499-503. Hoyoux takes these references as evidence of penal scalping, a reading vehemently contested by Ekkehard Kaufmann, 'Über das Scheren abgesetzter Merowingerkönige,' *Zeitschrift der Savigny-Stiftung für Rechtsgeschichte. Germanistische Abteilung* 72 (1955): 177-85, at 180-5. See also Floyd Seyward Lear, 'The Public Law of the Visigothic Code,' *Speculum* 26, no. 1 (1951): 1-23, at 15-16 (Appendix B: Decalvation); Averil Cameron, 'How did the Merovingian Kings Wear their Hair?' *Revue belge de philologie et d'histoire* 43, no. 4 (1965): 1203-16; and Michael McCormick, *Eternal Victory: Triumphal Rulership in Late Antiquity, Byzantium, and the Early Medieval West*, Past and Present Publications (Cambridge 1986), 303 n.30, 307 n.49, 313-14 (who stresses the probable Byzantine source of Visigothic rites, esp. 303-4, 312-14; cf. R.S. Lopez, 'Byzantine Law in the Seventh Century and its Reception by the Germans and the Arabs,' *Byzantion: International Journal of Byzantine Studies (American Series, II)* 16, no. 2 [1944 for 1942-3]: 445-61, at 450).

[22] Fifth- and sixth-century canons actually mandate that the clergy wear beards: 'Clericus nec comam nutriat nec barbam radat' (A cleric shall neither cultivate his hair nor shave his beard) states, for instance, a late fifth-century decree (attributed in the Middle Ages to the Fourth Council of Carthage in 436; *Statuta ecclesiae antiqua* §25 [XLIV], in *Concilia Galliae, A. 314 — A. 506*, ed. C. Munier; CCSL 148 [Turnhout 1963], 171; dating and misattribution discussed at 163).

Only from Carolingian times do beards appear to have gone into decline
again, at least in the aristocratic circles of Western Europe, to re-emerge with
a vengeance in the sixteenth century.[23]

But while, on the continent, the occidental contemporaries of both
Gísli and his anonymous Icelandic biographer may have shaved regularly – if
no more frequently than every other week or three[24] — Norsemen, like most
medieval men beyond the pale of Latin Christendom, seem to have sported
beards. When the deacon Bodo converted to Judaism in 839, his sprouting
hair and beard screamed apostasy to his former coreligionists no less clearly
than his circumcision; almost 150 years later, Adalbert of Prague's despair in
his mission to the Slavs was similarly marked by thoughts of forsaking the
razor.[25] Even the somewhat backward Anglo-Saxons, allegedly liable to

---

Beards did come back into fashion in the eastern Mediterranean around this time and were adopted
(also) by the clergy, but in the West such rulings were creatively reinterpreted to make them
conform to what they ought to have said. At least as early as the ninth century, e.g., this canon was
altered to enjoin rather than forbid shaving: 'Clericus nec comam nutriat sed barbam radat' (A
cleric shall not grow his hair but shall shave his beard), or simply 'Clericus nec comam nutriat nec
barbam' (A cleric shall grow neither his hair nor his beard) (Constable and Huygens,
'Introduction,' 103-12).

[23] Constable and Huygens, 'Introduction,' 88-102; the first few decades of the eleventh century seem
to have seen a temporary revival of beards (93-4). The Carolingian kings themselves, including even
Charlemagne, whose facial hair attains such celebrity in later literature (see D.D.R. Owen, 'Beards
in the *Chanson de Roland*,' *Forum for Modern Language Studies* 24, no. 2 [1988]: 175-9, and Robert
Morrissey, *L'empereur à la barbe fleurie: Charlemagne dans la mythologie et l'histoire de France*,
Bibliothèque des histoires [Mesnil-sur-l'Estrée 1997], 20), were all beardless (Constable and
Huygens, 'Introduction,' 91).

[24] Monastic rules from the ninth century to the twelfth prescribe shaving schedules of between once
every fifteen days and once in two months; Constable and Huygens, 'Introduction,' 116-17. Given
the late onset and sparseness of beard growth in premodern societies (see Herbert Moller, 'The
Accelerated Development of Youth: Beard Growth as a Biological Marker,' *Comparative Studies in
Society and History* 29, no. 4 [1987]: 748-62, at 750-7), even such a low frequency may have sufficed to
ensure that most men would normally display only minimal stubble.

[25] On Bodo, see *Annales Bertiniani* s.a. 839: 'Circumcisus, capillisque ac barba crescentibus' (ed. G.
Waitz, MGH SS *rerum Germanicarum* 5 [Hanover 1883], 17; cf. anno 847, 34-5) (Circumcised,
with growing hair and beard), and [Pseudo-]Amulo of Lyon, 'Epistola, seu Liber contra Judæos ad
Carolum Regem' §42: 'Ita ut et superstitione et habitu totus Judæus effectus, quotidie in
synagogis Satanæ barbatus et conjugatus, cum cæteris blasphemet Christum et Ecclesiam ejus' (PL
116: 171c) (So, as he has become fully Jewish in superstition and attire, he daily blasphemes Christ
and his church with the others, bearded and married, in Satan's synagogue). On Adalbert, see
Brunonis Vita S. Adalberti, chap. 26: 'Videns adleta Christi, nullum fructum animarum sequi et
desideratae mortis spem auferri, deiecit animum; tristicia magna affectus ... dixitque fratribus: ...
"vestimenta mutemus clericalia, pendentibus capillis surgere sinamus, tonsae barbae truncas comas
prodire permittamus"' (ed. Georg Heinrich Pertz, MGH SS in fol. 4 [Leipzig 1841], 609)

mistake clean-shaven Norman knights for clerics, only wore moustaches, keeping their chins and cheeks bare.[26] In contrast, Jews (and Muslims) and Slavs were uncouth enough to run around with hair framing their mouths.[27] In all likelihood, so were Norsemen.[28] Facial hair is ubiquitous in both Viking Age iconography and later literary sources, suggesting that beards were a routine feature on medieval Scandinavian visages.[29] And, although Norse jurists

(Christ's athlete, seeing no harvest of souls come forth and hope borne off by longed-for death, became dispirited; and, affected with great sadness, he said to the brothers: 'Let us change [our] clerical garb, let our swaying locks grow, allow the clipped hairs of our shaven beards to emerge').

[26] William of Malmesbury, *Gesta regum Anglorum* 3.239, ed. William Stubbs, Rolls Series 90 (London, 1887-90), 2.301: Harold's spies 'serio addiderunt, pene omnes in exercitu illo presbyteros videri, quod totam faciem cum utroque labio rasam haberent; Angli enim superius labrum pilis incessante fructicantibus intonsum dimittunt' (actually [reported] that almost all in that army appear to be priests, as they have the entire face, with both lips, shaved; for the English left the upper lip unshaved, [its] hairs ceaselessly blossoming); cf. 3.245, 2.305; as well as the pictorial evidence of the so-called Bayeux Tapestry (reproduced with an introduction, description and commentary by David Wilson [New York 1985], plates *passim*, and 208).

[27] Modern scholarly consensus holds that Jews, in fact, followed the customs of the gentiles among whom they lived, wearing beards in Byzantine and Muslim lands but not in Latin Europe. 'Cela n'empêcha pas les artistes chrétiens, notamment durant le Bas Moyen Age, d'adopter une stratégie iconographique qui consistait à dépeindre des juifs aux traits barbus, alors même qu'ils ne l'étaient évidemment pas' (Elliott Horowitz, 'Visages du Judaisme: De la barbe en monde juif et de l'élaboration de ses significations,' trans. Isabelle Rozenbaumas, *Annales: Histoire, Sciences Sociales* 49, no. 5 [1994]: 1065-90, at 1080) (This did not deter Christian artists, especially during the Later Middle Ages, from adopting an iconographic strategy of depicting Jews with bearded features, which they, clearly, did not have).

[28] Around the middle of the twelfth century, for example, the Orcadian Jarl Rǫgnvaldr kali is able to use the phrase 'meðan upp heldk skeggi' (while I wear a beard) to mean 'as long as I live' (*Skj* B1, 486; *Orkneyinga saga*, chap. 90, ÍF 34:238; cf. LP (1913-16), s. *skegg*).

[29] Despite his title, Per Gjærder ('The Beard as an Iconographical Feature in the Viking Period and Early Middle Ages,' *Acta Archaeologica* [Copenhagen] 35 [1964]: 95-114) offers little systematic description of the Scandinavian evidence. My assertion concerning the frequency of Norse representations of bearded faces is based on an informal, impressionistic survey of published runic images, carvings and statues, wall paintings in churches, MS illuminations, etc. Nearly all recognizably male faces represented, e.g., in James Graham Campbell's *The Viking World* (London 1980) and in Magnus Magnusson's *Vikings!* (London 1980) are bearded; of those that are not, either gender or features are usually indistinct, and only a tiny minority are clearly clean-shaven men. In Eddic verse, two of Karl and Snør's boys, e.g., have names that suggest they are bearded (*Rígsþula* 24, in *Edda. Die Lieder des Codex Regius nebst verwandten Denkmälern*, ed. Gustav Neckel, rev. Hans Kuhn, 2 vols, 5th edn. [Heidelberg 1983], 1:283). For mentions of facial hair in skaldic verse, see LP (1913-16), s. *grǫn* (entry 2), *kanpr*, and *skegg*. Saga examples are of course more numerous, including many which incorporate proverbial-sounding comments; see, e.g., *Vatnsdœla saga*, chap. 18 (ÍF 8:51): '[Hrolleifr] kvazk ætla, at hann myndi eigi skríða undir skegg þeim' ([Hrolleifr] said he had no mind to creep under their beard).

did not use the appearance of facial and body hair as an indicator of legal
majority (unlike the author of the thirteenth-century *Sachsenspiegel*),[30] saga
evidence substantiates that beards were not mere appurtenances of men — they
were synecdochic of manhood.

An *obiter dictum* in *Eiríks saga rauða* nicely proclaims the self-evidence
of beards as markers of mature male identity. Setting off from Vínland, the
land of plenty that had proved too dangerous for them to tame, Þorfinnr
Karlsefni and his men make one last-minute appropriation of New World
trophies: they stop over briefly to abduct two native boys. The youths are
members of a small family, it seems, but the adults, two women and a man,
manage to elude capture. The description of the fivesome as the Norse first see
them is noteworthy: 'Þeir [Karlsefni] fundu Skrælinga fimm; var einn
skeggjaðr ok tvær konur, bprn tvau' (chap. 12, ÍF 4:432, cf. 233) ([Karlsefni's
men] found five natives; there was one bearded and two women, two
children). Such casual use of *skeggjaðr* to designate mature male gender is
revealing of underlying concepts; all the more revealing if the man so
described is thought to have been an American Native, who is all but certain
not to have worn a beard.[31] Just as the biblical author might speak of 'any that
pisseth against the wall' to signify 'men' in general[32] — irrespective of their

---

[30] See Eike von Repgow, *Landrecht*, 1:42, §1: 'Swelkes mannes alder men nicht ne weiz, hât her hâr
in dem barde unde nedene unde under iewelkeme arme, sô sal men wizen, daz her zu sînen tagen
comen is' (*Sachsenspiegel III-V*, ed. Karl August Eckhardt, 2nd edn, Bibliotheca rerum
historicarum, Rechtsbücher 3 [Aalen 1973], 26) ([When] people do not know a man's age, [if] he
has hair in the beard and down below and under each arm, then people are to know that he has come
of age). The presence of beard and pubic hair likewise indexes maturity in Irish epic and legal texts;
William Sayers ('Early Irish Attitudes toward Hair and Beards, Baldness and Tonsure,' *Zeitschrift
für celtische Philologie* 44 [1991]: 154-89, at 166-7) surveys the evidence.

[31] One Native American feature consistently noted by Europeans since 1492 has been paucity of
body and facial hair; see Elliott Horowitz, 'The New World and the Changing Face of Europe,'
Sixteenth Century Journal 27, no. 4 (1997): 1181-1201. Bare Native American faces probably owe
something to genetics (though the disrepute into which anthropometrics have rightly fallen since
the 1940s has inhibited the assembly of reliable data and interpretations; see, e.g., Dick Edgar
Ibarra Grasso, *Los Hombres Barbados en la América Precolombina (Razas indígenas americanas)*
[Buenos Aires 1997]), but much also to cultural proscription of beards; see, e.g., Reginald
Reynolds, *Beards: An Omnium Gatherum* (London 1950), 19, 29, 36, 43; Josephine Paterek,
Encyclopedia of American Indian Costume (Denver 1994), 21, 24, 105, 122, 130, 142, 154, 203, 231,
254, 259, 277, 279, 280, 306, 308, 322, 325, 327, 339, 354, 370, 377. On the occurrence of *skeggjaðr* in
Eiríks saga rauða, cf. Geraldine Barnes, *Viking America: The First Millennium* (Cambridge 2001),
20-1 n.65.

[32] See, e.g., 1 Kings 25:22 (Douai-Rheims; 1 Sam. 25:22, King James Version), accurately rendering
the Hebrew 'maštîn bĕqîr.'

actual attitude to masonry when relieving themselves — so, for the Norse, the notional presence of facial hair unequivocally indexed manliness.[33]

The same conviction in the one-to-one correspondence between manhood and beardedness is apparent in Hallgerðr's sneer that Njáll Þorgeirsson 'ók eigi í skegg sér, at hann væri sem aðrir karlmenn' (*Brennu-Njáls saga* chap. 44, ÍF 12:113) (didn't [tend to] his beard so that he might be like other men).[34] Tugging Njáll's absent beard, Hallgerðr openly implies that he falls short of other men in his conduct as well as in his appearance: 'Hverr mun hefna' — she sniggers when her son-in-law expresses reluctance to murder his mark, one of Njáll's household men – 'hvárt karl inn skegglausi?' (chap. 41, ÍF 12:107) (Who will avenge [this]? ... The beardless chap?).[35] Egill Skalla-Grímsson manifests a similarly nasty attitude when he has brought to bay his enemy, the hapless Ármóðr skegg. Uncharacteristically agreeing to spare Ármóðr's life, Egill nevertheless subjects him to an involuntary shave (and gouges out one of his eyes for good measure; *Egils saga* chap. 72, ÍF

---

[33] The distinction may seem at first glance trans-cultural and ahistorical. As Will Fisher emphasizes, however ('The Renaissance Beard: Masculinity in Early Modern England,' *Renaissance Quarterly* 54, no. 1 [2001]: 155-87), societies differ in their choice of sex attributes to highlight as gender markers: 'genitocentrism seems to be predicated upon a modern notion of sexual difference in which physiological features are hierarchized (classed as either primary or secondary characteristics) and in which genital morphology comes to stand in for sex ... [In the past,] I believe that the beard was as important as the genitals and that it too "made the man"' (158). Moreover, '[t]he distribution of [facial] hair growth between the sexes,' imagined in early modern England (and in medieval Scandinavia) as bipolar, is in fact 'bimodal (that is to say that while the majority of males are more hairy than the majority of females, there are nevertheless some females who are more hirsute than some males, and [vice versa])' (166). The Norse attitude is succinctly expressed in the inclusion 'af skeggi konunnar' (of a woman's beard) among the list of impossible ingredients (cat's footfall, fish's breath, etc.) of which the gods have the dwarfs forge Gleipnir, Fenrisúlfr's leash (*Gylfaginning*, chap. 33, in *Edda*, 33).
[34] Sayers, 'Early Irish Attitudes,' 175-6, cites an Irish parallel and muses on 'the scene [as] a concise example of I.-E. tripartition' (176 n. 54). Cf. also his 'Njáll's Beard, Hallgerðr's Hair and Gunnarr's Hay: Homological Patterning in *Njáls saga*,' *Tijdschrift voor Skandinavistiek* 15, no. 2 (1994): 5-31.
[35] Njáll is referred to as *skegglauss* on numerous occasions: *Brennu-Njáls saga*, chaps 35, 41, 44, 91, 123 (ÍF 12:91, 107, 113, 114, 229, 314; cf. chap. 20, ÍF 12:57). Hallgerðr twice insists on bestowing the nickname on him with ritual formality: 'kǫllum hann nú karl inn skegglausa' (let's call him now "the beardless [old] man") (chap. 44, ÍF 12:113; cf. chap. 91, ÍF 12:229: 'Munu vér [kalla] heðan af ... fǫður yðvarn karl inn skegglausa' [From here on we shall (call) your father "the beardless (old) man"]). That Njáll's homestead, Bergþórshváll, is named after his wife may cast further doubts on his manliness.

2:228) – an eloquently cruel punishment, given his victim's nickname. Egill himself, though bald like his father, has a bushy beard (chap. 55, ÍF 2:143.) Thus, even if Norse legislators make no provision directly comparable to those King Alfred in the ninth century or the Emperor Barbarossa in the twelfth had put forth against violence to another's beard,[16] the sagas recognize assaults on the beard as an extreme form of aggression. The scribe who copied out *Grágás* into the Codex Regius may also hint at such a sensibility (though probably with as much regard for what grows on top of one's head as to cheek and jowl). In the *Vígslóði* paragraph enumerating the more serious types of harm, he initially wrote:

þessi averk metaz sem in meire sár. Ef maðr sceR tungo or hofde manne eða stingr avgo or höfðe manz eða brytr teN or höfðe manz. eða sceR har af manne nef eða eyro.[17]

These injuries are appraised like the major wounds: if one cuts the tongue out of a person's head or pokes the eyes out of a person's head or breaks the teeth out of a person's head; or cuts a person's hair off, the nose or the eyes.

He later expunged *har* from the list.[18] Yet the scribe's *faute de plume* seems predicated on a prevalent cultural assumption: that clipping a man's hair by

---

[16] See Ælfred 35 (*Das Gesetzbuch der Könige Aelfred – Ine*) §5: 'Gif he ðone beard ófascire, mid XX scill. gebete' (*Gesetze der Angelsachsen*, ed. F. Liebermann [Aalen, 1903-16; repr. 1960], 1:68) (If [someone] cuts off [someone else's] beard, [he shall] compensate by [paying] twenty shillings); Friedrich I, DF.I.25 (*Landfrieden*) §4: 'Si quis alium ceperit et absque sanguinis effusione ... crines eius aut barbam expilaverit, decem libras ei ... per compositionem impendat et iudici viginti persolvat' (*Die Urkunden der deutschen Könige und Kaiser*, ed. Heinrich Appelt, MGH *Diplomata regum et imperatorum Germaniae*, 10, no. 1 [Hanover 1975-90], 42) (If someone has seized another and, without drawing blood, despoiled his hair or beard, he is to hand him ten pounds in compensation and pay the judge twenty). Other so-called Germanic law codes similarly protect the beard: see the references cited by Constable and Huygens, 'Introduction,' 62 n. 75. (Even if such law codes reflect little more than eighth- and ninth-century Frankish impositions of 'national' customs on subjugated peoples, they are significant as indications of the Carolingian image of Others as people who value facial hair.) Likewise, early Irish texts recognize that touching or cutting another's hair is a serious offence; see Sayers, 'Early Irish Attitudes,' 174-6.

[17] *Grágás* Ia, 147-8. Note the close correspondence between the offences against hair and eyes in *Grágás* and the injuries Egill inflicts on Ármóðr.

[18] See *Grágás* Ia, 148 n. 1. In contrast, *Jónsbók* retains the cutting of a man's hair as a punishable offence, comparable, e.g., to the killing of a horse under its rider or to involuntary confinement

force seriously disfigured him, no less so than any other major trauma to the face.[39]

By claiming to beard Skeggi to his face, then, Gísli might offer offence aplenty. An attack on Skeggi's *skegg* would shed, however, the smutty overlay of the preceding lines. Below, I should like to canvass the potential for recapturing Gísli's sophisticated vulgarity by retaining the traditional understanding of *skeggja* as an inflection of the noun *skeggi*; it is the strict meaning of this noun that requires closer inspection.

Skeggi is, of course, closely related to *skegg*. If we set aside the prose context, it might simply be taken to mean 'man': the dictionaries maintain that it does, implying that it should mean 'bearded [person].'[40] To trade the specificity of the adversary's identity for a more general statement that 'I took a swing at the guy' hardly seems to enhance Gísli's literary stature, however. Nor is the common noun all that well attested, least of all as a simplex; and its exact denotation is less secure than the lexicographers would lead one to believe.[41]

(*Mandhelgebolk*, chap. 22, NGL 4:220). Norwegian legislation is even more specific in criminalizing offences against facial hair: the highest damages are to be paid for seizing a man violently by his whiskers, according to the *Ældre Gulathings-Lov* (chap. 195; NGL 1:69-70), while the compensation for amputating a man's nose is doubled if the blow also shears off his *grön*, 'moustache' (*Ældre Frostathings-Lov* [IV], chap. 45, and *Ældre Bjarkö-Ret*, chaps 19, 78; NGL 1:171, 1:307, 1:319).

[39] Further (ironic) illustration of the apparent equation between well-groomed facial hair and sovereignty is provided by Þorkell Eyjólfsson's prophetic vision in *Laxdæla saga* (chap. 74, ÍF 5:215): 'Þat dreymði mik ... at ek þóttumk eiga skegg svá mikit, at tœki um allan Breiðafjǫrð' (I dreamt that I seemed to have such a huge beard that it encompassed all of Breiðafjǫrð). He then glosses his dream: 'Auðsætt þykki mér þat, at þar mun standa ríki mitt um allan Breiðafjǫrð' (It seems to me obvious, that this [shows] my dominion will extend over all of Breiðafjǫrð). Guðrún is less optimistic: 'Vera má, at svá sé ... en heldr mynda ek ætla, at þar myndir þú drepa skeggi í Breiðafjǫrð niðr' (It may be that it shall be so; but I should rather imagine that it [shows] you'll dip your beard into Breiðafjǫrð). Þorkell drowns two chapters later.

[40] See esp. de Vries, *Wörterbuch*, s. *skegg*, and LP (1913-16), s. *skeggi*.

[41] The evidence that *skeggi* means (generic) 'man' is, in fact, rather slender; its specific denotations tend to cluster around the Faeroe Islands. The Götuskeggjar, for instance, were one of the most prominent families in the Faeroes in the thirteenth century (see Ólafur Halldórsson's introduction to *Færeyinga saga*, Stofnun Árna Magnússonar á Íslandi 30 [Reykjavík 1987], xiv-xv, ccix-ccxii, ccxxxii-ccxxxix). Their name may go back to an ancestral Skeggi. Similarly, *eyjarskeggjar* usually means 'inhabitants of the Faeroe Islands' (for a rare exception, see *Pals saga postola I*, chap. 21, in *Postola Sögur*, ed. C.R. Unger [Christiania 1874], 234). Other compounds (such as the *hapax legomenon* – usually glossed 'wild man' – *hraunskeggi*, a dismissive reference to a fugitive in the Greenlandic outback in *Flóamanna saga*, chap. 30, ÍF 13:315) may be jocular imitations (cf. a readily

But what if *skeggi* means, not 'bearded [one],' but 'bearded [thing]'?
ON *skeggja* (or *skeggøx* or *barða*), sometimes calqued 'bearded axe,' offers a
convenient analogue: an axe whose blade extended backwards, parallel to the
shaft, was likened to a human face sporting a protrusion on its chin.⁴² We may
suspect that *skeggi* relates to *skegg* in much the same way that *typpi* (an apparent
neologism of Arnórr jarlaskáld's) probably relates to *toppr*, 'top':⁴³

> Uppi glóðu élmars typpi
> eldi glík. (*Hrynhenda* 10)⁴⁴

The blizzard-steed's forelocks glowed aloft like fire.

Working through an extended marine metaphor, Arnórr weaves a dazzling
pattern in which the gilded tip of a ship's mast is also, simultaneously, the
fiery mane of a shaggy beast.⁴⁵ It may be particularly appropriate that the
bucking storm-rider with ruddy coat is a vessel named *Visundr*, 'Bison.'⁴⁶ Even

comprehensible formation like 'guesstimate,' which does not evince the existence of '*-stimate' as a
generally productive suffix). In Old Irish, too, *Sciggire* means 'The Faroe Islands' (E.G. Quin, ed.,
Dictionary of the Irish Language, Based Mainly on Old and Middle Irish Materials, Compact Edn
[Dublin 1983], s.v.); de Vries, *Wörterbuch*, s. *skegg*, derives *Sciggire* from ON *Skeggjar*. Might not its
confinement, in both Irish and Norse, to a specific geographic contact zone suggest instead a Celtic
origin (or an obscure local dialect), which Norse folk etymology could then assimilate to a
seemingly meaningful ON form? (Carl J.S. Marstrander, on the contrary, proposes assimilation of a
Norse form to the Irish homonym *sciggire*, 'fool, jester'; *Bidrag til det norske Sprogs Historie i Irland*,
Videnskapsselskapets Skrifter, II. Hist.-Filos Klasse, 1915 5 [Christiania 1915], 92.) Cleasby-
Vigfusson's imaginative definition of *eyjarskeggi* ('prob. originally a sort of sobriquet, owing to the
notion that islanders were more rough and wild in their habits than other men,' s. *skeggi*; cf. LP
(1913-16), s. *eyjarskeggi*) smacks of just such etiological rationalization.
⁴² See Falk, *Waffenkunde*, 108-10, and de Vries, *Wörterbuch*, s. *skegg*.
⁴³ See Diana Whaley, *The Poetry of Arnórr jarlaskáld: An Edition and Study*, Westfield Publications
in Medieval Studies 8 (Turnhout 1998), 77, 164.
⁴⁴ *Skj* Bi, 308; translation adapted from Whaley, *Poetry of Arnórr*, 77, 163.
⁴⁵ Judith Jesch has recently suggested that 'élmars typpi' may refer not to the masthead but to a gilt
copper weathervane fastened to the fore-stem (*Ships and Men in the Late Viking Age: The
Vocabulary of Runic Inscriptions and Skaldic Verse* [Woodbridge 2001], 162, cf. fig. 4.8 at 161; cf.,
however, Sigvatr's verse, cited in the following note). Right or wrong, her interpretation has no
bearing on my argument.
⁴⁶ Earlier in the same strophe, Árnorr terms the ship 'goll et rauða' (the red gold). It is perhaps no
coincidence that Sigvatr Þórðarson also alludes to Visundr's golden mast-top (in his *Erfidrápa
Ólafs helga* 16, referring to the king as 'hyrsendir ... húna' (distributor of the mast-top's fire [i.e.
gold] (?)) (*Skj* Bi, 242-3); see Whaley, *Poetry of Arnórr*, 163-4, citing Finn Reinskou's suggestion

more so than the workaday nautical noun *toppr*, the by-form *typpi* may help sustain both its proximate literal sense, 'masthead,' and its metaphorical and etymological base sense, 'tuft [of hair]' or 'forelock,'[47] underscoring the ontological continuity between the top of the mast and the animal's fleece. Just as *typpi* locates and concretizes an ersatz cowlick, so a ghostly beard may limn every *skeggi*.

What, then, might be the bearded thing to which Gísli points? Given the harshly pornographic idiom of the preceding lines, it hardly seems an obscene stretch to suspect that he might have in mind that region of his opponent's physiology which, like Alisoun's 'ers,' is garlanded with a 'berd ... al rough and long yherd.'[48] The juxtaposition of facial, armpit, and pubic hair in the *Sachsenspiegel*'s characterization of adult masculinity, cited above, further clarifies how hair above and below the tunic might become conceptually interchangeable. Moreover, a tradition of superimposing facial features on the pudenda is firmly rooted in skaldic usage. Interlacing anatomical and botanical metaphors, Eilífr Goðrúnarson calls the deluge of urine and menstrual blood foaming from between a giantess's thighs 'Fríðar fen svarðrunnit' ('Fríðr's sward-runoff fen,' as well as 'Fríðr's hair-swamp

---

that this was the first Norse ship with gilt vanes ('Olav den helliges vimpel?' *MM* 14, no. 1 [1922]: 32-6, at 34-5). European bison typically have golden-brown coats; for photos, see the website ⟨http://bison.zbs.bialowieza.pl/puszcza/zubry.htm⟩. Note also that both Árnorr and Sigvatr base their kennings on terms drawn from the animal kingdom, *marr*, 'steed,' and *húnn*, 'bear cub'; on the literary effects of such consistency of metaphor, see Roberta Frank, *Old Norse Court Poetry: The Dróttkvætt Stanza*, Islandica 42 (Ithaca and London 1978), 46-9, and cf. Jesch, *Ships and Men*, 137.

[47] To ON *toppr*, cf. such cognates as OE *top*, 'top, tassel, tuft,' OF *top*, 'tuft, sheaf, bundle' (whence English 'toupee'), OHG *zopf*, 'lock [of hair], curl'; all cited by de Vries, *Wörterbuch*, s.v. While the root sense may have been 'top, apex,' 'tip, protrusion,' or 'tail, penis, extension' (traced back to the reconstructed IE roots *dub-* or *deu-*), in ON and in most other European languages hirsute (or leafy) senses predominate; see, e.g., Cleasby-Vigfusson, s.v., sense 1; Fritzner, s.v., sense 2; LP (1913-16), s.v. ('top, nedhængende hårdusk,' 'top, swaying locks'); Oskar Schade, *Althochdeutsches Wörterbuch*, 2 vols (Halle a.S., 1872-82), s. *zoph, zopf. Toppr* can even be used as a metaphor for a moustache: 'toppr fyr nefi' (forelock in front of the nose) a giantess calls it in a verse (*Skj*, B2, 316; Qrvar-Odds saga, chap. 18, FSN 2:274).

[48] See Geoffrey Chaucer, 'The Miller's Tale,' ll. 3734-8 (in Larry D. Benson, ed., *The Riverside Chaucer* 3rd edn [New York 1987], 75). Middle English medical texts routinely refer to pubic hair as the 'neþir berd' (or even 'berde' *tout court*; see *MED*, s. *berd*, sense 4a [a]). Absolon, incidentally, underlines the prevalence of the general cultural principle that genders may be demarcated by facial hair: like Gangleri, 'wel he wiste a womman hath no berd' (l. 3737; cf. *Gylfaginning*, chap. 33: 'Sét munt þú hafa, at konan hefir ekki skegg' [You will have noticed that a woman has no beard] in *Edda*, 33).

spillage').[49] Later in the same poem, Eilífr seems to hint again at female pubes with the kenning *gránhǫttr* ('grey hood' but perhaps also 'foul head-hair').[50] 'The extension of *svǫrðr* in [the former] kenning from the basic sense of "skin of the head and its attached hair" to the pubic hair is, of course, dependent on the equation of the mouth with the vagina,' as Margaret Clunies Ross notes.[51] Eilífr's syllogism implies that, if all female orifices may be collapsed together, then the hair contiguous with any one of them must be identical with that adjacent to any other.

By a different para-logical displacement – dependent on the wagging, motile, and darting analogy between tongue, penis, and weaponry – men's genitalia may also be linked to their faces.[52] Skaldic kennings refer to a sword's blade as its tongue ('meðalkafla tunga,' for instance [tongue of the hand-grip])[53] or, conversely, to the tongue as a 'góma sverð' [sword of the gums].[54] 'Vâpn þat, er stendr meðal fóta manni,' a late paper copy of *Snorra Edda* explains, 'heitir sverð eða brandr ok öllum sverðs heitum' [That weapon which stands between a man's legs is called sword or sabre, as well as by all sword appellations].[55] Perhaps the most forthright (if also most baroque) analogy between men's oral and genital parts is drawn by the declining Egill who, in a

[49] *Þórsdrápa* 6 (*Skj* B1, 140). Fríðr is a generic feminine *heiti*. For a detailed gloss of this phrase, see Margaret Clunies Ross, 'An Interpretation of the Myth of Þórr's Encounter with Geirrøðr and his Daughters,' in *Speculum Norroenum*, 370-91, at 375.

[50] *Þórsdrápa* 13 (*Skj* B1, 142). See Clunies Ross, 'An Interpretation,' 381-2, and, for the alternative reading of the kenning, Vilhelm Kiil, 'Eilífr Guðrúnarson's *Þórsdrápa*,' *Arkiv för nordisk filologi* 71 (1956): 89-167, at 141-2.

[51] 'An Interpretation,' 375 n. 21 (n. continued at 376).

[52] Cf. Carol J. Clover's discussion in 'Regardless of Sex: Men, Women, and Power in Early Northern Europe,' *Speculum* 68, no. 2 (1993): 363-87, at 384-5.

[53] See LP (1913-16), s. *tunga*, drawing on Óláfr Þórðarson hvítaskáld (*Skj* B2, 107).

[54] See Meissner, *Kenningar*, 133.

[55] See *Edda Snorra Sturlusonar: Edda Snorronis Sturlæi*, ed. Jón Sigurðsson et al., 3 vols (Copenhagen 1848-87), 1:542-3 n. 21 (at 543), v.l. to *Skáldskaparmál*, chap. 71. The reading (apparently from the late eighteenth-century MS JS 198, 4to; see the editors' description of the MS at 1:vii and cf. §5089 in *Skrá um handritasöfn Landsbókasafnsins*, ed. Páll Eggert Ólason, 3 vols [Reykjavík 1918-37], 2:525) can only be traced back with certainty as far as the 1609 Laufás copy of the *Edda* (see Almqvist, *Niddiktning*, 1:177 n. 70). Cf. OE gender terminology: men are *wæpned* — 'wepned & wif geworhte hiæ God' (male and female created them God), says the Rushworth St Matthew, 19:4 in *The Lindisfarne and Rushworth Gospels*, ed. Joseph Stevenson, Publications of the Surtees Society 28 (Edinburgh 1854), 162 – probably an allusion to their physiology rather than to their accoutrement, since it can also be applied to male children or even plants (BT, s. *wæpned-bearn, wæpned-cild, wæpned-mann* [sense II]).

famous catalogue of geriatric ills, complains of his 'blautr ... bergifótar borr.'[56] 'Blautr borr' clearly means 'soft drill bit,' but what the 'bergifótr' qualifying it might be is more of a vexed question. Sveinbjörn Egilsson understands 'bergi' as 'rocks,' synonymous with *klettar,* which recall their homonym *kletti,* 'loins'; the kenning as a whole thus bewails the 'yielding tip of the limb of the loins.'[57] Finnur Jónsson, on the other hand, takes 'bergifótr' to mean 'head,' whose waxen bore is thus Egill's leaden tongue.[58] But the full impact of Egill's lament over his lost youth, over the virility that no longer infuses any of his vital members, only registers '[i]f one assumes,' like Carol Clover, 'that the art of the line lies precisely in its duplicity and that *both* meanings (penis *and* tongue) inhere in it (skaldic verse is nothing if not a poetry of the double entendre).'[59] With the very words that bemoan his inability to do so, Egill shoots from the hip, sticking out a sassy tongue at any who would mock his frailty.[60]

As densely compacted as Egill's 'bergifótr,' *skeggi* attains meaning by enhancing one attribute of manhood out of all proportion. The choice of attribute thus magnified is a matter of cultural consequence, just as the imputation of 'ravishing' beauty to those women after whom men lust tells us much about the assumptions behind the way language serves up our own

---

[56] *Skj* B1, 52; see also *Egils saga,* chap. 85 (ÍF 2:294), where the reading *bergis fót*[r] is preferred.
[57] See LP (1860), s. *bergi.* (Sveinbjörn also offers a less likely alternative interpretation, taking 'berg fótar' [sic] as 'buttocks' and unpacking the kenning in its entirety as a reference to shaky legs.) Cf. Erik Noreen, 'Om Egilssagans lausavísur,' in his 'Studier i fornvästnordisk diktning, andra samlingen,' *Uppsala Universitets årsskrift: Filosofi, språkvetenskap och historiska vetenskaper* 4 (1922): 31-6, at 35-6 n. 4, and Sigurður Nordal's remarks in ÍF 2:294 n., both citing Óláfr hvítaskáld's recognition of the verse as veiled obscenity (*Den tredje og fjærde grammatiske Afhandling i Snorres Edda,* ed. Björn Magnússon Ólsen, STUAGNL 12 [Copenhagen 1884], 114); also mentioned by Frank, *Old Norse Court Poetry,* 162.
[58] See LP (1913-16), s. *bergifótr.* Meissner disagrees with Finnur's interpretation of the base term, but concurs on the sense of the kenning as a whole: 'Eher ist *bergifótr* selbst als Zunge aufzufassen (*borr,* Spitze der Zunge?)' (*Kenningar,* 134) (It is better to take *bergifótr* itself as tongue [*borr,* the tip of the tongue?]).
[59] 'Regardless of Sex,' 384 (emphases hers).
[60] Cf. *Ketils saga hængs,* chap. 5, where the villain Framarr taunts Ketill during their duel: 'Skelfr skegg á karli, skeika vápn gǫmlum' (the [old] fellow's beard trembles, the geezer's blade wobbles); Ketill's infuriated response ('Þarfatt oss eggja!' [You ought not bait me]; *Skj* B2, 307-8, cf. FSN 2:179-80) suggests that he takes the insinuation rather personally, more so, it seems, than a mere slight to his swordsmanship.

world to us.[61] It is surely significant that, in opposition to women's soggy, lush 'mǫrnis mór' (moor of the cock), 'háfs mǫrk' (forest of the fish-weir), or 'læra skógr' (grove of the thighs),[62] men's pudenda are characterized by their unkempt shag.[63] (We may begin to wonder whether Ragnarr did, in fact, feel the need to wear breeches at all.) Contrary to Clover's insightful and influential suggestion of a Norse 'one-sex system,'[64] the overlap of concrete bearded pubes with abstract masculinity seems to hint at a conceptual system where gender is determined not only by manly behaviour but also by physical sex. It takes more than conduct as a *drengr*, 'stalwart,' to gain admission into the company of those who are *hvatr*, 'butch.'

An episode in the fourteenth-century *Þorleifs þáttr jarlsskálds* helps clinch the metaphoric link between upper and nether beards. The protagonist of the tale, the poet Þorleifr, has been sorely mistreated by Jarl Hákon. To wreak his revenge, Þorleifr comes before Hákon in disguise and offers to perform a poem in his honour. At first, 'þykkir jarli lof í hverri vísu' (it seemed to the jarl that there was praise in every strophe); but soon the defamatory venom with which the verse is laced begins to work its magical affliction on him, producing dire symptoms:

Er á leið kvæðit, þá bregðr jarli nǫkkut undarliga við, at óværi ok klái hleypr svá mikill um allan búkinn á honum ok einna mest um þjóin, at hann mátti hvergi kyrr þola, ok svá mikil bysn fylgdi þessum óværa, at hann lét hrífa sér með kǫmbum, þar sem þeim kom at; en þar sem þeim kom eigi at, lét hann taka strigadúk ok ríða á þrjá knúta ok draga tvá menn milli þjóanna á sér. (chap. 5, ÍF 9:222)

---

[61] On the displacement of 'ravishment' from its male subject to its female object, see Kathryn Gravdal, *Ravishing Maidens: Writing Rape in Medieval French Literature and Law* (Philadelphia 1991), 5.

[62] For these kennings, see, respectively, Almqvist, *Niddiktning*, 1.166-78, citing the *níð* Icelanders composed against Haraldr Gormsson (*Skj* B1, 166; Snorri Sturluson, *Óláfs saga Tryggvasonar*, chap. 33, in his *Heimskringla*, ÍF 26:270); Roberta Frank, 'Hand Tools and Power Tools in Eilífr's *Þórsdrápa*,' in John Lindow, Lars Lönnroth, and Gerd Wolfgang Weber, eds, *Structure and Meaning in Old Norse Literature: New Approaches to Textual Analysis and Literary Criticism*, (Odense 1986), 94-109, at 97, citing *Þórsdrápa* 6 (*Skj* B1, 140); and LP (1913-16), s. *skógr*, citing *Grettis saga*, chap. 75 (ÍF 7:241; *Skj* B2, 474).

[63] In dialectical Swedish, however, *skägga-mumma*, 'bearded-mouth (?),' occurs as a term for the vulva; see §143:28 in Torild W. Arnoldson, *Parts of the Body in Older Germanic and Scandinavian*, Linguistic Studies in Germanic 2 (Chicago 1915), 175.

[64] 'Regardless of Sex.'

As the poem wore on, the jarl was rather remarkably startled that a discomfort and itching started up all around his belly and most of all about his thighs, so great that he was utterly unable to endure it in silence, and the discomfort was so ominous that he had himself scraped with combs wherever they could reach; and where they could not reach, he had three knots tied in a length of burlap and two men pulled it between his thighs.[65]

Clearly, Hákon is contending with unnatural ants in his pants. Things only get worse as Þorleifr snuffs the lights, sends weapons flying through the hall and then makes a clean escape. When the dust settles, it is discovered that 'af var rotnat skegg allt af jarli ok hárit ǫðrum megin reikar ok kom aldri upp síðan' (chap. 5, ÍF 9:223) (the jarl's beard had entirely putrefied, as well as the hair across from his parting, and it never grew afterwards). While modern readers of the story resist any direct connection with the preceding itch in Hákon's groin, taking this blight to mean that he was rendered half-bald and beardless, a medieval Norse audience would likely have inferred that the unbearable irritation causes him hair loss down under.[66] One late paper MS attests to just such an understanding, stating that 'hánum var rifit allt kviðskeggit' (his belly-beard was all torn).[67] Gísli's term *skeggi* should, perhaps,

---

[65] Several words here are capable of various translations, which would slightly (but significantly) alter the meaning. For instance, *búkr* (cognate with German 'Bauch') may mean either 'the torso, trunk' or, more specifically, its lower portion, 'the belly'; *þjó* (cognate with English 'thigh'), usually taken to mean 'buttocks' (esp. in the pl.), may refer more generally to the upper leg. See Cleasby-Vigfusson, s.vv., and Fritzner, s.vv. My choice of meanings is obviously guided by the reading I espouse but, inasmuch as it seems to contribute to the coherence of the passage, is not arbitrary. Note, incidentally, the parody of hagiographic motifs in this passage: torment by raking of the flesh (cf., e.g., the martyrdoms of St Agatha or St Theodore, in Jacobus de Voragine's *Legenda aurea*, ed. Th. Graesse, 2nd edn [Leipzig 1850], 172, 740-1) and the wearing of sackcloth (cf., e.g., the Life of St Radegund, *Legenda aurea*, 953).

[66] The reference to the hair 'ǫðrum megin reikar' (on one side of the parting) may be particularly suggestive: fem. *reik*, 'Skillelinie paa Menneskets Hoved fra Panden til Nakken, hvorfra Haaret deler sig og falder nedover til begge Sider' (Fritzner, s.v.) (demarcation line on a person's head from the forehead to the occiput, from which the hair divides and falls down both ways), may be compared to such terms as *gil* (cleft) or *skarð* (pass, gap), used of women's vaginal opening as well as (in *níð*) of the slit between a man's buttocks (see, e.g., *Króka-Refs saga*, chap. 17, ÍF 14:154-5; *Ǫlkofra þáttr*, chap. 4, ÍF 11:94). 'Hárit ǫðrum megin reikar' should perhaps be translated as 'the hair on one side of the crotch.'

[67] MS AM 563a 4to (of the latter half of the seventeenth century; see *Katalog over den arnamagnæanske Håndskriftsamling*, [ed. Kristian Kålund,] 2 vols [Copenhagen 1888-94], 1:716),

be taken as synonymous with this more transparent form *kviðskegg*, just as *skeggja* corresponds to the compound *skeggøx*.[68]

Interpreting *skeggi* as Skeggi's private parts reintegrates the final line of Gísli's verse into the violent, cerebral, and unflinchingly bawdy exchange which Sørensen has uncovered in the first three lines of these *kviðlingar*. Such a reading also allows Gísli's *níð* to needle his adversary at every interpretative turn of the verbal phrase. Whether 'hjók til' implies a devastating blow or a mere grazing flick of the blade, Gísli here asserts that he has mussed his enemy's private hairdo, if not circumcised or castrated him outright.

Furthermore, with Skeggi's proper name pried loose of the verse, my reading implies that the *kviðlingar* no longer contain any internal evidence anchoring them to the story of Gísli, much less to the specific context the saga supplies. Holtsmark and Sørensen have shown how the saga author, striving to make sense of the enigmatic *Saxa*, invented an island Skeggi could call home; it now seems possible that the resident of this island, too, might be a prosaic mirage. Sublimated to an entirely symbolic language of sexual one-upmanship, the *kviðlingar* could well have circulated independent of any specific historical circumstance. Indeed, they may have been proverbial. Gísli's later exchange with his treacherous brother-in-law Þorgrímr (*Gísla saga* chap. 15, ÍF 6:50; *Skj* B1, 95, 97) — a structural parallel of opaque and vicious couplets – may argue for the traditional attribution, confirming that our *kviðlingar*, too, bear Gísli's stylistic fingerprint. But it could just as easily suggest that an enterprising saga author, noting the similarities with the tradition of Gísli and Þorgrímr's dialogue, deemed the style of these *kviðlingar* appropriately Gíslian and decided to incorporate them into his narrative.[69]

Still, even without conclusive proof, I am inclined to believe that the verses in question do belong in Gísli's oeuvre. In the opening chapters of the

cited as v.l. in Guðmundur Þorláksson and Finnur Jónsson, eds, *Íslenzkar fornsögur*, 3 vols (Copenhagen 1880-3), 3:125. The scribe responsible for this MS covered all his bases: 'Hánum var rifit allt kviðskeggit ok hárit á höfðinu' (His belly-beard was all torn, as well as the hair on his head), he writes.

[68] Cf. Grettir's reference to his 'lágr faxi' (*Grettis saga*, chap. 75, ÍF 7:241; *Skj* B2, 474): in glossing this expression as 'penis' (lit. 'nether horse'), Finnur Jónsson and Guðni Jónsson both feel obliged to point out that *faxi*, 'stallion,' here means more generically 'something with a mane' (see LP [1913-16], s.v.; ÍF 7:241 n.). If my reading of *skeggi* is accepted, might not Grettir's *faxi* simply be a weak by-form of *fax*, implying a 'mane down below'?

[69] As Holtsmark, following Magnus Olsen ('Om Gísla saga's opbygning,' *Arkiv för nordisk filologi* 46 [1930]: 150-60, at 153-4, esp. 153 n. 1), suggests (*Studies*, 27).

saga, Sørensen exposes a general obsession with establishing and maintaining one's own gender identity while calling into question one's opponents'; the recurring idiom in which this gender warfare is waged centres on sexual assault and degradation, precisely the sort of language the two antagonists who utter these *kviðlingar* wield. The saga's obscene obsession will climax in the account of Þorgrímr's murder. Having inadvertently grasped his sister's breast in the dark, Gísli waits by the bedside as Þórdís and Þorgrímr snuggle: 'Þorgrímr mælti: "Viltu at ek snúumk at þér?" Hon hugði, at hann legði hǫndina yfir hana' (chap. 16, ÍF 6:53) [Þorgrímr spoke: "Do you want me to turn to you?" She thought he had put his arm around her).[70] Only after the two fall back to sleep does Gísli nudge Þorgrímr again, running him through when the latter turns towards his wife. In this scene, Gísli switches roles from incestuous (but gentle and heterosexual) male to furtive voyeur, then impersonates female heterosexual propriety, inviting his 'husband' to take the initiative in the sex act, finally reverting abruptly to (metaphorical) male homosexual aggression and countering Þorgrímr's pelvic thrust with a far keener stab of his own: ['Þorgrímr] snerisk þá at henni. Gísli [leggr] í gegnum Þorgrím með Grásíðu, svá at í beðinum nam stað' (chap. 16, ÍF 6:54) ([Þorgrímr] then turned towards her. Gísli [lays] into Þorgrím with [the spear] Grásíða, so that it lodged in the bed).[71]

The layered ironies of the bedroom scene are matched by those of the sword-personae projected in Skeggi and Gísli's *kviðlingar*. Gísli's blade at first appears as a receptive, heterosexual female, yielding to the aggressive advances of a male of the species; the would-be sexual predator is next exposed as an

---

[70] To put an arm or a leg over a woman (*leggja hǫnd* [or *arm* or *lær*] *yfir*), as well as to turn towards her (in this context; *snúask til* [or *at*]), is, in ON, to have intercourse with her; see Andersson, 'Some Ambiguities,' 37-8, and Jenny Jochens, *Women in Old Norse Society* (Ithaca and London 1995), 72-3.

[71] The themes of incest and homosexuality, which recur faintly all through *Gísla saga*, have so far received little critical attention (beyond noting the consistent zeal with which Gísli terminates his sister's amorous ties). Auðr and Ásgerðr, respectively Gísli's wife and his brother Þorkell's, discuss cooperating to make items of intimate apparel – a task which, presumably, only a wife should handle – for the former's brother and two brothers-in-law (chap. 9, ÍF 6:30-1); later in the saga, in an otherwise empty house, Auðr lies close by her brother's side on the night he is murdered (chap. 13, ÍF 6:43). Thematizing on the basis of such hints, Ágúst Guðmundsson's 1981 film adaptation of the saga, *Útlaginn*, depicts Þórdís as the erotic and menacing dream woman who haunts Gísli's nights. Note also that Gísli's apparently affectionate marriage to Auðr produces no children; perhaps Skeggi knew something we do not when he undertook to represent Gísli and Kolbjǫrn as lovers.

impotent pervert; finally, Gísli emerges as a male homosexual aggressor, boasting of having crippled his foe in a genital encounter. The particular aesthetics I impute to Gísli may not pass for polished elegance in the twenty-first century, but medieval sensibilities seem to have been less squeamish when it came to taking credit for mortifying and maiming an enemy. One can easily imagine how the warrior-poet behind all this butting of belly-beards must have 'brugðit grǫnum' (stretched back his whiskers), baring well-honed skaldic teeth in a satisfied grin.

13

Prophetic Dreams and Visions in the Sagas of the Early Icelandic Saints

BERNADINE MCCREESH

The belief that revelations can be sent via dreams is widespread. As A.C. Spearing says: 'Most people cling instinctively to the notion that dreams are composed in a language which is intelligible in principle, though it requires interpretation.' Many ancient peoples in particular believed that the future could be revealed while a person slept. In the Old Testament, for example, dreams were considered to be divine in origin. Although prophetic dreams could be sent to non-Jews, only Jewish prophets had the power to decipher them, as can be seen from the stories of Joseph's interpretation of Pharaoh's dreams (Gen. 40-1) and, especially, Daniel's interpretation of Nebuchadnezzar's (Dan. 2-4).² For the ancient Greeks, who believed that the soul separated from the body in sleep, dreams provided a gateway to an otherwise inaccessible world.³ Among the Romans, a belief in prophetic dreams also seems to have been widespread, if the examples in Cicero's *De divinatione* are anything to go by (though Cicero himself expresses scepticism); in official circles, however, the Romans had recourse to augurs rather than to dream interpreters.⁴

---

¹ *Medieval Dream-Poetry* (Cambridge 1976), 10. On the development of Western views on dreaming, see Susan Parman, *Dreams and Culture: An Anthropological Study of the Western Tradition* (New York 1991).
² See Jean-Marie Husser, *Dreams and Dream Narratives in the Biblical World*, trans. Jill M. Munro (Sheffield 1999).
³ See E.R. Dodds, *The Greeks and the Irrational* (Berkeley 1951), 102-34; Angelo Brelich, 'The Place of Dreams in the Religious World Concept of the Greeks,' in G.E. von Grunebaum and Roger Callois, eds, *The Dream and Human Sciences* (Berkeley and Los Angeles 1966), 293-301; A.H.M. Kessels, *Studies on the Dream in Greek Literature* (Utrecht 1978); and R.G.A. van Lieshout, *Greeks on Dreams* (Utrecht 1980).
⁴ Still useful on Greek and Roman dream theories is Francis X. Newman, 'Somnium: Medieval Theories of Dreaming and the Form of Vision Poetry' (diss. Princeton University 1962), 1-128. On dream theory and interpretation up to the later Roman period, see Patricia Cox Miller, *Dreams in*

The Church's attitude to prophecy and prophetic dreams was somewhat ambivalent at first. In the early days of Christianity, even though people still believed in the power of dreams to give a glimpse of the future, dream interpreters were banned from baptism.[5] Then the Church decided to appropriate prophecy for its own use, as Valerie Flint explains:

> Much of the demonic magic and witchcraft of the non-Jewish and non-Christian dispensations was ... concerned with looking into and, if possible, determining the future ... No true Christian could doubt that this was wrong. It was an affront both to the idea of Divine foreknowledge and Providence, and to the doctrine of the freedom of the will; but there was a way out of the problem. Though the Old Testament hated diviners (Numbers 22:7, 23:23), the Jews had been allowed their prophets by their God ... Some form of looking into the future must, therefore, be allowable in its own right ... Augustine [354-430 A.D.] came positively to defend the idea of prophecy in the Late Antique Christian Church, and again, it seems, as both a defence against, and a substitute for, the older consolations pagan divination offered.[6]

By the late sixth century, both prophecy and prophetic dreams and visions were fully accepted by the Church as gifts of God, as St Gregory the Great explains:

> By granting these men the spirit of prophecy he [God] raises their minds high above the world, and by withdrawing it again he safeguards their humility. All this reflects God's boundless wisdom and love.[7]

Late Antiquity: Studies in the Imagination of a Culture (Princeton 1994), 14-105; on Cicero 44-6. On Ciceronian and later scepticism regarding dream interpretation, see Steven F. Kruger, *Dreaming in the Middle Ages* (Cambridge 1992), 87-8.

[5] Guy Stroumsa, 'Dreams and Visions in Early Christian Discourse,' in David Shulmann and Guy G. Stroumsa, eds, *Dream Cultures: Explorations in the Comparative History of Dreaming* (Oxford and New York 1999), 189-212.

[6] *The Athlone History of Witchcraft and Magic in Europe* (London 1999), 2:338-9.

[7] St Gregory the Great, *Dialogues*, trans. Odo John Zimmerman (New York 1959), 191.

This gift was, however, limited to people who were distinguished by their holiness; dream interpretation among the laity still met with disapproval.[8]

Once saintly dreams and visions were legitimized by the Church, they became an integral part of the hagiographic tradition.[9] Their authenticity, however, does not seem to have been a matter of great concern to medieval hagiographers. For example, in the lives of both St Dominic and St Francis, founders of orders of friars, the pope is supposed to have dreamed of a falling church propped up on the saint's shoulders before he gave permission for the new order to be founded. Thomas Heffernan explains the legitimizing effect of employing conventional motifs:

> For sacred biographers, there existed a veritable thesaurus of established approved actions which they could employ in their texts. The repetition of actions taken from Scripture or from earlier saints' lives ... ensured the authenticity of the subject's sanctity.[10]

Within the hagiographic tradition, dreams tend to appear at certain key points in saints' lives. Their mothers often dream of their future greatness before they are born. Strange happenings in childhood predict events in their adult life. When an important decision has to be made, an angelic messenger may appear to suggest the right course of action. At the moment of death, dying monks and nuns or their companions may see saints welcoming them into heaven. In addition, many saints are able to see what is happening at another time or in another place. The purpose of these supernatural dreams and visions is to show that 'their [the saints'] world was infused with divine purpose, and for their hagiographers, that the saints' success was predetermined.'[11]

Dreams and visions also play an important part in Old Icelandic literature. Here their purpose is not to show that the world is infused with

---

[8] For a discussion of the Church's attitude to dreams, see Kruger, *Dreaming in the Middle Ages*, 7-16.

[9] On the development of Christian attitudes towards dreams, especially ecclesiastical control and the authorization of a dreaming elite, see Jacques Le Goff, *The Medieval Imagination*, trans. Arthur Goldhammer (Chicago and London 1988), 193-231, incl. a list of dreams in the OT (229-31).

[10] *Sacred Biography: Saints and their Biographers in the Middle Ages* (Oxford and New York 1988), 6.

[11] Isabel Moreira, *Dreams, Visions, and Spiritual Authority in Merovingian Gaul* (Ithaca and London 2000), 173.

divine purpose but to prepare the audience for the imminent death of one or more characters. In parts of sagas set in pre-Christian times, men tend to see *fylgjur* (fetches, usually in animal form and bearing some sort of resemblance to the man they represent) shortly before they die. The *fylgjur* seem to derive from a pre-Christian belief in an animal-soul or alter ego. In the case of witches and magicians, this alter ego can be sent forth in animal form while the body lies in a restless sleep; if the alter ego is injured, so too is the dreamer. In the case of ordinary men, animal-*fylgjur*, which can represent either the man to be attacked or his enemies or both, usually appear in a dream or vision shortly before the person concerned embarks on his last fatal journey.[12] E.O.G. Turville-Petre has already pointed out that many *fylgjur* appear in the form of animals not found in Iceland, such as bears, wolves, and foxes.[13] Given that these animals are found on the mainland of northern Europe, their presence in the Icelandic sagas might be taken to suggest that the belief in the *fylgja* antedates the settlement of Iceland. However, Turville-Petre has also pointed out that the interpretation of *fylgja*-motifs agrees with the interpretation of similar dream symbols in the *Somniale Danielis*, a manual originally written in Greek in the fourth century A.D. and translated into Latin three centuries later. The conclusion he draws is:

> For the most part, the dreams of which we read in sagas must be regarded as artistic embellishment. The symbols published in the *Somniale* were made to accord with the literary tastes of Icelanders and with certain occult beliefs which they already held.[14]

In a similar vein, Paul Schach has pointed out European analogues to the dreams in *Sverris saga* and has come to the conclusion that Sverrir's four dreams of future kingship 'were in all probability the fabrication of the king or his biographer or both of them.'[15] Diana Whaley makes similar remarks:

[12] The standard work on dreams in Old Icelandic literature is Gloria Dunham Kelchner, *Dreams in Old Norse Literature and their Affinities in Folklore* (Cambridge 1935). See also Richard Perkins, 'The Dreams of *Flóamanna saga*,' *Saga-Book* 80 (1974): 191-238; and W. Henzen, *Über die Träume in der altnordischen Sagaliteratur* (Leipzig 1890).
[13] 'Dreams in Icelandic Tradition,' *Folklore* 69 (1958): 93-111.
[14] E.O.G. Turville-Petre, 'An Icelandic Version of the *Somniale Danielis*,' in Allan H. Orrick, ed., *Nordica et Anglica* (The Hague 1968), 19-36, at 31.
[15] 'Symbolic Dreams of Future Renown in Old Icelandic Literature,' *Mosaic* 4 (1971): 51-73.

'Even *Sturlunga saga* ... makes use of imagined dialogue, dreams and prophecies which, like the feud structures which prevail in the Íslendingasögur, represent actual experience honed into literary conventions.'[16]

Prophetic dreams, then, often function as artistic embellishments in both the hagiographical tradition of Europe and the historical tradition of Iceland. What happens to the motif when history and hagiography meet in the early literature of Iceland? This meeting point can be found in the lives of the early Icelandic saints. Note that the word 'saint' needs to be taken rather loosely in this context, because not all people regarded as saints were actually canonized. Their *vitae* were, however, written in anticipation of the happy event and as such fall into the domain of saints' lives. The Icelandic bishops for whom we have sagas or lives are St Þorlákr Þórhallsson (1176-93) and Bishops Páll Jónsson (1195-1211) and Árni Þorláksson (1269-98) of Skálholt, and St Jón Ögmundarson (1106-21) and Bishops Guðmundr Arason (1203-37) and Laurentius Kálfsson (1324-31) of Hólar.[17] Of these bishops, Páll Jónsson, Árni Þorláksson, and Laurentius Kálfsson appear not to have been candidates for canonization, and *Páls saga* and *Árna saga* display hardly any of the usual features of saints' lives. By contrast, the later *Laurentius saga* displays all the motifs found in Icelandic hagiography and is, in fact, the culmination of the genre. In addition to these bishops, the Icelanders also revered certain warrior-saints, such as St Magnús of the Orkneys, and, in particular, Ólafr Tryggvason, who, although never canonized, was still looked on as a saint by the Icelanders because he was the one responsible for converting their country to Christianity.

The prophecy or miracle at birth is very common in hagiographic literature and probably has its origin in the Bible, from the message of the angel at the Annunciation (Luke 1:26-38), from Elizabeth's exclamation at the Visitation (Luke 1:39-56), from the portents at the Nativity (Luke 2:10-14), or

---

[16] *Heimskringla: an Introduction* (London 1991), 135.
[17] *Byskupa Sögur*, ed. Guðni Jónsson, 3 vols (Reykjavík 1953). The versions of the bishops' lives used in this essay are *Árna saga byskups* in *Byskupa Sögur* I, 285-457; *Guðmundar saga Arasonar* in *Byskupa Sögur* II, 167-389; *Jóns saga Helga eftir Gunnlaug munk* in *Byskupa Sögur* II, 1-74; *Laurentius saga* in *Byskupa Sögur* III, 1-144; *Páls saga byskups* in *Byskupa Sögur* I, 251-83; *Þorláks saga byskups* in *Byskupa Sögur* I, 33-129.

from Anna's prophecy at the Presentation (Luke 2:36-8).[18] The purpose of the motif is to emphasize the saint's sanctity, to show how he or she has been chosen by God from birth or early childhood, or even before birth. In the Family Sagas, on the other hand, prebirth and childhood prophecies are extremely rare and the few examples that do occur refer to girls. A prebirth prophecy is found in *Gunnlaugs saga ormstungu*, in which the father of the as yet unborn heroine sees in a dream his future daughter, her suitors and her eventual husband in the form of birds (chap. 2, ÍF 3:55). A childhood prophecy occurs in *Njáls saga*, with a reference to Hallgerðr's 'thief's eyes' (chap. 1, ÍF 12:7). In the *Laxdœla saga*, Guðrún, who is about fifteen at the time, dreams of her four future husbands (chap. 33, ÍF 5:88-91). If the future of young men is hinted at, it is usually with reference to their deaths, as can be seen in the case of Kjartan and Bolli, also in *Laxdœla saga* (chap. 33, ÍF 5:88).

In the Bishops' Sagas, on the other hand, birth and childhood prophecies are relatively common. In *Laurentius saga,* for example, the saint's future career is revealed to his mother in a dream before his birth. She imagines that she is led through a crowded church to the high altar, where a cloth with a bishop's signet-ring is pressed into her hand (*Bysk.* III, chap. 2, p. 3). As for Guðmundr and Jón, their future glory is revealed in predictions, in the case of the former by a wise man, and in the case of the latter by King Óláfr and Queen Ástríðr, mother of King Sveinn of Denmark (*Bysk.* II, chap. 4, pp. 5-6). Guðmundr's birth prophecy is not very specific: the wise man merely says that 'þat barn mundi verða afbragð annarra manna, ef lífi heldi' (*Bysk.* II, chap. 2, p. 172) (the child would surpass all other men if he survived). It is only when Guðmundr becomes a boy and always takes the part of a bishop when playing with a friend that his future becomes more obvious (*Bysk.* II, chap. 6, p. 183). Jón's destiny, on the other hand, is clearly revealed through incidents concerning his mother. When she is only eight years old and staying at the Norwegian court of St Óláfr, the saintly king says of her:

Hon verðr gæfumaðr mikill, ok sá mun göfgastr ættbogi á Íslandi, er frá henni mun koma. (*Bysk.* II, chap. 2, p. 80)

---

[18] For further examples, see Grant Loomis, *White Magic: An Introduction to the Folklore of Christian Legend* (Cambridge, MA 1948), 15-26.

She will be a very fortunate person, and the noblest family in Iceland will descend from her.[19]

After her marriage and Jón's birth, when the family is staying at the court of Denmark, Ástríðr the queen mother tells Jón's mother not to slap the child's hands when he tries to take food before the feast has started, 'því at þetta eru byskups hendr' (*Bysk.* II, chap. 2, p. 79) (because those are bishop's hands).[20] Although these court stories may be apocryphal, their purpose is clear: on the secular plane, they emphasize Jón's noble ancestry; on the spiritual plane, they show that his holiness has been established for generations. In addition, they make his mother into a saintlike figure, an understandable embellishment when one realizes that both Bishop Páll and Bishop Guðmundr were illegitimate.

Birth and childhood prophecies are also found in the versions of King Óláfr Tryggvason's life written by monks for the purpose of promoting Óláfr's sanctity and possible canonization. They are, however, omitted in the historical version of his life, found in Snorri Sturluson's *Heimskringla*. In *Óláfs saga Tryggvasonar eftir Odd Munk*,[21] believed to be a close Icelandic translation of a Latin original written towards the end of the twelfth century by Brother Oddr Snorrason of Þingeyrar, Óláfr's future glory is emphasized by prophecies made both at birth and in childhood. The first is pronounced shortly after his birth by a pagan seeress in Garðaríki, a Scandinavian settlement in Russia where Óláfr later takes refuge (*Konunga sögur* I, chap. 6, p. 20). The seeress seems to be based on the figure of the *vǫlva* or pagan seeress, with whom she has some traits in common, such as being called on to prophesy at a feast;[22] she is, however, never referred to as a *vǫlva* but as a

---

[19] This scene is reminiscent of the one in *Eiríks saga rauða* in which Þorbjǫrg litilvǫlva says of Guðríðr: 'Ok man þar koma frá þér bæði mikil ætt ok góð, ok yfir þínum kynkvíslum skína bjartari geislar' (chap. 4, ÍF 4:208) (And there will come from you a race which is both great and good, and over the branches of your family will shine bright beams). The author of *Eiríks saga* may have been inspired by the scene in *Jóns saga*.

[20] This remark may have provided the inspiration for the already mentioned þjófsaugu, 'thief's eyes' in *Njáls saga* (chap. 1, ÍF 12:7).

[21] *Konunga Sögur* I, ed. Guðni Jónsson (Reykjavík 1957), 1-192.

[22] For an example of a *vǫlva*, see Þorbjǫrg litilvǫlva in *Eiríks saga rauða* (chap. 4, ÍF 4:206-9). The word *vǫlva* seems to have pagan connotations, whereas *spákona* (m. *spámaðr*) is used for biblical prophets as well as for people in both pre-Christian and Christian times who can see into the future. On the development and use of the figure in Old Norse literature, see Kees Samplonius,

spákona, 'prophetess,' and her gift of prophecy is termed *fítonsandi*, 'the spirit of the pythia.' The second prophecy is made by *spámenn*, 'prophets or wise men,' when Óláfr finally arrives in Garðaríki:

> Aldri fyrr höfðu þeir sét né eins manns *fylgjur* bjartari né fegri ... En svá sögðu þeir mikils háttar vera hans hamingju, at þat ljós, er yfir henni skein, at þat dreifðist um allt Garðaríki ok víða um austrhálfu heimsins. (*KS* I, chap. 8, pp. 25-6)

> Never before had they seen any man's *fylgjur* brighter or fairer ... And they said his *hamingja* was so significant that the light which shone over it extended over all Garðaríki and far into the eastern part of the world.

Interestingly enough, probably because they are still pagans, these men refer to Óláfr's *hamingja*, 'luck or guardian spirit,' and *fylgjur*, 'fetches'; however, to these traditional motifs is added the brightness associated with Christianity and Christian saints.

The next time a prophetic dream occurs is shortly before the future bishop hears he has been elected to a see. The format of the dream is standard in all the sagas: the priest sees himself in or near a church, with holy objects, doing something the meaning of which is unclear to him. Laurentius, for example, has this dream:

> Hann þóttist standa upp yfir lestrarkór. Hann þóttist halda á einni oblátu, svá hátt upp sem þá er prestr heldr upp í messu. Á þessari *oblacione* var merkt *Alpha* ok Ó. (*Bysk.* III, chap. 28, p. 56)

> He thought he was standing above the choir lectern. He thought he was holding a host as high up as the priest holds it up at Mass. On this *oblacione* was marked Alpha and O.

Guðmundr has this dream:

Hann þóttist koma í kirkju þar á Völlum í Svarfaðardal, en honum þótti altarit falla í fang sér ok þótti skrýtt vera inu bezta skrúði. (*Bysk.* II, chap. 40, p. 256)

He thought he had come to the church there at Vellir in Svarfaðardale, and it seemed to him that the altar had fallen into his arms and seemed to be dressed in the best vestments.

This is Þorlákr's dream:

Hann þóttist ganga frá kirkju þar á þinginu heim til búðar sinnar ok bera höfuð ins heilaga Martini í faðmi sér. (*Bysk.* I, chap. 17, p. 68)

He thought he was walking from the church there at the Thing home to his booth carrying the head of St Martin in his arms.

In no case is the meaning of the dream clear to the future bishop, who has to call upon a much wiser priest to interpret. Páll, the priest from Reykjaholt, 'dyrðligr maðr' (a worthy man) explains to Þorlákr that the dream means that he too will bear the head of (that is, be) a holy bishop. In Laurentius's case, an old priest from over the heath who is 'sæmiliga kunnandi' (suitably learned) makes a threefold interpretation of his dream: standing up over the choir lectern indicates that he will be appointed to stand over the choir of clergy in Hólar; the host stands for the highest authority; the alpha and omega mean that, just as he began his life at the school in Hólar, he will also end it there. Although these saintly future bishops have the future revealed to them in dreams, they do not have the power to decode the symbols. This part of the motif seems to be taken from native Icelandic literature, in which dreamers of dreams frequently need to have what they have seen interpreted for them, sometimes by their wives, but other times by a wiser man, such as the Norwegian who interprets the bird-dream in *Gunnlaugs saga ormstungu* (chap. 2, ÍF 3:55) or Gestr Oddleifsson, who interprets Guðrún's dreams for her in *Laxdæla saga* (chap. 33, ÍF 5:88-91).[23] From the point of view of the

---

[23] Of all the dreams in the Family Sagas, it is probably Guðrún's dreams of her four husbands, who are represented by rings and fine headgear, that come closest to the symbolic dreams in the Bishops' Sagas.

hagiographer, the reporting of the dream serves a double function: not only does it confirm that the bishop has indeed been divinely chosen, but it also provides a trustworthy witness to the fact, in the shape of the learned priest to whom the dream has been related.

The motif of the preconsecration dream appears to be peculiar to Icelandic hagiography; none of the bishops or abbots in the *Legenda aurea*, for example, has a dream of this sort before acquiring a bishopric or monastery.[24] It would seem, therefore, that the motif was specifically created by Icelandic monks by combining the motif of a dream from both the native and the hagiographic tradition with specific symbols from Roman Catholic Christianity.[25] Once one looks at historical conditions in Iceland at the time, the reason for the creation of the motif becomes clear. Two of the bishops, Þorlákr and Guðmundr, spent most of their lives at loggerheads with secular authorities. Þorlákr attempted to carry out the reforms demanded by Archbishop Eysteinn; he upheld the claims of the Church against the State and challenged the right of laymen to own the churches built on their land. He also strove to raise the moral standards of both clergy and laity. These attitudes brought him into conflict with a powerful local chieftain, Jón Loptsson, and it was only after Jón's death that the process of his canonization started. Guðmundr, who had a reputation as a miracle worker while still a priest, also had a strong belief in his divine mission. He too became embroiled in fights with local *goðar* (chieftains); in addition, he travelled around the countryside with a large following of unruly beggars, which did not endear him to those he stayed with. In the case of these two bishops, their biographers probably found it necessary to point out that, even if their actions were not altogether pleasing to the laity, they were elected by the power of God and were carrying out his will. In addition, there was a strong movement to have the two canonized,

---

[24] Although the *Legenda aurea* was compiled around 1260 and so postdates most of the Bishops' Sagas, it contains saints' lives that were part of the common European stock-in-trade and which, as a result, are likely to have been known to Icelandic clerics, especially those who studied abroad. The version of the *Legenda aurea* used here is Jacobus de Voragine, *Legenda aurea*, ed. T. Graesse, 2nd edn (Leipzig 1850), trans. William Granger Ryan, *The Golden Legend: Readings on the Saints*, 2 vols (Princeton 1993).
[25] The idea of a preconsecration dream may have been suggested by the second dream in *Sverris saga*, in which Sverrir sees a bird covering the country. The man with him comments: 'Vera kann, at þú verðir erkibiskup' (You may become an archbishop). Sverrir replies: 'Ólíkligt þykki mér þat' (I don't think that's likely) (*KS* II, chap. 2, p. 7).

successful in Þorlákr's case but not in Guðmundr's, and any features that emphasized the divine aspect of their lives would be welcome.

In the case of the other bishops, their lives were not so controversial, and most of them were not blessed with a preconsecration dream. St Jón's holiness was well documented, and he was generally regarded as a saint. Páll did not pursue the aggressive ecclesiastical policy introduced by Þorlákr, and his saga is more historical than hagiographical. Laurentius, who did have a prophetic dream, came into conflict not with the laity but with his bishop, Jǫrundr; his attempts to denounce his superior's laxity ended in his own disgrace. It is when Laurentius is at the lowest ebb in his career, after he has been refused permission to say Mass, that he sees the vision which, although he is unable to interpret it at the time, promises him a better life in the future. He is understandably sceptical about its veracity once he has it interpreted, but another priest, Síra Hafliði Steinsson, who was 'í mörgum hlutum forspár' (foresighted in many respects) shortly afterwards announces to the assembled company when Laurentius is staying with him, 'hann mun verða byskup á Hólum' (Bysk. III, chap. 28, p. 58) (he will be bishop at Hólar). Laurentius's life was written in the fourteenth century, a century after Þorlákr's and Guðmundr's. Since there was neither a movement to have him canonized nor great objections to him among the laity, it seems reasonable to assume that by this time the preconsecration dream had become a literary motif and could be used for purposes other than those mentioned in connection with Þorlákr and Guðmundr. In Laurentius's case, the dream shows how God does not forget his chosen saints but sends them consolation in adversity.

Guðmundr's dream is not the only one that precedes his consecration; his uncle Þorvarðr claims that he too has had prophetic dreams, in one of which he saw himself in King Óláfr's hall in Trondheim. Óláfr embraced him, saying, 'Kom þú heill ok sæll, Þorvarðr, ok skaltu blessaðr vera um öll Norðrlönd' (Bysk. II, chap. 42, p. 260) (Hail and welcome, Þorvarðr; blessed shall you be throughout the North). Þorvarðr interprets the dream as referring to Guðmundr. The reason for this second dream is that Guðmundr is extremely reluctant to become a bishop, to the point where family pressure has to be put on him to accept. Þorvarðr in fact falls back on the traditional Icelandic belief that fate is immutable and what has been seen in a dream must come to pass: 'Þú munt byskup vera, svá hefir mik dreymt til' (Bysk. II, chap. 42, p. 260) (You will become a bishop; so I have dreamed it). Guðmundr finally gives in and agrees to the nomination.²⁶ From a literary point of view, this scene is highly ironical, for Guðmundr's family later come to regret forcing the bishopric on him.

A variation on the preconsecration dream occurs in *Óláfs saga Tryggvasonar*. Since the high point of Óláfr's career is not his consecration as bishop but his conversion to Christianity, it is before his conversion that we find a symbolic vision similar to those experienced by the saintly bishops:²⁷

> Honum sýndist einn mikill steinn, ok þóttist hann ganga langt upp eftir honum allt til þess, er hann kom at ofanverðum. Honum þótti þá sem hann væri upp hafiðr í loftit yfir skýin. (*Konunga sögur* I, chap. 13, p. 38)

> A huge stone appeared before him, and he thought he climbed up it a long way until he finally came to the topmost part. It seemed to him then that he was lifted up into the heavens above the clouds.²⁸

A voice then tells Óláfr to go to Greece to learn about God. He is also granted a vision of heaven and hell, in which he sees King Valdamar, his queen and those who sacrifice to idols. He then goes to Greece, becomes instructed, and while still unbaptized returns to convert first the queen and then the king. This whole episode seems highly improbable, and Snorri simply omits it.²⁹

---

²⁶ Orri Vésteinsson, basing his idea on this passage and on passages in *Sturlunga saga,* assumes that Guðmundr's biographer is here recording a historical fact, but the motif of the reluctant bishop is also known from medieval hagiography; for example, St Gregory became pope and St Ambrose bishop very unwillingly in the versions of their lives recorded in *The Golden Legend* (*Legenda aurea,* chaps 46 and 57). See Vésteinsson, *The Christianization of Iceland* (New York and Oxford 2000), 205.

²⁷ Preconversion dreams are common in the hagiographic tradition (see Kruger, *Dreaming in the Middle Ages,* 151–65).

²⁸ The motif of a ladder, rather than a stone, leading up to heaven is very common in Judaeo-Christian literature, its first manifestation being Jacob's ladder in Gen. 28:12.

²⁹ This scene may be inspired by an incident in some versions of the life of St Martin, when the saint is 'admonished in a dream that he ought to visit his native country and his home, and father and mother who were wickedly heathen' (W.W. Skeat, *Ælfric's Lives of Saints,* EETS 94 and 114 (Oxford 1966 [reprint of 1890 and 1900 edns]), 2:229).

A further hagiographic feature found in the Bishops' Sagas is the use of dreams and dream messengers to explain an unusual aspect of a saint's life. Laurentius read the Hours of the Holy Spirit every day because of a dream he had (*Bysk.* III, chap. 29, p. 59). Jón was an accomplished harp-player, a gift which, according to his biographer, had come to him after he heard the biblical King David playing his harp, also in a dream (*Bysk.* II, chap. 8, pp. 9-10).[10] The ultimate source of the motif is the Bible, where, for example, an angel appears in a dream telling Joseph first to take Mary as his wife and later to flee with her to Egypt (Matt. 1:20-1; 2:13-15). Dream-messengers also appear in the Family Sagas, often in the form of a female *fylgja*, or oversized woman, who appears when there is, or will be, a death in the family. An example of this type of dream messenger is Án's 'óþekkilig' (repulsive) dream-woman in the *Laxdœla saga*, who appears to him before he receives a near-fatal wound in the abdomen (chap. 48, ÍF 5:149). A dream messenger of another sort is the 'svartr ok illiligr' (black and evil-looking) man who appears to Earl Hákon's thrall before both earl and thrall are killed (*Konunga sögur* I, chap. 21, p. 70). In direct contrast to these visions are the pleasant and very human-looking messengers of the Bishops' Sagas. For example, Laurentius's message was delivered to him by a person 'í kennimanns búnaði' (*Bysk.* III, chap. 29, p. 59) (in a clerk's clothes), and the person his mother saw was 'einn merkiligr maðr' (*Bysk.* III, chap. 2, p. 3) (a distinguished man). Þorlákr's visitor was 'göfugligr yfirlits ok með sæmiligum búningi' (*Bysk.* I, chap. 5, p. 42) (of noble appearance and attractively dressed). Unlike many of the angels in saints' lives and the New Testament, these Icelandic visitors are not surrounded by bright light, a feature which seems to be reserved for Óláfr Tryggvason.[11]

One of the functions of the messengers of hagiographic literature is to guide saints when they have a decision to make. According to Isabel Moreira, 'The *angelus Domini* was perhaps the most familiar figure to appear in visions

---

[10] A very similar story to that of the gift of music in *Jóns saga* is found in Bede's account of the poet Cædmon, who was taught to compose religious poetry in Old English metres by a man who appeared to him in his sleep (Bede, *The Ecclesiastical History of the English People*, ed. Judith McClure and Roger Collins [Oxford and New York 1994], p. 215). Although both stories may be from a common Germanic source, it seems more likely that Bede's account inspired this incident, since Bede's *Ecclesiastical History* was known in Iceland. See Régis Boyer, *La vie religieuse en Islande (1116-1263)* (Paris 1979), 180.

[11] For examples of brightness associated with angels, see Luke 24:4, Matt. 28:3, Acts 12:7. For examples of light being connected with King Óláfr, see my 'Structural Patterns in the *Eyrbyggja Saga* and other sagas of the Conversion,' *Mediaeval Scandinavia* 11 (1978-9): 271-80, at 279.

to saints ... It was the angel who conveyed divine will.'[12] The dream-man of
Þorláks saga is an angel of this type. Þorlákr never married, and the reason for
this is explained by a dream he had:

> Sá mælti, er honum sýndist í drauminum: 'Veit ek,' sagði hann, 'at þú
> ætlar þér hér konu at biðja, en þú skalt þat mál eigi upp láta koma, af
> því at þat mun eigi ráðit verða, ok er þér önnur brúðr miklu æðri
> huguð, ok skaltu engrar annarrar fá.' (*Bysk.* I, chap. 5, pp. 42-3)

> Then the man who appeared to him in the dream spoke. 'I know,' he
> said, 'that you intend to propose to a woman here, but you must not
> bring up the subject, because it will not be approved. There is another
> much worthier bride intended for you, and you are to take no other.'

Being celibate in Iceland was extremely unusual, even among the clergy, and
almost unheard of in secular life. To quote Roberta Frank: 'Part of the
difficulty Icelanders had in recognising celibacy as any kind of ideal state had
to do with their language: the Old Norse word for "bachelor" also designated
a "vagabond" or "wretch"; the term used to designate an "unmarried woman"
had the basic meaning of "unlucky."'[13] Þorlákr's unmarried state and his
campaign to improve the sexual morality of his flock are so peculiar that it
takes a visit from an angel to explain them!

Another conventional feature of hagiographic literature is the ability of saints
in holy orders to see what is happening elsewhere or will happen in the future.
This quality appears to have been considered a necessary adjunct to sanctity
and bishopdom by Icelandic hagiographers, for, once they are back home after
their consecration, Icelandic bishops suddenly acquire the gift of prophecy.
For example, although there has been nothing in the saga up to that point to
merit such a remark, the author of *Jóns saga* suddenly announces:

> Þessi inn heilagi byskup Jóhannes var prýddr af guði mörgum
> merkiligum hlutum ok fögrum vitrunum, sem fylgjandi frásögn váttar,

---

[12] Moreira, *Dreams, Visions,* 206.
[13] Roberta Frank, 'Marriage in Twelfth- and Thirteenth-Century Iceland,' *Viator* 4 (1973): 473-84,
at 482.

ok var þat eigi undarligt, at honum væri margir merkiligir hlutir í svefni sýndir, því at hann hafði eigi meira svefn en náttúran mátti minnstan nýta. (*Bysk.* II, chap. 34, p. 51)

This holy bishop John was then granted by God many remarkable things and fair visions, to which the following story bears witness, and it was not wonderful that many remarkable things were shown to him in sleep, because he slept no more than the least that nature could make do with.[14]

Then, to back up his claim, the author quotes three foresighted dreams of Jón's. In two cases, Jón knows of the passing of a priest before word has arrived of his death[15] and in the other he has a vision inspired by the contents of a holy book two days before the book arrives. Similarly, once he is bishop of Hólar, Laurentius knows in advance how the archbishop will judge a case: 'Sagðist hann þat vita af draumum sínum' (*Bysk.* III, chap. 60, p. 129) (He said he knew that from his dreams).

Another example given by the author of the same saga is that Laurentius knew cattle should have been slaughtered before a harsh winter,[16] to which the comment is added: 'Var hann maðr svo forspár, at margt gekk eftir því, sem hann sagði' (*Bysk.* III, chap. 64, p. 138) (He was so foresighted a person that many things happened as he said). Guðmundr's prophetic ability seems more like a capacity to lay curses: when a farmer refuses hospitality to the bishop and his followers, Guðmundr foretells that something evil will befall him:

En þat spámæli gekk svá eftir, at annat sumar fyrir Máríumessu ina síðari brann upp bærinn allr at köldum kolum. (*Bysk.* II, chap. 69, p. 315)

---

[14] Jón's lack of sleep is another common motif in saints' lives; in *The Golden Legend*, SS Bernard and Arsenius barely slept either (*Legenda aurea*, chaps 120 and 178).

[15] Knowing of the death of a fellow clergyman is also well illustrated in medieval hagiography.

[16] One of the pagan farmers in the *Landnámabók*, Þorsteinn rauðnefr, who showed great devotion to a waterfall, or to the spirit within it, knows which sheep should be slaughtered each autumn and prospers greatly as a result (ÍF 1:358, S chap. 355, H chap. 313). Since the *Landnámabók* antedates *Laurentius saga*, the story of Þorsteinn rauðnefr may have suggested to the author of *Laurentius saga* that Laurentius's common sense could be interpreted as prophetic ability.

And the sequel to that prophecy was that the following summer, before the Feast of the Virgin Mary [8 Sept.], the homestead burned to the ground.

Þorlákr's prophetic powers appear only on his deathbed, when he hands his episcopal ring on to his nephew, who becomes bishop after him; the author of this saga comments: 'Ok var þat forspá hans tígnar' (*Bysk.* I, chap. 18, p. 69) (And that was a presage of his distinction). Once a saint reaches the rank of bishop, he apparently acquires foresight, and examples must be found to illustrate this new-found gift.

The problem here is that none of the Icelandic bishops seems in reality to have possessed any prophetic powers. Laurentius's knowledge that the cattle would not survive the winter was a common-sense deduction based on the amount of hay he had in his barn. Guðmundr's curse was undoubtedly a coincidence that was reinterpreted by the faithful as a prophecy. That Þorlákr's nephew would become bishop after him was not improbable, since bishoprics tended to run in families in early Iceland. The author of *Jóns saga*, who was writing over a hundred years after his subject's death and so had more latitude to introduce motifs from fiction, does take a topos from the hagiographic tradition, that of one holy man being aware of the passing of another. However, since the examples of Jón's prophetic ability are all clustered together at the end of his life and are used to defend a hitherto unsubstantiated statement, they do not come across as particularly convincing. In short, the use of the motif of the prophetic bishop appears to have presented the writers of the Bishops' Sagas with a problem for which they did not find any particularly successful solutions.

The final use to which prophetic dreams and visions are put is to underline the death of the protagonist. In the Family Saga tradition, this is the most common use of the motif. The death omen usually occurs in a dream or a vision that comes to the hero shortly before he embarks on his last journey. A very clear example of the motif occurs in *Óláfs saga Tryggvasonar*.[37] Here the pagan, or rather apostate, Earl Hákon and his slave are hiding in a pit under a pigpen when the slave has some strange dreams:

[37] This scene occurs, with minor variations, in all three versons of *Óláfs saga Tryggvasonar*. The version quoted here is from *Óláfs saga Tryggvasonar eftir Odd Munk*.

Eftir þat sofnar þrællinn. Ok er hann vaknaði, þá sá hann jarl vaka, ok þá mælti hann: 'Enn sá ek einn draum. Mér sýndist maðr einn mikill ok gekk ofan frá fjallinu ok mælti: "Nú eru lokin sund öll."'
Jarlinn mælti þá: 'Skammt segir þú þá eftir lífdaga várra.'
Þrællinn mælti: 'Þat dreymdi mik enn, at Óláfr gæfi mér hest mikinn ákafliga.'
Jarlinn mælti: 'Þar mun hann festa þik á inn hæsta gálga, er hann fær til.' (*Konunga sögur* I, chap. 21, p. 71)

After that the thrall slept. And when he woke, he saw that the earl was awake and said: 'I had a dream again. A big man appeared to me coming down from the mountain and said: "Now all the straits are closed."'
Then the earl said: 'From what you say, short are the days of life left to us.' The thrall said: 'Moreover, I dreamed that Óláfr gave me an exceedingly large horse.' The earl said: 'There he will tie you on the highest gallows he can obtain.'

These dreams, like most of those found in similar circumstances in the Family Sagas, are symbolic, and Earl Hákon's interpretation of them is in fact correct, for the thrall kills his master shortly afterwards and is subsequently hanged by Óláfr.

Omens also appear in the sagas of the warrior-kings, Magnús and Óláfr, who both die violent deaths. In *Magnús saga*, which is incorporated into *Orkneyinga saga,* the death-omen takes the form of a breaker:

Ok er þeir røru í logni ok sækyrru, þá reis boði hjá skipi því, er jarl stýrði, ok fell yfir skipit, þar er jarl sat ... Þá sagði jarl: 'Eigi er þat kynligt, at þér undrizk þetta, en þat er hugsan mín, at þetta sé fyrirboðan lífláts míns.' (chap. 46, ÍF 34:106)

And as they were rowing in a calm and smooth sea, a breaker rose up beside the ship the earl was steering, and it fell over the ship where the earl was sitting ... Then the earl said: 'It is not surprising that you're wondering at this. It is my opinion that this betokens my death.'

A wave does not usually portend death in the Family Sagas.[38] However, according to Bo Almqvist, 'Waves as harbingers of death are frequently met with in Gaelic popular legends and beliefs.'[39] The reason for the use of a Gaelic motif is twofold: first, since Magnús was earl of the Orkneys, a part of the British Isles with a large Gaelic population, the use of the wave adds local colour; second, by using a Gaelic motif to indicate upcoming death, the author can avoid putting a pagan motif into a Christian part of a saga.[40]

A similar avoidance of pagan symbols can also be seen before Óláfr Tryggvason's death: an old blind man with the gift of prophecy ('framsýnn mjök'), not knowing that Óláfr is beside him, inadvertently reveals the imminent loss of the king, his queen, his boat, and his dog (*Konunga Sögur* I, chap. 64, pp. 150-1). In some ways this old man is reminiscent of the foresighted *fóstra*[41] of the Family Sagas who knows of the upcoming death of members of the household; on the other hand, the motif of the prescient man of God is very common in religious literature. What we seem to have here is a blending of two traditions: we have the foresighted aged person of the sagas, with a change of gender to bring the motif into line with hagiography. So, even though the authors of early Icelandic saints' lives continue to use the motif of the death-omen in the case of saints who die violent deaths, they avoid using supernatural creatures with pagan connotations, such as *fylgjur,* 'fetches' and *hamingjur,* 'guardian spirits,' and employ motifs that are not unknown in the Family Sagas but to which they give a slightly unusual twist.

The death omen is almost entirely absent from the Bishops' Sagas. One reason is undoubtedly that the bishops passed away quietly in their beds, whereas Icelandic men who have intimations of mortality die violently. In

---

[38] In *Laxdæla saga*, the Kotkell clan of sorcerers conjure up a similar breaker, with disastrous consequences for those sailing past. In this case, though, the wave is an instrument of death, not merely an omen: 'Síðan reis boði skammt frá landi, sá er engi maðr munði, at fyrr hefði uppi verit, ok laust skipit svá, at þegar horfði upp kjölrinn' (chap. 35, ÍF 5:100) (Then a breaker rose up a short distance from the land which nobody remembered being there before, and struck the ship in such a way that it immediately turned keel uppermost).

[39] *Viking Ale: Studies on Folklore Contacts between the Northern and Western Worlds* (Aberystwyth 1991), 24.

[40] Russell Poole (personal communication) suggests that there may not be Gaelic influence here, given the obvious verbal similarity between *boði,* 'breaker' and *fyrirboðan,* 'foreboding, omen'.

[41] The word literally means 'foster-mother,' but it is often used of a woman with supernatural powers.

fact, the only Bishop's Saga in which there is a death omen is *Páls saga*. The night sky is strange before the bishop's death:

En viku fyrir andlát Páls byskups sýndist tungl svá sem roðað væri ok gaf eigi ljós af sér um miðnætti í heiðviðri. (*Bysk.* I, chap. 18, p. 279)

But a week before the death of bishop Paul, the moon looked as if it were covered in sacrificial blood and gave no light at midnight in a clear sky.

This may, however, be not a death omen but an example of pathetic fallacy. When Páll actually dies, the whole of nature is perturbed:

Jörðin skalf öll ok pipraði af ótta, himinn ok skýin grétu, svá at mikill hlutr spilltist jarðar ávaxtarins. (*Bysk.* I, chap. 18, p. 279)

All the earth shook and quivered with fear, the sky and the clouds wept, so that a large part of the earth's produce was destroyed.

The author of *Páls saga* states that he took his inspiration for this scene from Ari, 'prestr inn fróði,' who told 'hvé mjök várt land drúpti eftir fráfall Gizurar byskups' (*Bysk.* I, chap. 18, p. 279) (how greatly our land drooped after the death of Bishop Gizurr); on the other hand, visions of blood before a person dies are common in parts of Family Sagas set in Christian times.[42] The ultimate source of the motif of nature being perturbed is the Bible, which describes darkness falling over the earth and the veil of the Temple being rent asunder when Christ died (Luke 23:44-5; Mark 15: 3-8). So it is difficult to say whether the blood-red moon of *Páls saga* has its roots in religious or secular literature or a combination of the two.

Although pathetic fallacy occurs in the Bible, a more common motif in hagiographic literature is to have visions occur as the saint lies dying. Either the *mourant* or those keeping him or her company may see saints welcoming the departing saint into heaven, or else the deceased's soul may be seen going

---

[42] For example, in *Njáls saga*, before Njáll and his family are attacked, Njáll sees the gable wall of his house gone and the table covered in blood (chap. 126, ÍF 12:324).

up to heaven in the form of a dove or a ball of fire.[41] A variation on the theme occurs when the saint's passing is seen in a dream by a fellow saint. Only one of the Bishops' Sagas makes use of this theme. On the night before Páll's death, a wise chieftain has a holy dream:

> Dreymdi Þorvaldr Gizurarson, inn vitrasta höfðingja, at Jón Loftsson fæli Pétri postula á hendi þá hjörð er Páll byskup, sonr hans, hafði gætt. (*Bysk.* I, chap. 18, p. 280)

> Þorvaldr Gizurarson, the wisest of the chiefs, dreamed that Jón Loptsson commended to the Apostle Peter the flock of which his son, Bishop Páll, had charge.

The reason why no other episcopal biographers make use of the motif of the death-bed vision probably stems from the fact that the Icelandic *vitae* were written not too long after the bishop's death, and those who were witnesses to the good man's passing knew that neither he nor they had seen saints calling him from heaven. Truth and common knowledge forbade the adding of such an embellishment.

Jón's biographer, who was writing beyond the time of living memory, would have had more latitude to add dreams and visions. He does not, though. What he does add is a miracle related to the bishop's ring. Jón's corpse cannot be transported to the grave until his mislaid episcopal ring is returned to his finger:

> Þeir tóku þá gullit ok drógu á hönd honum, ok eftir þat gengu til inir sömu menn sem fyrr ok tóku þá upp líkit léttliga ok báru til graftar. (*Bysk.* II, chap. 22, p. 113)

> Then they took the ring and drew it onto his hand, and after that the same men as before went and picked up the corpse easily and carried it to the grave.

The inspiration for this scene may have come from traditional Icelandic ghost stories, from tales of unpleasant men who become *draugar*, 'undead,' after

---

death and are brought to their burial place only with great difficulty. The author of this saga seems to have taken a pagan motif and turned it into a Christian miracle, thereby illustrating both Jón's sanctity and the importance of episcopal rings in early Icelandic society. Other sagas also make use of the motif of the episcopal ring. In *Þorláks saga*, Þorlákr's bequeathing of his ring to his nephew illustrates the bishop's prophetic powers. In *Laurentius saga*, the ring is again important, but the handing on of it provides some possibly unintentional humour:

> Þá dró hann þat sama gull af hendi sér ok fekk honum, ok svo sem hann síra Egill hafði ætlat at geyma gullit, þá greip byskup af honum gullit, svo segjandi: 'Ekki skaltu gullit fá fyrri en ek er dauðr.' (*Bysk.* III, chap. 65, p. 144)

> Then he took that same ring from his hand and gave it to him, and as Reverend Egill was intending to keep the ring, the bishop grabbed it from him, saying: 'You'll not get the ring before I'm dead.'

This scene, and the one in *Þorláks saga*, may easily be based on what actually happened. Be that as it may, the author of *Laurentius saga* has seen the literary possibilities of the motif of the bishop's ring and uses it to emphasize the beginning and the end of Laurentius's life: his mother dreamed that a 'byskups innsigli' (*Bysk.* III, chap. 2, p. 3) was pressed into her hand when she was pregnant, and Laurentius's own ring will be passed on once he is dead.

What happens when hagiography meets history? In the early sagas, if bishops are not candidates for canonization, a mainly historical and factual format is followed. In later sagas, or in those written in support of would-be saints, writers to a large extent follow the European hagiographic tradition, while managing at the same time to incorporate certain features, such as the wise man who interprets dreams, from their native literary tradition. Dreams and prophecies are used, as in the European tradition, to underline the most important events in the saint's life. In the case of bishops, these events are the divine selection of the future saint in early childhood and the secular election of the saint to a see in later life. In addition, a dream may also be used to explain a particularly holy or otherwise unusual aspect of the saint's life. The bishop himself is granted the gift of prophecy once he takes possession of his diocese. His passing is foreshadowed not by a death omen, as in the case of the warrior-saints, but by the handing on of the episcopal ring. In addition, the prophecies in saints' lives show a clear progression, from prophecies or dreams about the saint, to dreams dreamed by the saint but interpreted by another, to the acquisition of the gift of prophecy itself. Although all the motifs do not occur in every saga, a definite pattern still emerges.

The Bishops' Sagas are least successful when hagiography and history come into conflict. The problem is most acute in the motif of the prophetic bishop, when unconvincing examples are dragged in to illustrate a nonexistent gift. In the case of the saints' deaths, their biographers, with one exception, abandon the hagiographic and biblical formats entirely, probably because most saints' lives were written in nearby monasteries shortly after their subjects died, making it a little difficult for clerics to introduce into their works unusual phenomena of nature or celestial visions that nobody could remember experiencing. Some other European motifs, such as the dream messenger, are skilfully integrated. But the most effectively used motif is undoubtedly the one that is original to Icelandic hagiography: the preconsecration dream. Here, saga writers show how well they can combine the symbolic dream vision, which seems to have its roots in both native and foreign tradition, with elements from the Christian religion. The author of *Laurentius saga* then extends the motif so that it illustrates not only that bishops are chosen by God but also that they are not abandoned by him in time of trouble. The same author also expands the use of the bishop's ring motif, using it to indicate not so much his subject's sanctity as the beginning and the end of the holy man's life.

In many ways, *Laurentius saga*, the last of the Bishops' Sagas, exemplifies Icelandic hagiography at its best: the cleric's birth and death are linked; his pregnant mother's dream is vivid, with religious imagery appropriate to the child she is carrying; Laurentius's preconsecration dream illustrates how God brings consolation to those unjustly condemned; and Laurentius, the nonsaint, shows a very human side as he holds on to his episcopal ring until the last minute. In short, the European tradition may have shown Icelandic clerics how to write hagiography but the monks felt free to adapt and elaborate upon that tradition, creating a new and specifically Icelandic format.

14

Claiming Kin Skaldic-Style

RUSSELL POOLE

> 'However, 'tis well to be kin to a coach,
> even if you don't ride in 'en.'
> (*Tess of the d'Urbervilles*)

We think of early English and Scandinavian poets as eager seekers after gifts, not always overly fussy about which patrons they obtain them from.[1] Widsith, the archetypal and obviously fictive travelling poet, has gift-giving occasions at the warm centre of his speech:

> Swylce ic wæs on Eatule   mid Ælfwine,
> se hæfde moncynnes,   mine gefræge,
> leohteste hond   lofes to wyrcenne,
> heortan unhneaweste   hringa gedales,
> beorhtra beaga,   bearn Eadwines. (Wid 70-4)

Likewise I was in Italy with Ælfwine, who, to my knowledge, of mankind, had the readiest hand to win praise, the least niggardly heart in the sharing out of rings, bright circlets, son of Eadwin.

But the poets' opportunism, however lucrative, must often have been attended with feelings of insecurity, as this representation of the widely travelled Widsith appears to acknowledge:

> Swa ic geondferde fela   fremdra londa
> geond ginne grund.   Godes ond yfles
> þær ic cunnade   cnosle bidæled,
> freomægum feor   folgade wide. (Wid 50-3)

[1] I should like to thank Roberta Frank, Guðrún Nordal, and Martin Chase for organizing or presiding over two earlier presentations of ideas incorporated into this essay.

Thus I travelled through many foreign lands, across the vast earth. There I experienced good and evil, cut off from my kindred, remote from my dear relatives, was in attendance far and wide.

Here, like an exile, the itinerant poet is made to speak plangently of separation from his kinsfolk. Such a person, exceptionally vulnerable in a social system that relied heavily upon kinship ties, must have sought to create surrogate ties, entered into at the courts he visited. At the least he could enjoy the companionship and comradeship of the *comitatus* in this new community:

> Ðonan ic ealne geondhwearf   eþel Gotena,
> sohte ic a gesiþa   þa selestan;
> þæt wæs innweorud   Earmanrices. (Wid 109-11)

From there I travelled through the entire territory of the Goths, always sought the best of comrades; that was the following of Eormanric.

Meanwhile, nevertheless, his closest patronage, like his declared family relationships, remains at his point of origin: he has been close to Eormanric, but there is no suggestion that he has entered into any sworn or foster-relationship to the king.

> Ond ic wæs mid Eormanrice   ealle þrage,
> þær me Gotena cyning   gode dohte;
> se me beag forgeaf,   burgwarena fruma,
> ...
> þone ic Eadgilse   on æht sealde,
> minum hleodryhtne,   þa ic to ham bicwom,
> leofum to leane,   þæs þe he me lond forgeaf,
> mines fæder eþel,   frea Myrginga.
> Ond me þa Ealhhild   oþerne forgeaf,
> dryhtcwen duguþe,   dohtor Eadwines.
> Hyre lof lengde   geond londa fela,
> þonne ic be songe   secgan sceolde
> hwær ic under swegle   selast wisse
> goldhrodene cwen   giefe bryttian. (Wid 88-102)

And I was with Eormanric throughout; there the king of the Goths
looked after me well. He gave me a ring, the greatest of city-dwellers
... I passed it into the possession of Eadgils, my protecting lord, when
I came home, as a reward to the beloved man, lord of the Myrgings,
for bestowing land on me, my father's estate. And Ealhhild presented
me with another ring, daughter of Eadwine, noble queen to the
following. Her renown spread through many lands when in my song I
had to declare where beneath the heavens I knew the best gold-
ornamented queen to distribute gifts.

If similarly we consider the assumptions held by Deor, the other
archetypal and no doubt equally fictive court poet in Old English poetry, they
appear to be at the same comparatively modest level, despite his manifest
personal bitterness at the slights he has incurred. He is dear to his royal patron,
who in turn has been *hold* (loyal/gracious) to him, but there is no implication
that the two men are linked in sworn kinship.

Þæt ic bi me sylfum   secgan wille,
þæt ic hwile wæs   Heodeninga scop,
dryhtne dyre. Me wæs Deor noma.
Ahte ic fela wintra   folgað tilne,
holdne hlaford,   oþþæt Heorrenda nu,
leoðcræftig monn   londryht geþah,
þæt me eorla hleo   ær gesealde. (Deor 35-41)

This I will say about myself, that for a time I was the poet of the
Heodenings, dear to my lord. My name was Deor. For many years I
enjoyed a good place, a gracious lord, until now Heorrenda, a man
skilled in songs, received the title to land that the protector of warriors
had earlier assigned to me.

Although the early Scandinavian evidence for the tenor of relationships
between poet and patron is naturally much richer and more diverse, it too
centres on a reciprocation of gifts and comradeship between the two figures.
Aspirations to anything more suggestive of familial relationships would be
hard to document. Exceptionally, however, two skalds, namely Hallfreðr
Óttarsson vandræðaskáld and Sigvatr Þórðarson, extend their claims in that

direction. The most overt examples centre on the newly Christian surrogate relationship of godfather to godson or goddaughter, probably a tie that newly Christianized Scandinavians would have understood most readily as an adaptation of the time-honoured foster-father and foster-son tie in their own culture. In one of his verses, Hallfreðr expresses satisfaction — if that is not too mild a word — at having found a very distinguished godfather in his patron, the tenth-century warlord and would-be Christianizer of Norway, Óláfr Tryggvason.

> Hlautk þanns œztr vas einna
> (ek sanna þat) manna
> und niðbyrði Norðra
> norðr goðfǫður orðinn.   (*Skj.* B1:156, v. 26)

I gained as my godfather (this I affirm) him who had become the greatest man of all under the heavens in the North.

Correspondingly, Sigvatr, the leading skald of the next generation, expresses perhaps a quieter gratification that the subsequent Norwegian leader, Óláfr helgi, stood sponsor at the baptism of his daughter.

> Dróttinn, hjalp þeims dóttur
> (dyrr's þínn vili) mína
> heim ór heiðnum dómi
> hóf ok nafn gaf Tófu;
> helt und vatn[2] enn vitri

---

[2] It is perhaps merely a curiosity that the two texts of this verse preserved in *Flateyjarbók* contain the readings 'vottr' and 'vatr' for 'vatn.' For details of these readings see Finnur Jónsson, ed., *Den norsk-islandske skjaldedigtning*, vols A1-2, *Tekst efter håndskrifterne*, vols B1-2, *Rettet tekst* (Copenhagen 1912-15), A1:268-9, v. 11 (hereafter *Skj.*). Probably the copyist has erred through some confusion with *váttr*, 'witness,' or anticipation of the *-tr-* in 'vitri.' A remoter possibility, but one worth entertaining, is that Sigvatr, who quite frequently uses forms discrepant from those familiar to us in early Icelandic and Norwegian, here avails himself of the older nominative form of the word for 'water,' parallel to OE *wæter* and implied by the Swedish lake name Vättern. That would be a unique attestation in skaldic poetry, so far as I am aware, but vestiges of the ancient heteroclitic declension of the word for 'fire' (*funi* and *fúrr/fýri*) are more overtly preserved in OI poetic language: cf. Jan de Vries, *Altisländisches etymologisches Wörterbuch*, 3rd edn (Leiden 1977), s.vv.

(varðk þeim feginn harða
morni) mínu barni
móðrakkr Haralds bróðir. (*Skj.* B1:248, v. 11)

Lord, help him — mighty is thy will — who lifted my daughter
home from heathendom and gave her the name Tófa. The wise,
courageous brother of Haraldr held my child under the [baptismal]
water. I was most joyful that morning.³

Much later, Sigvatr was to integrate himself still further into the family of
Óláfr when he stood sponsor to his son Magnús. Other strong overtones of a
familial relationship between poet and patron can be seen in a verse ascribed to
Sigvatr where he speaks, seemingly addressing his fellow poet Óttarr, about
having received a gift of nuts from the king. According to the king's own
express instructions, this gift was to be divided with Óttarr as if it were a
paternal legacy.

Sendi mér enn mæri
— man þengill sá drengi —
síð munk heldr at hróðri —
hnytr þjóðkonungr — snytrask.
Opt en okr bað skipta,
Óttarr, í tvau dróttinn —
endask mál — sem myndim
manndjarfr fǫðurarfi. (*Skj.* B1:248, v. 10)

To me the renowned king of the people sent nuts; this king does not
forget his men; it will be a long time before I devote more art to
praise-poetry. But the lord, bold towards men, often bade us divide
them in two, Óttarr, just as we would a father's legacy: my speeches are
ended.⁴

---

³ For a discussion of this touching and beautiful stanza, with suggestions that, like Hallfreðr's
stanza quoted above, it was composed shortly after the king's death, see Magnus Olsen, 'Tova
Sigvatsdatter,' MM (1954): 189-96.
⁴ Cf. *Skj.* A1:268; E.A. Kock, ed., *Den norsk-isländska skaldediktningen* (Lund 1946), 1:128, v. 10
and E.A. Kock, *Notationes norrænæ: anteckningar till edda och skaldediktning* (Lund 1923-44), §§
675, 2010, and 2338 (hereafter *NN*). Font changes, here and henceforward, are intended to clarify

To judge from extant verses ascribed to the two skalds, these close relationships were not easily won. Neither poet could rely on his productions being accorded an automatic hearing but had to petition for it first. While perhaps that was a matter of ancient ritual, testing the newcomer, it might in this specific context have had more to do with a newly suspicious attitude to skaldic poetry on the part of the two missionary kings. To hear recurrent mentions of the names of mythological figures such as Freyja and Njörðr, when you as ruler had made determined efforts to supplant their cults and perhaps even to assert that you yourself possessed some of their key powers, would scarcely be welcome.[5] Yet in a few verses the two poets appear to push their hints of royal closeness even further, verging on the risky or inappropriate. In doing so they employ highly allusive and stylized language, couched in atavistic terms that were fading from currency at the steadily Europeanizing courts of Scandinavia.

In the first two of the verses I shall cite, Hallfreðr acknowledges the gift of a sword from Óláfr Tryggvason.[6] Some two decades later, Sigvatr composes a single verse, with some apparently studied parallels to verses by Hallfreðr, so as to acknowledge the gift of a sword from Óláfr helgi.[7] We shall begin by examining the Hallfreðr texts closely.

> Veitk at vísu skreyti
> víðlendr konungr sendi
> nøkðan hjǫr af nøkkvi;
> nú ák Sýrar mey dýra.
> **Verða hjǫlt fyr herði**
> *hǫfum gramr* – **kera** – *framðan* –

---

word order. I have followed Kock in postulating a word *snytra 'make wise, artful' but not in other aspects of his interpretation. The placement of 'opt' is especially tricky. I have assumed that the king 'repeatedly' urged Sigvatr to share the nuts fairly. Such fulsomeness would not be strange in the context of a 'father' leaving a legacy. One might compare Hróðgar as Beowulf's surrogate father in *Beowulf*, uttering a sententious speech upon parting, also the effusiveness of the father in the OE *Precepts*. It is notable that examples of *snottor* and its derivatives, cognates of *snotr* and therefore *snytrir/*snytra*, tend to cluster in these sententious types of poetry.

[5] Cf. Roberta Frank, *Old Norse Court Poetry: The Dróttkvætt Stanza*, Islandica 42 (Ithaca 1978), 66-7, and Russell Poole, 'The 'Conversion Verses' of Hallfreðr vandræðaskáld,' MM (2002), 1:15-37, at 23-4.

[6] *Hallfreðar saga*, vv. 8 and 14.

[7] Bjarni Aðalbjarnarson, ed., *Heimskringla*, ÍF 26-8 (Reykjavik 1941-51), vol. 27:55, v. 35.

skǫlkving of þák – **skjalga**
skrautlig – *konungsnauti*. (v. 8)

I know that the king of extensive territories sent the skald (embellisher of verse) a naked sword for some reason; now I own the precious treasure (daughter of Sýr). Thanks to the warrior (i.e. the king, the hardener of the fish of the chest), the hilts become embellished; the king has honoured me with his possession; I received the sword.[8]

Eitt es sverð – þats – sverða –
sverðauðgan mik gerði;
fyr svip-Njǫrðum sverða
sverðótt mun nú verða.
Muna vansverðat verða –
verðr emk þriggja sverða
jarðarmens – ef yrði
umbgerð at því sverði. (v. 14)

That is a sword of swords, which made me sword-rich; now there will be sword-plenty in the presence of warriors (agile gods-of-plenty of swords). There will be no deficiency of sword if a scabbard is supplied for that sword; I am worthy of three scabbards (the turf arch of three swords).[9]

These stanzas, as is usual with skaldic verses, appear in a prose narrative context. In two major redactions, represented by *Möðruvallabók* and the *Óláfs*

---

[8] The revised edition of v. 8 offered here takes into account all previous editions known to me. For critical apparatus for both verses see *Skj.* A1:169 (v. 11); Bjarni Einarsson, ed., *Hallfreðar saga* (Reykjavík 1977), 55; and Ólafur Halldórsson, ed., *Óláfs saga Tryggvasonar en mesta*, Editiones Arnamagnæanæ A1 (Copenhagen 1958), 394. Bjarni's reading 'vatnsverðat' for AM 61 lacks support both in the manuscript itself and in other editions and is doubtless a mere slip. The clause analysis yields an interpretation of the second *helmingr* without recourse to emendation. Although the demarcation of clauses is complicated, such complexity is possible to parallel elsewhere in the Hallfreðr corpus.

[9] Here I follow the interpretation offered in Einar Ól. Sveinsson, ed., *Vatnsdœla saga*, ÍF 8 (Reykjavík 1939), 162, n. ad loc. (hereafter *Hallfreðar saga* 1939). It seems likeliest that, despite Finnur Jónsson in *Skj* B1:159 (v. 11), both 'sverðótt' and 'vansverðat' are used impersonally, rather than referring to the constituents of the verse itself.

saga Tryggvasonar en mesta,[10] vv. 8 and 14 are placed at quite separate stages in the chronology, so that the sword has been gifted by the king and in Hallfreðr's possession for some time before he requests the scabbard. *Heimskringla* cites only the second stanza. The various prose accounts of the verses differ markedly, as does the partially related account of Hallfreðr's acquisition of his nickname, also reportedly conferred by the king. A ready explanation is that these accounts represent secondary accretions and amplifications in which the potential of v. 14 for ex post facto aetiological anecdotage is exploited.[11] If we ignore the prose-based chronology and consider the verses in and of themselves, it looks probable that, rather than being distinct compositions, both belong to the same chronological stage and form part of a single composition.

Hallfreðr parades his virtuosic verbal wit and agility in these stanzas, which clearly were celebrated in the skaldic tradition. The first stanza appears to constitute a securely documented case of highly complex word and clause order in skaldic poetry (so many other proposed examples are debatable, depending as they do on uncertain interpretations and emendations). Among subtler points, suspicions of erotic wordplay involving the nakedness of the sword, the hardness of the fish (used as base-word in the kenning for 'sword'), and the poet's possession of Freyja's maiden (treasure) are difficult to discount.[12] Only a step away, but this step is perhaps prudently not taken, lies the atavistic notion that the conquering warlord takes the land as a bride or a forced female prize, a trope that Hallfreðr had used extensively in an earlier eulogy for the aggressively heathen Hákon jarl.[13] Here he contents himself with calling the Christian king 'víðlendr.' Otherwise, as I shall unravel in greater detail presently, a neat reciprocity exists between king and skald.

[10] *Hallfreðar saga* 1977, 54-5.

[11] For details see Russell Poole, 'The Relation between Verses and Prose in *Hallfreðar saga* and *Gunnlaugs saga*,' in Poole, ed., *Skaldsagas: Text, Vocation, and Desire in the Icelandic Sagas of Poets* (Berlin 2000), 125-71.

[12] Compare Roberta Frank, 'Anatomy of a Skaldic Double Entendre: Rǫgnvaldr Kali's *Lausavísa* 7,' in E.S. Firchow et al., eds, *Studies for Einar Haugen Presented by Friends and Colleagues* (The Hague 1972), 227-35.

[13] For a discussion of this trope, see Frank, *Old Norse Court Poetry*, 63-5 and 85-6; also Folke Ström, 'Poetry as an Instrument of Propaganda: Jarl Hákon and his Poets,' in Ursula Dronke et al., eds, *Speculum Norroenum: Norse Studies in Memory of Gabriel Turville-Petre* (Odense 1981), 440-58.

In the remarkable second stanza, a tour de force with its intricate word repetition, we find the equally remarkable kenning 'þriggja sverða jarðarmens,' (the turf arch of three swords). It is the 'jarðarmen' (or turf arch) that is most singular in this collocation. It is decidedly a word to pause over. Some copyists of the manuscripts and perhaps reciters of the verse appear to have stumbled over it, offering the alternative readings 'jarðarleggs' (-legs) and even 'sverð.'[14] Of these the former two appear to represent substitutions of a more familiar kenning element, since the 'leg of earth' is well attested in the meaning 'stone.' The latter can only represent an outright cutting of the Gordian knot. In *Skjaldedigtning* Finnur Jónsson cut the knot in a different way by taking up the emendation 'jarðar hljótr' (B1:159), refining on 'jarðar valdr' earlier proposed by Konráð Gíslason.[15] This gives us a vocative (skald addressing the successor to territories) and leaves the skald claiming he is worthy of three swords, which is possible although even by skaldic standards a little immodest. But it would seem bad methodology to discard a reading which, aside from being the *lectio difficilior*, is shared by representatives of different branches of manuscripts – those of *Heimskringla* (*Fríssbók*), of the separate saga (*Möðruvallabók*), and of the conflation of *Hallfreðar saga* with the saga of Óláfr Tryggvason found in *Óláfs saga Tryggvasonar en mesta*.

Two interpretations, while adopting the reading 'jarðarmens,' do so on the assumption that this word should be interpreted in some ad hoc fashion. Guðbrandur Vigfússon suggests that 'jarðarmen' is a pun on *svǫrðr* 'sward,' a word which, according to Guðbrandur, 'means also leather.'[16] More recently, Sverrir Tómasson has suggested that 'jarðarmens' should be understood as a *heiti* for 'snake' and that in turn as a cryptic expression for 'sword.'[17] Both proposals involve a double inference that may not be strictly necessary. Instead, let us start by finding out what *jarðarmen* means in plain prose before we try to assimilate it into the kenning system.

---

[14] For further documentation see *Skj.* A1:169, v. 11; Kock *NN* §1089; *Hallfreðar saga* 1939, 162; Aðalbjarnarson, ed., *Heimskringla*, 26:331-2; and *Hallfreðar saga* 1977, 55.
[15] Konráð Gíslason, ed., *Udvalg af oldnordiske skjaldekvad med anmærkninger* (Copenhagen 1892), 110.
[16] Gudbrand Vigfusson and F. York Powell, ed. and trans., *Corpus Poeticum Boreale: The Poetry of the Old Northern Tongue from the Earliest Times to the Thirteenth Century*, 2 vols (Oxford 1883), 2:575.
[17] 'Hugleiðingar um horfna bókmenntagrein,' *Tímarit Máls og Menningar* 50, no. 2 (1989): 211-26, at 225.

A *jarðarmen*, to judge from our chief prose source, an account in *Gísla saga*,[18] was formed by separating a strip of turf from the underlying soil along its length while leaving it attached at the ends. At the middle it was propped up above the ground on a spear, so as to form a crude arch. This arch could no doubt be imagined as the visible part of an arm- or finger-'ring' (*men*), hence the name ('ring of earth'). Many kennings are founded on the notion that parts of the earth map on to parts of the body or originate from the body of some chthonic being and this phrase would be a natural extension from them.[19] The *jarðarmen*, once formed, became the focal point of a ritual where initiands would crawl through the arch or ring. As they went, they scraped their hands against the nail in the spearshaft. The blood shed in this process was mixed in the final stage of the ceremony. The mixing of blood from the different initiands betokened the assumption of a common purpose such as revenge or ritual self-humiliation or the formation of a foster-brotherhood.[20] In both *Fóstbrœðra saga* and *Vatnsdœla saga* a set of three turf arches is stipulated for the rite (although in the latter case special contextual reasons appear to have motivated the precise choice of number).

Turning now to the inner workings of the kenning, we can start with the idea that our two operative words are 'sverða jarðamens.' It follows from the previous discussion that the 'jarðarmen' of a sword (or swords) is what it 'crawls' or slips or slides into (remembering that the verb that would be used in this context, *skríða*, cognate with Old English *scríðan*, covers this range of meanings). What is slid into has an arc- or hoop-like section and is wide enough to form a partially enclosed area. The referent can hardly be other than a belt or scabbard.[21] The belt would provide the best visual parallel but from the final line of v. 14 it is apparent that the scabbard must be intended. Kennings of this general type elsewhere are based on a tacit comparison between the sword sliding out of the scabbard and a serpent or snake sliding out of its barrow or burrow. This kenning type is conceptually easy in that

[18] Björn K. Þórólfsson and Guðni Jónsson, eds, *Vestfirðinga sögur*, ÍF 6 (Reykjavík 1943), 23 n. 1 (hereafter *Gísla saga* 1943).
[19] Guðrún Nordal, *Tools of Literacy: The Role of Skaldic Verse in the Icelandic Textual Culture of the Twelfth and Thirteenth Centuries* (Toronto 2001), 271-308, esp. 301 and 303.
[20] For a very clear analysis of the different attested types of common purpose see Johan Fritzner, *Ordbog over det gamle norske sprog*, 2nd edn (1883-96), 3 vols, repr. including vol. 4, *Tillegg og rettelser*, ed. Didrik Arup Seip and Trygve Knudsen (Oslo 1954), s.v.
[21] Here for the most part I follow the analysis in *Hallfreðar saga* 1939, 162.

sword kennings can be based on words for 'snake.' Hallfreðr's kenning appears to be an elaboration on this type, using as its point of departure the notion that just as a snake slides out of its hole so men can be envisaged sliding out of a low arch just above ground level. The parallel is not perfect — indeed involves some conceptual strain — and that is all part of the boldness of the effect, other aspects of which I shall discuss presently.

A semiotic analysis of the skald's response to the scabbardless sword will bring out further aspects of this boldness. We should first note that in the rituals of gift giving, gifts mattered in terms of not merely the material aspects of the object (its value, aesthetic qualities, and utility) but also the symbolic implications for the relationship between donor and recipient: indeed we could say that those two facets coexisted in a classic 'signified/signifier' reciprocity.[22] As a material object the sword is obviously a most valuable acquisition, comparable with cloaks and rings and other customary gifts. It is moreover not just decorative but also serviceable, albeit not quite as serviceable as it might be because of the lack of its logical complement, the scabbard. It is probably not accidental that the only specific part of the sword to be praised by Hallfreðr is the hilts, which would be seen even when the sword was safely lodged in its as yet absent scabbard. If we turn to the symbolic import of the sword, a degree of ambivalence also exists: it could betoken the maintenance of peace or justice, but for many beholders it would as readily evoke associations of conflict and death.[23]

Then if we consider the verses per se, the poet's return gift of verses has a distinct cutting edge, like the king's gift of the sword, since it supplements the expected acknowledgment with an overt petition – virtually a reproach. If, as I have argued, Hallfreðr has structured his verse making as a pair of stanzas,

---

[22] For a contrary opinion, see Ross Samson, 'Economic Anthropology and Vikings,' in Samson, ed., *Social Approaches to Viking Studies* (Glasgow 1991), 87-96, at 90.

[23] Jane Martindale, 'The Sword on the Stone: Some Resonances of a Medieval Symbol of Power (The Tomb of King John in Worcester Cathedral),' *Anglo-Norman Studies* 15 (1992), ed. Marjorie Chibnall (Woodbridge 1993), 199-241, at 232. For further discussion in relation to traditional Germanic practice, see Michael J. Enright, 'The Warband Context of the Unferth Episode,' *Speculum* 73 (1998): 297-338, at 316-17. See Gerd Wolfgang Weber, 'Saint Óláfr's Sword. Einarr Skúlason's *Geisli* and its Trondheim Performance AD 1153. A Turning Point in Norwego-Icelandic Scaldic Poetry,' in *Sagas and the Norwegian Experience. Sagaene og Noreg. Preprints of the 10th International Saga Conference* (Trondheim 1997), 655-61, at 661, for a discussion of the spiritual sword of the *sacerdotium* vis-à-vis the worldly sword of the *imperium*, in relation to the twelfth-century *Geisli* by Einarr Skúlason.

that is to say two parts or instalments, the implicit logic is that the king's gift of the sword ought to be two-part in structure as well, with a scabbard as the complement. Thus the attainment of perfect symmetry in the gift making will depend upon the king's living up to the obligations imputed to him by the skald. Reciprocity is presupposed when the speaker, calling himself a 'vísu skreytir' (ornamenter of verses), praises a sword that has expressly been made 'skrautlig' (ornamented) at the king's behest (v. 8).

Finally, the semiosis of the skald and his verses could be read as equally double-edged. The absence of the scabbard means that the attribute signalled by the nickname 'vandræðaskáld' applies to both the skald and the gift: they both make for 'difficulty, trouble' (*vandræði*).[24] The symmetry here is one that Óláfr himself is made to point out in certain versions of the Hallfreðr story. This skald, and in principle any skald, had the potential to bring about harmony, by fostering rapport between the leader and the community, but likewise disharmony. Aside from the skald's familiar recourse to satire so as to amplify and disseminate grievances, personal or communal, it may likewise have been the skald who incited warriors to battle. As Michael J. Enright remarks, 'Provocative wordplay and weapon play go together; hence the god of war is also the god of poetry.'[25] The corpus of verses attributed to Hallfreðr makes his abilities in most of these different capacities evident. Thus through his gift the king both signals Hallfreðr's status as an especially favoured underling[26] and singles him out as a potentially unruly element.

This contemplation of gift giving brings us back to *jarðarmen* 'ring of earth.' When Hallfreðr incorporates this lexical item within a kenning for 'scabbard,' we find ourselves devoid of parallels elsewhere in any kind of kenning. While certainly that could be an accident of preservation, it is at the least suggestive of some special significance. We can reasonably assume, as an inference from the documentation already given, that this specific choice of word calls up rich associations with ritual and particularly with initiation into foster-brotherhood. Who could have heard such a distinctive word, even

---

[24] See Enright, 'Warband Context,' 316 and 319-23, for discussion of possible traditional beliefs in an animistic link between swords and their owners.

[25] Enright, 'Warband Context,' 329. Compare Roberta Frank's comments on this aspect of the skald's functions in 'The Unbearable Lightness of Being a Philologist,' *JEGP* 96 (1997): 486-513, at 509.

[26] Cf. Vilhelm Grønbech, *Hellighed og Helligdom. Vor Folkeæt i Oldtiden*, 4 vols (Copenhagen 1911-12), 3:83.

'buried' in a kenning, without visualizing the archaic and no doubt painful initiation ceremony at whose heart the ring of earth stood? But, this granted, what rhetorical or pragmatic purpose might Hallfreðr's use of the word have served?

In answering this question, consider fosterage as an institution in early Scandinavian society. To judge from frequent references, it was widely practised not merely in Hallfreðr's kin group but in Norway and Iceland much more generally. Foster-brotherhood normally sealed a relationship of mutual obligation between just two men, although *Gísla saga* and some of the *fornaldarsögur* reckon with larger numbers.[27] When someone was accepted into this exclusive relationship, in effect he joined the family; duties of solidarity and vengeance extended to him.[28] The formation of a sworn and at least symbolically 'blood' relationship was especially prevalent among warriors and magnates who had, like Widsith, to cope with periods of absence from home. In occasional predicaments as dangerous as those attending the existence of an exile, such itinerants would have recognized the need for staunch friends upon whose support they could rely as surely as they would have on the support of kin when at home. If Hallfreðr's position in Norway was as precarious as the prose narratives suggest, he would undoubtedly have benefited from such support. In v. 14, then, he alludes to the central motif of foster-brotherhood while stopping short of actually claiming this relationship to the king. That would be the ultimate gift the king could give him. That a compact of foster-brotherhood formed part of the broader gift-giving system was seen by Aron Gurevich, who subsumed it under his 'give and take principle.'[29] Hallfreðr's verse therefore figuratively invokes one kind of gift transaction (commitment to foster-brotherhood) in the course of literally describing another (the presentation of the sword). The *Hallfreðar saga* traditions may have picked up on this idea when they tell us of Hallfreðr's expectation that the king must never reject him, regardless of eventualities.[30]

---

[27] *Gísla saga* 1943, 23 n. 1.

[28] See Jakob Benediktsson and Magnús Már Lárusson, eds., *Kulturhistorisk leksikon for nordisk middelalder fra vikingetid til reformationstid* (Copenhagen 1956-78), 22 vols, s. *fostring* and *fostbrorskap*.

[29] Aron Gurevich, 'Wealth and Gift-Bestowal among the Ancient Scandinavians,' *Scandinavica* 7 (1968): 126-38, at 135.

[30] *Lokasenna* 9-10 contains a mythic enactment of the code that once 'blood has been blended' even the malignant and outrageously misbehaved Loki cannot be excluded from hospitality: see, in particular, Ursula Dronke, ed., *Poetic Edda* II *Mythological Poems* (Oxford 1997), 335.

Let us now consider in the same light a verse attributed to Sigvatr in *Óláfs saga helga* and *Heimskringla*:[31]

> **Ek tók lystr**, né ek lasta –
> *leyfð íð es þat* – síðan,
> sóknar Njǫrðr, **við sverði** –
> *sá es mínn vili* – **þínu**.
> **Þollr, gaztu húskarl hollan** –
> *hǫfum ráðit vel báðir* –
> **látrs**, en ek lánardróttin,
> **linns blóða**, mér góðan.

I accepted your sword eagerly, warrior ('god-of-plenty of the dispute') nor do I criticize that in hindsight; it is a praised action; that is my will. Patron ('tree of the resting place of the snake's blood-brother, i.e., gold'), you have gained a loyal retainer and I a liege-lord good to me: we have both decided well.

The kenning for 'gold,' 'resting place of the snake's blood-brother,' draws on the traditional idea of serpents or dragons jealously guarding the treasures in burial mounds. In itself it is a very common type, probably almost formulaic in the form 'resting place of the snake.' But the addition of the very rare word *blóði* 'blood-brother' to the kenning makes it decidedly less routine. This word stands in close proximity to the semantically related expressions 'húskarl hollan,' 'góðan,' and 'lánardróttin.' The Old English and Icelandic verses quoted earlier in this paper will suffice to suggest the charge attaching to the time-honoured words *hold/hollr*, *god/góðr*, and *dryhten/dróttinn*, which often appear in collocation. Similarly, the metaphorical *látr* of the snake suggests the congenial resting-place or berth for the poet at Óláfr's court. In such a context, the word *blóði* carries a political or institutional association, as invoking a quasi-familial relationship between poet and king. Although there is no precise verbal parallel, the general similarity in kenning conceit and sentiment between this stanza and Hallfreðr's v. 14 is apparent. Once again, Sigvatr makes no express claim to foster-brotherhood in this verse about his

---

[31] *Heimskringla* 1941-51, 27:55, v. 35.

relationship with the king. He merely alludes to such ties in passing, within the kenning.

This is atavistic material, redolent of heathendom and insinuated into a newly Christian context. Sigvatr augments the piquancy of this moment of cultural transition by reaching in the same verse and indeed the same *vísuorð* for the highly modern term *lánardróttinn*. The first element in this compound marks a departure from the time-honoured collocations listed in the above paragraph. Its presence here evidently startled Finnur Jónsson, who tried to explain it away as meaning something like '(the lord) one was gifted with/fated to have.'[32] But the only cogent explanation is by comparison with the medieval German noun *lehan/lehen*, as used in German-speaking territories to translate *beneficium*.[33] The new compound refers to the feudal system, where the lord grants (or 'lends') a benefice or tenement of land to the vassal, often for the term of the life of one or other or both parties.[34] Deor and Widsith had claimed broadly similar land rights in the deep past, as we have seen, but with Sigvatr we have made the transition into a social dynamic of lordship, vassalage, and benefice. His 'sá es mínn vili' (such is my will) could perhaps even be interpreted in this context as the prospective vassal's 'volo' or 'declaration of intention.'[35] His self-identification as a 'húskarl' could encapsulate the vassal's duty to provide *auxilium*. Meanwhile, other terms, notably 'hollr' and 'ráð[a],' have meaning within both the traditional and the newly feudal systems.

In traditional *comitatus* practice, the degree of 'relatedness' acquired by the recipient of gifts of weaponry from a king was more frequently at the foster-son, not foster-brother level.[36] Nevertheless, exceptions could be made: so much is clear from customs in England. When the Danish leader Guthrum was baptized under the sponsorship of Alfred the Great, his newly-chosen baptismal name was Æðelstan. This name just happens to have been borne by one of Alfred's own brothers, subking of Kent from 830 until the early 850s —

---

[32] Finnur Jónsson, ed., *Lexicon Poeticum antiquae linguae septentrionalis: Ordbog over det norsk-islandske skjaldesprog oprindelig forfattet af Sveinbjörn Egilsson*, 2nd edn (Copenhagen 1931; repr. 1966), s.v.
[33] F.L. Ganshof, *Feudalism*, trans. Philip Grierson, 3rd edn (London 1964), 112-13.
[34] Ganshof, *Feudalism*, 40.
[35] Ganshof, *Feudalism*, 70-2.
[36] David C. Van Meter, 'The Ritualized Presentation of Weapons and the Ideology of Nobility,' *JEGP* 95 (1996): 175-89, at 180.

though to be sure it was also borne by other, earlier-generation members of Alfred's family.[37] England seems to have exerted a key influence on Norway in this era, not least through Alfred's grandson Æðelstan's adoption of Hákon (later to be styled 'inn góði') as a foster-son, as also through the infiltration of Christianity into Norway, culminating in outright proselytization.

The Hallfreðr and Sigvatr allusions to foster-brotherhood, conveyed via the oblique and veiled language of kennings, made for an ideal way to construct a similarly familial relationship by implication, rather than outright arrogation, and to hint at a continuity from the heathen past. Once again, the older poet is more atavistic on that front than the younger, whose diction marks a transition into a European feudal ideology and to that extent brings Icelanders into contact and developing rapport with metropolitan realities.

---

[37] Paul Kershaw, 'The Alfred-Guthrum Treaty: Scripting Accommodation and Interaction in Viking Age England,' in Dawn Hadley and Julian Richards, eds, *Cultures in Contact: Scandinavian Settlement in the Ninth and Tenth Centuries* (Turnhout 2000), 43-64, at 51; and Simon Keynes, 'The Control of Kent in the Ninth Century,' *Early Medieval Europe* 2, no. 2 (1993): 111-31, at 124. Olsen, 'Tova Sigvatsdatter,' 194-5, traces the somewhat different process through which Óláfr honoured Sigvatr and his daughter by choosing for her the Danish name Tófa, borne by Tófa Strút-Haraldsdóttir, the sister of the famous Þorkell inn hávi. This name evokes long years of comradeship and loyalty, not merely on Sigvatr's and Óláfr's part but also on the part of Sigvatr's father Þórðr Sigvaldaskáld and Sigvaldi jarl. See also Roberta Frank, 'The Ideal of Men Dying with their Lord in *The Battle of Maldon*: Anachronism or *Nouvelle Vague*,' in Ian Wood and Niels Lund, eds, *People and Places in Northern Europe 500 - 1600: Essays in Honour of Peter Hayes Sawyer* (Woodbridge 1991), 95-106.

NOTES ON CONTRIBUTORS

Don Chapman teaches Old English at Brigham Young University.

Martin Chase is assistant professor of English and Associate Director of the Centre for Medieval Studies at Fordham University.

Robert DiNapoli has taught Old and Middle English at the University of Manchester, Lancaster University, Royal Holloway, and the University of Birmingham.

Oren Falk is an assistant professor in the Department of History, Cornell University.

Dorothy Haines is a drafting editor at the *Dictionary of Old English* at the University of Toronto.

Antonina Harbus is a lecturer in the Department of English at Macquarie University, Sydney.

Pauline Head teaches Old English at York University, Ontario.

Christopher A. Jones teaches in the Department of English at the University of Notre Dame.

Soon-Ai Low has taught Old English at the University of Baltimore.

Bernadine McCreesh teaches English in the Départment des Artes et Lettres, at the Université du Québec à Chicoutimi.

Haruko Momma is an associate professor of English at New York University.

Karin Olsen is a lecturer in English language and literature of the Middle Ages at the University of Groningen.

Russell Poole is a professor of English in the Department of English, University of Western Ontario.

Carin Ruff teaches Old English at John Carroll University in Cleveland, Ohio.

INDEX

Toronto Old English Series